FERNÁNDEZ DE OVIEDO'S CHRONICLE OF AMERICA

FERNÁNDEZ DE OVIEDO'S CHRONICLE OF AMERICA

A New History for a New World

KATHLEEN ANN MYERS
TRANSLATIONS BY NINA M. SCOTT

UNIVERSITY OF TEXAS PRESS
Austin

Printed in the United States of America
First edition, 2007

Requests for permission to reproduce material from this work should be sent to:
Permissions
University of Texas Press
P.O. Box 7819
Austin, TX 78713-7819
www.utexas.edu/utpress/about/bpermission.html

∞ The paper used in this book meets the minimum requirements of ANSI/NISO Z39.48-1992 (R1997) (Permanence of Paper).

Library of Congress Cataloging-in-Publication Data

Myers, Kathleen Ann.
Fernández de Oviedo's chronicle of America : a new history for a New World / Kathleen Ann Myers ; translations by Nina M. Scott. — 1st ed.
p. cm.
"Translations of passages from Fernández de Oviedo's Historia general y natural de las Indias": p.
Includes bibliographical references and index.
ISBN 978-0-292-71703-9 (cloth : alk. paper)
1. Fernández de Oviedo y Valdés, Gonzalo, 1478–1557 Historia general y natural de las Indias. 2. America—Early accounts to 1600. 3. America—Discovery and exploration—Historiography. 4. America—Discovery and exploration—Biography. 5. Historians—America—Biography. 6. Historians—Spain—Biography. 7. Explorers—America—Biography. 8. Explorers—Spain—Biography. I. Scott, Nina M. II. Fernández de Oviedo y Valdés, Gonzalo, 1478–1557. Historia general y natural de las Indias. English. Selections. III. Title.
E141.O96M94 2007
970.01'6—dc22

2007021076

For my parents,
Mary Tyrrell Myers and Richard James Myers

CONTENTS

LIST OF ILLUSTRATIONS

Note: In an attempt to publish as complete a record as possible of Oviedo's illustrations in the *History*, I have drawn on a variety of sources. When possible, I first provide a photograph of images in the extant autograph manuscript (at the RAH and HEH). If the autograph image has been lost, I first use the contemporary Trujillos' copy (at the BC and PR), which is very true to the original except that the illustrations are in color. When that is unavailable, I include the woodcut from one of the early editions, which closely follow Oviedo's drawings (1535, 1547, 1557). When none of the above were available, I reproduce the eighteenth-century copy, made by Juan Bautista Muñoz, who appears to have copied the images fairly faithfully (at the RAH).

The numbers in parentheses refer to the nineteenth-century edition by José Amador de los Ríos.

ACKNOWLEDGMENTS

Gonzalo Fernández de Oviedo took decades to complete his lengthy history of the New World. My study of his five-volume text has spanned nearly two decades as well. While at Brown University, I took a course with Alan S. Trueblood on Renaissance dialogue, and Stephanie Merrim suggested I study Fernández de Oviedo's dialogue about Hernán Cortés. That seminar paper became the first of several articles I published on Oviedo in the early 1990s. These two professors, along with José Amor y Vázquez, Roberto González Echevarría, and Geoffrey Ribbans, continually encouraged me as I headed into new territory. During these years, I also had the good fortune to discover a section of Oviedo's autograph manuscript, the most extensively illustrated volumes, at the Huntington Library in San Marino, California. This serendipitous event led to years of tracking down all extant sections of the manuscript, a search that included trips to nine libraries in the United States and Spain.

I owe a tremendous debt of gratitude to the numerous people and institutions who helped me with research, funding, and early drafts of articles. Rolena Adorno guided my research at a National Endowment for the Humanities Summer Institute held at the Newberry Library. William Frank, Amy Meyers, Jane Munro, and Carla Pestana worked with me during my fellowships at the Huntington Library. Linda Curcio-Nagy, Charles Ganelin, Amanda Powell, Enrique Pulpo-Walker, and Jerry Williams read and commented on drafts of several articles, as did my colleagues at Indiana University, Gordon Brotherston, Catherine Larson, James Mandrell, and Frances Wyers. Chapters 4 to 6 of this book are revised versions of these three articles from the early 1990s. My thanks to the editors at *Hispania* and the University of Arizona Press for the rights to republish them.

After a five-year hiatus from working on Oviedo's *General and Natural History of the Indies* while I completed several other projects, I was awarded a research grant from Spain's Ministry for Education and Science to work with Dr. Fermín del Pino at the Consejo Superior de Investigaciones Científicas in Madrid. There I continued the task of weaving together a book that would take into account three aspects of Oviedo's work that deeply influenced the writing of his text: the complex story of Oviedo's drafts of the *History,* Oviedo's personal and political ambitions, and period rhetorical structures and genres. I found that most of the existing studies about his *History* tended to focus on only one or two of these aspects, or focused on either the general or natural history, leaving aside how the two work together. Fermín served as an enthusiastic and knowledgeable interlocutor, and our discussions were often enriched by Jesús Carrillo and Luis Millones, two scholars who were completing their dissertations at the time. The staffs at the Madrid libraries that hold portions of Oviedo's manuscript, the Biblioteca Nacional, Real Academia de Historia, and Palacio Real, all in Madrid, also offered enormous help. Arantxa Domingo was particularly helpful.

The final stage of my archival work and drafts of book chapters took place in the past few years, when Indiana University, the American Philosophical Society, and the Ministry for Cultural Cooperation Between Spain and the United States all provided generous financial support for travel to Spain in order to attain photographs of the manuscript and to carry out research at the Archive of the Indies, which houses nearly two hundred documents that deal with Oviedo's life and works. My stay in Seville was greatly enhanced by the collegial reception Berta Ares Queija and Salvador Bernabeu offered me at the Escuela de Estudios Hispanoamericanos and by the staff at the Biblioteca Colombina. My thanks also go to the staff at the Hispanic Society of New York, which houses a rare nineteenth-century copy of Oviedo's *History.*

Upon completion of my book, Álvaro Félix Bolaños, Mark Feddersen, William L. Myers, and Nina M. Scott provided valuable comments on the whole manuscript. Licia Weber skillfully and enthusiastically collated and formatted the illustrations. My graduate students at Indiana University, Hernán Feldman, Eric Harzman, and Amber Ray García, helped prepare the manuscript for publication. In particular, Pablo García worked tirelessly as a research assistant, reader, and computer guru. With grace and expertise Lynne Chapman, my editor at the University of Texas Press, guided the manuscript into its final form.

As always, friends and family played an important role in keeping me going during all these years. A big thanks goes to my good friends Rob and Karen Green Stone, who provided a quiet haven many summers for me to write, and to my husband, Mark Feddersen, who, besides being the best editor around, served as a constant source of encouragement.

Finally, I owe my deepest gratitude to my parents, Mary Tyrrell Myers and Richard James Myers. My dad was the first historian I knew and is still the best. My mom has been my biggest fan, even reading all my footnotes. They have inspired me in countless ways during my life.

FERNÁNDEZ DE OVIEDO'S CHRONICLE OF AMERICA

NEW WORLD, NEW HISTORY AND THE WRITING OF AMERICA

In 1493 a fourteen-year-old boy serving as a page for the Spanish prince Don Juan stood in awe as Christopher Columbus met with the Catholic Kings, Ferdinand and Isabella. Columbus unveiled to the royal court in Barcelona his findings from his first voyage, displaying colorful parrots, enticing bits of gold, and native people. Nearly forty years later this boy, Gonzalo Fernández de Oviedo, would write about this first presence of the New World on European land in his *General and Natural History of the Indies* (1535, 1850s). Appointed official royal chronicler of the Indies by the king of Spain and Holy Roman Emperor Charles V (the Catholic Kings' grandson), a post he held from 1532 until his death in 1557, Oviedo lived in the midst of radical changes in western Europe: the Age of Exploration and the birth of the Hapsburg Empire as well as the new intellectual and religious trends born out of the Renaissance and the Reformation. Writing from the island of Hispaniola, the crossroads for the Spanish enterprise in the New World during the sixteenth century, Oviedo composed the most comprehensive history of the discovery, conquest, and colonization of the Americas from 1492 to 1547. Both a chronicle of the Spanish domination of America and a description of its flora, fauna, and indigenous peoples, the two-thousand-page general and natural history is the most authoritative text on the Americas from the first half of the sixteenth century. Granted a royal decree, Oviedo had access to all the official reports about America. In addition, he knew or interviewed many of the major figures of the period. In Europe, Oviedo worked with three generations of Spanish monarchs (the Catholic Kings, Charles V, and Philip II) and an array of prominent political and religious men. In America, Oviedo knew Columbus and his sons, Juan Ponce de León, Bernal Díaz del Castillo, Francisco, Gonzalo, Juan, and Hernando Pizarro, Diego de Almagro, Hernando de Soto, Vasco Núñez de Balboa, and many others. He also met a number of important indigenous leaders in the Caribbean and Central America. The only other comparable history from the period, the *History of the Indies* by the Dominican friar Bartolomé de Las Casas, does not include an extensive natural history and was not published until the late eighteenth century. The *General and Natural History* can help modern readers understand how the new "discovery" became a catalyst for change in European historiography, geography, politics, and philosophy. Indeed, Oviedo's text itself served as a catalyst for European historiographical change.

Oviedo's dilemma was to write a history of a new world at a time when only two types of textual precedents were available: military and navigational accounts and histories written in Europe. The military accounts, for example, Hernán Cortés's letter about the Conquest of Mexico (1520), addressed specific expeditions and concerns. The histories, such as Peter Martyr's *De Orbe Novo* (1530), lacked the authority of an eyewitness account. Oviedo also looked to contemporary European histories and to the Greco-Roman tradition of Herodotus, Pliny, and Thucydides, among others, but these models fell short. The ancients did not know, much less write, about the Western Hemisphere. Oviedo had to reconcile the established histories with his own observations, frequently citing the ancients while also insisting that this New World required a different kind of history.

Writing over the course of nearly thirty-five years (ca. 1514–1549), Oviedo found that he had to shift his strategies, developing them according to the nature of his topic, as the exploration and conquest actually unfolded. His narrative and rhetorical strategies tell the story of history—both as a written practice and as a series of events—at a crossroads. Faced with an ongoing process of exploration, conquest, and colonization, with multiple and often competing reports from the field, and with an abundant new natural world, Oviedo attempted to give his patron the king the fullest possible account about the American territories, while also promoting his innovations on traditional historiographical methods. He justified his deviations from canonical texts and authorities by creating a central role for himself as the transcriber of his own eyewitness testimony and that of others.

Trained in the Castilian royal court at the beginning of the sixteenth century, exposed to the arts and philosophy of humanist Italy, and charged with official duties in America, Oviedo took a multifaceted approach to constructing his text. He wrote numerous explanatory prologues, interviewed conquistadors, transcribed field reports, debated the existence of mythical creatures, detailed indigenous customs, wrote autobiographical vignettes, and drew illustrations of American flora and fauna. In every case, Oviedo is the central vehicle or filter through which the reader receives valuable information. Future generations will be "awestruck," he boasts, that "a single man could have written such a multitude of histories and secrets of nature" (bk. 39, *Proemio*). Moreover, he states that the history is "not one of the least but rather one of the most high and copious that has been written by any man since Adam" (bk. 22, *Proemio*). As the author of both a natural and general history, Oviedo determinedly sought fame as the Pliny and the Herodotus of the New World. His vivid first-person interjections and omnipresence as mediator of sources, information, and meaning constitute the focus of this book. Oviedo's narrative reflects his official duties as chronicler of the Spanish Empire's American possessions and his own agenda as an author and actor within history. He was a man between worlds: he fervently defended the interests of the Spanish monarchy and projected the norms of early modern European culture, and yet he realized that the New World needed a different historical approach.

Oviedo's massive *General and Natural History of the Indies* follows a rough overall chronological and geographical organization that parallels the conquest and colonization of the Indies. Books 1–19 cover Columbus's trips and the Antilles. Beginning with book 20, the author describes Ferdinand Magellan's voyage to the Moluccas and his subsequent explorations of the Southern Cone, rounding the Río de la Plata area and returning to the Caribbean, to what today is Trinidad, Venezuela, and Colombia. He then describes the expeditions to and settlement of Panama, parts of Central America, and the Yucatán. Books 33–40 detail the Conquest of Mexico and some of the North American territories. Oviedo then turns back to Central America, but this time to Honduras, Nicaragua, and Panama, before continuing down the Pacific coast to Peru and Chile (bks. 46–49). Book 50, the so-called Shipwreck Narratives, is a collection of the unfortunate stories of some expeditions.

In 1535, the first nineteen books (of what would become fifty books) were published along with what would become the fiftieth book. Within twenty years it was reprinted (1547) and translated into French (1555) and Italian (selections, 1556).[1] Although it was not published in full until the mid–nineteenth century, the importance of Oviedo's *History* was immediately recognized by his contemporaries. The text offered the most comprehensive coverage of the Indies in the first half of the sixteenth century, and it provided the best access to a large number of primary sources. While men close to the events in the Indies, for example, Fernando Columbus and Las Casas, often criticized Oviedo's narrative renditions of historical events, a circle of Venetian scholars comment that the history is "the most pleasant which any person has ever got to read."[2] In fact, Oviedo's text became a crucial source of information for many people dealing with a variety of issues raised by the Spanish Conquest. The Spanish humanist Juan Ginés de Sepúlveda, for example, drew on it to bolster his arguments in the famous mid-sixteenth-century debates with Las Casas about the justice of the conquest. Another humanist historian, Francisco López de Gómara, refers to Oviedo's and Martyr's histories as the only true accounts.

In subsequent decades and centuries, historians and scientists discussed the chronicler's contributions, often pointing to his work as the first to describe natural phenomena in the Indies. The history written by the mid-sixteenth-century Jesuit natural historian Bernabé Cobo follows Oviedo's, the eighteenth-century Italian forerunner of cultural anthropology, Giambattista Vico, mentions Oviedo on the subject of human sacrifice, and Alexander von Humboldt considered him, along with José de Acosta, the founder of physical geography. Oviedo's writings about America's natural world were the first of their kind; Spain's other notable early natural historians, such as José de Acosta, Nicolás Monardes, and Francisco Hernández, did not write until the second part of the sixteenth century. Nonetheless, Oviedo's work was often cast in the shadow of his archrival Las Casas. As the discourse about the conquest shifted during the sixteenth century, Oviedo's *History* came to represent the darker side of the conquest, while Las Casas's writings were seen as defending the Indians (a point I will take up in chapter 7).

In an attempt to recover Spain's leadership in the development of science, the Spanish Royal Academy of History in the eighteenth century tried to collect and publish for the first time the complete fifty-book *General and Natural History.* This was part of a larger plan to publish many of Spain's early chronicles of America. As María Teresa Nava notes in her studies on the topic, at various times during the course of a century scholars, among them Juan Batista Muñoz (whose partial copy is still extant), began the lengthy process of preparing Oviedo's work for publication. The effort to publish the entire *History* finally came to fruition in the 1850s with José Amador de los Ríos's monumental edition.[3] Amador's panegyric introductory study portrayed the chronicler as a Renaissance man and a Spanish hero of a lost American empire. Nearly a hundred years elapsed before scholars produced more critical studies of Oviedo. First with the four-hundred-year commemoration of his death (1957) and later with the five-hundred-year commemoration of his birth (1978), some Spanish scholars created the portrait of an imperial hero, while others severely criticized Oviedo's view of Native Americans and the wordy style of his history. Notable exceptions to this trend were Juan Pérez de Tudela's introduction to a reprinted edition of the history in 1959 and Antonello Gerbi's extensive study, *Nature and the New World* (1975). Both authors attempt to correct biographical errors and provide a more balanced context for understanding Oviedo's life. In addition, several scholars, such as Daymond Turner, wrote a series of articles and a bibliography which help document the historical setting in which Oviedo lived and worked.[4] With the dynamic reevaluation of colonial texts and contexts that occurred around the quincentenary of Columbus's landfall, scholars increasingly began to analyze the representational strategies the chronicler employed (for example, Bolaños, Greenblatt, Merrim, Pagden) and his political motivation (for example, Brading, Kohut, Mojica, Rabasa). But they have been limited to articles or book chapters in their scope and length. They often focus on a single aspect of Oviedo's history: for example, a study of the natural history without regard to its role in the general history or a study of a specific conquest without taking into account Oviedo's general plan for the Spanish imperial project. The tide may be turning, however, as a handful of valuable dissertations in Spain, Britain, and the United States have been devoted to studying Oviedo from literary and historical perspectives (for example, Beckjord, Carrillo, Méndez, Rodríguez, Romano, Sampedro). One of these theses, *De la naturaleza y el nuevo mundo* (2002) by Alexandre Coello de la Rosa, was published as a monograph. These studies exemplify the renewed interest in Oviedo as a figure who merits full-length study.

There is a significant gap between this scholarly production—much of which is available only in Spanish—and the frequency with which Oviedo's work is invoked in a myriad of fields, including, among others, botany, ethnography, history, literary studies, and zoology. People turn to his text for the first descriptions of pineapples, sloths, and canoes as well as of native Taíno dance (*areitos*) and detailed information recorded from now lost sources, such as Alvar Núñez Cabeza de Vaca's report about his trek across what is today the Southwest United States.[5] This frequent reliance on Oviedo as a source begs the question of why this lacuna in scholarship exists. A large part of the answer lies in the text itself. At over two thousand pages filled with multiple accounts of a single event, the history can be unwieldy. The author's uneven narrative flow and style make for difficult reading in some passages, yet vivid reading in others. These variances in style and narrative strategies have too often been tagged as proof of Oviedo's poor authorial capacity. In addition, perhaps because of this, we lack an authoritative edition and an English translation. The only full edition of the history, that of Amador de los Ríos, is a hundred and fifty years old, and it is full of inaccuracies, perhaps the most serious being that it drastically altered many of Oviedo's original illustrations and moved them to an appendix.[6] Access to Oviedo's work is further complicated by the lack of a complete autograph manuscript; only about half of the *History* is extant, and it is dispersed among several libraries.[7]

In this book I aim to address, at least in part, several of the gaps with regard to the accessibility and reliability of the *General and Natural History of the Indies*. I reproduce, to the extent possible, his original field drawings, which were among the first European images made of the New World. In addition, Nina M. Scott provides in English translation samples of several genre types found in the history, and these furnish the keys with which to interpret Oviedo's representational strategies. To date there are no translations of sections of Oviedo's history that reveal his overall purpose and method. In general, translators have excerpted material dealing with specific historical figures, such as Cabeza de Vaca, de Soto, and Columbus, or have focused on a particular geographical region, such as the Amazon or Puerto Rico. Scott's passages in translation offer a sampling of the range of material covered in Oviedo's text. The selections highlight his historiographical material: discussion about historical method (prologues), autobiographical accounts (the colonization of Central America), natural history (the pineapple), general history—which included secondhand reports about mythical human beings (Amazon women) and interviews with witnesses of the conquest (Mexico-Tenochtitlan)—and descriptions of Native American cultures. Many of these deal in particular with Oviedo's acute consciousness as a historiographer living in a new world.

Each of the six translated selections corresponds to one of my six chapter studies and illustrates the historian's complex intermingling of New World topics, representational strategies, Spanish politics, and personal ambition. I study Oviedo's efforts to convey graphically American reality to European readers and explain them by placing his efforts in the context of the intellectual and cultural transformations taking place in the early modern period. In particular, I focus on Oviedo's compositional challenges as a writer of the New World and suggest how period conventions may have informed the author's choice of genre and representational practices. In so doing, my studies encompass theories of knowledge, sight, genre, and experience.

Besides being a dedicated writer sensitive to the representational dilemma facing a historian of the Indies, Oviedo was a contentious Crown bureaucrat and an ambitious Spaniard seeking his own fame and fortune in America. Thus, each chapter also situates Oviedo's discussion of nature, history, Native Americans, and conquistadors within the context of relevant biographical data about the author and the overarching politics of the Crown and courts at the time Oviedo records specific information. His legal battles and changing administrative positions in the Indies often deeply influenced his historical account. Writing from about 1514 to 1549, Oviedo began his life in the Indies as one of the early settlers and Crown administrators in Central America but later became an established keeper of the fort in Santo Domingo and the royal chronicler of the Indies. His perspective changed from that of a colonizer fighting for rights to profits to that of an opinionated historian who observes and records what he sees and hears, for the king and for posterity.

In order to accomplish the cultural, historical, and biographical contextualization of Oviedo's representational practices and influences, I have based my reading of the *History* on knowledge of his entire work—including, most significantly, the complex process of composing and recomposing the text. As mentioned above, Oviedo wrote over decades, decades that reflect important changes in European intellectual practices, in the conquest of America, and in the author's circumstances. Through extensive archival research on sections of Oviedo's extant manuscript, contemporary copies, and the nineteenth-century edition, my book sets out for the first time a detailed chronology of the author's constant, at times obsessive, revisions and additions to the *History*. Oviedo considered his text to be an open repository for new information. He made continual revisions and updates and added testimony as he collected it, practices that have caused confusion in earlier studies. A systematic chronology can throw new light on our interpretation of Oviedo's natural, general, and autobiographical history and reveal his concept of writing and making history. He did not produce a fixed text but rather conducted an ongoing project in which he created a central—though changing—role for himself within the shifting nature of the conquest and updated information about a new world.

A focus on the complex, changing text and context will allow us to see the epistemological and philological underpinnings of Oviedo's discussion of the Indies as well as the economic, political, and moral contours of the text. The historian's representation of America and his own role within it had deep ethical and political implications for himself and others. In my analysis, I open the reading of Oviedo to a complex matrix of considerations that helps uncover Oviedo's worldview, neither adopting it nor ignoring the fact that a violent conquest took place with his full engagement in it.[8] As we will see in the chapters that follow, as Oviedo became less concerned with participating in the governance of the newly colonized areas and, after 1532, more concerned with his role as the royal chronicler, he tended to focus more on the methodological challenges of writing a history of the Indies, which often involved more detailed descriptions and moralizing and less schematic information and legalistic reports. Through a reconstruction of Oviedo's writing of certain parts of his text, we see the explicit and implicit purposes of his *History*. The author's uneven style, repetitions, and contradictions often tell the story of his evolving roles as historian and actor in history.

I use a series of case studies to analyze Oviedo's historiographic strategies; they include an examination of his self-portraits, drawings of American phenomena, approaches to myth, process of revision, and depictions of Native Americans. In every case I reconstruct key aspects of cultural practices, political and personal contexts, and compositional dates. Before beginning the case studies, in an opening chapter, "Between Two Worlds: The Life and Writings of Gonzalo Fernández de Oviedo y Valdés," I detail Oviedo's career as a court page, author, Italian courtier, and New World bureaucrat. This chapter places the historian in the context of the emerging Hapsburg Empire, Renaissance Italy, and the conquest of America. Oviedo was a man between two worlds. He lived for nearly equal periods of time on both sides of the Atlantic. While in Europe, he worked as a bureaucrat and in the royal courts. In the New World, Oviedo had a long and varied career as town councilman, supervisor of the king's gold, and keeper of a fort. In the few trips he made back to Spain after 1515, Oviedo presented numerous legal cases about the governing of the Indies and information about Native Americans. This chapter also sketches the relationship between Oviedo's life and his writings. His most important legacy is a corpus of about ten major books, works that display his knowledge of a broad range of historical events, literary genres, and historical, ecclesiastic, and juridical discourses. He was a prolific writer who played many roles as a participant-observer of the tumultuous politics of America and Spain in the early modern era. His life was driven equally by loyalty to the monarchy, personal ambition, and a love of America.

The next chapter, "A Reader's Guide to a New World History," examines the prologues to each of the three parts of the *History*. The first prologue, in particular, reveals Oviedo's careful manipulation of historiographic and linguistic norms as he explains why a new world required a new historical method. Between the lines, we glimpse the linchpin of the entire text: the author's own central, authoritative role as the on-site historian. Oviedo states that information about the Indies cannot be learned from the great texts of classical antiquity or in the hallowed halls of any of Europe's best universities. This chapter contextualizes Oviedo's prologue, placing it within period debates about the limits of book learning and the value of experience. By the time Oviedo wrote the prologue to the third and final part of his *History,* some dozen years after the first, he broadened his role as scribe and interpreter of America: he increasingly became a judge of men's actions and an avid advocate for imperial policies.

Chapter 3, "The Historian as Actor and Autobiographer: Tierra Firme 1514," takes a closer look at Oviedo's role in the early years of the conquest and colonization of Central America—the years when he served as a royal bureaucrat rather than as a historian—and examines the abundant stories and autobiographic details within the *History* (bks. 26, 29). The author blends elements from classical history with the emerging autobiographical genres of the period, especially the legalistic *relación* and confessional narrative (*vida*), to create a narrative space and authority for his personal role as a good governor and as a good witness for both king and God. Upon closer examination, this self-portrait is telling: it coincides with Oviedo's repeated efforts to obtain a coveted governorship and to censor the governor of Castilla del Oro, Pedro Arias de Ávila, or Pedrarias Dávila.

Subsequent chapters turn to Oviedo's representational strategies for both the natural and general history. Studying first the depiction of the natural world, in chapter 4, "Eyewitness to America's Wonders: Illustrating a Natural History of the Indies," I study the complex relationship between Oviedo's verbal description of New World phenomena and his nearly eighty field drawings. I look in particular at his discussions of the link between sight and truth, between the writing of history and the attaining of knowledge. The author's illustrations and commentary help us to understand better the role of visual epistemology during the period and the role of experience within it. This relationship between the creator of text and image, and the reader and knowledge, however, was not static. As Oviedo revised sections of the history and wrote new chapters, his ideology about the role of images and the author evolved. A study of the illustrations reveals Oviedo's transformation as a historian over time and the emerging concepts of scientific illustration.

Continuing a close interrogation of the construction of Oviedo's text over time and its implications for understanding the evolution of his historiographic method, chapter 5, "Amazon Women and New World Realities: Documenting an Expanding World," discusses the major changes in Oviedo's writing project. Composing his text about the Indies over a period of thirty-five years, the author changed his method and organizational structure—most importantly in the early 1540s. After examining the deep revisions he made to his text at this time, I turn to a case study that reveals how Oviedo continued to debate the "truth" of New World realities, even when he became more of an official transcriber than a personal witness of events. Nearly a dozen passages in the *History* address the possibility of republics of women, "Amazon-like" women, living in America. As evidence mounted that these women, if indeed they existed, did not look like the Amazon women portrayed in the Greek myth, Oviedo was reluctant to let go completely of the association of the New World reality with the Old World myth. We see this through a study of revisions made to the original accounts in the autograph manuscript. As a man who knew how to use myths to attract readers, he may have resisted discarding well-known fabulous and fantastic stories. Clearly, the development of a more modern historiographic practice was not always a linear process.

Chapter 6, "Cortés and the Conquest of Mexico: Truth and Multiple Testimonies," delves further into Oviedo's emphasis on eyewitness testimony, his own role as the mediator of truth, and the need for constant revisions. Taking a key chapter from the history of the Conquest of Mexico (bk. 33, chap. 54), I study Oviedo's transcription of an interview with an informant in which polemical issues about the conquest are discussed. By the mid-1540s new versions of the events of the Conquest of Mexico made clear that the material Oviedo had included earlier, based on Cortés's letters, was inaccurate. By including verbatim his own questions and the responses of a dissenting view of Cortés's role, the historian manipulates the material to revise the previous account and to reestablish the veracity and authority of his own history. Oviedo's use of dialogued prose rather than of summarizing historical narrative is central to understanding the author's justification of his historiographic method and indirect criticism of Cortés.

Chapter 7, "Native Americans in Oviedo's *History,*" turns to the controversial issues surrounding Oviedo's representation of Native Americans. No study of the historiographical method and ideology he employs in his general and natural history would be complete without an attempt to sort out the often contradictory portraits he paints. His text had important political implications in the discussion of and ultimate ill-treatment of the Indians. On the one hand Oviedo accused Native Americans in the Caribbean of being idolatrous. On the other he praised certain aspects of their culture and provided some of the first extensive ethnographic information about indigenous communities. Based on the approximate dates of composition and types of indigenous groups depicted, I trace the trajectory of Oviedo's descriptions of Indians. In particular, I examine three influences on his text: knowledge about his subjects, policy about the Indians, and his role at the moment of writing. As we see throughout Oviedo's text, history and representation are far from static. Moreover, we see clearly the limitations of European models and worldviews for describing and understanding vastly different cultures.

My reading of Oviedo's *History* as a complete text, using a threefold approach of rhetorical conventions, biographical and political contexts, and compositional dates, helps us broaden and deepen our understanding of this key Spanish chronicler. We glimpse the myriad philosophical, representational, political, and personal challenges facing a European writer of America and see that Oviedo was as complex and contradictory as the times in which he lived.

ONE

BETWEEN TWO WORLDS

The Life and Writings of Gonzalo Fernández de Oviedo y Valdés

Gonzalo Fernández de Oviedo y Valdés was a man between two worlds. He spent nearly equal time on both sides of the Atlantic and endured the dangerous transatlantic crossing between Spain and America eleven times. While in Europe, Oviedo played many roles in the royal courts, from bureaucrat and chronicler to wardrobe keeper and entertainer. In the New World, too, he had a long and varied career that included town councilman and supervisor of the king's gold, slaveholder and pearl merchant. Oviedo was also a prolific writer who had many talents and played many roles in the tumultuous politics of America and Spain in the early modern era. He wrote about medieval mythical creatures and knights errant and yet cited contemporary humanists and employed a method of inquiry into the natural world that prefigured modern scientific empirical methods. Oviedo described this in-between-worlds status when he announced he would write about "another half of the world" (otra mitad del mundo) that famous ancient Greco-Roman authors never knew. By understanding the diversity of Oviedo's worlds and life, we will better understand the complexities of his *General and Natural History.*

Oviedo began his lifelong service to the monarchs of Castile and Aragón in early childhood.[1] Born of Asturian ancestry in Madrid in 1478 to Miguel de Sobrepeña and Juana de Oviedo, Gonzalo entered the service of the family households of King Ferdinand de Aragón in 1490.[2] He first served as a page to the duke of Villahermosa, the king's nephew. By at least 1493, at age fourteen, he was a *mozo de cámara,* in charge of the wardrobe for the Catholic King's only son and heir to the throne, Prince Don Juan.[3]

During these years at the court, Oviedo saw the consolidation of a confederation of kingdoms under the leadership of the Catholic Kings, a development that laid the foundation for the emergence of Spain as a nation and an imperial power. In 1492 he witnessed the surrender of Granada by the Moors after five hundred years of rule and observed the negotiations between Queen Isabella and Columbus that led to the funding of Columbus's first voyage. A year later, Oviedo was present upon Columbus's triumphal return to the court. Indeed, years later the chronicler remarked that the event served as the catalyst for his lifelong project of writing about America. Just as his father had done, Oviedo began to write memoranda of the personalities and events he observed. This privileged court position came to an abrupt end when the young prince Don Juan suddenly died in 1497. Apparently no longer needed at the court, Oviedo embarked within a year or so for Italy, a destination of many young, ambitious Spaniards of the time.

THE ITALIAN YEARS (1499–1502)

From about 1499 to 1502 Oviedo lived an itinerant life in the noble and royal households of Italy. Drawn into the complex political struggle for control among the Italian states, the papacy, Spain, and France, Oviedo first worked in the court of the duke of Milan. When the duke was defeated by French troops and the powerful son of Pope Alexander VI, Cesar Borgia, Oviedo moved briefly to the court of Isabella d'Este in Mantua before joining the military campaigns of the Borgias in central Italy. Given his background, Oviedo probably was not a soldier but rather worked as a supply clerk or quartermaster sergeant.[4] In 1500 he visited Rome for the Jubilee Year and went on to serve as steward, entertainer, and clothes designer for King Ferdinand's relative, King Frederick of Aragón, and Queen Juana in Naples. He aroused curiosity and amused the court with unusual diversions, such as his deft use of scissors to create paper designs. His position, however, was short-lived. The royal house of Naples was forced into exile by the Spanish and French in 1501, and Oviedo followed Queen Juana's exiled court to Sicily for a year before returning to Spain with her.[5]

Oviedo's three years in Italy greatly influenced him. During this time he traveled through much of the country, meeting many of its prominent leaders and artists. Oviedo met Leonardo da Vinci and the Neapolitan poet Jacob Sannazaro, who served in the household of King Frederick, and witnessed the emergence of Machiavellian politics at the instigation of Borgia, Pope Alexander VI, and the French. While in Naples, Oviedo attended lectures by the great author and director of the humanist academy, Giovanni Pontano.[6] In Milan, he made contact with a circle of Venetian intellectuals who later helped him with the Italian translation and publication of his work and with whom he formed a business venture.[7] Oviedo became deeply acquainted with Italian literature and acquired numerous books. Later in life, he wrote, "I travelled all over Italy, where I gave all that I could of myself to know, and read and understand the Tuscan language [from which Italian evolved], and looked for books in [Tuscan], of which I possess some which have accompanied me for over fifty-five years" (cited in Turner 1971, 140).[8] Among other authors, he cites Ovid, Virgil, Petrarch, and Dante as well as Caesar and Cicero.[9] Some years later, it appears he even planned to translate several works from Tuscan into Spanish.[10]

TURN-OF-THE-CENTURY SPAIN (1502–1513)

After his sojourn in Italy and return to Spain, Oviedo spent the next ten years as part of the bureaucratic system being developed by the Castilian monarchy. This system fostered the transition from the Trastamara dynasty to an imperial project, which later took form with Charles V's reign and his victory in the Comunero revolt of 1522. Although the information we have from this period is sketchy, Oviedo seems to have held a variety of important positions that required good writing skills. Most scholars agree that Oviedo held posts as a notary for the Inquisition and for the town of Madrid. Around 1503, he was ordered into the service of the duke of Calabria, Don Fernando de Aragón, by the Catholic King. In 1512, he enlisted as secretary for the massive, but aborted, military campaign to Naples led by the "Great Captain," Gonzalo de Córdoba. Around this time, Oviedo began his work as chronicler. About 1505, King Ferdinand asked him to chronicle the history of the Castilian monarchy. This initial work established a framework for his three-volume genealogy of the monarchy three decades later (the *Catálogo Real* [1532]).

During these years, Oviedo married twice and had a son. First married in 1502 to the beautiful Margarita de Vergara, he was widowed within several years when his wife died in childbirth. This tragedy remained vivid in his mind; years later the author interjects into his history a personal observation about the event.[11] By 1509, Oviedo had a natural son, Francisco González de Valdés, and had married Isabel de Aguilar. Isabel bore several children, but both she and the children would die within several years of joining Oviedo in America.

TIERRA FIRME (1514–1532)

After about fifteen years of filling various posts but never attaining a steady court position, Oviedo embarked for America at the mature age of thirty-seven. It is at this point that the materials in the Royal Academy of History and in the Archives of the Indies in particular take up the story of Oviedo's tumultuous, multifaceted career and life in the early years of the Spanish occupation of the West Indies and Central America.[12] Although best known to posterity as a historian, Oviedo was a very active administrator in the Indies. Passage to and from America was tightly controlled, and conquistadors, bureaucrats, and colonizers tended to be contentious—and often litigious. Archival materials from 1513 to 1557 describe various lawsuits brought against Oviedo as well as his numerous bureaucratic positions, advocacy for newly established towns in the New World, efforts to protect his person and wealth, and petitions to bring his household to America.

In 1513, the royal secretary for American affairs, Lope Conchillos, chose Oviedo to be an imperial bureaucrat for the king's new territories in Castilla del Oro (later known as Tierra Firme, the continental southern rim of the Caribbean, now part of Central America). Lope Conchillos gave him a portfolio of appointments, most notably those as *veedor,* or inspector of the mines, and *escribano general,* or judicial notary.[13] Oviedo set sail for the city of Santa María del Antigua del Darién (in present-day Panama; hereafter referred to as Darién) in 1514 with the soon-to-be-notorious conquistador Pedrarias Dávila in one of the first large-scale expeditions to America and the mainland, known as the Splendid Armada. The expedition, charged with conquering and settling the area, followed the historic voyage of Núñez de Balboa during which he claimed the Pacific Ocean for the Crown of Castile (1513). Most of the Spaniards on this expedition settled in Darién, but within several months more than half had died of famine and illness.

As was typical of most other campaigns of the Conquest of America, no sooner had the expedition arrived than differences of opinion emerged over how to manage the processes of conquest, settlement, and evangelization. Núñez de Balboa had established a policy of peace with the Indians, but Pedrarias's governorship of Castilla del Oro became a reign of greed, misrule, and cruelty. In fact, Balboa was executed by the governor in 1519 on trumped-up charges of treason. It is in relation to Pedrarias's administration of the colony that we first see Oviedo's fierce loyalty to the monarchy and his personal ambition. Within a year, he returned to Spain, transporting thousands of pesos of gold and planning his request that the king intervene in Pedrarias's governorship. The veedor officially accused the governor of maladministration and abuse of power. Soon after Oviedo's audience with the king, Ferdinand died. Oviedo lost no time, leaving for Brussels soon after Ferdinand's death to meet with the new king, Charles V, and present his petition. This initiative started nearly a decade of lawsuits, petitions, and political wars over the governance of Tierra Firme.[14] Although initially the new king did not support Oviedo's pleas for reforms, later, in 1519, he offered the veedor the governorship of one of the provinces of Castilla del Oro, Santa Marta, and replaced Pedrarias with a new governor.[15] Neither of these efforts succeeded, however. In a move that suggests Oviedo's nostalgia for a heroic feudal world, he accepted the governorship on the condition he be given one hundred knights to help him rule. The king refused, and Oviedo declined the position, preferring to remain in his post as *veedor.* Meanwhile, the newly appointed governor and replacement for Pedrarias, Lope de Sosa, died as soon as he reached America (1520), and Pedrarias easily took power again. He transferred the administrative center to the Pacific side of the isthmus, to the city of Panama. For a short while, Oviedo served as Pedrarias's lieutenant governor in Darién, but the dispute between them continued, and Pedrarias replaced Oviedo by 1522/3. Around 1525, the case was settled when Pedrarias was removed again as governor by the king.

Curiously, during these tumultuous years Oviedo began in earnest his career as an author. During his stay in Spain in 1515–1519 he published his first and last fictional work, a chivalric romance about a knight errant who conquers Constantinople and eventually becomes both emperor and pope (*Don Claribalte* [1519]). The author says he wrote it during his short stay in Castilla del Oro. It is also during these years in Spain that Oviedo had the first of many famous confrontations with the Dominican friar and court-appointed "Defender of the Indians," Bartolomé de Las Casas, in a debate about the royal policy dealing with the Native Americans (1519). This encounter solidified an animosity between the two that would last the rest of their lives.

Oviedo returned to the Indies in 1520, bringing with him for the first time his wife, children, and eight servants.[16] They settled in the city of Darién and built a luxurious house, one "fit for a prince," as he tells us.[17]

But both his wife and her children were dead by 1522, leaving only his natural son Francisco alive. Personal tragedy struck again fourteen years later (1536) when the twenty-six-year-old Francisco died during a trip he made as *veedor,* a position he had inherited from his father; he drowned when crossing a river in Arequipa, Peru. During a brief trip to Santo Domingo while en route to Spain in 1523, Oviedo married for a third and final time. He married Catalina de Ribafranca, with whom he had at least one daughter, Juana. The family settled in Santo Domingo, perhaps remaining there while Oviedo was away for much of the next decade.

Oviedo's talent and passion as a historical writer became apparent in 1525–1526. As mentioned, he had returned to Spain two years earlier and had been following the peripatetic court in order to present further charges against Pedrarias Dávila and to secure his removal as governor.[18] While in Spain, he wrote and published his first book about American flora, fauna, and native peoples, *De la Natural Historia de las Indias* (widely referred to as the *Sumario* [1526]). Sections of this work later were expanded in the *General and Natural History.* Widely published and translated, the *Sumario* is a product of the times. It paints a deliciously rich, vivid portrait of the novelty of American nature in a triumphant, providentialist tone. Dedicated to Charles V, who now was sovereign of the Netherlands, duke of Burgundy, king of Castile, holy Roman emperor in Germany, and ruler over the ever-expanding territories in the Americas, the *Sumario* jubilantly frames American nature as part of Charles's massive empire. Only five years earlier, the new emperor had to put down an uprising of Castilian subjects in the Comunero revolt, an act that had helped establish the authority of his reign in Spain. In the ten years since Oviedo's first trip to America, Cortés had overthrown the great Aztec empire (1521), and Ferdinand Magellan and his men had circumnavigated the globe (1519–1522).

During his stay in Spain, the chronicler attended an important general meeting of the Castilian parliament (*cortes*) in Toledo and Charles's royal wedding to the sister of the king of Portugal, Isabel, in Seville, an event that strengthened ties between the two countries. In addition, Oviedo interviewed Francis I, king of France, who had been taken captive when Charles's army defeated the French at the battle of Pavia in 1525. Oviedo took notes about this event and several years later wrote the *Relación de lo Sucedido en la Prisión del Rey Francisco de Francia* (ca. 1532). As a loyal civil servant caught up in the events of the time, Oviedo reflected the euphoria of the epoch. Curiously, in these same few years, Oviedo rediscovered his love of Italian culture: he obtained a license to publish a Spanish translation of Giovanni Boccaccio's *Il corvaccio (Laberinto de amor),* but it appears he never published it.[19]

Finally accepting an appointment as governor, this time of Cartagena (in present-day Colombia), and having settled the Pedrarias Dávila affair with the appointment of Pedro de los Ríos as governor of Castilla del Oro, Oviedo returned again to America in 1526.[20] But his tenure as governor was short-lived. Upon arriving in Panama and learning about the disastrous state of affairs left by an indigenous uprising against his predecessor and apparently lacking sufficient funding to establish himself there, Oviedo declined the position and returned to his post as *veedor,* which he held until 1532, when his son Francisco inherited it.

These years were punctuated by more writing and more travels on both sides of the Atlantic. Never laying down his pen for long, Oviedo finished a still-unpublished treatise on heraldry, the *Libro de blasón* (ca. 1528), and continued work on the *Catálogo Real* (1532). While in Central America, he lived for several years in Nicaragua and visited its lagoons and volcanoes. There he witnessed the devastation of many Native American populations, which he would write about in his *History.* While in Spain from 1530 to 1532 as an agent (*procurador*) representing the interests of Panama and Santo Domingo,[21] he talked with the queen in Ávila about American food products and marveled at the healthy maize now growing in the plains of Castile. All of these experiences became material for his history.

SANTO DOMINGO, HISPANIOLA (1532–1549)

Fifteen thirty-two initiated the second and final stage of Oviedo's American career. During his trip to Spain in 1530, Charles V had granted Oviedo's request to fill the vacancy left by the death of the first royal chronicler of the Indies, Peter Martyr D'Anghiera (d. 1526). At age fifty-four, Oviedo had finally achieved royal approval to write America's next official general and natural history, a task for which he had been grooming himself and a role that finally brought him fame. Within the year, Oviedo was also given a second official position as garrison commander (*alcaide*) of the royal fortress at Santo Domingo. Both were lifelong appointments that he held until his death twenty-five years later. The Council of the Indies, a body Charles created to help govern the new lands, first recommended Oviedo as chronicler to Charles:

> Gonzalo Hernández de Oviedo, resident of Hispaniola, has had the care and inclination to write of affairs of the Indies; he offers to carry forward his work if he is given some salary towards the expense of collecting material and maintaining a clerk. It appears appropriate that it be included in the *Chronicle of Spain*. He displays more ability than anyone over there. It would be well to order him to examine all those lands where he has not been and to send the reports to this council in order that here they may be edited and incorporated in the *Chronicle* and he should be given an annual subsidy. (cited in Turner 1964, 267)

The king then instructed Oviedo in the duties of his new position as royal chronicler of the Indies and offered him the salary of thirty thousand *maravedíes* (significantly less than the seventy thousand he had received as *veedor*). Responding to the Council of the Indies' recommendation that Oviedo write a thorough history of the Indies,[22] a royal decree states,

> What you say about writing down matters concerning the Indies seems good, so that there will be a record of them, and since it appears to you that Gonzalo Hernández de Oviedo will do this well, as he has been over there for such a long time, and because of his experience and the information he has of things over there, charge him to do this, with the proviso that before any of his writings are printed or published, he must present us with a copy thereof so that we can have it examined . . . have it be done thus, and since he will be granted this salary [thirty thousand *maravedíes*], have him write down matters concerning the Indies in due order and in a good style.[23]

While these instructions and his predecessor's model, *Decadas de novo orbe* (1516, 1530), gave Oviedo some guidelines for his history, he conceived of a whole new scheme for writing about the Indies. He was the first European with firsthand experience to attempt such a project. Oviedo had lived in America for many years and had his own ideas about writing a complete, official history of the nature and events of America from 1492 to 1532. In addition, Oviedo negotiated with royal officials for the right to have access to and request written reports on the Indies so that he would not have to continue traveling. He was duly granted this wish. Now in his midfifties, he carved out a role for himself not as field interviewer but as historian, which required a stable office and library in Santo Domingo. From the information we have, it seems that this project consumed Oviedo's time and efforts for the next sixteen years and that he had been taking notes for decades already. He is probably the most dedicated, if not obsessive, historian of America from the period, surpassing even his archrival Las Casas. Nonetheless, as documents in the archives demonstrate, Oviedo continued to be an active administrator. He petitioned—and often received—monies and privileges for the city and fort of Santo Domingo as well as for himself, including the right to a *repartimiento* (a forced labor draft by which a Spaniard was given an allocation of Indians to provide labor) and body guards.[24]

Upon his return to Santo Domingo in 1533, Oviedo eagerly gathered more material to add to his already extensive notes and, perhaps, draft of the *General and Natural History.* There he continued to meet eyewitnesses of and participants in the conquest. Besides vanquishing the Caribbean, Central America, and Mexico, Spaniards had traveled to and conquered the Inca capital of Cuzco and other regions of South America. Oviedo interviewed Diego de Almagro, Francisco Pizarro, Andrés de Urdaneta, Hernando de Soto, Juan Ponce de León, Pánfilo de Narváez, Alonso de Santa Cruz, Alvar Núñez Cabeza de Vaca, Alonso de Solís, Francisco de Orellana, and García de Lerma, and he collected and read the accounts of many others.[25] The historian also continued observing the natural wonders of America, even maintaining a zoo at the fortress. One year later (1534), he sailed for Spain to seek personal concessions from the court and to turn over the completed first part of his history to the Council of the Indies for approval.[26] Eager to see his work in print, Oviedo financed its publication (Seville, 1535).

Although he wrote it for Charles V and his Council of the Indies, Oviedo clearly had greater ambitions for his history. His text aimed at a wide audience, and he ensured that it would reach many readers by overseeing the publication and paying all publication costs. These first books, totaling more than three hundred pages, develop and expand the description of marvelous natural phenomena depicted in the *Sumario.* In addition, they detail the first decades of exploration and conquest (1492–1520) and describe the indigenous cultures encountered. It is difficult to summarize such a vast range of material, but in general the conquest is depicted in a positive light, with portraits of Spaniards as heroes and portraits of Native Americans as inferiors who nonetheless have some noteworthy ethnographic artifacts.

After successfully presenting his causes and publishing his history, Oviedo returned to Santo Domingo the next year. There he rebuilt the fort and oversaw the estates and property he now possessed on the Haina River, at San Juan de la Maguana, and in Santo Domingo. He also kept busy writing. Oviedo took on the role of quasi-counselor to the king and his council by writing numerous informative letters about the state of affairs in the Indies.[27] And, of course, he diligently continued parts II and III of the *History*. These parts increasingly recount his disillusionment with the conquest. The sections recount cruel acts by Spaniards toward each other in civil wars and, sometimes, toward innocent indigenous populations as well as a general decline in the population and riches produced in some areas of the new territories. Parts II and III focus more exclusively on general rather than natural history. By the 1540s, Oviedo's home city of Santo Domingo was beginning to decline as gold production slowed and a labor shortage developed, a decline that resulted in an all-out crisis by the 1550s. The island's native populations had been decimated by disease and forced labor. In Peru, the devastating civil wars spurred by the Pizarro brothers' greed, which culminated in the killing of the viceroy, revealed a shocking lawlessness among Spaniards. In Spain, Las Casas campaigned hard and with varying degrees of success against the *repartimiento* system. Oviedo favored this scheme, no doubt because he benefited from it. Las Casas enjoyed success in 1542 with the passage of the New Laws, which prohibited the system. Despite the fact that these laws were partially revoked in 1544 and were continuously debated and often ignored for the next decade or more, Oviedo's early portrayals of many Native Americans as inferior devil worshipers often brought him into the debate—at times on the losing side of it.

Originally setting out to publish a revised version of part I as well as parts II and III in 1542, Oviedo could not travel to Spain because of battles in the Caribbean with French corsairs. He did not receive permission to leave Hispaniola until 1546. Upon Oviedo's arrival in Spain with his completed manuscript, he discovered that it would be very costly to publish the full *History* and that Las Casas intended to block its publication. In the political climate of the times, there was little the chronicler could do to obtain a license to publish his work. The Crown's energies and resources were absorbed by a severe famine in Castile, and for the most part the king's son Prince Philip, who greatly esteemed Las Casas, ruled in Charles's absence. Nonetheless, a second edition of the largely unrevised first part of the *History* was published in Salamanca the following year (1547). During his two-year stay in Spain, Oviedo continued to revise all three parts of the manuscript, and in 1549 he finally deposited the final version in a monastery in Seville for safekeeping before returning to Santo Domingo.[28] During this time in Spain, the historian also devoted time to collecting information for his manual about the household of Prince Don Juan, *Libro de la cámara,* which Prince Philip had requested, and for the *Batallas y Quinquagenas,* which he had begun years earlier but had suspended while he completed the *General and Natural History.* In a more spiritual turn, Oviedo apparently translated and published a best-selling book in Tuscan, *Reglas de la vida y secreta teología* (Seville 1548).[29] This was Oviedo's last trip to Spain.

THE FINAL YEARS (1549–1557)

Oviedo returned to his post as constable of the fortress in 1549 and for the next eight years of his life continued to write diligently. Notably, however, he shifted his focus away from America and toward Europe—both its past and present. Oviedo promised a fourth part to the *General and Natural History,* and there is even a copy of an outline for it, but there is no evidence that he continued the history of the Indies during these final years.[30] Instead, the author dedicated his final writings to two multifaceted moralistic biographical works on virtuous individuals: he finished the *Quinquagenas* and resumed the *Batallas y Quinquagenas.*

One final attempt to publish the *History* in 1556 resulted in the publication of the first book of part II, but the effort was cut short by Oviedo's death,[31] in his adopted city of Santo Domingo on June 27, 1557. One of the salient characteristics of Oviedo's two final works and his history is his often frank and disarming observations about his own life. For example, he tells us that in these final years he had a full head of white hair and was toothless and nearly deaf, having to place his ear on a guitar in order to hear it.[32] Through these comments we glimpse him as a person. He had a sensual appetite, a deep curiosity for novelty, a penchant for promoting his career, and a strong sense of morality. He was also highly critical and at times contentious. In chapter 3 of this book we will see more of Oviedo as a man who lived between the Old and the New worlds and as a man who constantly negotiated his changing roles.

By the time Oviedo died, the great emperor Charles V had abdicated, Europe had endured a series of costly wars, and Hispaniola was in a state of crisis. Both Europe and America had dramatically changed since 1492. The post of royal chronicler of the Indies left vacant by Oviedo's death would not be filled by the new king until the appointment of Juan López de Velasco in 1571.[33] For more than a decade, no other Spaniard would attempt an extensive description of America's general and natural history.

AN OVERVIEW OF OVIEDO'S WORKS

Fernández de Oviedo's most important legacy is a corpus of about ten major books (several are multivolume works). As a writer he was versatile and prolific, ambitious and professional. His writing displays not only a knowledge of a broad range of historical events, but also a mastery of several literary genres, and they contain historical, ecclesiastic, and juridical discourses. Keeping in mind the cost and relative newness of the printing press, one can say Oviedo enjoyed a good deal of editorial success: three of his nine works were published or partially published in his lifetime, and two were widely translated. Subsequently, all but two have been published, at least in part. (For a complete listing of Oviedo's extant autograph manuscripts and publications, see the bibliography.) Although Oviedo's official duties as a writer included being a secretary and notary to important political figures and a chronicler for three kings, he also wrote a novel, biographical dialogues, and moralistic poetic musings. In addition, he translated works in the Tuscan language into Spanish. A product of his times, Oviedo's choice of genres span the gamut from legal depositions and historical narrative to octosyllabic poetic verse and translation. Many works also include a visual dimension: illustrations and coats-of-arms are drawn into manuscripts with beautiful calligraphy (for example, see fig. 82).

Taken as a whole, Oviedo's works reveal an aesthetic sensitivity, concern for representational practices of the period, insistence on a moral dimension, and a keen personal ambition. Depending on the text, Oviedo focused more carefully on aesthetic considerations and moral concerns, as we see in his last work (*Quinquagenas*), or more doggedly on the bureaucratic details and his own role and loyalty to the Crown, as we see in the manual for Philip about the organization of Prince Don Juan's household (*Libro de la cámara*). Together, these works provide an important aesthetic and political context for understanding Oviedo's masterpiece, the *General and Natural History*. In 1519, the chivalric romance best known as the *Don Claribalte* was published and dedicated to Oviedo's former patron the duke of Calabria, Fernando de Aragón, to give him good reading during his imprisonment. Reportedly written during Oviedo's first trip to America, the book has an Arthurian hero who echoes to a degree Charles

V's political aspirations: the knight errant becomes emperor of Constantinople and eventually pope. By 1526 the first natural history and illustrations of the Indies exotica, known as the *Sumario,* was written, dedicated to Charles V, and published in Toledo. Upon his return to Nicaragua, Oviedo finished a work that is still unpublished: a book of heraldry and genealogy, *Libro del blasón* (ca. 1528). About five years later, Oviedo wrote his report relating his interview of the king of France, Francis I, during his imprisonment after the battle of Pavia, *Relación de lo sucedido.* During this same period, the author presented the first of a three-part genealogical history of the Spanish monarchy, from its mythic origins to the reign of Juan II (father of Queen Isabella) to Charles's wife, the empress Isabel. Including genealogical trees, poetry by Juan de Mena, his own octosyllabic verse and stories, this *Catálogo Real de Castilla* is a synthesis of Spanish historiography (1532). Only one volume survives, and it has been published only as part of a recent dissertation.[34]

Three years later, Oviedo's *General and Natural History* continued the political agenda of mapping and legitimizing the Spanish empire, but this time the New World is his focus. The first part (bks. 1–19 and bk. 50 of part III) was published in 1535 and republished in 1547 and 1557.[35] Parts II and III were composed between at least 1535 and 1542, revised and augmented from 1542 to 1549, and published in full only in the 1850s, in spite of the editorial success of part I.

After the disappointment of not seeing his beloved history published in 1548, Oviedo spent his final years on projects that had been left unfinished while he wrote historical narratives about America.[36] He now turned to European subjects and new genre types, especially dialogue and poetry. He completed the *Batallas* in 1552, a work in the tradition of the biographies of illustrious Spanish aristocrats written by Pérez de Guzmán and Hernando del Pulgar. Oviedo, in the persona of his role as *alcaide,* interviews a night watchman (*sereno*), and each of the 150 interviews, or dialogues (three sets of 50 *quinquagenas*), gives a biographical sketch of the life and achievements of Spanish aristocrats whom Oviedo had met. The work is surprisingly devoid of New World individuals and is filled with remembrances and echoes of Oviedo's youthful years in Italy. Most of volumes 1 and 2 were published in the twentieth century, but the third is still unpublished. His last work, the *Quinquagenas de los generosos e ilustres e no menos famosos reyes, príncipes, duques* (ca. 1555), also focuses on the chivalric feats and individual valor of Spaniards in Italy, but it is written as a series of three *quinquagenas,* each of 50 poems, each with its own gloss. The tone is more clearly spiritual and moralistic than in any of Oviedo's other works. Presented as a memento to Philip, the three-volume manuscript has beautiful calligraphy and illustrations. Only sections of it have been published, first in the 1880s and later in 1974.

As noted earlier, Oviedo appears to have also intended to translate two works written in Tuscan. The first was a literary work by the famous fourteenth-century Italian author Giovanni Boccaccio. The second appears to have been a best-selling late fifteenth-century Italian religious manual entitled *Rules for the Spiritual Life*.[37] The first translation coincides with Oviedo's literary interest of the 1510s and early 1520s, the second with his increasing concern in later years with moral conduct and behavior. There is no evidence that either of the translations ever reached the publisher, in spite of licenses having been granted.

Most of Oviedo's texts are filled with glosses, citations, and allusions to the textual authorities of his epoch. On the basis of Oviedo's citations, Daymond Turner's important study reconstructs Oviedo's possible library, which was full of literary and historical works that provided ancient, humanist, and Castilian models for his own texts.[38] Writing at a time when the individual author's voice was increasingly valued—but only if the author could first establish his knowledge of the canon—Oviedo parades his textual universe before readers. Although he did not master Latin, he quotes many classical texts in Latin in the *History*, and others were probably based on Italian or Spanish translations or summaries.[39] Oviedo was fairly learned. He had contact with such great Spanish humanists as Hernán Núñez and Antonio Nebrija and, according to some scholars, was trained alongside his masters in various courts, especially that of Don Juan.[40] But Oviedo clearly was not a university man and therefore often attempted to compensate for this lack by proving his bookish knowledge. His works reflect a didactic impulse and a need to assert his own importance in the events he chronicles. From books about knight errantry and genealogy to reflections on men he met in America and Italy, Oviedo's texts reveal the ideological perspective of an ambitious man who lived between two worlds and considered himself an emissary for God and king. As we will see in subsequent chapters, his most famous book, *The General and Natural History of the Indies*, the focus of this study, reveals a man who worked constantly to navigate the complex politics and ambiguities of living and working in a colonial setting and in a period of rapid change in both Western history and historiographical practices.

TWO

A READER'S GUIDE TO A NEW WORLD HISTORY

(Proemio, *bk. 1)*

What I have said cannot be learned in Salamanca, in Bologna, or Paris, but only in the lecture hall of the quarterdeck . . . just because a person studies Cosmography, and knows it better than Ptolemy, he will not know, by means of all the words ever written, how to navigate until he tries it. Nor will reading Medicine enable one to cure the sick as one should, until one gains experience, such as taking a pulse, and by means of it understanding the paroxysms and precise terms which should be applied to the illness. . . . Of relevance here is a courtly proverb which sly people often say: he who has not been a page always smells like a mule driver. (bk. 2, chap. 9)

Early in the *General and Natural History of the Indies* Oviedo proclaims that the route to the Indies and the Indies themselves could not be learned in the great texts of classical antiquity or in the hallowed halls of any of Europe's best universities. Indeed, the new cosmography that was emerging contradicted the wisdom of the ancients. Information provided by New World explorers raised the thorny issue of how to incorporate "another half of the world" into a philosophical and intellectual framework that was thousands of years old. To deal with this issue Oviedo inscribes his "true and new history" (verdadera y nueva historia) in the historiography of the Hapsburg Empire and of the canon. Echoing his most direct model, the well-known Roman historian Pliny the Elder, who wrote for his own emperor, Oviedo presents the topic of writing with authority about new things: "As Pliny said of his own [pen] in the prologue to his *Natural History*: it is hard to make old things new; to bestow authority on what is new . . . and authenticity on what is doubtful" (Prologue, part I).[1] In writing about a new era, empire, and hemisphere, Oviedo discusses the definition, method, language, and purpose of a written history of Charles V's American territories. They become motifs throughout Oviedo's self-conscious narrative and provide a basis for his theories of narrative authority and truth. Nowhere are these elements addressed as methodically as in the preface (*proemio*) that opens the first edition of the history (1535).

Three general prefaces demarcate the three-part *General and Natural History;* each part opens with its own preface to the reader (and most of the fifty books within the three parts open with their own prefaces). Part I, published in 1535, comprises the first nineteen books, corresponding to the years 1492–1520. Its publication followed Oviedo's first editorial success, the *Sumario* (1526), Charles V's victories in Spain and Europe, and the conquest of the Aztec capital and Pizarro's remarkable conquest of Cajamarca. The overall tone of part I is jubilant and triumphant, and extensive sections treat the natural world. Parts II and III focus more specifically on the general history from 1520 to 1549 and reflect a growing disillusionment with the conquest. Their two prefaces date from between 1544 and 1549.

Although generally written last, the preface is meant to be read first, as the author's instructions to the reader before embarking upon the main text. It is a guide, a key for understanding textual issues—both direct and indirect—such as the author's role, sources, and practical concerns. During the Renaissance the preface held a prominent place in the makeup of a text. There the author usually revealed the basic parameters of the work: the patron/addressee(s), the genre type and its specific rhetorical conventions, the purpose of the text, and the place of enunciation. In addition, and perhaps more important, it is here that the author establishes his ongoing dialogue with the reader. Oviedo's preface to part I is an extremely valuable guide to understanding both the pragmatics of the *History* and the larger intellectual debates it engages. In four pages the author explains his role as loyal vassal and scribe for an imperial monarch, and, therefore, his need to write a useful, worthy, decorous official history. The emperor hired him to be an informant-counselor, assigning him the duty of reporting truthfully about empire. The two subsequent prefaces, corresponding to parts II and III, are more concerned with the development of the conquest and with changes in the empire than with Oviedo's historical method.

When the official chronicler set out to write the first preface he made clear the dilemma he and other early modern writers faced. The cultural tradition for accessing knowledge and what is knowable was constituted primarily as a textual tradition: books were considered the sources and the authorities for gaining knowledge. Although experience and empiricism could add to the store of knowledge, as in the case of medieval travel accounts about Asia, such as those by Marco Polo and Pero Tafir, knowledge was based on a mostly textual universe. Indeed, by Columbus's generation, Polo's enormously popular account had become yet another text for interpreting the world. Well-established books set the limits on the knowable world. The Age of Exploration, and Europe's discovery of America in particular, brought a new set of data and questions to European minds. The data often challenged the canon; traditional knowledge literarily no longer fit the New World view. One of the clearest examples of this, of course, was the ancient texts' calculations of the size of the globe, especially the distance from western Europe to Japan, the lands, if any, that lay between the two, and the percentage of the world that was deemed inhabitable. The distance between Europe and Asia was greater than that calculated by the Greek geographer and astronomer Ptolemy; an entire hemisphere lay between the two Old World continents; and, again contrary to the opinion of the ancients, more than one-fifth of the globe was habitable by human beings—the torrid zone below the equator was full of people.

New World reality challenged the sixteenth-century canon, and writers like Oviedo had to devise a method to reconcile the Old World system with new empirical information. The responses, even in a single author's work, often were delayed and inconsistent. Oviedo reveals a remarkable range of reactions and strategies as he writes over the course of several decades. The responses to the cracks in the canon depended on many factors, but two stand out. First, although access to knowledge was seen as primarily a bookish endeavor, the era of exploration saw important inventions, such as the compass and the printing press, which altered how knowledge was gained and disseminated.

Second, the culture of the book varied in different intellectual circles. As Anthony Grafton points out in his study *New World, Ancient Texts,* at the turn of the sixteenth century there was an encyclopedic tendency that envisioned the book as being able to contain all the knowledge necessary to know completely the cosmos. Moreover, these works, such as the *Nuremberg Chronicle* (1493), mixed authorities without regard to chronology when presenting a world history (18–19). In the university, however, textual knowledge was less static. As professors and students followed scholastic methods and used examples from books for lecture and disputation, knowledge became layered, and textual contradictions were explained away through commentary and allegory. When humanists came on the scene, they emphasized the *studia humanitatis*: grammar, rhetoric, and dialectic—the arts that gave the student a command of Latin, which then helped him read the great texts of the ancients in order to study poetry, history, and philosophy. Humanists argued with scholastics about how to use the canon, but even within the humanist school there were lively debates about whether ancient texts should be read as sources of fairly static information or reinterpreted to be more relevant to modern times. One paradigmatic debate centered on the question of whether the works of the Roman rhetorical theorist Cicero should be imitated exactly as he wrote them or whether they should be updated, as if Cicero were a contemporary. The great humanist Erasmus of Rotterdam wrote an entire dialogue on the subject. While learned men discussed the role of the canon, explorers had a certain culture of the book as well. As Grafton points out, most men gained a sense of the world through the Bible, chivalric romances, family genealogies, and travel accounts. Some of these accounts were fictitious and other were not; an example of the former is John Mandeville's popular fourteenth-century travels of a fabulous knight who sees Amazon women and one-eyed monsters, while Polo's more factual *Travels* illustrates the latter trend (72). We know that Columbus relied on, for example, Polo's text, Pliny's *Natural History,* Pierre d'Ailly's *Imago Mundi,* Aeneas Sylvius's *History,* and, of course, the Bible.

Over one hundred books formed Oviedo's textual universe. Daymond Turner's study of the books Oviedo cites in his works (1971) reveals that the chronicler demonstrated knowledge of a broad spectrum of classical, humanist, Castilian, and New World historiographical texts.[2] Oviedo cites, among other Greco-Roman authorities, Cicero, Herodotus, Plutarch, Pliny, Ptolemy, and Thucydides; he mentions humanists such as Giovanni Pontano and Leonardo Bruni; he looks to Castilian chronicles on Enrique II and Alfonso VIII as well as that by Hernán Pérez de Gúzman; he cites Alfonso X's legal text the *Siete Partidas;* and he discusses New World authors' texts, such as Amerigo Vespucci's letter of 1504, Peter Martyr's *De Orbe Novo,* and the manuscript version of the work by the cosmographer Alonso de Santa Cruz. In addition to these historiographical works, Oviedo cites numerous literary works, ranging from the chivalric romance *Amadís de Gaula* to works by Dante, Petrarch, and the fifteenth-century Spanish poet Juan de Mena; philosophical and philological works, such as those by the humanists Erasmus, Antonio Nebrija, and Juan Luis Vives, who was deeply influenced by Erasmus; and religious and moral works, such as the popular lives of the saints, the *Flos Sanctorum,* Ludolphus's *Life of Christ,* and numerous works by St. Augustine. Each of these textual categories established a set of knowledge and range of conventions for writing a history.

Beyond any writer's a priori textual framing of the world and knowledge, his official role in and exposure to the New World also deeply influenced his point of view. Early Europeans who wrote about America tended to fall into three categories: explorers/conquistadors, churchmen, and Crown officials. Explorers and conquistadors often wrote specific accounts about their missions in order to petition for reward or to justify their actions, as we see in Columbus's and Cortés's letters. Men of the Church, depending on their affiliation with mendicant orders or not, often devoted themselves to producing catechisms in local languages and pictographs or to writing systematic descriptions of natives (for example, the Franciscan school of Bernardino de Sahagún) or treatises defending the Native Americans (for example, Bartolomé de Las Casas). Crown bureaucrats, such as Martyr and Oviedo, presented their writings as a service to the Crown, usually promoting its agendas while carving out an important role for themselves within the Crown's agenda. An author's textual universe, his firsthand experience (or lack of it) in America, and his official position (if any) certainly influenced his access to information as well as his interpretation of it.

Oviedo's *General and Natural History of the Indies* responds to paradigm shifts between the worldview of scholastics and humanists, between European textual framing of knowledge and lived experience in a new world, between personal and religious objectives and a new imperial power. The intellectual traditions and canon for writing a general (based on men's actions) and natural (based on nature) history are the underpinnings for Oviedo's text, even as he expands and revises them. He self-consciously and insistently evoked these debates and traditions in order to design a new hybrid historiographic practice and work. The chronicler drew upon a diverse textual universe. As we have seen, he quotes frequently from ancient and contemporary books; he knew famous humanists, such as Pontano and Nebrija; he was trained in the Castilian court and had been hired by King Ferdinand of Aragón to participate in a Castilian historiographic project; and he read a multitude of explorers', conquistadors', governors', and missionaries' reports from the New World because of the royal edict he received which allowed him access to them. These texts and traditions dictated certain historiographical practices and norms that the official chronicler had to confront when he embarked upon his own "new" history.

In broad terms, Renaissance historians agreed with Aristotle that history reports specific events without adornment, which distinguishes it from the realm of the probable and universal treated in fiction and poetry.

This definition, however, centered on the nature and value of truth. Was a history truthful if it presented a moral or artistic truth? Or did a truthful history need to be based on documented, eyewitness accounts? Vives, the great contemporary Spanish humanist whom Oviedo cites, stated in a work from the 1530s, *De Ratione Dicendi,* that history should be like a mirror, narrated so as to reflect the truth (*El Arte de hablar* 780). This in turn served a didactic end, teaching its readers how to live their lives, as *magistra vitae*. Nonetheless, Vives argues in humanist style that history may employ a slightly embellished style. In a dialogued treatise entitled "Truth Dressed Up," he expounds upon the idea that truth, if completely naked of adornment, is too harsh. Thus, for the humanist, history's defining component was its truthful narration, but the narrative needed philological and moral components as well: good style and a solid moral purpose. In addition to these parameters, humanists' translations, critiques, and restorations of ancient histories, such as those by Herodotus, Tacitus, Pliny, and Thucydides, transformed critical methods used for interpreting historical documents: humanist translations heightened the awareness of the relativity and uniqueness of cultures distant in time or space. New sources revolutionized the writing of history. For instance, humanists such as Lorenzo Valla had translated the Greek history about Egypt by Herodotus and had written his own historical texts. Oviedo was well aware of these humanist debates and practices.

In sixteenth-century Castile, there was also a well-established historiographical tradition upon which Oviedo drew (Carbia 15–44). As R. B. Tate demonstrates, historiography in the era of the Catholic Kings reflects the expansionist goals of the monarchy. The post of royal chronicler was increasingly separated from the post of secretary (*cancellería*) and seen as a distinct duty and salaried position. Histories were educational, written in Latin for an international public, and they mapped the expansion of territory both in Castile's past and present. Queen Isabella dismissed the longtime royal chronicler Palencia and replaced him with Hernando del Pulgar because the latter proved a more willing messenger of official politics (Tate 18). As Richard Kagan discusses in his article on the Hapsburg monarch, the Catholic Kings' grandson, Charles V, continued to prize historians for their role in legitimizing his monarchy. He employed numerous chroniclers for his European enterprises; some, like Juan Ginés de Sepúlveda, portrayed the emperor in humanist, classical terms as a king with both positive and negative traits, while others, such as Pedro Mexía, depicted Charles in a traditional Castilian providentialist light. Curiously, however, none of these European histories were published during Charles

V's reign, and only Sepúlveda's was completed. (Sepúlveda would later use Oviedo's history as support in his debate against Las Casas.) Regardless of their approach, as Tate notes, the historians after 1490 developed a more individual voice, one in which the narrator is inseparable from the narrative (20).

This Castilian historiographic tradition is crucial to understanding the background of Oviedo's *General and Natural History.* Although based in America for much of his career, Oviedo actively participated in this development of the historian playing a stronger role within the empire's political agenda and of the historian carving out a strong authorial presence for himself within the text. While the royal chronicler of the Indies blended elements from the various historiographic traditions, he also deviated significantly from the trend of writing a more international, learned history in Latin. Most notably, Oviedo chose to write in Castilian, unlike his only predecessor as royal chronicler of the Indies, the Italian humanist Martyr. (Oviedo had met him in 1515 and refers to his history and letters about America.) The decision to write in Castilian was probably the result of several factors. First, Oviedo's command of Latin was not good enough to enable him to write in that language. He laments in the *History* that his Latin is not as good as that of his friend the Italian poet Pietro Bembo. (Bembo, however, was known for writing in the vernacular as well.) Second, he argues that Castilian is a noble, imperial language. Oviedo may have expanded upon the implications of the first Castilian grammar, penned by Oviedo's contemporary Nebrija at Queen Isabella's request in 1492. Nebrija proclaims in his preface to the grammar that the vernacular, in this case Castilian, was an important tool for expansion: "It is the handmaid of the Empire" (es la doncella del imperio). Nebrija wrote his providentialist history in the international, learned language of the day, but he opened the door for someone like Oviedo to use the vernacular, ennobling a return to a tradition begun with Alfonso the Wise's twelfth-century chronicle. Moreover, the same year Oviedo published his history, Charles V, in a letter to the pope, stipulated Spanish as the official language (1536).[3]

By 1611, these historiographical theories and practices were well codified in a treatise by the Spaniard Luis Cabrera de Córdoba. He explains that history is "the relating of truths by a wise man to teach how to live well" (xli).[4] And, while truth is the soul of history (40), history serves as "the feet of the empire" (29). Historians should employ a concise, decorous style, a task that Cabrera admits was difficult to adhere to during the rapid expansion of Charles V's and Philip II's empires. The treatise recommends, in addition, the imitation of only one authoritative text as a way to improve both style and content: imitation is "the companion of eloquence, [which is] the educator of ignorance" (148).[5]

A concern for the nature of history, the role of language, and the definition of truth emerges at every turn in Oviedo's history. The preface to nearly every one of the fifty books insists on some aspect of historiographical practice. As a royal chronicler trained in Europe, Oviedo was well acquainted with the debates about and pitfalls of writing in an evolving genre. Nowhere is this more evident than in his first preface.[6]

PREFACES IN THE *HISTORY*

In his first preface, addressed to his employer King Charles V and his royal counselors, Oviedo discusses the empire's urgent need for a new history and the key role he, the writer, plays in creating that history. The lengthy preface defines the historical project within the demands of the genre and as part of a providential plan for the Spanish empire. The preface opens with an erudite reference to an ancient authority, El Tostado, on the location of the East Indies and closes with a mention of contemporary historians writing about Charles's European territories. In between ancient and contemporary histories, the chronicler for the West Indies carves out a space for his history, one which mixes traditional concepts with new empirical data, true love for America with imperial politics. The preface covers a good deal of ground but emphasizes four areas: the vastness and abundance of the new territories, the need for knowledge of these lands, the reliability of his historical method, and his qualifications for the task.

First, Oviedo discusses the need for a "true cosmography," one which would record the novelty, abundance, and riches of the New World. Other parts of the world have been mapped; now Oviedo must map New World peoples, fauna, and flora. Pitting the wisdom of the traditional canon, such as Ptolemy and Pliny, against his own experiential knowledge, the chronicler declares,

> Some cosmographers would have it that much less than a fifth thereof [the world] is inhabited, from which opinion I am very far removed, as a man who, apart from all that Ptolemy wrote, knows that in this empire of the Indies . . . there are such great kingdoms . . . far removed from anything which has been recorded, *ab initio* up to our

> own time, that the span of a man's life is hardly sufficient [either] to see it, to begin to comprehend, or [even] to conjecture upon it.

He will write about a new hemisphere teeming with people, plants, and animals—all proof of a dynamic worldview in which man was destined to take over the globe.[7] The ancients never recorded such abundance:

> What mortal understanding can comprehend such diversity of languages, habits, [or] customs among the people of the Indies? Such variety of animals, from domestic to wild and savage? Such an unutterable multitude of trees, [some] laden with diverse kinds of fruit and others barren, both those which the Indians cultivate as those produced by Nature's own work without the aid of human hands?

He first portrays the Indies as a cornucopia of aromatic plants and fruit-bearing trees. In addition, there are rich mercantile possibilities in America. Besides its coveted silver, gold, and pearls, the New World offers fertile lands for agriculture and cattle, "products which are desired by many kingdoms of this world."[8] This natural and mercantile paradise belongs to his patron, the king, "with one and all under your rule."[9] Oviedo moves beyond what had been literary topoi about the wonderous novelty of the New World in Columbus's and Martyr's texts and catalogues American phenomena, naming objects and mapping them in specific geographical regions. For a monarch who continually needed funds to finance his far-flung military campaigns and to rule his vast empire, this information was crucial. With intentions typical of those of a Renaissance historian, Oviedo promises that his work will help the emperor rule; through Oviedo's eyes and text, Charles V will know his new peoples and lands and their commercial potential, even though his life span will surely be too short to "see" (ver) and "comprehend" (entender) the immensity of these new lands.

Oviedo recognized that knowledge served many ends and that the more he established the utility of his knowledge of the Indies, the more important his history would be. But he attempted to place his work on a higher plane. Glossing his most direct model, Pliny, the New World historian addresses a more general reader with reference to a divine plan. He argues that all men have a God-given curiosity to know about the world beyond their own experience. The *General and Natural History* satisfies this curiosity while also moving it toward a good end, as praise of God's handiwork. His history reveals nature's secret wonders. The chronicler's ambition is to describe nothing less than God's Book of Nature, making divine creation accessible to all. Last, if published, Oviedo argues, the history will reach many readers who may recognize in its pages the signs of a divine plan in Charles V's Holy Roman Empire. The text encourages the emperor's desire for fame and glory: "so that all the world should know the extension and greatness of these states which God set aside for your royal Castilian crown for the good fortune and merits of Your Imperial Majesty."[10] When Christians and infidels alike hear of America's marvels, they will be obliged to praise God. The chronicler links his eye and word with the divine Book of Nature and makes providentialist claims for Charles's reign in America. Oviedo's ultimate goal is to position his text as the official history of the empire.

Much of the preface sets out Oviedo's specific conception of a historiographical project that documents a new land for a providential emperor and the greater glory of God. Engaging indirectly, and at times directly, with period debates about the nature of history, Oviedo discusses the choice of models, method, and structure. At the base of his argument lies the belief that a "new history" requires new methods to assure its authority. The chronicler emphasizes the difference between his history and previous ones. Oviedo chooses Pliny the Elder's encyclopedic *Natural History,* written for the Roman emperor, as a comparable model for compiling vast amounts of real and fantastic information. Indeed, Pliny's own prologue discusses many of the same issues Oviedo's covers: the problem of novelty, foreign words, a lack of textual models, the reliability of sources, the amount of information, and detractors. But the Spaniard emphatically asserts a certain independence from his model: Oviedo writes about another part of the world and includes its general history, the contemporaneous events of the conquest and early colonization from 1492 until "the end of his life." Just as important, the *General and Natural History* differs in method and, therefore, truthfulness. Pliny's work depended more on literary sources than on empirical investigation. The Spaniard announces that he uses only eyewitness testimony, even though gathering it entailed many hardships:

> I have not culled them from two hundred thousand volumes I might have read, as Pliny wrote . . . where it seems that he related what he had read. . . . I, however, compiled what I here write from two hundred thousand hardships, privations and dangers in the more than

> twenty-two years that I have personally witnessed and experienced these things, serving God and my king in these Indies, and having crossed the wide ocean eight times.

Whereas Pliny is the explicit ancient model for his history, Martyr is the implicit contemporary countermodel. Oviedo never mentions Martyr's successful *Decades* or *De Orbe Novo* in the preface, but he accuses historians who never traveled to the Indies of falsely representing America. Martyr never set foot in the New World, yet his elegant Latin texts were enormously popular. Oviedo had a hard act to follow, and his claim to difference—and authoritative truth—rests on his years of experience in America. He pits the humanist reliance on a textual world and sources against a more empirical method, yet one that was only just beginning to be developed. Oviedo tirelessly interviewed conquistadors, explorers, and missionaries, read countless eyewitness reports, and traveled widely to gather source material.

The relative silence about his countermodel also provides a backdrop for understanding the chronicler's insistence on the role of language and style in the *History*. As we have seen, most humanist histories demonstrated a great concern for eloquence and were written in Latin; even most contemporary Castilian histories were written in Latin. Oviedo's choice of Castilian set his history apart from the writings of many of his contemporaries, even though it harkened back to an earlier Castilian historiographical tradition. Moreover, Oviedo's style is a far cry from the carefully crafted rhetorical and stylistic elegance of a humanist like Martyr. Recognizing the gap between his work and that of university-trained writers, Oviedo employs the language of the debate about history and language to defend and underscore the truthfulness of his text. Oviedo's combative insecurity helps to explain his verbose, legalistic style. He argues he may have a poor style, but it is simple, direct, and true, free of the excessive "ornamentation" (*ornamento*), "artifice" (*artificio*), and "cleverness" (*industria*) which are the trademarks of fiction. Others, he asserts, write more elegantly, but their accounts are full of lies (*fábulas*). Linked with the dilemma of style and language is the problem of nomenclature. Reflecting philosophical and linguistic debates about the relationship between a thing and its name, the chronicler deliberately chooses to use Native American words for certain objects and practices that do not have a close equivalent in the Old World. These include, for example, the hammock, the canoe, and Caribbean sacred objects like the *semí* and dances such as the *areito*. He anticipates critics who might question his command of Castilian and flaunts his credentials: "I was born in Madrid, grew up in the royal household, conversed with noble folk, and have read a thing or two." Once again, the discussion centers on the crucial issue of establishing authority when writing about a new world.

The chronicler's qualifications are marshaled in support of the truthfulness of his *History.* Besides insisting on the validity of his empirical historical method, he creates a persona, the reliable chronicler, "escriptor vuestro," at the service of God, knowledge, and the emperor. A three-part strategy accomplishes these goals. First, the chronicler emphasizes his qualifications as a competent historian. Ten years ago, he says, at the emperor's behest he wrote a successful brief natural history, *De la naturaleza* (1526). The emperor, trusting Oviedo's work, then hired him to be the official royal chronicler of the Indies. Oviedo adds to this profile of a zealous historian that of a loyal vassal of forty years. Since his youth he has served the monarchy, first in the court of "your grandparents" then as a servant of the empire, taking the dangerous post of overseer of the gold foundries and captain in the early settlement of lands filled with warlike natives. He summarizes his profile: "For twenty-two years . . . I see and experience [all] . . . serving God and my king."[11]

Second, as a historian who has nothing to hide and who recognizes the hierarchical chain of command, Oviedo submits his history to Charles's Council of the Americas, or Consejo de Indias, as well as to the Church for "correction and emendation" (correción y enmienda). He positions himself as a loyal vassal to the king, council, and Church.

A third strategy permeates the preface. The chronicler casts himself into the archetypal roles of traveler, Christian witness, and near martyr. His self-portrait borrows the language of travel accounts and hagiographies in order to depict himself as a "pilgrim" (peregrino) who travels and "suffers" (padecer) a multitude of "dangers" and "travails" (peligros, trabajos), all for the greater good of the Christian empire (I discuss this point in depth in chapter 3). His pilgrimage began with the first trip to America, when Pedrarias Dávila joined Balboa in the settlement of Tierra Firme. Oviedo declares that of the twenty-five hundred Christian settlers of Darién, by 1535 no more than forty survived. According to the author, the land was depopulated because of the "savage Indians" and the natural dangers. Through the hardship early settlers endured, the region was finally Christianized.

No longer active in settling non-Christian lands at the time of writing the *History,* Oviedo states that his trials now serve a yet greater purpose. His firsthand experiences are transposed into a textual medium in order to bear witness for the king and others of "the pleasant lesson of hearing and understanding so many secrets of Nature" and to make manifest Spain's providential role.[12] The author links his "praiseworthy occupation" (loable ocupación) as historian to the great divine plan for Spain and all of Christendom. Oviedo writes of the pacification of native populations in America and of the victories of Charles's armies against Mohammad and the Turks. Notably, at the turn of the next century Cabrera de Córdoba treatise on Castilian historiographical practice called for the historian to be all that Oviedo attempts to be in his preface: educated, well traveled, a pilgrim, well versed in government, and a good investigator (*inquiador*) (29).

About fifteen to twenty years after publishing the preface to part I, Oviedo wrote prefaces to parts II and III. By the mid- to late 1540s Oviedo's perspective had evolved: part I had enjoyed editorial success while also coming under some criticism; he had further developed his methodology; and the nature of the American enterprise had changed. These two prefaces reflect a less jubilant, more contentious man who focuses far less on the divine secrets of a bountiful nature and far more on the politics of the conquest and the increasingly problematic relationship with his detractors and his primary textual model, Pliny. The preface to part II includes a brief reiteration of Oviedo's persona as a suffering vassal committed to a truthful yet dangerous empirical method. But the main thrust of the preface pits the accomplishments of contemporary imperial Spain against those of the ancient Roman Empire. The author focuses less on representing his own experience and more on the *History* as representative of a new truth, age, and empire. Echoing the genealogy of the Castilian monarchy found in his *Catálogo Real* (1532), Oviedo rejects the Roman Empire as the predecessor to the Spanish empire and creates instead a link with the medieval Iberian Visigoth kings. In an era when Charles's relationship with Rome was tense, the royal chronicler recalls the sins of Romans in Iberia: the number of Christians put to death by Roman rulers and the Roman traitor who gave Iberia to the Moors. By contrast he hails the glories of the Visigoths—to Oviedo's mind, a race without African or non-Christian bloodlines and one which reinforced the Castilian Crown's exclusionary policies against Moors, Jews, and many native cultures in the Indies.[13]

Taking up another sensitive topic in support of his king, Oviedo touches on the lawsuits of Columbus's heirs against the monarch but deliberately leaves these for chroniclers of Iberian history. Not long after the publication in 1535 of part I, Fernando Columbus wrote his own hagiographic history of his father and contested Oviedo's thesis that Columbus did not discover America, but that he knew about it through the written records given to him from an unknown "sailor" (piloto). This time around Oviedo seems to want to support the monarchy in its legal battles with the Columbus family but avoid further angering Columbus's sons, with whom he had served in Don Juan's court. The preface to part II clearly demonstrates the integral role Oviedo's history played in the imperial agenda and the similarities between his arguments in texts about America and Spain. Perhaps more significant, after living primarily in America for several decades, Oviedo creates a genealogy for himself and other Spaniards living in America, the so-called *Indianos*: "It was Goths and Spaniards who discovered these Indies."[14] His new history establishes a new identity for Spanish settlers.

The third and final preface returns to two key textual issues discussed in the opening preface, but in a distinct register. First, Oviedo speaks confidently and unambiguously about a new cosmography that made ancients' ideas, such as those of Pliny, obsolete. The "torrid" zone is not only inhabitable, but there are temperate places and areas with snow-capped mountains:

> As Pliny declared that of the five parts of the world only three were habitable, it follows that as people who knew less of the world, there was much more of which the Ancients had no knowledge . . . and this matter of the torrid zone . . . is surely an error which has now been amply shown as such, for every day our Spaniards travel from the Tropic of Cancer to the [Tropic] of Capricorn and back again. So you see, truth is completely the opposite of this.[15]

Part III of the *History* describes the geography and conquest of these lands. Ancient texts were still needed as tools to guide the interpretation and definition of new data, but the information they contained often was no longer valid. Second, the historian reiterates his empirically based methodology. However, his tone betrays a deep concern. Much had changed by the mid-1540s. He is no longer writing about his own experiences, since he had never traveled to South America. The author now has to depend completely on other witnesses' firsthand reports.

Moreover, part I had been widely read for over a decade and, while some people praised it, others harshly criticized it. The highly influential Las Casas, in particular, took issue with Oviedo's portraits of Native Americans as savage infidels, and he worked hard to block the publication of parts II and III. Perhaps more disturbing still, Oviedo had to recount a conquest gone awry in many regards. Part III deals with the conquest of Peru and the civil wars among tyrannical Spanish conquistadors, among other subjects. The presentation of his method in this preface has less to do with issues about historiographical process than fending off current and possibly future detractors and defending the monarch's imperial claims.

The first preface establishes Charles's victories against the Turks and French as well as the most rapid acquisition in history of an enormous overseas empire as proof of the divine favor bestowed upon the Hapsburg Empire and, by extension, the importance of Oviedo's role as historian within the monarchy and the divine plan. By the time he wrote the prefaces to parts II and III, Oviedo had broadened his role as scribe and interpreter of America; he increasingly judges men's actions and speaks on behalf of the monarchy's politics. An ambitious author, Oviedo created a strong central role for himself in the unfolding of the empire's history and historiographical project. He writes himself into the history in a myriad of ways: as mediator, judge, author, *veedor,* divine scribe, king's servant, and Crown historian.

THREE

THE HISTORIAN AS ACTOR AND AUTOBIOGRAPHER

Tierra Firme 1514 (bk. 29, chap. 6)

Many modern scholars have commented on Oviedo's emphatic authorial presence: most describe the text as a heterogeneous, multivoiced narrative. But no scholar has thoroughly analyzed how Oviedo's first-person interventions serve an evolving purpose, one that often matches the author's complex administrative and legal ambitions. Of all the sixteenth-century chroniclers, Oviedo is the one whose voice and role as author are probably the most multivalent. Individual parts of the history and the circumstances in which they were composed reveal a writer continually reconstructing his persona as author and actor. A detailed chronological analysis of sections of the text and the context in which they were written highlights his shifts in methodology and purpose.

One particularly compelling section of the *History* is Oviedo's depiction of himself in books 26 and 29 as an actor in the early years of the conquest and colonization of Tierra Firme. These books, two of the longest and most autobiographical in the history, reveal how Oviedo created various interrelated personas by mixing the rhetorical strategies, structures, and ideologies of several genres in order to cast himself in the best possible light. He needed a fluid, flexible narrative in order to write history even as his personal fortune shifted and as imperial policy in the Indies changed. Oviedo combined the lofty aims of the providential history, the Ciceronian idea of history as *magistra vitae* (as teaching men about life), the personal grievances and petitions of the first-person *relación,* and the role of Christian witness from confessional narratives, called *vitae.* He understood that the legitimacy of his actions as one of the early administrators and settlers of Castilla del Oro (later known as Tierra Firme) lay in the credibility and authority of his history.[1]

In 1514 Oviedo embarked for Castilla del Oro with Pedrarias Dávila, who had been chosen to replace Núñez de Balboa as governor of Santa

Marta, the central province of Castilla del Oro. The fleet, known as the Splendid Armada (the king had invested more than fifty thousand ducats in it), consisted of twenty-two ships, and the roughly two thousand men aboard ships included Bernal Díaz del Castillo, Ponce de León, Francisco Pizarro, Diego de Almagro, and Hernando de Soto (bk. 29, chap. 1), all of whom were to become legendary figures. These men had been paid to continue the exploration and colonization of Tierra Firme under Pedrarias's leadership. Oviedo, who had been trained in the court from an early age and had served occasionally as a general chronicler and notary for King Ferdinand since about 1505, was sent as the king's judicial notary (*escribano general*) and overseer of the gold foundries (*veedor*). He stayed only a year in America. By 1516, the *veedor* was back in Europe reporting Pedrarias's mismanagement of the province to the new king, Charles V. After several years of lobbying by Oviedo and others, the king replaced Pedrarias. Soon after, in 1520, Oviedo returned to Tierra Firme. However, the new governor died on board ship, and Oviedo had to endure another eight years of Pedrarias's corrupt administration.

These first experiences of America provided the material for Oviedo's famous exposition on the exotic and abundant nature of the New World, his *Sumario* of 1526, and for the books in part II of the *History* that describe the discovery and conquest of the provinces of Castilla del Oro.[2] Like the mostly geographical and chronological organization of the process of discovery found in the rest of the history, these books offer a political mapping of the rights, policies, and riches of the province; they align the rights and claims of the Crown and individuals with the historical process of conquering lands.

Many scholars have noted the highly autobiographical nature of books 26 and 29 in part II, which deal, respectively, with the governance of Santa Marta and Castilla del Oro. Largely on the basis of this section of the work, for example, Stephanie Merrim notes that book 29 serves as an intellectual and literary autobiography of the author ("Mar," 114–117). Alberto M. Salas goes a step further and proclaims that the *Historia general* could be called the *Historia de Oviedo;* the text is filled with the chronicler's spontaneous, often intimate anecdotes and interjections about his personal life (112). Oviedo tells us, for example, about his habit of standing nude in front of his window on hot tropical nights (bk. 29, chap. 19) and about his heartache upon the deaths of his wife and children (bk. 29, chap. 14). Scholars link the autobiographical details of these books to Oviedo's extensive firsthand experience in Tierra Firme and suggest that the often digressive details help account for the uneven style of the history. Yet, given the chronicler's insistence on the primacy of authoritative eyewitness testimony as the methodological basis of his history, these first-person interjections play an important role.

A closer examination of the historical context and text itself suggests, however, that much more than a simple autobiographical impulse was involved. Oviedo was writing about himself during a period of violent political upheaval in Tierra Firme (1514–1532) and during a period in which he was part of the Crown's administrative structure in the new colony. He had yet to land the highly regarded post of royal chronicler of the Indies, a post that would help legitimize his role and judgment of the situation. (He was appointed in 1532.) Oviedo was implicated in the events that ultimately led to the abandonment of an important early settlement, the beheading of Núñez de Balboa, the decimation of a large percentage of the native population, and decades of litigation over governorships and rights. By linking the historical context of Oviedo's situation to the rhetorical strategies he employed one discovers clues to understanding the author's insistent first-person presence in these chapters. They help reveal how the textual layering in the composition of the *History* over a period of several decades is crucial to understanding Oviedo's changing personal circumstances and agenda as well as his evolving sense of the requirements of writing a New World history. Book 29 is crucial for viewing this process because there is strong evidence that the first draft dates from much earlier than most other sections of the general history, predating Oviedo's appointment as chronicler of the Indies, and from a period before the author had a fully developed sense of his place in history and as part of a historiographical project.

GOVERNMENT ADMINISTRATION AND THE COLONIZATION OF TIERRA FIRME

Book 26 opens with a geographical description of Santa Marta, but it soon turns political with a special focus on the performance of its governors. A dozen chapters treat issues of governance, while only a half dozen detail the conquest of natives and the riches found.[3] Oviedo lists the governors and lieutenant governors and characterizes each as a failure. Some were too greedy, others too inexperienced or foolish. Each received his just reward according to his moral character. Oviedo's portrait of Governor

Rodrigo Bastidas, the most detailed sketch, sets the pattern. The chronicler criticizes Bastidas for provoking an ill-advised war with the natives and for failing to colonize the neighboring province of Cartagena (chaps. 2–5). Oviedo even suggests that Bastidas's murder was an example of divine justice (chap. 5). While these chapters are cast as a moral tale, they also reveal the chronicler's own agenda. As we will see below, Oviedo faults Bastidas for his loss of position, revenue, and prestige.

Book 29 continues the subject of Tierra Firme and its leaders. This time the narrative is twice as long and the central villain is Pedrarias Dávila, governor of Castilla del Oro and Oviedo's superior during much of his time in Tierra Firme. Oviedo goes to great lengths to list Spanish leaders and to describe their capacities for moral virtue and their destinies. But the portrait of the infamous Pedrarias dominates; he represents the ultimate traitor to the king. From the ominous opening scene in which the new governor imposes an unnecessarily severe punishment to the beheading of Núñez de Balboa and his men as traitors, Pedrarias wreaked havoc on the king's system of justice. The governor's greed and ambition blinded him. Pedrarias established a system of bribery by which he allowed expeditions to ignore the king's instructions as long as the governor received two shares of all the Native Americans and wealth.[4] In addition, he blatantly disregarded the monarch's instructions to help settle the important new Christian city of Darién, Oviedo's place of residence during these years. According to Oviedo, Pedrarias single-handedly depopulated the province's capital city: men died from hunger and fled from the violence, and soon Pedrarias moved the government seat to the city of Panama. By 1524 the city was abandoned. Notably, however, Oviedo never discusses the strategic advantage that moving the government to a town with access to the Pacific Ocean offered the military campaigns in the conquest of Peru. His diatribe reveals Oviedo's disappointment in losing his fortune and administrative status in Darién.

Moreover, according to Oviedo, Pedrarias was notoriously cruel to Native Americans. The author gruesomely details how the governor allowed massacres of innocent natives: they were stoned to death, eaten by dogs, and slaughtered without warning. Others were unlawfully enslaved. Oviedo illustrates how Pedrarias allowed his captains to ignore the king's instructions, which were supposed to ensure that natives understood the reading of the *requerimiento,* the document that gave indigenous groups the choice of willingly becoming Christians and subjects of the king or enduring warfare with the Spaniards; furthermore, he disregarded the royal dictate that only "cannibals" and "warlike" Indians (indios de guerra) could be enslaved. Oviedo establishes a cause-and-effect relationship between Spanish leaders' disobedience of the king and native uprisings and rebellions.[5] And yet, Oviedo himself highlights how he and others did not observe the *requerimiento* when he describes his own reading of the text to a depopulated town before torching the entire town and Palacios Rubios's laughter about having to carry out this legal ritual.[6]

The sharply drawn sketches of leaders—especially Bastidas in book 26 and Pedrarias and his treacherous attorney, the Bachiller Corral, who had a hand in "legalizing" the misdeeds, in book 29—offer negative examples for all of Oviedo's readers: the king, the Council of the Indies, and the general reading public. They also provide a springboard for his self-portrait as the authoritative voice on New World affairs and as an ideal leader who loyally served God and king. As unwise as Bastidas was and as tyrannical as Pedrarias was, Oviedo as a historical actor in the conquest and settlement of Tierra Firme generally portrayed himself as wise, just, and loyal. In his role as a faithful royal bureaucrat, for example, Oviedo periodically highlights his important position as head notary. He boasts that Lope Conchillos, the secretary of the Royal Council for King Ferdinand, had "delegated to me his rights as notary general. As such I had a royal commission to oversee for him all the notaries of the government's and chief justice's tribunal and other courts" (bk. 29, chap. 8).[7] He recorded government officials' meetings and chose notaries for expeditions. In his role as *veedor,* he assessed the net worth of gold and other booty of expeditions.[8] More dramatically, in the first weeks of the conquest he boasts of personally destroying a colossal gold statue of a pair of "sodomites"—to his mind he destroyed sinful "idolatry" while also increasing the king's treasury with the smelted gold (bk. 26, chap. 6). As a good colonizer (*poblador*), Oviedo brought his wife, children, and servants to Darién in 1520 and built a luxurious house. As an upright Christian, he says he upheld high moral standards, in spite of the chaos and temptations in the new lands; Oviedo reports that unlike the Bachiller Corral and other Spanish men, he never took a native mistress.[9] What the author fails to discuss is Corral's alternate view of colonization: both Corral and Balboa promoted a policy of creating alliances with native cultures, which included marrying local women.[10] In his self-representation as colonizer, Oviedo reveals his insistence on a more vertical rule, based on the racist "purity of blood" ideology that was promoted in the Spain of the Catholic Kings.

Oviedo's citing of his roles as notary, *veedor,* colonizer, and good Christian is only the start of his self-portrait as a just ruler.[11] For a brief period around 1522, when Pedrarias moved to Panama City, he granted Oviedo the position of lieutenant governor (*teniente*) in the city of Darién. When Oviedo recounts this period in books 26 and 29, he slows the narrative pace by including more direct speech. First, he cites Pedrarias's words when he empowers Oviedo with the position (bk. 26, chap. 4). Later he quotes himself as judge and leader (bk. 29, chap. 15). He also carefully describes what he considered to be an ingenious plan to pacify the natives of the area, who had become warlike in response to Pedrarias's injustices. He first sells axes to natives and confiscates their weapons. Then, when shipments of axes from Spain were halted because of the revolt of the Comuneros, Oviedo set up a ship that traveled along the coast to sharpen the axes already distributed. (Ironically, Oviedo was not as virtuous as he maintains. He betrays his self-portrait by telling the reader that he sold axes of inferior quality, thus deceiving the natives.) In the process of selling the axes, the *teniente* collected over ten thousand bows and arrows from the natives. The author boasts, "I was as anxious to disarm those Indian archers as I was to seek gold" (bk. 26, chap. 4).[12] In addition, Oviedo depicts himself as the representative of the king's justice and Christian morality during his short term. He bought houses and meat to give to people to encourage them to remain in the city; he outlawed prostitution and gambling as well as the practice of using Indian women as beasts of burden. He concludes, "And thus I did other things by means of which I thought to serve God and King, which were for the common good" (bk. 29, chap. 5).[13] Through contrasting examples, Oviedo would have his readers believe that no leader in these early years of Castilla del Oro lived up to the high standards he possessed; he alone served God, king, and the Republic. But he foreshadows his failure in the post: "My nature could not tolerate shameful or ugly things and to try to impose justice upon people accustomed to its absence and to evil living would not be without considerable risk to my person" (bk. 29, chap. 14).[14]

What was at stake in Oviedo's laudatory self-representation? One answer to this question lies in the opening chapters to book 26, in which Oviedo at first enigmatically and then directly relates his three bids for a governorship—and his three failures to take office—in Tierra Firme. The first chapter describes in third-person narration three candidates put forth for the governorships in the region of Castilla del Oro in 1519: one is briefly described as suspicious; another is full of lies (*fábulas*). But a third candidate's worthy plan for the government seat in Santa Marta is described in full. The plan would have settled one hundred knights on the land to pacify and edify the natives:

> I recall that, questioning the one who asked for this, why he needed these knights, he answered that it seemed to him the only solution and the best way of all to govern and settle this country, and also the speediest, with the Indians better treated, more quickly converted and well trained than any other way which had been attempted by other governors.[15] (bk. 26, chap. 1)

Oviedo as narrator states that if the plan had been adopted, the history he writes in book 29 would not have been so tumultuous. In fact, Oviedo himself, of course, was the third candidate. Elsewhere he meticulously lists the names of Spaniards involved in leadership roles, so his silence about the names of the three candidates, including himself, is resounding. He manipulates the use of narrative voice through omission and use of third-person pronouns to appear more objective. The author identifies himself as the wise candidate two chapters later, when he explains that the king offered him governorships a second and a third time. The king offered Oviedo the governorship of Santa Marta again in 1524, and the governorship of the neighboring province of Cartagena the following year.[16] Oviedo declined the offers for Santa Marta because the monarch refused his demand for one hundred knights. He accepted the third offer, but, upon his arrival in Cartagena, he discovered that Bastidas had provoked war with the natives by enslaving a *cacique*. According to Oviedo, he immediately realized he could not administer peacefully and resigned. Yet here again, a closer examination of the historical facts demonstrates that the author told only half of the story—the half that painted him in the best light. At least one historian notes that Oviedo lacked the funds to carry out the governorship of Cartagena and used the rebellion as an excuse to decline the office.[17]

Oviedo's dream of a governorship did not die after these three failures in the 1520s. Twenty years later, in 1546, after hearing about a political situation, Oviedo petitioned once again for the governorship of Cartagena. He continued to ask for the contract on similar terms and added yet more difficult ones: he would have a license that banned all university men, attorneys, and friars (*letrados, procuradores,* and *frailes*) from the region. No doubt Oviedo sought a situation in which his authority would not be challenged. His bid was turned down.[18]

Oviedo's narrative strategies in the opening chapters of book 26 make clear his purpose. The author indirectly complains that the king made poor choices, which dearly cost the monarch. Oviedo asserts that he was the only true royal servant: "My wish was always to serve His Majesties with my person and everything else" (bk. 26, chap. 3).[19]

Indeed, in the very next chapter the author asserts his leadership abilities to the king when he describes his successful pacification of "warring natives" (indios flecheros) during his brief term as *teniente.*

Another answer to the question of Oviedo's purpose becomes clear upon examination of the narrative structure of book 29. Oviedo's outline of his achievements as lieutenant governor occupies the narrative center of the book (chaps. 15 and 16).[20] Within a year Pedrarias removed Oviedo from office. Despite his ambition to obtain a post as governor, he did not succeed even as lieutenant governor. To defend his honor the author reproduces several of his lengthy speeches. These are not classical Greco-Roman speeches interpolated into a history, but rather self-defenses. First, he defends his position as *teniente,* next his judgment against Captain Martín de Murga, Pedrarias's *visitador de los indios,* and later his decision to renounce the post (bk. 29, chap. 15). He describes his renunciation:

> That having been said, I took the staff of office in the council chamber and placed it on the highest chair, on which I was seated and from which I presided in the governor's place, and sat in a lower seat, saying: "This is my place, which the Emperor gave me, and from which I shall serve Their Majesties as their official, and not as the governor's deputy. In all that I can do to please the governor with my person, and all I might attain in the service of my King and for the good and profit of this realm, I shall execute as I have sworn and am bound to do." And I took an oath never to take up the staff of justice on behalf of Pedrarias or of anyone else, unless it be for Your Majesties, without Their express order or that of the Royal Council. I requested written proof of this and had it officially recorded.[21] (bk. 29, chap. 15)

The author creates a scene in which he protects his honor, claiming he literally chose to step down from his post as leader. He attempts to disassociate himself from Pedrarias and link himself more closely to the Crown. The use of direct speech brings the situation to the narrative fore both to combat the impression that he had been an ineffective *teniente* and to set him apart from the corrupt Pedrarias administration.

In addition to explaining his poor luck in governorships, Oviedo needed to defend his position in courts of law and policy making. Book 29 includes a dizzying array of the numerous lawsuits in which he was variously the plaintiff, defendant, or prosecutor and represented himself, a whole city, a province, or the even king.[22] Oviedo had ongoing litigation with Pedrarias from a year after his arrival in America in 1514 until about 1529. He initially sought Pedrarias's removal from the governorship in 1515. He had a brief victory in 1519, but when the new governor, Lope de Sosa, died before setting foot in Tierra Firme, Pedrarias was not removed until 1524. In another twist of fate, Oviedo took a position in Nicaragua (1527), only to find upon his arrival that Pedrarias had recently been granted the governorship there. Oviedo stayed in Nicaragua until 1529 and continued to be entangled in personal grievances with Pedrarias.[23] He explains that at the time of Pedrarias's *residencia* (the process for claims by which people could make official claims of wrongdoing against outgoing government officials) "I had fourteen or fifteen claims against Pedrarias and was convinced that, if justice were done, I would have a verdict against him for more than eight thousand gold pesos" (bk. 29, chap. 24).[24] The author relates that because of Pedrarias's influence in Spain, he received only a fraction of his claim (seven hundred gold pesos).

From 1515 until 1546 (three years before Oviedo stopped writing the history), the chronicler returned to Spain five times for periods of one to five years each. Much of this time was spent in the courts and *audiencias* dealing with the policy and governance of the Indies. What began as Oviedo's personal campaign against Pedrarias in 1515 turned into a role as representative of the cities of Darién, Santo Domingo, and Panama in the Spanish courts.[25] But cases were also initiated against him during own his *residencia*. When Oviedo declared his intention of returning to Spain in 1523, he was briefly jailed and held on bond until the claims for his *residencia* were cleared. The author proudly notes that all the claims were ruled invalid, except two, which were then forwarded to the Spanish courts. In the end, Oviedo was fined for exiling Pedrarias's right-hand man, the Bachiller Corral, and for meting out too harsh a punishment (a woman's teeth were pulled out for falsely accusing her husband).[26] In both cases Oviedo defends his zeal, saying the acts were done to serve the king's justice. Tales of his own noble, loyal, just service to God and king depicted him as a reliable—if harsh—witness. Claims of injustice made against Pedrarias and his men added support to the charges. Oviedo's complex, manipulative self-representation reveals that money, position, and honor were all at stake for the chronicler.

GENRE CHOICES

Oviedo weaves together a myriad of defenses and apologia to defend his actions and life. Yet he places them in a broader framework of teaching the king about the mismanagement of the Indies and the general reader about the results of men's sinful greed. How does Oviedo achieve such diverse narrative ends? An author of works in multiple genres ranging from poetry, dialogues, and novel to court manuals and genealogy, Oviedo was keenly aware of the rhetorical and ideological weight of genre in the framing of information. In particular, he used two genres that featured a strong first-person presence, the legalistic *relación* and the confessional *vida*. He employed their narrative codes and rhetoric while also giving a general narrative frame to the history by the use of a third genre, the *magistra vitae*. Although some Greco-Roman historians such as Thucydides employed an authoritative first-person voice in their texts, early modern Spaniards could draw on a variety of genres to bolster their authority.[27]

Not surprisingly, Oviedo employed the first-person record of litigation, testimony, and petition—the *relación*—when recounting his role in the contentious history of Castilla del Oro. Typically a report to a superior to justify one's actions and seek recognition—often monetary or honorary—the *relación* was an extension of the notarial record. The narrator had to establish the truth value of his testimony by convincing others of his virtuous person as well as by producing corroborative evidence. As Roberto González Echevarría notes in his influential book on the topic, the *relación* as a notarial record demanded the inclusion of the particular and the anecdotal: "[The notarial record] is the fine mesh that traps everything into place, from domestic quarrels to the discovery of the Pacific" ("Myth," 67–68). He argues that a narrative tension and rhetorical confusion mark most histories of the Indies. Their implicit model is the *magistra vitae,* the eloquent universal humanist history with its didactic purpose. And yet, the *relación* is a competing structuring device. Whereas a model universal history required a unity of style, voice, and historical significance, the *relación* encouraged the revelation of personal experience in a direct forensic style. While the *relación* blended humanist elements with legal forms, it also dissolved the hierarchy of literary forms, which allowed the history to include everything from the quotidian to the transcendental ("Myth," 67–68).

Oviedo draws heavily on the juridical authority of the *relación* to recount his merits and service to the Crown. As a longtime notary in Spain and as *escribano general* in Tierra Firme, the chronicler was very familiar with the rhetorical possibilities of the *relación.* Indeed, he often mentions reports, accounts, and legal depositions he continually drafted and read, and later in the *History* these are often incorporated directly into his narrative. Elsewhere he acknowledges that he may be getting "litigious" when an account delves into great detail (bk. 29, chap. 20). He includes, among other verbatim documents, the king's initial instructions to Pedrarias (bk. 26, chap. 6), the 1513 *requerimiento* (bk. 29, chap. 7), and the letter that warns Oviedo of a plot to murder him (bk. 29, chap. 19). Essentially, these documents accuse Pedrarias Dávila and his men of failure to obey the king. The monarch's instructions to the governor outline his duties: the peaceful conversion and good treatment of Native Americans; the prohibition of lawyers in the new territories; the reading and observations of the terms of the *requerimiento;* and the joint decision-making process among Pedrarias, the bishop, and other officials. The text of the *requerimiento* made it abundantly clear that natives were to be given interpreters and adequate time to consider the edict's terms of conversion to Christianity or warfare (of course, this presentation contradicts Oviedo's own earlier abuse of the document when torching a town). The letter informing Oviedo of the conspiracy to murder him is an example of the dangers he encountered in his heroic efforts to bring justice to Darién. Oviedo deftly weaves these texts into his firsthand accounts of his exploits as colonizer and *teniente,* and the resulting narrative both contests his foe's reports and presents an inherent petition for recognition of his own feats and services.

In addition to the presentation of his merits, the author enumerates the losses he suffered in serving the king. Cast as a sort of pilgrim's narrative—describing his journey to the shrine to Saint James in Santiago and "journeys and troubles which did not cease"—Oviedo describes how he risked his life in 1514 during a dangerous crossing to Brussels to report on Pedrarias's misgovernment to the king. The author also complains of the king's failure to reimburse him for his journey (bk. 29, chap. 11). In Tierra Firme, Oviedo also discusses the loss of wealth, first in his pearl business because he spent all his time in pacifying the indigenous groups (bk. 26, chap. 6), and second when Darién was abandoned (bk. 29, chap. 24). The most poignant loss, however, is that of his family. Within several years of arriving at Darién, both his wife and a son had died: "God took one of my sons from me, of eight years of age"; "I buried my wife, who had been taken sick for ten days. And with the pain of such a sad loss for me, distaught and irrational, seeing her dead whom I had loved more than my own self, I was on the point of losing my mind" (bk. 29, chap. 14).[28]

In order to help link the anecdotal, juridical genre of the *relación* about his personal trials to the lofty universal aims of the humanist historical genre and the didactic Castilian providentialist history, Oviedo draws on another important early modern first-person genre, the confessional *vida*. He echoes the rhetoric of the Christian witness whose experiences reveal God's word. This rhetorical persona was abundant in biblical stories and sermons, but Oviedo also had a copy of Augustine's *Confessions,* the foundational text for the genre.[29] The Augustinian theme of conversion of the soul and the quest for the divine through spiritual pilgrimage was an important part of scholastic teachings. But Oviedo saw that the Augustinian model of personal endeavor experienced as a process of conversion for encountering one's self, offered another, nonscholastic approach to the world. The witness, often in the role of pilgrim, penitent, or martyr, experienced suffering and loss and was willing to risk his life for Christ. This experience demonstrated the subject's moral virtue and made him capable of directly revealing God's design (revelation) without basing his authority on canonical texts.

Significantly, the closing chapter about Oviedo's lieutenant governorship is a dramatic account of an attempt on his life, and it is introduced with the conventional set phrase "I confess" [yo confieso] of the confessional *vida* (chap. 17): "Each man's strengths are made manifest only by adversity, according to St. Gregory. I confess that the strength with which I resisted my adversities and which saved me from them was not mine but rather that of omnipotent God's." Next, the author anticipates his critics' charges that he records too many of his own "personal troubles" by listing why he must "confess" in writing to all that has happened to him:

> First, because I did my duty and upheld justice . . . second, even though St. Paul was incomparably better than I, his stripes were not lessened . . . third, because Christ, Our redeemer, is God yet He did not disdain His Passion. (Of course, these comparisons are very highly disproportionate. . . . I am and have been a sinner.) However, Divine Grace did not allow my enemies to accomplish their intentions.[30] (bk. 29, chap. 17)

He draws parallels between his enemies and those who accused St. Paul and Christ of wrongdoing and quotes St. Gregory on Job's trials. Typical of the *vida* genre, the author confesses to being a sinner while also illustrating God's mercies in his life. His claim to Divine Grace is only thinly veiled with the rhetoric of humility.

After this lofty opening, Oviedo briefly returns to a more litigious discourse: "Another reason I include these things in my histories is that those who wished me dead were friends of that Bachelor Corral, who was behind it all." Within this narrative frame, the author dramatically recounts how Simón Bernal stabbed him with a dagger and his response: "As I fell stunned to the ground I cried loudly: 'Mother of God, help me.' As a good Christian, I urgently sent for a confessor well aware of the danger I was facing."

Remarking on his recovery and God's plan, Oviedo continues to echo the rhetoric of the confessional narrative:

> It seems that God had reserved me for other tribulations. . . . I was not unaware that my trials came from God's Hand for my betterment, since as St. Gregory says: "When in this life we suffer what we do not wish, it is necessary that we incline our will to that of Him who cannot wish any unjust thing." It is a great consolation in adversity to think that everything happens by the disposition of God.[31] (bk. 29, chap. 17)

And yet, Oviedo's borrowing of the confessional mode never lasts long; in the same paragraph he asserts, "However, the glorious doctor's authority I cited notwithstanding, I suspected Pedrarias's hand in the accumulation of my troubles."[32] As soon as the author recovered he began another lawsuit. Indeed, Oviedo's confessional vow to forgive his would-be assassin, Simón Bernal, was soon forgotten. In the next chapter, the author complains that his assailant's punishment—the amputation of his arm and leg—was too lenient (bk. 29, chap. 18), but he seems satisfied to report in the following chapter that in the end justice prevailed: the man died within days of tetanus (bk. 29, chap. 19).[33] Oviedo undoes his own saintly portrait by revealing his vindictive inclinations and his own cruel streak.

Oviedo's use of the confessional mode is more credible when he is not also telling the story of his litigation. When writing about these years in Tierra Firme for the prologue to part I (1535), Oviedo convincingly draws on the persona of the Christian pilgrim ready to suffer for Christianity:

> Nor do I wish to be denied praise for a work which has taken me so long and with so many obstacles which I have suffered, compiling and inquiring in all the ways I was able to know the certainty of these subjects from the year 1513 of the birth of our Savior, when King Fer-

> dinand the Catholic, of glorious memory, grandfather of Your Imperial Majesty, sent me as his inspector of the gold foundries to Panama, where I fulfilled that office the best I could, such as in the conquest and pacification of some parts of those lands by means of arms, serving God and Your Majesties as captain and vassal during those harsh beginnings in which a number of cities and towns were settled, which now are populated by Christians, [and] where, with great glory for the royal sceptre of Spain, [our] holy religion has continued to be served. . . . And of these two thousand five hundred men I have mentioned, there are, I believe, today not forty left in or out of all of the Indies, for, to serve Your Majesties, and to assure the safety of the Christians who later went to those regions, it was best, or better said, essential, that this be accomplished. At the cost of our lives we endured the harsh nature of the territory, the climate, the dense vegetation and underbrush, the danger of the rivers there, great lizards and tigers, and testing water and food, in order to benefit the traders and settlers who, reaping what others sowed, now enjoy the fruits of other men's labors. . . . I, however, compiled what I here write from two hundred thousand hardships, privations and dangers in the more than twenty-two years that I have personally witnessed and experienced these things, serving God and my king in these Indies.[34] (*Proemio,* part I)

Over fifty years later, Cabrera de Córdoba's treatise on Castilian historiography codified the persona of historian as pilgrim (*peregrino*), a traveling, suffering witness of truth who served God and king. Oviedo likens his role to that of an "evangelist."[35] History is not a simple mirror but requires the historian to demonstrate personal virtue as the basis from which he sees reality and conveys it. In the *History* Oviedo offers his life as a touchstone by which others could perceive both a juridical and a universal truth. His life story, his *vita,* serves as a microcosm of the Ciceronian *magistra vitae.* In these books Oviedo is not just the overseer of the gold foundries, but also symbolically the one who "oversees" God's justice for the king. The preface to book 29 makes clear this aim: "The reader must be tired of certain things he has read up to now . . . but in this he will see the justice of God, and the reckoning which He effected to punish in this life those who went to take His own. Show us Your face, Lord, and we shall be saved."[36] As chronicler, his duty is to teach the king and his Council of the Indies about the needs of the new territories and to warn would-be settlers about the corrupting nature of riches in America. In an era when historians often wrote guides on good government for their princes, Oviedo ensures that his voice will be important in the king's decisions. He is the witness that will inform all about the human and divine consequences of the conquests of Tierra Firme.

HISTORICAL CONTEXT

If the borrowing of elements from the confessional subgenre provided added authority for Oviedo and his historiographical project, it also suggests that Oviedo's history and authority were on trial. Like the *relación,* the *vida* both exalted a life and responded to an inquiry into the validity of the subject's life and works. The church solicited the account and passed judgment. As official history, Oviedo's narrative is mediated by the Spanish Crown's interests in America. Although the first part of the history was published in 1535, Oviedo continued writing and rewriting the text for more than a dozen years. During this period, debates were raging about the justice of the conquest, the rights of Native Americans, the role of the Church, and the deeds of and rewards for the conquistadors. Was Oviedo or his history being questioned by the Crown? On the one hand, the historian's reports were used increasingly as direct testimony in policy making.[37] On the other, as we have seen, Oviedo was embroiled in many issues dealing with the Indies. Certainly his attempt in 1548 to publish the second part of his history had been foiled, in part by his longtime adversary Bartolomé de Las Casas.[38] By this time, Las Casas wielded power in the court, and the New Laws, which attempted to revoke or limit the *encomienda* system (Spaniards' right to service and tribute from Indians), had been passed (1542), although they were partially revoked in 1544 because of vast discontent among American settlers. Las Casas had traveled to the Indies in 1544 to campaign for the Native Americans, and upon his return to Spain he and Juan Ginés de Sepúlveda began their debates.

Since 1515, Oviedo and Las Casas had vied for the Crown's favor and for recognition as an authoritative voice of the Indies. By 1518 Las Casas's charges of foul play in the Indies were instrumental in forcing Oviedo's employer, Lope Conchillos, out of the new administrative staff formed by the new Hapsburg dynasty. As Charles V presided for the first time over the Council of the Indies in 1519 (Barcelona), Las Casas and Oviedo competed for land grants in Castilla del Oro. Oviedo presented his aristocratic plan of ruling with one hundred knights, and Las Casas presented his as creating a new order of knighthood with peaceful farmers.[39] By the 1540s legislation on the encomienda system threatened Oviedo's personal fortune as well as his honor and favor at court. He had long been a spokesman for the encomienda system. The chronicler had appeared before the Council of the Indies to give his views of it, and Sepúlveda, Las Casas's opponent in the famous debate in Valladolid in 1550, used Oviedo's writings to bolster his argument. In fact, a document from 1536 demonstrates how even at this late date Oviedo was petitioning the Crown for a *repartimiento* of Indians for his use in Santo Domingo.[40] In this political context, Oviedo's portrait of himself as loyal protagonist and of Pedrarias as corrupt antagonist in the tumultuous settling of Tierra Firme may have been more than an attempt to settle the score with his old foe. The chronicler may have used the notorious conquistador as a smokescreen for his own role in the bloody conquest of Tierra Firme.

Pedrarias died in 1531, so the author had relatively free rein in depicting his long-term antagonist.[41] Well connected in the court, Pedrarias received two prestigious governorships and—at least from Oviedo's point of view—literally got away with murder.[42] More to the point for Oviedo, the court required Pedrarias to reimburse Oviedo for only a small percentage of his loss of property when Darién had been abandoned. The unfair settlement and Pedrarias's luck in the Spanish courts rankled Oviedo. Book 29 often reads, as Merrim points out, like a personal vendetta against the ex-governor ("Un Mar," 114).

In spite of this animosity, Oviedo expresses strong convictions about the disastrous nature of the conquest of Tierra Firme.[43] It is remarkable that Oviedo, a bureaucrat who did not have a close connection to the royal court, promptly returned to Spain in order to request the removal of the governor whom the king had appointed only a year before. Given that it took nearly nine years (1515–1524) and several transatlantic journeys to achieve his goal—and then only in part because of Pedrarias's new appointment as governor of Nicaragua—Oviedo's insistence on Pedrarias's cruelty and corruption is understandable. Yet, he charged that "[Pedrarias] and his ministers and captains devastated and destroyed the land with robberies and cruelties, with no punishment meted out to them . . . and what he and they termed pacification was to lay waste and devastate, to murder and to destroy the land in many ways, robbing and exterminating the indigenous population thereof" (bk. 29, chap. 15).[44]

The accusations may serve another purpose as well. With the exception of only a handful of paragraphs out of the entire thirty-four chapters of book 29, Oviedo's description of the conquest and colonization under Pedrarias's leadership echoes Las Casas's systematic rhetoric of the destruction of the Indies. Most of the central chapters argue that the Spaniards' greed led to diabolical and unchristian acts while the natives were mostly friendly and civilized until provoked. In chapter 13, for example, Oviedo juxtaposes the portraits of the wise *cacique* Paris, who worked hard to protect his people, and of Captain Espinosa, who in his rage of greed and cruelty, executed an Indian with a cannon shot.[45] Oviedo writes in phrases that one might think were by Las Casas: "So began the destruction of the land (which they termed pacification and conquest)" (bk. 29, chap. 8); "there is neither time nor paper enough fully to describe all these captains did to annihilate the natives, to rob them and to destroy the land. . . . there had been two million Indians. . . . So many perished. . . . Many captains . . . although they had committed a thousand evil deeds and cruelties, were protected by the favor of the officials themselves. . . . Not one province nor part of the land was spared from sorrow" (bk. 29, chap. 10).[46] Unlike Las Casas's hyperbolic descriptions and one-conquest-fits-all sketches in his *Brevísima relación de la destrucción de las Indias* presented to Prince Philip in 1542, however, Oviedo's books on Tierra Firme are filled with careful, convincing historical detail: the Indian leaders are named, towns described, exact atrocities outlined, and dates specified.[47] In legalistic detail the author creates scenarios in which men under Pedrarias systematically ignored the king's instructions for a fair conquest. His account of Tierra Firme may have deflected Las Casas's charges that Oviedo was "an enemy of the Indians," implicated in the destruction of the Indies and guilty by association with Pedrarias's administration.[48] The author concludes, "In the end, it was left to me to fight against Pedrarias" (bk. 29, chap. 20) and seek justice. Books 26 and 29 provide a more permanent record of the governor's misdeeds and Oviedo's importance to the king even as policy about the administration of the Indies shifted and justice was unevenly meted out.

MANUSCRIPT DRAFTS AND REVISIONS

Unraveling the dates of composition of these books in the history would give a more definitive answer to the question about the author's agenda. As we will see in chapter 5, the historian's concept of the writing of history constantly evolved and resulted in multiple revisions. Unfortunately, Oviedo rarely included the dates of composition in his history, except when noting a later addition or revision of a passage. There are a few telling passages in this case, however. Although much of the history was completed by about 1540, from 1540 to 1542 Oviedo deeply revised and expanded part I, which was already published, and sections of parts II and III. When he was unable to travel to Spain in 1542 to publish this newly revised version, he spent another seven years updating the manuscript.[49] The autograph manuscript of book 26 is lost, but most of book 29 is extant.[50] The manuscript discloses essential information about Oviedo's changing agendas. In it we see updates and clarifications about such things as people's deaths (f. 25r) and amounts of money (f. 89r) as well as changes demarcating the new organizational structure of the history, such as the cross-referencing of books (f. 74v) and the substituting of Spanish translations for Latin quotes (f. 77r). Yet more significant for my purposes here, the internal dating—and the changes made to the dates—makes clear that most of book 29 was completed by at least 1540—and in some cases, much earlier. On multiple occasions the author deletes "Darién" and adds "this city of Santo Domingo where I live" (ff. 25r, 27r) to denote that he is now writing from Hispaniola (and therefore after 1532) and that the original account was drafted in Darién (therefore, before 1524, at which time the town was abandoned).[51] Other passages give the actual changes in dates: in chapter 30, for example, Oviedo dates the first draft to 1526 and states that it is now 1548; in chapter 31 he deletes 1527 and inserts 1535 (f. 121r). Throughout other chapters are inserts such as "ahora [presently], 1547." Second, passages dealing with Pedrarias Dávila and Bachiller Corral exhibit extensive textual revisions. Indeed, the chapters that recount the attempt on Oviedo's life and Pedrarias's residency have more internal revisions than any other section of the entire extant manuscript.[52] Books written later, such as books 30–40, have only minimal internal revisions. The author returns to early accounts that appear to implicate him; he meticulously deletes or adds passages in order to represent himself in a better light (or Pedrarias and Corral in a worse light). For example, he deletes from chapter 18 a key passage that highlights Oviedo-the-teniente's zealous judgments which were later overruled, including his order that a cacique be burned to death.[53] In another passage, the author adds a paragraph to discuss the effects of his notoriously rocky relationship with the governor:

> As far as I am concerned, all I have said about my travails and differences with Pedrarias and with the Licenciate Diego de Corral, was the principal reason why Darién became deserted, because in truth, the city could have maintained itself, had I not been destroyed and persecuted in the way it has been told. Thus, that settlement lasted from the

year 1509 to 1524. Pedrarias served God and King no less ill by letting [the city] fall into ruin than Enciso and those with him were notable and great for having won it, nor would it be a lesser good to restore and rebuild it, given the fertility and richness of its site and environs.[54] (RAH 9/553, f. 82v)

Generally added well after Pedrarias's and Corral's deaths and after court rulings that did not favor Oviedo, these changes set the record straight—at least from the author's perspective.[55]

Indeed, in the massive revisions of 1540–1542, Oviedo added several new chapters and books to part II to fill in lacuna about various expeditions. Book 29, for example, was originally book 26.[56] Also during the process of revision Oviedo added Gil González's expedition in 1548 (chap. 21) and information about the governorship of Pedro de los Ríos sometime after 1542 (chap. 25) as well as several more general chapters that detail the fates of leaders of expeditions and government officials (chaps. 33–34). The author announces, for example, that Oviedo's nemesis the Bachiller Corral died penniless in Seville. The final paragraphs of book 29 reflect a decidedly moralistic posture: "Think and contemplate if there are not sinners among these generations and different kinds of men, and not only enough of common [sinners], but the most perverse and rejected by their own countries, even exiled from other places because of their worth" (chap. 34).[57] All of these additions from the 1540s demonstrate the author's growing tendency to distance himself from the events and to create a moral tale about the men he knew, one which would illustrate how divine justice took care of men's misdeeds. A similar pattern is apparent in book 26; the autograph manuscript for this book, as noted, is not extant, but four stages of writing and revision are decipherable. They reflect not only the evolution of the conquest and the changing administrative structure in the Indies, but also Oviedo's tendency to add a more didactic frame to each chapter.[58] Additions from 1548 to chapters 2 and 17 highlight the role of fortune and the author's role as royal servant; and chapter 18 has an addition from this same year that describes the suffering and trials all Spaniards experience in the New World:

I will not pause to relate in detail the travails which this lieutenant governor [that is, Oviedo] and the Spaniards suffered in following him: it suffices that, as a man who has traversed the Indies for thirty-four years, I deserve credence, and I dare to say that the travails which

Christians suffer in the Indies are so great, that no one in any other part of the world in which Christians happen to be could be greater or more intolerable.[59] (bk. 26, chap. 18)

A study of the internal dating, passages added at a later date, and the resulting shifts in focus and tone suggests that many of the chapters in books 26 and 29 that read like a *relación* were written quite early, perhaps well before Oviedo began his grand historical project in the 1530s and well before the reconceptualization of the *History* from 1540 to 1542.[60] Indeed, many of the passages and chapters added during the 1540s elevate the circumstantial *relación* to a higher historical purpose. The additions coincide with the author's changing conception of his narrative as well as with a time when he was having difficulty publishing the second and third parts of his text and when imperial policy had changed radically.[61]

CONCLUSIONS

In the end Oviedo's use of the *relación* is not so different from that of his 1514 shipmate Bernal Díaz.[62] Many colonial writers justified their authority by demonstrating their moral superiority and sought self-affirmation by contrasting images of chaos and disintegration. As we have seen, Oviedo's account describes the failures of the Pedrarias expedition to Castilla del Oro in 1514. The king's policies regarding colonization, government, wealth, and treatment of Native Americans were disobeyed. Oviedo lost his wife and child, a high-ranking position, and some of his fortune. The author uses the *relación* to clear his name in regard to these failures, to accuse Pedrarias of wrongdoing, and to gain recognition of and reward for his own losses. But Oviedo goes further: the legalistic tone of the *relación* merges with the Christian witness's account and with the aims of a universal history to create a composite persona of a loyal servant worthy of trust and reward and even an evangelist capable of recording divine will. Each aspect of this persona is used to establish the reliability of the author as an expert on affairs in the Indies.

Part of the larger pattern of first-person discourses that emerged as individuals justified their lives to authorities and to the Hapsburg Empire's new ideological framework that favored multiple chroniclers and ones who had a closer relationship to the king, Oviedo's creation of a strong self-identity went beyond the pragmatic function of jockeying for a position at court or in the administrative structure of America. His use of the first person and the words he uses in his text provide the continuity between the separate worlds he continually bridged through his frequent transatlantic crossings and multiple writings. The dream of a lifelong career in the court of Prince Don Juan, shattered by the prince's untimely death in 1497 at age eighteen, still burned in Oviedo's imagination. In book 25, which initiates the history of Tierra Firme, the author wistfully reflects upon his destiny:

> God did not want me to stay in Spain, though I was raised in the royal house of Castile, but when God took away the most serene prince Don Juan, my lord, and I no longer had his royal presence, from whom I expected to be remunerated and given an inheritance in my own country, I had to wander about the world to render my services, and came to dwell in these lands which are so strange and different from those where I was born and originated.[63] (bk. 25, *Proemio*)

For the remainder of his life Oviedo constantly redefined himself. His self-characterization as a loyal servant, whether as *veedor, teniente,* or "loyal scribe," is more than just a stylistic motif. Oviedo affirms his identity as a faithful royal servant, creates a continuity with his position in Don Juan's court, and sets himself up as a moral force in opposition to the immorality and barbarism in which he lived in America.

Understanding the narrative complexity of Oviedo's history remains a challenging task. The more we recognize the hybrid nature of most narratives in the period and the ideological and practical purposes for using a variety of subgenres to structure events and language, the less we question the unity of the text and the more we appreciate its narrative and rhetorical richness. In a study of early modern narrative, Rosalie Colie argues that the concept of *nova reperta,* of the new genres that emerged out of old ones and of the mixture of genres to describe new situations, is as important to understanding the sixteenth century as other achievements of the era. Oviedo's history demonstrates how the American enterprise challenged European knowledge, authority, and textual traditions. As ideas about truth, genre, language, and knowledge were being debated in academic court circles, Oviedo explored their implications for himself and for his history as he lived and wrote in the middle of the political and cultural upheaval of the Conquest of America.

Although many scholars have criticized Oviedo for failing to fulfill his overt purpose of writing a grand history, it is the deviations from a formal historical mode—in particular, his lively firsthand observations—that most often captivate contemporary readers. A study of genre shifts as they correspond with dates of composition and Oviedo's complex administrative and legal circumstances reveals that the autobiographical elements in the history often serve as important indicators of the author's evolving purpose. In this chapter we have seen the shifting and layered voice of Oviedo as administrator-actor and chronicler. I want to turn in the remaining chapters to an examination of Oviedo as a full-fledged official historian who meticulously documents both the natural (chapter 4) and general (chapters 5–6) history of the Indies for his royal patron.

FOUR

EYEWITNESS TO AMERICA'S WONDERS

Illustrating a Natural History of the Indies (bk. 7, chap. 14)

When Oviedo stopped writing about events he had witnessed in Tierra Firme and devoted himself to natural history, to depicting American flora, fauna, and ethnographic items, he confronted a dilemma. How was he to convey in his natural history the particular novelty of the New World to an audience that had never seen America? In order to accomplish this task, Oviedo made his role as a witness and writer an integral part of a complex argument in which he proposed that through the record of his own experience he would enable the king to know the nature of the Indies. This account, the author argued, would help the king to formulate just laws based on truthful knowledge of the Indies and, upon beholding the secrets of New World phenomena, to praise God.

Yet just as the laws of the empire were being formulated for the New World in the course of the first fifty years after Spain's contact with America—laws that reflect, at times, the emergence of a broadened worldview of economics, the nature of man, and natural phenomena, among many other things—Oviedo was formulating his own theories and practices for representing the New World. The official chronicler's passages on natural history and, in particular, his illustrations open a window onto the complexities of rendering New World natural phenomena for the European reader. His visual depiction of America's flora, fauna, and ethnographic items in more than seventy field sketches as well as his theories on the role of sight, knowledge, and representation underscore the relationship between seeing, understanding, and visual epistemology during the period. To explicate the significance of these illustrations, I focus on the concept of visual epistemology during the early modern era and how it affected ideas of history and representation. I also discuss the epistemological problem that the New World presented to the Old World and how Oviedo responded to this challenge by supplying drawings, as epitomized by his chapter on the pineapple. In the process of contextualizing Oviedo's illustrations, I will discuss how their function changed as the chronicler's narrative purpose and methods evolved.

The full impact of Oviedo's drawings has never been completely felt because many of the illustrations have never been published in their original form. Furthermore, with the exception of a doctoral thesis by Jesús Carrillo (1997), scholars have primarily examined the drawings for their documentary and artistic value, ignoring their context within the *History*. The thirty-two woodcuts in the sixteenth-century editions were faithful to Oviedo's manuscript sketches. Most of the illustrations are embedded in the narrative itself, and the pictorial style is not altered.[1] The majority of the drawings are in the first part of the *History*, which is more clearly devoted to depicting the natural wonders of America (later parts increasingly focus on historical events), and generally illustrate a single item in a nonnarrative context.[2] However, only a quarter to a third of the text was published in the sixteenth century (part I, 1535 and 1547). After revising the published version of part I in the 1540s, Oviedo added at least eighteen more illustrations to books 1–19. Parts II and III include at least another twenty sketches. Although the first editor of the complete history, José Amador de los Ríos (1851–1855), used the final version of the autograph manuscript, his edition drastically altered the drawings so that they no longer convey a sense of the role the sketches played in the text. Making engravings based on the original sketches, Amador rendered some of them fairly faithfully (mostly the floral illustrations) while redrawing others according to nineteenth-century romantic conventions (see fig. 83). In addition, he removed the illustrations from the narrative and placed them in an appendix.[3] Regrettably, subsequent editions have followed this practice. Thus, many of Oviedo's sketches have never been published in their original form.[4] Moreover, about half of the fifty books of the original autograph manuscript used by Amador are now lost. Consequently scholars must rely on a sixteenth- and an eighteenth-century copy of sections of the *History* in order to reconstruct a more complete portfolio of the original illustrations. In appendix D, I reproduce the existing illustrations—either in their autograph form or in the most faithful copies available. I also document the drawings and their archival source and note which autograph books are extant.

Given that Oviedo's sketches of American phenomena are among the earliest of any that exist, they have caught the attention of many scholars. But because some of the original versions are inaccessible the attention has been brief and often misinformed.[5] In general, Oviedo's illustrations have been either condemned for a "lack of artistic talent" or praised as being among the first to depict accurately aspects of American flora, fauna, and ethnography.[6] William Sturtevant's survey of ethnographic drawings of the New World, for example, lists only six works or artists published before Oviedo's work appeared. They range from items etched into early maps (such as the armadillo in Diego Ribero's map of 1529) to a book for Maximilian I containing 137 woodcuts of ethnographic items by Hans Burgkmair. By the second half of the sixteenth century there were other illustrators, such as the doctor Francisco Hernández (1570s), who was sent to the Indies by Philip II to report, collect, and draw plants with medicinal value. In North America, Jacques Le Moyne (1580s) and John White (1580s) portrayed American subjects with relative loyalty to what they witnessed. Oviedo's work is one of the few series of eyewitness drawings of the New World's natural and man-made wonders in the early sixteenth century. Perhaps just as noteworthy, as Jesús Carrillo observes in his study of the figurative culture in Oviedo's time, is the fact that Oviedo began illustrating New World phenomena at a time when herbals and emblem books were yet to become popular in Europe ("The Representation," chap. 5).

Most sixteenth- and seventeenth-century artists' illustrations of America, argues Mercedes López-Baralt, reflect a Eurocentric mentality and serve the political ends of the text. The popular engravings of the New World by Theodore de Bry and family (1590–1634), for example, depict mythologized figures and create narrative scenes that promote the black legend, that is, the portrayal of the Spanish as cruel and inhuman conquerors of the Native Americans. Bernadette Bucher's insightful critical study of de Bry's work analyzes his illustrations as an ethnographic record not of America but of Europe's integration of knowledge about the New World and of the Old World's inability to overcome its ethnocentrism. In doing so, she examines de Bry's illustrations for their symbolic value. Taking a similar point of departure, I suggest we leave aside questions concerning the documentary value of Oviedo's ethnographic and botanical illustrations and examine them for what they reveal about his purposes in writing a natural history of the Indies. Although I will discuss how Oviedo's illustrations evolved during the decades that he wrote—and this will involve an analysis of the naturalism of his drawings—in general I will look beyond the mimetic value of the drawings in order to achieve a clearer understanding of why Oviedo wove illustrations into the fabric of his narrative history and what effect this visual, nonverbal form has on the history as a whole. Oviedo's own musings about his method in his prefaces and narrative will aid us in understanding his approach.

SIGHT AND KNOWLEDGE

As we saw in the analysis of Oviedo's prefaces (see chap. 2), the author often asserts that the truth of his work is linked with firsthand experience: "The blind man cannot distinguish colors, nor can one who is absent bear witness to these matters like one who sees them" (*Proemio,* part I).[7] Yet the natural historian faced a difficult prospect. At the most practical level, it was an overwhelming task to document the proliferation of unfamiliar natural objects, languages, and customs in America. At a more theoretical level, how does the writer who asserts that "without doubt the eyes play a great part in our intelligence of these things"[8] endow his text with the necessary authority for his reader to participate in the sight and experience, and therefore the knowledge, of the New World?[9] At the heart of this dynamic lie the epistemological and linguistic problems the New World presented to the Old. How does one know the New World? and how does one portray it? According to Oviedo, a new approach to the concept of knowledge and its written expression had to be devised. This search for a new method of recording history resulted in a renewed interest by many in Herodotus and the Greek sense of the historian as "an individual who sees and who recounts from the starting point of his own experience and sight" (Franklin, 130). While the role of sight in the apprehension of knowledge was a common medieval topos, passages of Oviedo's history show signs of moving away from medieval theories of visual epistemology and practices of representation toward a new form of expression inspired by the works of classical antiquity and the emerging emphasis on empiricism and natural observation.

The new, seemingly limitless wonders of the discovery of "one half" (una mitad) of the world served as a catalyst. The passages dedicated to reproducing visual images in the form of drawings and the verbal explanations of the items illuminate changes in early sixteenth-century representational practices—from a more medieval schematic or conceptual idea of an image to a more empirical image that attempted to convey the appearance of an object. As Forrest Robinson notes in his study *The Shape of Things Known,* medieval scholars saw the universe as "reducible to a series of spatial relationships that may be reproduced in abstract pictures" (29).

In this view, all material things, including art, hold a symbolic value. Accordingly, they attributed to the sense of sight a symbolic rather than an empirical value in apprehending knowledge and truth. For example, the revelation of truth—in particular, truth as God—was often described as coming in the form of light or a vision (58). Likewise, medieval histories used historical events to illustrate God's judgment of people: history was considered a symbolic record of this judgment.

With the reinterpretation of the works of classical antiquity and the new focus on textual erudition and empiricism in the early modern period, traditional theories about the relationship between the sense of sight and knowledge, and therefore the role of sight in art and history, shifted in emphasis. The focus "turned away from the divine itself and toward the divine found in nature," which encouraged a view of truth as quantifiable and based on the observation of nature (59). The association of knowledge with the sense of sight had originated in Plato's theory of knowledge, and it was elaborated by Aristotle and Cicero (the latter being one of Oviedo's models). Both Plato and Aristotle, in their attempts to bridge the gap between the human mind and the external world, resorted to explaining the phenomenon of knowing as integral to sight, but sight as linked to the intellect. Pliny, Oviedo's most direct model for his natural history, summed up the classical view of visual epistemology: "The mind is the real instrument of sight and observation, the eyes act as a sort of vessel receiving and transmitting the visible portion of the consciousness" (18). According to classical authors, then, the equation of seeing and knowing was largely figurative.

Renaissance scholars, in reading and reevaluating the works of these authors, both revitalized and changed this formula. The tradition of visual epistemology came to be taken more literally in the early modern period. With the new emphasis on empiricism, a new relationship emerged between vision and the apprehension of knowledge. Renaissance artists and scientists sought truth in the observation of nature and experimented with mathematical relationships that placed objects in spatial relationships that attempted to reflect how things are perceived by the eye but that were also linked to the intellect, or the mind's eye. Using geometry, emblems, and images, they asserted that a direct relationship existed between a pictorial image and a higher reality—whether it was the Aristotelian concept that artists give expression to forms of nature or the Neoplatonic belief in the ideal of Ideas within the mind. In turn, the belief that truth and knowledge are apprehended primarily through the sense of sight influenced theories of perspective and representation. For example, Leon

Alberti developed three-point perspective to create the illusion of three dimensions and developed practices in which ideological points could be made with perspective.[10]

A parallel tendency emerged in early modern historical writing, in which a new emphasis on the role of perspective in examining the past resulted in a distancing from the events that permitted sixteenth-century interpreters of classical antiquity to allow for the particular—in other words, to see history not as a record of judgment but as a window onto a unique society at a specific time. Histories of the period began to tend toward particularity and relativism, yet did not abandon a Christian framework or worldview. Along with the lively debates about the essence of truth, fiction, and history at the turn of the sixteenth century, the emerging concepts of perspective and relativity gave new importance to the role of sight and individual experience—for the author/artist as well as the reader/beholder—in the apprehension of truth in the overall scheme of God's world. Through his examination and configuration of experience and experiment, the author/artist played a more central role than his medieval or classical counterpart in establishing truth. This helps to explain the increase in autobiographical tendencies among works of the period. To state it another way, the reliance during the early modern period on the sense of sight led increasingly to the need for scientists, historians, and artists to experience through observation their subject of inquiry in order to establish their authority to represent the subject.

OVIEDO'S ILLUSTRATIONS

Many of Oviedo's works show a strong interest in and talent for illustration. In more conceptual figurative genres, Oviedo generously illustrated his chronicle of the Crown of Castile, *Catálogo Real* (see fig. 81), and his book with genealogical charts and coats of arms, *Batallas y Quinquagenas* (see fig. 82). As Carrillo notes, citing the aristocratic figurative culture of the emblem and the *impresse,* these illustrations tend to be fairly sophisticated and conceptual ("The Representation," chap. 3). The *impresse,* for example, depicts personal characteristics of families and individuals as animals and flora. But a different concept—and therefore a different level of artistic sophistication—informs Oviedo's New World drawings. The early modern impulse to quantify and visualize knowledge seems to have encouraged Oviedo to convey through pictorial images—both verbal and visual—what he actually saw. Oviedo had become familiar with Renaissance ideas and artists during his years in Italy. In trying to describe a tree, for example, he asserts,

> I will relate what I have learned about it [the tree], deferring to whomever knows best how to paint it or make it understood, because it would be preferable to have it rendered by the hand of Berruguete, or a painter as excellent as he, or Leonardo da Vinci, or Andrea Mantegna, famous painters I got to know in Italy, than to describe it by means of words. All of this is better seen than written about or painted.[11] (*Proemio,* bk. 10)

Notably, Leonardo da Vinci produced his own illustrated herbals.[12]

Oviedo's drawings and words attempt to place America in the mind's eye of the reader who cannot visit the Indies. Indeed, at times the author employed the strategy of comparing the exotic natural world, people, and artifacts of the New World with paintings and other visual arts of the period. Oviedo literarily and figuratively applies the advice of his model Pliny. Thus he evokes portraits of Suleiman Ottoman, king of the Turks, and his headpiece to describe the marvelous feathers of an American bird (bk. 6, chap. 2); the manner in which Spanish painters rendered arabesques and florets to help the reader imagine some Native American clothing (bk. 24, chap. 11); and the gilding of a Castilian altarpiece to depict the color of a Yucatán mask (bk. 17, chap. 13). In other instances, Oviedo simply evokes a visual image of the object without making comparisons to Old World archetypes. His descriptive technique generally moves from the appearance of an object and its nomenclature to its use and value.

Oviedo simultaneously places American phenomena within European conventions for the representation of known objects and practices and describes them as something completely new. The sheer number of terms he borrowed from indigenous languages rather than creating a semantic shift (a word based on a European word) demonstrates Oviedo's response to nomenclatorial pressure—a need to include new words.

At times Oviedo enhanced the descriptive power of words or the evocation of existing visual images with pen-and-ink illustrations integrated into the narrative. When confronted with the inadequacy of language to set forth what he had witnessed or if he wished to emphasize the significance of the object, he employed drawings as a means of rendering the essence of an object for the reader. He maintained that if direct observation was the most important element in the apprehension of a new subject, then a simple and relatively unembellished drawing was second best, the reader being, as it were, only once removed from actually observing the thing itself.

ILLUSTRATING THE INDIES

Of the approximately seventy-six surviving illustrations by Oviedo, the majority are of American phenomena: flora (twenty-three), fauna (twelve), indigenous ethnographic items (eighteen), and geographical scenes or maps (twelve). In addition to these, a couple are of Old World analogues that help the reader imagine New World phenomena.[13] Two others are coats of arms, and there are a couple of faint marginal sketches, of a serpent and a monstrous bird, that appear to have been rendered quickly. Nonetheless, Oviedo mentions in a note to the engraver that the sketches should be included. The majority of the illustrations were executed by Oviedo on the basis of his firsthand experience in Central America and the Caribbean islands. Thus, the majority are in part I (especially books 5–13), book 29 (Tierra Firme), and book 42 (Nicaragua). Oviedo's method of embedding illustrations in the historical narrative and the evolution of his drawing technique over several decades indicate the importance of the visual to the construction of the *History* and to the evolving aims of the historian over time.

Oviedo's opening illustrations document the coat of arms given to Columbus as discoverer and admiral of the ocean sea (see fig. 2) and the symbol of the Southern Cross given to Oviedo for his own coat of arms, which closes the 1535 edition of the *History* (see figs. 3 and 78). Both emphasize the newness of the Americas: Columbus's coat of arms carries the symbols of Castile and Leon in the upper section and an image of the abundant new world of gold and palms in the lower section. Oviedo highlights the new symbol added to his coat of arms by drawing the Southern Cross, the constellation that is visible only from within twenty-two degrees of the equator. Both symbols underscore Columbus's and Oviedo's importance—one as the discoverer of a new world, the other as the experienced scribe of New World novelty:

> I want to say another very noteworthy thing, one which those who have not sailed through these Indies cannot have seen. . . . [There are]

> four stars arranged in the shape of a cross which go around the edges of the antarctic pole, as they are shown in this drawing; stars which the Imperial Majesty gave as an improvement to my coat of arms, so that I and my successors, would put them together with our ancient ones of Valdés, in consideration of the services I have rendered in these parts and Indies and first in the Royal House of Castile, from the time I was thirteen years old.[14] (bk. 2, chap. 11)

These first illustrations establish a connection between sight, experience, novelty, and the important roles of discoverer and author.

Once he begins depicting American phenomena, the historian turns his gaze first to indigenous cultures. In general, ethnographic objects are presented straightforwardly and analytically, and the first drawings are introduced with either a formulaic phrase or a more elaborate rationale for the drawing. Oviedo's composite formula normally consists of a discussion of the construction and function of an item, a comparison with a European analogue, the introduction of the Native American name for the item, and, in some cases, a drawing of it. For example, after describing in detail (and in the process borrowing no fewer than seven indigenous words) the appearance, use, and utility—even for Christians—of the hammock, the author includes a drawing of it: "And if I have been able to make it understood, this bed is of the kind that is depicted here" (bk. 5, chap. 2; see fig. 6).[15] Likewise, two pen-and-ink depictions of native houses, or *caney,* follow a long passage that explains, using many Taino words, their construction and utility (bk. 6, chap. 1; see figs. 7, 8). They are then compared with the "field tents" (tiendas de campo) that Spanish armies carried. Finally, one drawing is presented with a short statement on the purpose it serves: "And that this may be better understood, I put here the manner or figure of this *caney,* so that it may be sufficient to be well understood" (bk. 6, chap. 1).[16] Rather than reduce it to a single form, he emphasizes the particular; he not only distinguishes its likeness to and difference from Spanish objects, but also details the many varieties of *caney.* He explains the need for a second illustration:

> Because in certain provinces there, they have a different shape, and some of these indeed are neither heard of nor seen except in that very land. But as the shape of the caney, or round house, was drawn [earlier], I now want to include the second kind of house that I have mentioned, which is like the one shown here, so that one may better understand what I said with respect to one and the other.[17] (bk. 6, chap. 1)

Here we see Oviedo's belief in the power of linking a visual depiction with the new name for an object. The equation of seeing with understanding makes a "painted bed" (cama pintada) become a "hammock" (hamaca) and a "round house" (casa redonda) a *caney* for the European reader/viewer. He links the act of beholding a drawing with an understanding of its nature "so that it may be sufficient to be well understood" (bk. 6, chap. 1).[18]

Whereas Oviedo attempts to delineate the particular qualities of the *caney* through a composite of various methods of representing it, he inscribes his chapter on the canoe into the works of classical antiquity (bk. 6, chap. 4). The chapter opens with a reference to Pliny's *Natural History* and the "little boats of a single log" (navecillas de un leño) that Pliny describes. Oviedo deduces that these must be the same as those he sees on Hispaniola. As with previous descriptions, he borrows Native American words to name the object: "boat" (canoa) or "ship" (piragua). He explains in detail its construction, measurements, and utility. He employs European analogues, weighing the value of the American object against its European counterpart (barca, navío). Finally, he incorporates two illustrations into the chapter "like the figure of it seen here"; "just as the *nahe,* or rowboat, and the *canoa* are depicted here" (bk. 6, chap. 4; fig. 11).[19] The distinction of this passage lies in Oviedo's intent to discuss the texts of antiquity (he mentions Ovid and Virgil, too) and to elevate his own standing and history by comparing his experience to that recorded in written authorities. By this rhetorical device he asserts that his history is at least as authoritative as those of antiquity, since he can corroborate what they say, and is perhaps more authoritative because his text includes a new discovery for Europeans.

Indeed, the next chapter (bk. 6, chap. 5) questions the need to rely on the authorities of classical antiquity at all. After Oviedo's usual analytical description of a new item—in this case, the fire drill used in Hispaniola—he introduces a drawing of it and invokes Pliny again (see fig. 12). This time, however, the official chronicler questions the conventional method of referring to traditional authorities and instead suggests that the reader play an active role in apprehending the idea of the fire drill:

> The [process], at least, of drawing fire from sticks, is included by Pliny in his *Natural History* . . . so that what Pliny relates and these Indians do (in this case) are one and the same thing. . . . But for what reason should I wish to call on classical authors regarding things that I

> myself have seen, much less for those which Nature shows to all, and are seen everyday?[20] (bk. 6, chap. 5)

He appeals to the reader's observation of the sparks that fly from carriage wheels in motion in order to secure in his reader's mind a better understanding of the nature of the fire drill: "Thus, this is a thing seen and found in nature" (bk. 6, chap. 5).[21] Although Oviedo encourages the reader to apprehend this device in the mind's eye, based on the reader's experience, he also acknowledges the role of the eye in the cognition of the essence of the object: "Its form is just as I show in the drawing, since, even without the picture, what I have said is enough to understand it. But it is still good to make as much use as possible of the picture, so that the eyes may become informed thereby, and these things may be better understood" (bk. 6, chap. 5).[22] Even drawings of ethnographic items that were executed after 1535, such as those in the books on Tierra Firma and Nicaragua, maintain the same formula for introducing illustrations. Several are simply included with no explanation ("as it is painted here"),[23] while others are presented for their documentary value—as novelties—as we see in the cases of the fire tower (bk. 20, chaps. 22/23; fig. 54) and the whirlabout (voladores) (bk. 42, chap. 13; fig. 71).

Thirteen maps and illustrations of geographical scenes, especially volcanoes—all from parts II and III of the *History*—reveal a similar inclination to document mostly firsthand experience so that the reader can better see and understand notable New World phenomena. The maps, in particular, focus on adding to the store of cartographic images that had begun to flood into the king. Oviedo includes six maps, all of Central America, and notes how they fit into current cartography. He renders, for example, the Lake of Maracaibo "because the painted image which was taken so that His Imperial Majesty might see it is very different from the map which I have set down here" (bk. 25, chap. 1; fig. 58).[24] He admits that his map of the Gulf of Nicoya is a first attempt, open to revision by others: "So that this Gulf may be better known, I have here put down its image, if I was even able to grasp it, and willing to accept the correction of anyone who might have understood it better than I" (bk. 29, chap. 21; fig. 59).[25] Six other images depict volcanoes, an island, and a plaza in Central America that he saw for himself: "When I saw it; it was a thing very much worth seeing" (bk. 42, chap. 5; fig. 72).[26] As in the case of Oviedo's cartography, we see glimpses of an increasingly scientific bent to his illustrations, such as in his diagram of the interior of a volcano (bk. 42, chap. 6; fig. 70). Two of the drawings in this category, however, are taken from other sources, which he carefully notes (a volcano in Mexico, bk. 33, chap. 33; fig. 64; a map of the Panama coast, bk. 43, chap. 1; fig. 57).

Oviedo's twelve illustrations of American fauna tell a different story. Only two of these animals—the armadillo and the manatee (figs. 45, 51)—appear to have been drawn before 1535. Both are in book 13 on sea animals (the armadillo was later moved to the chapter on land animals). The first is briefly introduced as "esta que aqui yo pinté," [This which I have painted here] and the second goes without comment. In the final version of the history, Oviedo added dozens of additional chapters (chaps. 9–40) and eight more drawings to book 12 on land animals. (He even mentions a proposed drawing of a cow that he never executed.) Although none of these survived in the sixteenth-century manuscript copies, Muñoz's eighteenth-century copy seems to have rendered them relatively faithfully. Curiously, none of these illustrations are accompanied by a verbal presentation of the sketch, and nearly half resemble symbolic figures in heraldry. Most of the fauna, such as the tiger and the bivana (figs. 42, 48), are diagrammatically sketched, with no resort to naturalism, and carry bold letters around the figure indicating its name. Only the anteater (fig. 44) is sketched naturalistically and is not set off with figurative lettering. Although it is difficult to draw any definitive conclusions about the role of these illustrations, it appears Oviedo saw little need to comment on the link of the illustrations with his historical narrative and method—assuming, of course, that Muñoz did not alter the original text. The only two post-1535 drawings for which we have the autograph manuscript, a monstrous bird (bk. 6, chap. 36; fig. 16) and a serpent (bk. 39, chap. 2; fig. 65), are lightly sketched in the margin and look more like doodles than full-fledged illustrations. But the historian comments on the former: "Pay attention to this bird; it will be painted in full size" (HEH, HM 177, f. 45v).[27]

Oviedo apparently encountered few problems in describing and depicting Native American ethnographic items, geographical scenes, and fauna. Verbal descriptions are extensive, and if pictorial images are introduced, they are concise, with only an occasional brief expression of doubt about the accuracy of the drawing. Such is not always the case with the representation of indigenous flora, perhaps because there were fewer European analogues and more varieties. In many cases, samples could not be sent to Europe. Thus the author's composite representation often includes a statement of the inadequacy of his drawings as representations of reality.

In a chapter devoted to a meticulous description of the planting of yuccas, the use of the fruit, and the varieties that exist, Oviedo mentions in passing that he has resorted to depicting particular aspects of two varieties of yucca leaves. Yet even this attempt is incomplete: "I have drawn here the shape of one and the other, notwithstanding that even in the same types of leaves there are particular features and different kinds or varieties of yucca" (bk. 7, chap. 2; fig. 17).[28]

THE PINEAPPLE

The predicament recurs in other chapters, such as the famous description of the wonders of the pineapple (bk. 7, chap. 14; fig. 20). This chapter is one of the clearest examples of the author's dilemma in talking to the European reader about unnamed, unordered American reality. In near rapture, Oviedo presents a dizzying proliferation of words. He begins with the problem of naming the fruit and continues with his struggle to classify and describe accurately its marvels. First, the act of naming the fruit causes a variety of difficulties. Oviedo explains that because the fruit from the *cardo* looked like pinecones, the first Christians in the New World named it "pinecone" (*piña*). He asserts, however, that *piña* could be construed as a misnomer:

> A person could inquire why, since it is a thistle, is this fruit not called an artichoke? I maintain that it was the responsibility of the first Christians who saw it over here, to give it one name or another. It seems to me that the better name would have been to call it an artichoke, with respect to the thistle and spines among which it grows, although it does resemble a pinecone more than an artichoke. The truth is that it is not totally unlike an artichoke.[29] (bk. 7, chap. 14)

In the process of pointing to an error of identification, however, Oviedo mistakenly identifies the pineapple as a type of thistle. He points, perhaps unwittingly, to the apparently arbitrary nature of naming things. Why should the pineapple be named according to its resemblance to something else rather than according to its natural classification? While the writer refers primarily to the fruit as "pinecone" (*piña*), he also resorts to a sort of double name, "pinecone or artichoke" (*piña o alcarchopha*). The relationship between a thing and its name in the New World is further complicated (as with the yucca) by the presence of many varieties of pineapples, which carry different indigenous names to identify them: "Some they call yayama, others boniama, and others yayagua" (bk. 7, chap. 14).[30]

Reducing the fruit that Oviedo believes is unequaled in the world to a single word proved problematic for the author. He therefore resorted to a detailed delineation of its qualities according to the four senses that could experience the fruit. Here, too, Oviedo finds words alone inadequate. Creating a circular narrative pattern, he reiterates the sensuous qualities of the pineapple and intersperses these passages with information about its cultivation and medicinal uses—as though by pure repetition he could render for his reader the nature of this fruit. In addition, the author employs the dual strategy of evoking an analogue, saying that the fruit tastes like a mixture of peach and other fruits known in Europe, while asserting the pineapple cannot be compared with any fruit he has known: "No other gives such contentment . . . there is no comparison between a good [pineapple] and any of the other fruits I have seen" (bk. 7, chap. 14).[31]

Halfway through this whirlwind of words, Oviedo acknowledges the obstacles involved in accurately portraying the fruit with words alone. Reflecting an uneasiness about things unseen that was characteristic of his times, Oviedo believed all things could be represented to the sense of vision in some form,[32] so he introduces a drawing of it:

> Neither the illustration of my pen nor my words can bestow on the original the accurate description or the glory of this fruit in a manner so wholly satisfactory as to be able to explain the matter without a brush or a drawing, and even with these it would be necessary to use colors to make it more alike (*if not entirely, at least in part*), to make it easier to understand than by what I do and say, *because in some manner the reader's sight would be able to share in this truth.* All this notwithstanding, I will include it the best way I know, as badly drawn as described; yet, for those who may have seen this fruit, that will suffice, and they will fill in the rest. And for those who never have seen it but here . . . I assure them that if ever they do see it they will pardon me if I did not know or was unable justly to praise this fruit.[33] (bk. 7, chap. 14, emphasis added)

Here we can clearly detect the limits of a literal interpretation of Oviedo's idea that seeing equals understanding when it is applied to his drawings. He tells his readers that the drawing will enable them to understand the wonders of the pineapple better, but that their comprehension of it will be only partial. Achieving a visual epistemology through drawings, no matter how unembellished, is not equal to actually seeing the object firsthand. He expands on this view, saying, "And if, because of a deficiency in the colors and in the drawing, I am unable *to make people understand what I would like to say,* blame my opinion, in which, to my eyes, it is the loveliest of all the fruits I have seen, the one which smells and tastes the best" (bk. 7, chap. 14, emphasis added).[34] In fact, the chronicler points here to his admittedly schematic drawing, which served as part of an act of mediation. The illustration does not so much render a naturalistic image of the pineapple as remind the reader that the author experiences the apprehension of the new and communicates that personal experience and process to the reader so that he may participate in it and understand it.

While the image can only indirectly convey truth to the reader, the author recognizes another problem: his drawing attempts to depict a particular type of pineapple and in doing so leaves out the other varieties: "The one called yayama is somewhat elongated, like the one I have here drawn, while the other two species of which I have spoken are rounder" (bk. 7, chap. 14).[35] Although he sets out to depict the particular, Oviedo also wishes to represent all pineapples, and thus a tension emerges. He draws one type of pineapple, which becomes a schema for all pineapples, and with some apprehension he compensates with his words for depicting only a single variety.

The author's revisions in the 1540s to the original 1535 chapter on the pineapple reveal the new weight he gives to the role of words and images to convey more accurately the appearance of an object. Oviedo augmented sections about the name and varieties of pineapple as well as the role of the senses. In addition, he rendered a new drawing of it, centering the fruit in the middle of the page and noting it in the margin. The illustration thus takes on a more important role while the new verbal additions further highlight the author's sense of frustration that words cannot capture the essence of this marvelous fruit.

In contrast both to Leonardo da Vinci's sketches of plants and to the herbals that began to circulate in the mid–sixteenth century, Oviedo's work increasingly strove to portray the particular reality of America. Whereas the earlier European woodcuts employed in herbals depicted generic forms in which the details of the particular types (and the resulting multiplicity) are replaced with a schema, Oviedo set out to portray the particular in his drawings. Nonetheless, he encountered difficulties similar to those he faced in trying to make words represent precisely America's novelties and abundance. E. H. Gombrich, writing about the use of the schema in art, explains the dilemma: "This tendency of our minds to classify and register our experience in terms of the known must present a real problem to the artist in his encounter with the particular" (168). He goes on to explain that seeing and knowing become seeing and noticing (172), where reality cannot be grasped by the intellect without some standard of comparison or interpretation (178). The tension between using analogies and schemas and attempting to fix an accurate verbal or visual image of the particular characteristics of American subjects is manifest in Oviedo's text.

By the 1540s, Oviedo relied on European formulas less frequently than he had earlier. In fact, in some cases the New World becomes the referent for introducing yet newer discoveries. He avoided the reductive tendency of many other early writers and attempted to reproduce the vast complexity and heterogeneity of the New World through both words and drawings. Although Oviedo also included statements on the cultivation and utility of the pineapple as well as people's opinions about it, his primary impulse in this passage seems to be an attempt to understand for himself the process of representing this new wonder, to break the spiral of confusion caused by trying to settle on a single word that reflects the essence of the pineapple. He delineates the qualities of the object by using analogues, describing the empirical aspects of the fruit, and rendering at first a schematic visual image of it and later a more natural one. The fact that Oviedo underscores the incompleteness of his representation of the pineapple emphasizes the inadequacy of his and other chroniclers' endeavors and the importance of his presence in America in order to approximate a truthful representation of the New World for the reader. Indeed, the author's early illustrations often focus more on the communication process between the writer and reader in apprehending American novelty than on attempting a realistic depiction of the object.

In several other introductions to his drawings, aspects of this near-miss quality emerge. Oviedo continues to draw new objects and periodically insists that the drawing aids the verbal description but does not replace the actual witnessing of the object. Rather, Oviedo positions himself as a mediator and translator of American reality for his reader. By asserting the superiority of a firsthand experience of America, Oviedo claims a place for his own authority as a chronicler who devoted forty-three years to living in and writing about America. His words and drawings, he maintains, are based on his own experience. They cannot supplant the experience itself.

Characteristically, however, Oviedo's insistence on this stance leads to an ironic situation in later parts of the text as his historical method evolves. The pineapple is not the only drawing that the author revised after 1535. Many of his early illustrations underwent a thorough process of revision, a process that in general increasingly allowed the image to look like the thing itself. The increased sense of naturalism in the drawings is not a question of artistic skill. As we saw in the case of his heraldry books, he had this skill early on. Instead, it reveals a shift in the relationship between the role of illustrations and the historian. By the 1540s Oviedo's drawings were for the most part less schematic and more naturalistic. The images often included precise details of the appearance of the object, especially in the case of flora, or a clearer rendition of the use of ethnographic objects. For example, whereas the 1535 edition renders a series of schematic tree leaves (for example, figs. 21–24), the 1540s illustrations of most plants reveal the entire plant with roots, shading, and instructions to the engraver about the precise dimensions of plant stems (for example, figs. 40, 41). In the case of early ethnographic images, the author creates more realism: the illustration of the human figure in the canoe is done with more *contrapposto,* the artistic technique of showing a human figure twisting on an axis, in order to demonstrate the motion necessary to move the canoe (bk. 6, chap. 4; fig. 11); a pair of hands are added to the drawing of the fire drill to show more precisely how it was used (bk. 6, chap. 5; fig. 12); and the hammock is completely redrawn, this time with a human figure in it, in order to show how it is used (bk. 5, chap. 2; fig. 6). Little verbal commentary is changed, but in a significant passage from a chapter and image that were added after 1535, Oviedo notes his new awareness of the naturalism in his images: "The true leaf of this plant, in its natural state, is like the one I have drawn" (bk. 11, chap. 4; fig. 37).[36] The new direction toward a more empirical, autonomous image reflects a meaningful shift: the author's role is no longer that of mediator between New World reality and reader but that of transcriber, a scientist documenting an ever-expanding American world.

Another element signals a shift in Oviedo's initial insistence that he translates only his own firsthand experience: several of the later drawings are based on secondhand accounts. He illustrates in book 20, for example, a fire tower he has never seen, basing his drawing on a captain's verbal description of it: "And since they are a new shape of building, I have here drawn one of the same shape which this captain described to me" (bk. 20, chap. 6; fig. 54).[37] The new form of the tower justifies the inclusion of the drawing, but in the process Oviedo acknowledges both his inability to experience everything for himself and his indebtedness to other individuals' firsthand accounts in order to complete his history. Elsewhere, he includes a map made by Diego de Almagro, verifying that it came from a reliable witness and therefore that the chronicler considers it as trustworthy as his own firsthand experience (bk. 43, chap. 1; fig. 74).

CONCLUSIONS

By examining Oviedo's drawings, we come to understand how he linked seeing with understanding. But we must also note the author's recognition that this formula is limited in two ways. First, the European reader can view a picture of an American subject yet cannot witness the thing itself. Second, the abundance of American marvels prohibits Oviedo from witnessing everything firsthand, so he must rely on accounts by others who were eyewitnesses. The reader must rely on Oviedo's sense of sight and trust his methods of representing what he witnesses.

The rhetorical device of repetition of certain words and their synonyms in the general preface to part I, which was written in 1535 and was not revised for the final *History,* as well as their sequence reveals that Oviedo linked his travels in the New World with "trials" (*trabajos*) and "dangers" (*peligros*) that he underwent in order to "witness" (*ver*) and thus to "understand" (*entender*) the marvels of American phenomena. He asserts that being an "eyewitness" (*un testigo*) enabled him to "name" or represent (*nombrar*) American reality truthfully. This "truthful and new account" (*verdadera y nueva historia*), in turn, gives him "authority" (*autoridad*) as the official chronicler and enables the reader to "praise" (*loar*) God's creation and Spain's imperial destiny. According to Oviedo, the authority of his history depends on a chain of actions in which sight and experience are the crucial links; to travel (*viajar*), suffer (*padecer*), see (*ver*), experience (*experimentar*), understand (*entender*), write the truth (*escribir verdad*), and praise (*loar*) are all interconnected. In the instances in which he encounters the most difficulty in portraying American phenomena (as we see in his chapter on the pineapple), his words circumscribe the central issue of his text, pointing to his history as an authoritative medium through which the reader can praise the wonders of God's creation.

We have seen that the illustrations are integral to the descriptions of the natural history of America as well as to the underlying principle of the *History.* Oviedo promotes the theory that everything is capable of visual representation, but at times only to the mind's eye. That is, Oviedo's outer or corporeal eye must serve as a link to the reader's own corporeal eyes—vis-à-vis the drawings—and to the reader's inner eye. Images are not simply illustrations; image and text function as one.[38] Basing his inclusion of drawings on theories of visual epistemology, Oviedo asserts the importance of the sense of sight in apprehending the essence of the New World. Yet in most cases the reader is unable to experience America firsthand. Oviedo positions himself and his text as the essential link between America and his reader. Accepting his *History* as the first full and true representation of America depends on accepting the author's experience of the New World. Through his firsthand knowledge of New World natural phenomena, Oviedo sought to bring the original experience closer to his reader.[39] Responding to the Renaissance concern with the nature of truth and its relationship to history as well as to concern with how best to apprehend a new reality, Oviedo resorted to creating visual images of America and in the process constructed a theory of authority and representation. At key junctures, he placed more importance on the image of America than on words about it: "Because it is better seen in drawings . . . than understood with words" (bk. 7, chap. 14).[40]

Oviedo's illustrations and musings about them reveal his theory and practice of representation and showcase the European writer's predicament when describing a new world. The *History* reveals much about the dilemma America posed to historians—in finding both an adequate means for Europeans to convey America's essence and the credentials to write about it. Since traditional European authorities did have direct experience of the Indies, authority increasingly became a relative term based on individual experience. Each chronicler therefore invented his own "true" picture of America according to his own particular point of view and purpose. Through the use of drawings in his text, Oviedo asserts that the criterion of the truth of history, both human and natural, is sight and experience. The historian worked through various methods of representation, both verbal and visual, to make known particular American phenomena. As we have seen, even though Oviedo's method of drawing images changed over time, both his old and his new methods helped convey knowledge of the New World to the reader through the sense of sight. Early illustrations in the *History* tend to be schematic and subordinated to the narrative, part of a plan to convey New World novelty and the chronicler's experience. Later illustrations document the object itself with greater care and detail, focusing more on Oviedo as an observer and collector.

FIVE

AMAZON WOMEN AND NEW WORLD REALITIES

Documenting an Expanding World (bk. 6, chap. 33)

Caught between two eras—one that would recognize the contribution of empiricism to historiography and one that often viewed history as writing a variation of a primal text—Spanish chroniclers of the New World frequently revised traditional historiography, but they rarely broke completely from it. In his efforts to document all he saw and heard in the Indies, Gonzalo Fernández de Oviedo conceived of his historiographical project as an open-ended process of recovering new information about a vast area from dozens of informants. Thus the *History* became a sort of repository of information that required continual revision—revision of canonical histories and revision of his own previous accounts. A study of Oviedo's process of rewriting history brings into sharper focus the relationship between traditional historiography and the emerging ideas of empiricism. Multiple contemporary testimonies, new information appended to previous chapters in the *History,* and citations from traditional histories all reveal Oviedo's attempts to come to grips with heterogeneous American reality.

As we saw in the case of Oviedo's illustrations, there were significant changes in his historiographical method over the decades that he wrote. Study of the 1535 edition and of the extant autograph manuscript reveals at least four distinct stages in the writing and revision of the *History.* The first stage is the publication of part I in 1535; no autograph manuscript of this version exists. Yet passages from it are taken directly from the *Sumario* (1526) and expanded, pointing to the author's penchant for accumulating information in an ongoing process. The second stage is a version of the three parts of the *History* written as early as 1535 and 1540, a version he attempted to publish in 1541. This draft appears to have been dismantled and reworked during a third stage, around 1541–1542, when the historian reconfigured the whole historiographic project and vastly expanded it. Extant autograph manuscript sections date from this period. This 1542 version greatly expanded the number of chapters about American flora and fauna and placed them into discrete books about natural history, as a separate category from the history of different provinces. The natural world was seen increasingly as separate from the general history of conquests and government. Indeed, the general history was now thoroughly organized according to geographical regions, which corresponded to administrative divisions for provinces. Thus, when the administrative territory changed for New Spain, for example, its placement changed in the *History*: what had been book 28 changed four times until it finally became book 33. Oviedo attempted to leave for Spain in 1542 in order to publish this vastly reorganized three-part history, but he was prevented from traveling by a prohibition on ships leaving for Spain because of battles in the Caribbean with French corsairs. This ushered in the final stage of revision. For the next six years, until his attempt in 1548 to publish the *History,* Oviedo continually updated the text. Finally, he left the manuscript for safekeeping in a monastery in Seville (1549). Throughout the three parts there are marginal notes, deleted information, and insertions of new material. In other sections the author appended entire chapters and books to previous ones (books 29 and 33, for example).

Almost all modern scholars who have studied the *History* note the chronicler's continual revisions, but they often overlook the full implications of this process or fail to examine it systematically. In the first complete edition of the *History* (1850s), José Amador de los Ríos included nearly all of Oviedo's changes but only sporadically footnoted them. He attributes most of the revisions to changing circumstances rather than to Oviedo's methodological concerns. Alberto M. Salas proposes that Oviedo "doesn't [so much] write as he is in the process of writing" (no escribe, sino está escribiendo) because he lacks the confidence in man's ability to tell the whole story (100). The historian must produce all known accounts to ensure he has not left out anything. Salas concludes that Oviedo "looks for safety in detail" (busca refugio en el detalle) (101). Likewise, Antonello Gerbi perceives this "open" nature of the history and adds a nuance to Salas's observation. Oviedo, as "the high priest of truth," believes that multiple accounts and revisions help the truth emerge, clarifying the naturally clouded ways in which humans perceive events and revealing all of nature's marvels (245). Gerbi sees Oviedo's efforts as having an almost legal precision, a point I will return to later. One of the chronicler's most recent editors, Juan Pérez de Tudela, also notes Oviedo's zeal for including new accounts to revise previous versions. He concludes, as does Gerbi, that Oviedo rarely viewed his material as having achieved a final, unalterable form. Significantly, Pérez de Tudela suggests that the additions to the history reveal a movement away from the glorification of Spain and the justification of the conquest and toward "the physiognomy of an interpreter of the essentially distinct New World" (la fisonomía de un exégeta del Nuevo Mundo esencialmente distinto) (cxl); in other words, as the imperial aims of the *History* faded, the New World itself came into clearer view. If this is true, how do the revisions achieve this effect? The two printed versions of part I of the *History* (1535, 1850s) we can use to study Oviedo's changes reveal that he is only partially successful in this attempt to view the New World in a completely new way.

Oviedo's revisions can serve to illuminate his historiographic process. First, I look at the differences between the first edition of the history published in 1535 and the final version published in the 1850s. Second, I study the changes made to the autograph manuscript of the final version of the *History,* written from no later than 1535 to 1549. The editions and the manuscript reveal that Oviedo sought to represent the New World by means of a dual approach. He set out to mirror nature by rendering American phenomena and events as he and his witnesses observed them, demonstrating an empirical bent, but he also imitated authoritative texts, especially general and natural histories from classical antiquity, in order to highlight America's differences from the Old World. Both approaches, he argues, prove that his historical method rendered the most accurate picture of America. Furthermore, his narrative strategies for dealing with reports of Amazon women living in the New World manifest the collision of Old World myths with New World reality. While Oviedo's method hints at what will later become the method of scientific observation and reporting, his training was steeped in the early modern precept of *imitatio,* imitation. Based on the humanist revival of Cicero's method of instruction through the practical exercise of imitating authoritative texts, the discipline of imitation complemented the learning of rhetorical theory.[1] Oviedo relied on the conventions of *imitatio* while simultaneously criticizing and even attempting to usurp classical authorities.

THE REVISIONS

The most obvious difference between the 1535 edition of the *History* and the final version is the inclusion of parts II and III, which the author had promised in the 1535 edition of part I. Because parts II and III generally treat new information, however, the revisions to part I are more revealing of Oviedo's historical method and will be the focus of my comments here.[2] Boasting that his work was the most extensive since the time of Adam, the chronicler added over one hundred new chapters to part I and revised large sections of the earlier version.[3] There are changes in some chapter titles as well as in the chapters themselves. These textual revisions tend to fall into two main categories: the addition of new information on New World phenomena and events, and the inclusion of further sources and textual authorities.

Encouraged by the instructions he received as official court chronicler of the Indies to render his accounts as fully as possible, Oviedo expanded his material on New World phenomena and events by more than a third in the final version of part I.[4] The new descriptions of American flora and fauna reflect, for the most part, Oviedo's own observation and further experience of subjects first described in the 1535 edition. As we saw in the last chapter, the author doubles the number of illustrations and renders them in a more naturalistic style in the final draft of the *History*. In addition, he offers more practical details on habitat, utility, and appearance of American phenomena. In the case of the description of the pineapple, for example, Oviedo expands his almost formulaic two-page description of something new and wonderful to a much longer description that attempts to give the reader the experience of the pineapple through each of four senses.

The new details demonstrate Oviedo's almost inexhaustible efforts to keep his accounts up to date with the most recent discoveries, conquests, and colonizations. For example, books 16–19 include new information about Hernando de Soto's expedition. The pattern of revision that emerges is complicated because of the ever-changing nature of events and the complex network of informants. A typical example of the layers of change occurs in a chapter on the Columbus family and includes alterations from three periods (bk. 6, chap. 7). First, Oviedo adds new information about the efforts of the vicereine, Columbus's wife, to secure from the Crown inheritance rights for her children. He explains that this account was written for the revised history "because for the second printing of this first part or history we shall go on adding and revising that which will complete it, and which time has changed."[5] Later he returns to the already "completed" account to add yet more news, saying, "I arrived here with this material when a clean copy of [the manuscript] was being prepared, the end of March of the year 1539."[6] Finally, the manuscript for the final history renders the first two emendations as part of a whole continuous narration, smoothing over the additions from two different periods, but there is one last layer of revision in the manuscript: the insertion of the phrase "of glorious memory" (*de gloriosa memoria*) next to the vicereine's name. By the time Oviedo deposited the manuscript in Seville, the vicereine had died. This pattern of emendation permeates the history.

The historian's extensive additions of newly observed phenomena and events are part of his "open" history written by, as Gerbi says, a "high priest of truth," someone willing to expand on truth as it is revealed over time (241–245). Perhaps the key to Oviedo's precision is his philosophy of "we are adding and revising" (*vamos añadiendo y enmendando*). As Kathleen Ann Ross has noted in her work on the seventeenth-century Mexican intellectual Carlos de Sigüenza y Góngora, *enmendar* held a dual meaning: "to correct," connoting an error in the original source, and "to propose a variation," implying that an added source will confer more veracity on the original account (47). Ross views this layering as characteristic of the baroque style in colonial Spanish America, but it clearly emerges in Oviedo's case in the descriptions of the seemingly infinite variety of nature in the New World and the proliferation of accounts about the ongoing Spanish enterprise. Oviedo both corrects and adds variations to his previous accounts, hoping that by adding multiple testimonies he would add a juridical authority to his observations.

As Oviedo includes more observations about the conquest and about American nature, he appends entire paragraphs that discuss the inadequacy of emulating canonical texts when writing about America. Conventions of the time may have dictated that the official chronicler refer to textual authorities in his second edition. However, Oviedo often cites them and then takes issue with their writings. Indeed, the inadequacies of canonical texts become the justification for his new theories about the nature of the New World and its inhabitants. Chapter 2 of his book on agricultural practices (bk. 7), for example, adds detail to his previous description of the cultivation of maize; he mentions four established authors on the topic—three ancients and one contemporary. Outlining canonical views on the subject and drawing a parallel with Native American practices, the author portrays the natives as natural authorities, needing no precepts to guide them: "What I mean is that these Indians, although they are ignorant of these precepts, are taught by Nature what is best in this case" (bk. 7, chap. 2).[7] Furthermore, Oviedo notes that Pliny does not talk about a certain kind of maize found in the New World ("It could be that Pliny did not see this in its entire spectrum").[8] Just as the New World illustrates aspects of the Old and offers new material, Oviedo's discussion of the limits of previous texts to explain the New World implies a revision of those texts and a new reliance on observation and experience.[9]

A second source, the extant manuscript sections of the final history with which Amador worked for his edition, further illuminates Oviedo's additive strategies.[10] A study of the manuscript reveals that even the completed revision of sections of part I was continually modified until 1549, when it was deposited in Seville and was finally out of reach of further emendation. First, Oviedo perfects his verbal description of the natural and general history of the New World by making his accounts more detailed. He elaborated on the location and workings of gold mines (bk. 6, chap. 8), and he reworked many manuscript drawings that originally appeared in 1535, all in order to depict objects more accurately. As mentioned in chapter 4, the one-dimensional hammock of the 1535 edition, for example, is rendered in three dimensions, and a human figure is added to illustrate its function. The chronicler also carefully updated the passage of time and the emergence of new sources. A passage that specifies the current year originally reads 1540 and is successively changed five times (to 1541, 1543, 1545, 1547, and 1548; bk. 6, *Proemio*).[11]

These manuscript emendations once again reveal Oviedo's commitment to a juridical-like precision in history. As we saw in the discussion of the prologues, Oviedo was inspired by the Erasmian *libro de verdad* and by the new humanist philology that saw language as a "return to reality" and history as concerned with the particular incident, or *caso*. As a bureaucrat and former scribe, Oviedo mixes these rhetorical and discursive traditions with the Castilian legalistic tradition. Like a notarial scribe or judge, he depends on eyewitness testimony to determine the truth, and therefore all versions were seen as valid in their own way "as leading to the truth" and should not be deleted. All observations and details were considered essential. Although the revisions dealing with nature and events still reflected in part the medieval impulse to write a catalog of *novedades,*[12] or novelties, they anticipated an empirical age, adducing detailed information in order to represent more accurately the New World.

Oviedo's emendation of passages referencing theories of the ancients regarding general and natural history emphasizes, however, that he could not rely wholly on the empirical method. He was charged with writing Spain's official history of the Indies. Historical decorum, an essential consideration for any medieval or Renaissance historian, dictated that his history inscribe itself in conventional historiography. However, while the theory and practice of *imitatio* informed every aspect of a writer's language and treatment of a subject, its use was constantly shifting during the period. On the one hand, following medieval tradition, Oviedo occasionally inserts references to authorities as proof of his point. For example, a passage from St. Isidore is given as proof of the existence of an improbable half-feline, half-bird creature (bk. 6, chap. 52). On the other hand, and more frequently, he searches for a continuity between the old and the new but ultimately suggests a historical distance between them. Perhaps following Erasmus's lead, Oviedo raises the question of the appropriateness of imitating the methods of ancients, since he was living in a different historical age and a new world.[13] In a discussion of the origins of *pelota,* for example, he proposes that the Taíno may have invented the game before Pliny knew of it. Oviedo also brings his Latin model in as a second authority in a chapter about the fire drill but then firmly pushes Pliny's account aside: "For what reason would I want to bring in the authority of the Ancients for things which I have seen, or for those in which Nature instructs us every day?" (bk. 6, chap. 5).[14] Oviedo acknowledges the authorities but deeply revises their work. His manuscript additions, like those in the revised edition of part I, often dispute the role and utility of texts from antiquity.

IMITATIO

In fact, over time Oviedo demonstrates an increasing knowledge of canonical texts along with a growing sense of their irrelevance in the New World. If Oviedo's initial reports about America betray a certain naiveté, the revised text underscores the tension between the direct observation of American novelty and his textual universe. If personal experience and contemporary testimony are more reliable than previously written texts, why interpolate these texts into the already "final" version of the manuscript and then revise them by challenging their authority? He increasingly sees the Indies' difference but acknowledges the need—complicated though it may be—to place the New World into the existing universe of knowledge. That Oviedo tells the reader he will base his history on Pliny's *Natural History* demonstrates that emulation is the foundational structure for his text.[15] But clearly this is not a case of simple mirroring, in which the model is used as a frame for the new text and does not attempt to compete with the original. Oviedo renders a complex comparison in which two periods of history and texts are interwoven and questioned:

unlike Pliny, Oviedo will not just rewrite previous texts, but rather include his experience in the discovery of the Indies:

> I have not culled them from two hundred thousand volumes I might have read, as Pliny wrote in the example discussed above, where it seems that he related what he had read . . . , I, however, compiled what I here write from two hundred thousand hardships, privations, and dangers in the more than twenty-two years that I have personally witnessed and experienced these things. . . . In one way my book will differ from Pliny's model: this will be to relate something of the conquest of these Indies, and . . . justify the reason for their discovery.[16] (*Proemio,* bk. 1)

The ancients did not know the New World, and, according to most Europeans' view, America was without a recorded history. And yet the New World sometimes coincided with the ancients' writings. While Oviedo increasingly perceived the need to use the past to interpret the present for the reader, he also understood the increasing inadequacy of the past to explain the present.

A type of *imitatio* known as *aemulatio,* or an imitation that competes with and attempts to surpass its model, may suggest an answer. In a landmark book on Renaissance imitation, Thomas M. Greene studies the humanists' varied uses of that device, uses which reflect differing views of history and which encompass the notion of emulation (*aemulatio*).[17] One of the more complex uses, heuristic imitation, actively engages with a sense of history as being comprised of distinct historical ages (40–46). It singles out a model, or subtext, and then rewrites it, modernizing it through a process of *aggiornamento* (updating). Rejecting the notion of a primal text that must be followed closely, this strategy attempts to bridge the gap between two periods. It becomes "a double process of discovery," of the "otherness" of the past and of the author's own context and voice (41).[18]

The difficulty of pinpointing an author's adherence to a single type of imitation strategy, as noted by Greene, is clear in Oviedo's work. While at times moving toward a dialectical strategy, in which the author engages fully the past and the present, Oviedo's practice tends to be more heuristic, an attempt to bridge the gap, to use his writing as a "double process of discovery" of self and other. Oviedo singles out Pliny's text as his primary model and then sets out to modernize and surpass it. His modifications include the seemingly infinite and expanding New World phenomena and events. By including further references to Pliny in the manuscript,

Oviedo at once acknowledges Pliny's work and revises it, adding more information to the ancient's *Natural History* and rendering his own *General and Natural History* more comprehensive.

AMAZON WOMEN

What happens, however, when the historian dedicated to writing a truthful history of a new world confronts reports that appear to corroborate Old World texts that describe mythical Amazon women? When Oviedo encountered multiple accounts, in both Spanish and indigenous sources, of republics of women living without men in several regions of America, his historiographic method of using eyewitness testimony and creating a new space in textual traditions is tested. Elsewhere in the *History* Oviedo tends to reject the existence of monstrous beings, such as sirens and Patagonian giants. Adhering to the Erasmian ideal, the *libro de verdad,* Oviedo often states that fables are no longer necessary. The New World outshines fiction by offering even more marvelous and wonderful tales: "All the more as these things are in themselves so distinct and new that there is no need for fictions to amaze people, nor to omit giving infinite thanks to the Master of Nature" (bk. 6, *Proemio*).[19] Yet when he encounters a report from the royal cosmographer Alonso de Santa Cruz about the existence of mermen (*hombres marinos*) on the River Paraná, Oviedo carefully weighs the cosmographer's testimony against reports from other witnesses and against evidence from textual authorities such as Pliny and the humanist El Tostado (bk. 23, chap. 5). Oviedo concludes, taking into account all the reports, that it must be true that mermen lived in the region. He does not revisit the question. But the case of sightings of republics of women in the Indies was not so clear-cut. In nearly ten separate passages in the *History* the author brings to the fore the debate about the existence of such women and their relationship to the Old World myth of Amazon women. The recurrence of the topic and his changing statements about it reveal Oviedo's ambivalence.

One of the most telling examples of the author's negotiation of eyewitness testimony and Old World texts is the chapter in book 6 on miscellany, about a sighting of Amazon women in the New World (chap. 33). The chapter is unusual because it contains deletions as well as the usual additions.[20] As we have seen, his revisions in descriptions of nature and events in general follow an inclination to include new data, to reveal the fullest and therefore the most truthful representation of the New World, in order to eradicate errors and myths. In keeping with this historical method, Oviedo removes from this chapter (bk. 6, chap. 33) his original portrayal of the female warriors that Nuño de Guzmán encountered in his expedition to the town of Ciguatán in New Galicia (which Oviedo tells the reader means "town of women" in the native language). The women are first portrayed as single-breasted female warriors who carry bows and arrows and frighten the Spanish soldiers with their bold words. This depiction mirrors the portrait of the legendary tribe from classical antiquity as described in Justin's *Epitomy* (II: 4), which Oviedo mentions at the beginning of the chapter. Interestingly, in the revision process as seen in the autograph manuscript, anything that links the portrayal directly to the classical source is deleted: the new version carries no mention of the Amazonians' practice of burning off their right breasts in order to improve their archery skills or of the arms they carry. Oviedo first deletes a passage in which the women threaten the Spaniards ("They themselves sent messengers to the Spaniards warning them not to dare to come into their territory because they were women . . . their deeds seemed to them the acts of men of great valor and spirit" (HEH, HM 177, f. 43r).[21]

Another stricken passage describes their appearance and how they arrayed their army in preparation for battle ("Another day he got within sight of the settlement and near that city encountered a large army of women in the countryside, on the point of war, waiting for the Christians, and all of them with their bows, arrows and quivers. Dressed in white shifts . . . the majority of them have but one left breast" f. 43r).[22] One last deleted passage further removes a direct association of these republics of girls and women with the classical Amazon myth: "When they are young they remove or burn off their right breast for exercising their arms, which are bows and arrows, in which they are very skilled" (f. 43r).[23] These deletions may have been executed at the same moment the author added an important passage, the paragraph in which he reveals that in 1547 he interviewed one of the original explorers, Nuño de Guzmán, who unequivocally denies the existence of a tribe of women living without men:

> Back in Spain I wanted to gather information from this same Nuño de Guzmán. . . . He told me it was a hoax, and they were not Amazon. . . . I maintain that it could be that, finding them in a married state, he went there during the time of their relationships, but let us leave this matter and go on.[24] (f. 43v)

Oviedo does not easily reject the idea of Amazon-like women living in the New World. By proposing that Nuño de Guzmán happened upon the women in the period when they allowed men into their camps for reproductive purposes, the author debates the reliability of his informant's testimony. He then creates a case for the plausibility of the existence of a republic of women by recurring to textual antecedents and to the reader's own experience: besides stories from antiquity about communities of men living together, the reader can see how European women live without men in convents. The chronicler makes no final judgment. A narrative tension becomes apparent. Oviedo's source, after a second trip to the area, withdraws his original testimony about the existence of a colony of women. Yet Oviedo lets the original account stand, although with significant deletions, and speculates on the possible error in Nuño de Guzmán's observation during his second trip to the colony.

The resulting account is one that removes the most obvious Old World iconography for the Amazons but does not eliminate the possibility of their existence.[25] In other words, Oviedo's retention of the account may suggest a reliance on Old World myths that at times supersedes the lack of evidence of the existence of such a group of women in the New World. Whether by design or through an oversight, in another book Oviedo retells the story of Nuño's encounter with the republic of women and leaves several sentences verbatim from the passages deleted in the previous account—though only those that refer to the women's dress (bk. 34, chap. 8). Indeed, a closer look at Oviedo's later additions and other accounts of Amazon women suggests that he never rejected the possibility that an Amazon-like tribe of women might well exist in the New World.

At least two other accounts of colonies of women (bk. 21, chap. 8; bk. 26, chap. 29) support the observation that Oviedo tends to remove the most irrelevant characteristics of Old World myths from his text while continuing to define the New World phenomenon through association to a well-known Old World myth. Reflecting his much-noted anxiety about the ability of language to depict New World phenomena, Oviedo discusses the etymology of the word *amazona* and how it has been inappropriately applied in the New World: "In Greek *a* means 'without' and *zona* means 'breast,' and for that reason Amazon means 'without a breast . . .' Thus the Christians began to call them Amazons without their being so" (bk. 26, chap. 29).[26] In a move that is reminiscent of his strategy for naming the pineapple, Oviedo attempts to disassociate the Old World word from the New World reality but sees no linguistic alternative. Thus, he renders these figures as "women who live in imitation of the Amazons" (mujeres que viven a imitación de las amazonas) (bk. 6, chap. 33).[27] For Oviedo this linguistic imitation both explains the New World in Old World terms and demonstrates its difference. If Amazon women were merely a myth in ancient times, republics of women, at least according to some testimony, were a New World reality.

The trajectory of Oviedo's accounts of "women who live in imitation of the Amazons" also demonstrates that he did not always abandon preconceived notions of the New World as the marvelous land where Old World myths became real. When Amazons are first mentioned in the 1535 text (bk. 2, chap. 8), the chronicler unequivocally rejects the possibility of a tribe of women living in the Caribbean:

> Some chroniclers say that [Matinio] was settled by Amazons, and other fables very far from the truth. . . . for those of us who have seen it . . . it is completely false what has been said of this island as far as being settled only by women, because it is not, nor does anyone know if it ever was.[28] (bk. 2, chap. 8)

By contrast, subsequent chapters, mostly written after 1535, fail to take a stand on the matter. We have seen how Oviedo wavers with respect to Nuño de Guzmán's second testimony, challenging its veracity in book 6, but then allowing the first testimony to stand along with another update from Nuño in book 34, chapter 8.

Nonetheless, the *History* never records a Christian eyewitness's definitive testimony of Amazon women; expeditions were often sent to explore for the republics but returned with vague findings. Spanish explorers questioned groups of indigenous women, reported sightings of such groups, and yet were unable to ascertain if the women lived by themselves (bk. 34, chap. 8). In other cases, after an initial period of searching for republics of women, expeditions opted not to deviate from the main goal of the expedition (bk. 25, chap. 14). In later renditions, Oviedo increasingly turns to indigenous informants (bk. 25, chap. 14 and bk. 33, chap. 36). He substitutes New World witnesses for Old World ones, even though the veracity of the natives' reports was generally questioned—for instance, Oviedo records how one conquistador suggested that the Indians' accounts contained discrepancies (bk. 26, chap. 29)—and Oviedo asserts that few Christians believed them (bk. 33, chap. 36). The Spaniards listened to their native sources, set out on expeditions, and wrote about Amazon-like women. Oviedo returns time and again to write about "the Amazons (if one can call them that)" despite the lack of "identifiable" (that is, Christian) eyewitness accounts.[29] He acknowledges that the jury is still out on the question and that he must await more testimony:

> But because of [a lack of] clarity and particular information nothing more certain is known at present, I wanted to put this here . . . to be in agreement with what might happen in the future and what would be appropriate to write when these lands and provinces are better known and examined. . . . And so, to understand this better, I would advise the reader who has reached this point not to read on, but to consult Chapter XXIV of the last book of this *General History of the Indies,* so that he may be more satisfied with what he will discover there.[30] (bk. 49, chap. 4)

Typically, Oviedo's final account on a debatable topic often is a key to his judgment on it, one he frequently introduces with someone else's words, as a secondary speech. In the last book of the history, Gaspar de Carvajal, the friar who accompanied the expedition to the Amazon River, is given the last word on the question of Amazon women (bk. 50, chap. 24). Oviedo sets up the authority of Carvajal's account in an earlier chapter when he speculates on the existence of Amazons living between the rivers La Plata and Marañón. As noted above, he at once informs the reader that too little is known about these women to confirm the truthfulness of stories about them, and he tells the reader to skip directly to Carvajal's *relación* in book 50 for a full account. Removing the responsibility from his own shoulders, Oviedo lets a reliable friar have the final say on the Amazons. Carvajal's account, however, is based on the testimony of a Native American noted for his trustworthiness: "[As] there was no discrepancy with what . . . other Indians said . . . we hold this information to be very true" (bk. 50, chap. 24).[31] The friar reports further that some Native Americans told him about Amazon women "without having been asked" (sin le ser preguntado); in his view, information offered without prompting was a sure sign of its truthfulness.

Despite earlier questions about Native Americans' trustworthiness, they emerge in Oviedo's history as the new authorities who affirm the existence of Amazon-like women. If the New World women seem to "imitate those whom the ancients called Amazons" (bk. 50, chap. 24), the native reports now emulate, by both affirming and replacing, the authority of the accounts of antiquity.[32] Wondrous American difference is knowable only by comparing it to Old World texts and myths, but perhaps this New World reality makes Old World myths more real. In keeping with the rest of the history, Oviedo juggles New World and Old World authorities, suggesting that the New supplants the Old. But the chronicler fails to follow this schema completely: he gives added authority to native testimony with his use of a reliable "Christian" interlocutor.

One last twist reveals the chronicler's narrative strategy here. Fray Gaspar de Carvajal's first-person account moves to the forefront of the history's narration in book 50, but the nearly exact repetition from two previous chapters in the *History* on the etymology of the word *Amazon,* now recorded as Carvajal's words, unwittingly reveals Oviedo's manipulation of the friar's account for his own ends in the *History.* Carvajal's words are really Oviedo's (or Oviedo's words are really Carvajal's).

MYTH AND HISTORY

Why does Oviedo first reject the possibility of Amazon women living in the Caribbean, then draft a chapter modeled on Greek mythology, only later to eliminate sections that directly relate it to that myth, and finally affirm the existence of a republic of Amazon-like women in South America, using a native (via Carvajal) as a spokesperson?[33] Formerly the author of fantasy and wonder (as the author of America's first novel of chivalry), Oviedo perhaps capitalized on the one area where Renaissance historians had license: history that was temporally or geographically remote. Building on Aristotle's theories, the early modern theorist López Pinciano explains that the domain of history (in contrast to that of poetry) was the particular, the *caso,* and therefore the historian could elaborate on his material only if the particularities were vague. This precept ruled out the possibility of elaborating on natural history ("because it does not change" [porque no se muda]) and on history in which many of the actual circumstances were well known, leaving only the more remote historical ages or areas open to the historical imagination (78–83). If few facts were available, the historian could elaborate as he wished, without violating the important precept of verisimilitude, the notion that an author must make his account plausible.

The vague geographical location of Amazon-like women—not to mention the general remoteness of America to the typical Europe reader—allowed Oviedo more license to elaborate on classical myth. The New World republics of women are typically reported as living just over the next mountain range, further up the river, or just beyond any given location. They are always just out of reach. To further the verisimilitude of his account, and in keeping with his inclination to find authorities in the New World, Oviedo deletes all direct references—the name and the breast-burning tradition—that relate the colonies of women to the Old World myth. He maintains, however, a more subtle iconography that maintains a link to European culture. According to Juan Gil's study of New World myths, in the European tradition Amazons were always warriors associated with water—they always lived on an island or at the intersection of two rivers—and possessed great riches (34–39). These characteristics are mentioned without fail in Oviedo's accounts.

Oviedo does not completely reject the rhetorical emulation of legends found in ancient texts; rather he uses them as a backdrop to show how the New World surpasses the Old. The ancients' accounts are rewritten in a New World context. The myths acquire credibility in the Indies through the authority of indigenous testimony of women living *a imitación de las amazonas*.[34] By representing the New World as both mirroring and changing Old World myths, Oviedo bridges the gap between the two worlds and shows how America often replaces its model.[35]

We find in Oviedo's revisions and his use of imitation a historical method that sets out to represent the truth of nature as superior to the use of models or texts. The author states that there will be a more empirical frame to his history than Pliny's and that previous texts will play a limited role. His text will be a manual for others to imitate. In general, the revisions Oviedo makes often underscore his legalistic, empirical bent, by which he attempts to document as fully as possible the American phenomena and to reorganize them according to their place in the universe of knowledge.

Characteristic of Oviedo's work, however, are tensions and ironies that undermine the goal of rendering a text that is a verbal reflection of nature, one that does not rely on a preexisting textual universe. The multiple accounts and revisions of reports about Amazon-like women in the Indies reveal that although the historian at times questions the ability of previous histories and narrative structures to tell the story of America, he backs away from the full implication of this discovery of the "otherness" of both the past and the reality he sees before him; he often returns to the texts of the classical world for points of reference to bridge the gap between the Old and the New worlds. The repetition of accounts of the Amazon women serves an indispensable function in the *History*: the classical world is a necessary backdrop to the New World, investing it with meaning for the European reader.[36] Consequently Oviedo retreats from the implications and recognition of the subversive nature of his line of questioning—one that might lead to the conclusion that histories from the past have nothing to offer a new historical age and continent. He settles, at times unevenly, into negotiating several types of discourse, both old and new, in order to discover the meaning of America and the relationship between the Old and the New worlds. The Old World myth ultimately reinforces the plausibility of a reported New World reality. In a sense, Oviedo rewrites the myth to shape it to American novelty. The repetition of the account throughout the text indicates the longevity, interest, and importance of the phenomenon.

The *History* becomes a layered narrative that creates a more dynamic role for the author himself, who negotiates between previous models and the new reality. Oviedo reinterprets and, at times, rejects classical texts. At other times he attempts to sort out contradictory testimony, rewriting his text along the way. He defines his historical subject as both part of and distinct from the Old World. As the author who interprets, translates, and revises knowledge about the New World, he becomes the medium for the representation of this new history.

SIX

CORTÉS AND THE CONQUEST OF MEXICO

Truth and Multiple Testimonies (bk. 33, chap. 54)

As we have seen in the last two chapters, the increased availability of information about the natural world and reports from new expeditions led Oviedo to use multiple strategies for revising his text. I noted, for example, the historian's evolving theory of illustration and his use of Fray Gaspar de Carvajal's account of Amazon women to authorize his own beliefs. By the 1540s, Oviedo began to reduce his autobiographical presence in order to emphasize his persona as official historian and substitute an authoritative, even sanctified voice of imperial policy. His self-concealing strategy is most prominent when he receives new testimony that contradicts previous accounts, accounts already recorded—and in some cases published—in the *History*. He often comments at length on variations, especially when they deal with the important conquests of Mexico (bk. 33) and Peru (bks. 46, 48, 49), in order to establish his loyalty to truth and his ability to rise above egotistical concerns.

The historian's dedication to the humanist idea of a history that would mirror as closely as possible men's actions as they actually occurred, as the omnipresent God would have witnessed them, helps to explain Oviedo's use of multiple reports of a single incident.[1] In keeping with the biblical model of using multiple representations to indicate the author's desire for accuracy as well as the all-pervasive juridical model of collecting multiple testimony, Oviedo often revised an account or wrote another version of it in order to afford a new perspective on the events he had recorded. He hoped this methodology would reveal the true moral and natural history of the Indies.[2] His exposure to Erasmian and juridical ideas about truth, Italian humanism, and the classical historian's moralizing tendency, as well as the author's own belief in Spain's destiny to establish a universal Catholic empire, are all influences that inform Oviedo's work. In this case, the author's strategic choice of genre, rather than references to Old

World myth, provides the basis for his revisions and musings about his authority as an historian.

One of the most famous and extensively revised sections of the *History* is Oviedo's interview with Juan Cano, Montezuma's Spanish son-in-law, who fought with Cortés and later testified against him. Appended to the lengthy book about the Conquest of Mexico (bk. 33, chap. 54), the interview follows chapters based on a variety of sources, including Cortés's *Relaciones* about the conquest and the letters written by the first viceroy of Mexico, Antonio de Mendoza (1535–1550). The interview reflects Oviedo's data-collecting methods and his inclusion of multiple reports about the same historical event.[3] Given the frequency with which Oviedo employs multiple accounts, it is not surprising that he returns in chapter 54 to material he treated earlier (chaps. 14–16). What is notable, however, is the historian's use of a new genre. Much of the history before this chapter consists of written and oral accounts the author gathered and then transposed into summarizing narration. Why, then, at this particular narrative juncture, does Oviedo choose to deviate from the norm of narrative summary and turn to a dialogue form—a choice he makes only one other time in his lengthy text (in the book on Nicaragua, bk. 42, chaps. 2, 3)? What does the historian achieve by employing direct discourse in the passage on the Conquest of Mexico?

The most obvious reason to use dialogue is that it dramatizes the historical material. The narration of facts fades into the background as the dialogue moves to the foreground and unfolds, apparently with no mediation, before the reader. However, unlike classical or humanist histories enlivened by direct discourse (and in particular by eloquent dramatic monologues), Oviedo's dialogue lacks the eloquence that stems from the classicist's consideration of history as a branch of literature.[4] He reports that he subjugates style to content in order to avoid disguising the basic historical facts: "But it will cleave to simplicity and the manner of speaking which ought to concur in true history. I call simplicity that which the grammarian attributes to this term, which is to speak simply, without cajolery nor flattery, which is of the essence" (bk. 33, chap. 21).[5] Another explanation for the use of dialogue is that its inquiry-and-response format enables Oviedo to treat more disparate material than narrative technique allows. The author can disregard chronological order and focus on specific details, revising them as necessary.

Several other elements may have factored into Oviedo's decision to use the genre. First, the existence of a voice other than his own, transcribed within the history as direct discourse, lends more credibility to the newly revised account; the dialogue format shares more directly with the reader one of the author's sources for his history. Moreover, the objective of most Renaissance dialogue was to arrive at a truth. In its first moments the Conquest of Mexico by Hernán Cortés (1519–1521) marked Spain's first glorious conquest in the New World: a populous, wealthy New World civilization had been overthrown by Spanish soldiers. Primarily basing his report on Cortés's own *Segunda Relación* and other documents about the events, Oviedo wrote about these heroic events in the first thirty-five chapters of book 33. But later reports called into question Cortés's and Oviedo's initial representations of the conquistador and the Conquest of Tenochtitlan. The sixteenth-century dialogue format provided Oviedo with the perfect vehicle to reshape his depiction of both the conquest and its leader while also reestablishing the truthfulness of his *History*.

TRUTH AND DIALOGUE

As we saw in the discussion of the *History*'s preface, Oviedo found it necessary to elaborate on the challenges facing a historian writing about a new era and a new world. I noted in chapter 1 that, as the author of America's first novel, *Don Claribalte* (1519), and later as Europe's first official historian writing in the New World, Oviedo was well versed in the early modern debate about the interrelationship of truth and history and how this differed from the truth of fiction.[6] Until the sixteenth century, history was considered a branch of literature and depended greatly on rhetorical considerations for its composition and on moral truths for its raison d'être. By the sixteenth and seventeenth centuries the consideration of history as rhetoric was being debated, and there existed an increased interest in the representation of historical accounts as compendia of documentable facts. Histories of classical antiquity were no longer adequate to describe a broadened worldview, and this contributed further to the ambiguity of the early modern concept and genre of history. The emphasis on the authority of direct experience to supplement or, at times, to improve on the authorities of classical antiquity was accompanied by an increased interest in linguistics.[7]

Before I turn to Oviedo's musings about the truthful representation of the Conquest of Mexico in book 33, a brief review of the origins and the popularity of dialogue in the sixteenth century may help to illuminate the link between history, truth, and the dialogue form in Oviedo's work. Plato first fused common speech and dialectic to enliven the presentation of his ideas to his reader. The primary objective of the dialogic process, however, was to discriminate truth from error. Stemming from the concept of *mayeutics* (Greek for midwifery), the Socratic method, as expounded by Plato, held that every man possessed an innate wisdom, and one need only ask the proper questions to arrive at the truth, which was achieved through a drawing-out process that dialogue of an inquiry and response type aided. Cicero's later adaptation of the dialogue form into Latin as a vehicle to present moral questions became an important model for the Quattrocento dialogue, from which the humanist dialogue was born.[8] David Marsh notes that to Quattrocentists dialogue was considered to be useful both for the examination of a topic that may not have a definitive answer at the time of exposition and for the discussion of a potentially dangerous topic (12).[9] These two purposes, as we will see below, illuminate Oviedo's possible intentions.

Furthermore, as natural, rational, and universal tendencies flooded the Renaissance literary scene, dialogue became a more popular genre through which learning might be achieved with naturalistic speech. Erasmus employed this form in his famous *Colloquies*.[10] Oviedo's acquaintance with several of the leading authors of Quattrocento dialogues (in particular, Leonardo Bruni and Giovanni Pontano) as well as his knowledge of other dialogues (for example, those of Petrarch, Juan Luis Vives, and Erasmus) highlights the Spanish author's familiarity with the form and its purpose.[11] Indeed, one of Oviedo's historical-literary projects, put on hold while he finished the *History* and resumed in the 1550s, was written as dialogued prose: the *Batallas y Quinquagenas*. In the persona of the keeper of the fort (*alcaide*) Oviedo interviews a night watchman (*sereno*), and each of their 150 dialogues (three sets of 50 *quinquagenas*) gives a biographical sketch of the life and achievements of illustrious individuals whom the author had met. The dialogue format here, however, serves merely as an expository vehicle for information; it is not employed, as in the *History*, as a means to critique information.

THE INTERVIEW WITH JUAN CANO

The most striking characteristic of Oviedo's interview with Juan Cano is its rendition as a colloquy that opens and closes with an extensive narrative section. The chapter title and narrative passage introduce the new form, its purpose and tone. The title announces:

> In which the author explains why he stopped his journey and voyage to Spain, and relates other matters and events of New Spain; he tells of some particular subjects which have come to his attention, which are of the sort which the history has told, for the greater verification and truthfulness of some passages which were written in another manner, as [the author] was not as accurately informed as will be told now. And other matters of this sort will be related, in this way correcting several topics noted earlier, thus making known and perfecting others of which the readers must be apprised.[12] (bk. 33, chap. 54)

Oviedo openly underscores his dependency on the testimony of other writers and eyewitnesses to the events he records. He emphasizes his own commitment, at the cost of appearing repetitive, to present his readers with the most truthful historical narrative possible. The lexicon employed by Oviedo (*verificación, verdad, informando, enmendando, declarando, perficionando*) points to his explicit intention in the chapter: to persuade the reader of the veracity of his newly written version of the events surrounding the Noche Triste, the night the Spaniards were forced to flee Tenochtitlan.[13] The introductory narrative reveals Oviedo's self-awareness as an official court chronicler. The narrative frame serves a threefold purpose: it presents Oviedo's criteria for his history, it aims to persuade the reader to trust the new account, and it introduces the circumstances that produced the dialogue. The overriding goal here is to assert the author's credibility.

The narrative opens with a lofty statement about the utility of history and its role in instructing rulers, in this case, Charles V. His purpose, Oviedo argues, is to serve the king by providing him with information about the Indies, information that should help the king to rule wisely and promote the imperial vision. Portraying himself as "obedient and faithful keeper and servant," the author emphasizes his trustworthy service to the monarch.[14] Perhaps more important, Oviedo highlights his role as royal historian of the monarchy when he mentions the royal genealogy he was writing simultaneously with the *History,* the *Catálogo Real.* Furthermore, as a historian, Oviedo gives authority to his account by indirectly drawing parallels between his work and the works of well-respected contemporary and classical historians. Joanis Carionis, Oviedo tells us, also writes in the vernacular with much "utility" (utilidad) and "artifice" (artificio), and Thucydides' history is a "treasure trove" (tesoro) of human truths.[15] Last, he asserts the authority of eyewitness account over secondhand information. Twice he brings up Spanish enterprises in Europe, Asia, and Africa, and each time he deliberately drops the topic saying "let those who live [in these places] tell them."[16] In doing so, Oviedo underlines his own authority to write about events in the Indies.

The historical criteria presented in these opening paragraphs echo previous prefaces and passages in the *History,* but the final two paragraphs aim to persuade the reader to accept this new account of Mexico as the objective truth. In an attempt to reassert his credibility, Oviedo only indirectly accepts the blame for the presence of incorrect information in his previous account of the Conquest of Mexico. Instead, he employs a dual strategy: he excuses his poorly informed sources ("I . . . put them in this volume in good faith, assuming that they were true, as the witnesses affirmed they were. However, as men's understanding may be much better in some [persons] than in others, it is no wonder that they differ in their utterances and even in their deeds, especially in such cases in which intention, partiality, and individual interest cause these differences in the information");[17] and he invokes the hand of Divine Will ("In truth it appears that Our Lord permits my eyes not to close and indeed gain greater clarity with respect to the history which I hold in my hands").[18] Both strategies enabled Oviedo to protect himself by absolving him of responsibility for the material at hand and attempting to secure the reader's trust.

Before the dialogue begins, one last narrative paragraph states pertinent situational information: the year (1544), the location (Santo Domingo), the interlocutors (Cano and Oviedo), and the purpose (the correction of past accounts). In so doing, the author gives the colloquy the three aspects attributed to dialogue by Jan Mukařovský in his seminal work on the verbal act—the relation between the interlocutors, their surrounding situation, and a thematic structure—thus enabling him to bridge the gap between dialogue and narrative, oral and written history, history as events and history as recorded representation (86–88). The actual process of the dialogue is brought closer to the reader when Oviedo reveals the technique he has used: "With me asking and Juan Cano answering, I will relate those things of which we spoke, as there was no time for more."[19] The author's method of inquiry results in the alternation of short and long exchanges between the questioner and the respondent. Oviedo uses both the historian's interviewing method and juridical techniques, revealing his continual attempt to focus questions in order to clarify historical reality.

Oviedo's choice of two interlocutors—himself, in his historical role as keeper of the fortress at Santo Domingo (*alcaide*) and official court chronicler, and Juan Cano—allows the author to present his account as a personal testimony and, at the same time, as an objective historical account. The voices of the *alcaide* and the historian merge and give the reader insight into the difficulty of Oviedo's task as compiler of a history and as a man of action within the history itself. The autograph manuscript shows a clear demarcation of his role: each time he speaks is marked with "ALC" for *alcaide* (RAH 9/555 f. 199v). Indeed, the main purpose appears to be to reveal his dual roles as protagonist and historian. The transcription of Cano's words enables Oviedo directly to reassert his technique as interviewer and compiler of the *History* as well as to reveal the dilemma he has faced as a historian. To a certain extent this interview technique highlights his reliance on informants and relieves him of responsibility for errors of information. He thus asserts the need for the present revision and establishes the importance of trustworthy informants.

Anticipating his critics' scrutiny, Oviedo begins by establishing his interlocutor's credentials. He states that he knew Cano's uncle, who was from a good family, and that Cano is "an intelligent man" (un hombre de buen entendimiento). Furthermore, in his roles as eyewitness of the events discussed and husband of Montezuma's daughter (Doña Isabel), Cano was in a unique position to inform Oviedo about the Spanish and Mexica points of view about the Conquest. He is presented as a legitimate link between the Old and the New worlds. Oviedo tells the reader that Cano first came to Mexico with Pánfilo de Narváez's army (to subdue Cortés). But he fails to mention that Cano then was forced to join Cortés's army and ultimately testified against Cortés in the first Real Audiencia.

The establishment of Cano's reliability as a source is paramount for the achievement of Oviedo's goals. The author portrays himself as an intermediary, limiting his role and responsibility to that of a sort of prosecuting attorney and scribe, and he portrays Cano as the best authority on the subject at hand. In using this strategy, Oviedo attempts to revise errors in earlier chapters and to regain credibility for his *History*. Through the apparent objectivity of the interview process, the historian manipulates the dialogue for his own ends. Oviedo's dialogue is double focused. On one hand, he undertakes to draw out the truth of an event by correcting his own earlier accounts. On the other hand, he enters into a discussion with other texts. Often the overt intention of correcting the representation of reality hides a critique or criticism of another author and, in the process, serves to reassert Oviedo's own authority as official historian of the Indies. As we will see, the author places the blame for his earlier incorrect account on Cortés and attempts to set the record straight with regard to Las Casas's criticism of his history.

COVERT POLEMICS

The author emphasizes his integration of recent written and oral reports with previous accounts in the Oviedo-Cano dialogue itself. Oviedo's speech as interlocutor abounds with words and phrases such as "I heard" (oí), "they say" (*dicen*), "certain information" (cierta información), "it was said" (así dizque) interwoven with "as I wrote in chapter XVI" (como lo he escrito en el capítulo XVI), "thus I have written this differently" (así lo he yo escrito diferenciadamente). By employing these phrases, the historian suggests to the reader the nature of his task: to transpose oral and written information ("dicen," etc.) into a narrative history ("como lo he yo escrito"). Another narrative strategy is the repetition of words that establish the veracity of the information presented, for example, "it is true" (es verdad), "without a doubt" (sin duda), "he is right" (razón tiene), "this is a very important truth" (muy gran verdad es). Both strategies aim to establish the accuracy of the information treated. The author employs words and phrases that serve as a sort of code, inviting the reader to trust the new account. A closer look at these rhetorical strategies, however, reveals that Oviedo often uses these very phrases about credibility and truth in order to disguise his manipulation of the dialogue itself. The author weaves together apparently objective questions or statements and evaluative remarks, which Mukařovský calls "semantic reversals." These are phrases found at the beginning or end of an utterance—often of an evaluative nature—that prompt a certain response from the other interlocutor (89).[20]

The use of apparently objective questions or statements coincides with the presentation of information about the Conquest that was generally accepted as fact during the era. For example, inquiring into the murder of Cuauhtemoc, or Guatimucín, the last ruler of the Mexicas, Oviedo asks, "Señor Juan Cano, I beg you to tell me: why did Hernán Cortés kill Guatimucín? Did he rebel later on, or what did he do so that he had to die?"[21] Cano responds with a testimony on Cortés's torture of the Mexicas and the killing of Guatimucín. The interviewer then refers directly to Cortés's account about Guatimucín, which differs from Cano's testimony, and to the appearance of this information in chapter 15 of the *History.* This in turn allows the author, through Cano's response, to cast doubt on the veracity of Cortés's *Relaciones* and to highlight the reliability of his current informant: "Well, Your Grace may write what he likes, as the Marquis Hernán Cortés [may say] what he wishes, but I tell the truth before God and my conscience, and this is very well known."[22]

To illuminate the events precipitating the war for Tenochtitlan and Cortés's moral character, Oviedo typically uses a semantic reversal: "I have heard much about these things, and I would like to write the truth, may God save my soul."[23] To which Cano responds, "Señor Alcaide, what you are asking is a question which few who dwell on earth will be able to explain, although the matter was most notorious and the injustice done the Indians obvious."[24] He goes on to explain that the cruel massacre of natives during their ceremonial dance by Cortés's lieutenant, Pedro de Alvarado, who was left in charge of Tenochtitlan during Cortés's absence, led to the Mexica uprising. Cano concludes his testimony with another semantic reversal, "as they had more than enough cause to do this."[25] Oviedo allows Cano's words to stand on their own; he makes no comment and proceeds directly to the next question: "How did Montezuma die? For I have heard differing accounts and thus have written different versions of it."[26] Through this technique Oviedo portrays himself as an objective interviewer, allowing Cano's words to appear unmediated by the author and leaving the reader to judge for himself. In a sense, Oviedo leads the witness.

A look at other examples of Oviedo's use of evaluative statements woven together with references to his account in chapters 14 and 15 reveals his attempt to establish his credentials as a reliable historian. Referring again to the controversial events of the Noche Triste, he states, "It was a great pity so much treasure was lost, as well as one hundred and fifty-four Spaniards, forty-five mares and more than two thousand Indians. . . . I have it written thus in chapter XIV in this history."[27] To this Cano responds emphatically that many more died than Cortés reported:

> In truth, Señor Alcaide, the person who told you that either did not see [what happened], or know the truth, or wanted to conceal it. I guarantee that the Spaniards who were killed in this action . . . numbered more than one thousand one hundred and seventy, as a review of the troops showed. With respect to the Indians, you refer to two thousand of our Tlaxcalan allies, but doubtless there were more than eight thousand.[28]

In essence, through Cano's speech Oviedo is suggesting that Cortés is a liar. Although the author manipulates the dialogue and employs a code to partly disguise his purposes, ultimately the reader is led to doubt Cortés's testimony as recorded in an earlier chapter of the *History*.

The use of evaluative language to direct the interviewee's response increases as the dialogue continues, particularly as the list of Cortés's misrepresentations in his *Relaciones* grows longer. The language, however, takes on an ironic tone. Not long after Cano criticizes Cortés's attitude toward the Native Americans ("he said the Indians were dogs" [dijo que (los indios) eran unos perros]) and suggests that it provoked the Mexica rebellion that culminated in the Noche Triste, Oviedo addresses Cortés's claim that he lost two fingers during the Conquest of Mexico. The author carefully constructs his dialogue with a series of linguistic devices and progression of material to make his inquiry appear objective, but in reality the passage is a covert attack on Cortés's character and writings. Oviedo apparently praises the conqueror's bravery:

> The Marquis is quite a man, and is worthy of all he has and much more. I am sorry to see such a valiant gentleman maimed, missing two fingers on his left hand—as I wrote down and got from his account, and put in Chapter XV—but that is how war is: the honors and the palm of victory are not acquired by sleeping.[29]

There is, however, a hint of sarcasm in the last phrase ("los honores e la palma de la victoria no se adquieren durmiendo"). When Cano responds by saying that no miracle or surgeon was needed to restore Cortés's fingers, the ironic nature of Oviedo's praise for Cortés becomes clear. Replying in a similar tone, Cano sets the record straight with regard to Cortés's claim about his fingers:

> God did not have to work hard to heal him, and you can forget about your concern: the fingers which he brought with him out of Castile when he first came here he still has now in Spain, as he never lost them nor are they missing. He never needed either a surgeon or a miracle to recover from this trial.[30]

Here, as in the previous example, Oviedo leaves the reader to judge the account because he moves directly to another area of controversy: "Señor Juan Cano, is the brutality true which they say the Marquis used against Cholula, a city through which he passed the first time he went to Mexico?"[31] His commentary is disguised in the form of another query eliciting evidence of Cortés's mistreatment of Native Americans and constitutes another thinly veiled attack on Cortés's character. Through Cano's utterances Oviedo portrays Cortés as one of the conquistadors who most mistreated indigenous populations. In light of the attack on Las Casas which follows this passage, Oviedo may be attempting to shift to Cortés the criticism Oviedo received from Las Casas about his view of Native Americans. Mikhail Bakhtin's studies on the role of dialogue in narrative helps to elucidate Oviedo's possible authorial intention when employing Cano's direct speech. Bakhtin states, "The author's ultimate conceptual authority (the author's intention) is brought out, not in the author's direct speech, but by manipulating the utterances of another addresser" (179). By asking certain questions of Cano, Oviedo elicits specific information that calls into question Cortés's heroic image.

By the time Oviedo wrote this chapter, sometime between 1544 and 1547, he had been drawn into the highly charged debates about the nature of Native Americans. Las Casas had branded Oviedo as "an enemy of the Indians" and had achieved some success at changing the laws dealing with Native American populations. On the other hand, by 1544 Cortés, once held in high esteem by Europeans, had abandoned his estates in Mexico and was living out his last years in relative poverty in Castile. His *Carta de relación* about the Conquest of Mexico had gone into multiple editions and been widely translated in the 1520s, but it was banned and included in book burnings within the decade.[32] Cortés was now an easy target and served as a smokescreen for the criticism Oviedo had received.

Although Oviedo's use of the dialogue form is a method of pointing to the truths about Cortés's character and the facts of the Conquest, the dialogue simultaneously serves as a method of self-protection for the author. Literary critics often point to the ambiguity of meaning that dialogue can introduce into a text. For example, Robert Alter has examined how biblical dialogue employs first-person direct discourse in order to question the authority of a trustworthy narrator and to allow the reader "to ponder the different possible connections between the author's spoken words and his actual feelings or intention" (67). Another critic, David Marsh, asserts that the Quattrocento dialogues intentionally create ambiguities (such as the discrepancies between historical figures and their literary portrayal) to protect the author of the dialogue from possible detractors (15). The use of Cano's testimony about the Conquest (which contradicted

Cortés's version) and Oviedo's questions about Cortés may be a way to undermine the credibility of the conqueror of Mexico without directly criticizing him.

A look at the preface to book 33 supports the argument proposed above and more specifically elucidates the author's purpose. The narrative sequence of the preface moves from a reiteration of Oviedo's central concern, the importance of a truthful representation of history, to a defensive statement directed to his critics. The statement acknowledges that not everyone will be content with his revisions, which were necessary for presenting a truthful rendering of history, but, he says, God will be the judge of them all. The preface concludes with an attack on Cortés's failure to comply fully with the king's order, which required that certain government officials send accounts to Oviedo upon request:

> Besides this, I state that I have royal documents so that governors should send me word of that which pertains to the history of their governorships, for these chronicles. I wrote and informed the Marquis del Valle, Don Hernando Cortés, so that he would send me his . . . and he sent me some letters he had written His Majesty . . . and did not bother to do more.[33]

Perhaps some of Oviedo's representation of Cortés in this new version reflects his own hurt pride. Oviedo implicates Cortés as the cause of the misinformation that appeared in his earlier accounts. Moreover, the author had to not only reestablish his credibility, but also confront the popularity and therefore the wide dissemination of the misinformation contained in the conqueror's *Relaciones.* In that Oviedo was writing more than twenty years after the first edition of the *Segunda Relación,* Cortés's central account of the Conquest, and following subsequent multiple editions, his readers may have had another version of the Conquest of Mexico in mind, one eminently more favorable to Cortés.

Cortés, however, is not the only object of Oviedo's criticism of writers of the New World. After making his statement on Cortés's cruel treatment of the Mexica, Oviedo turns his attention to the recently passed New Laws of the Indies and their instigator, Las Casas. The friar's criticism of Oviedo's earlier critical view of the indigenous populations was well known; some critics have suggested that Las Casas blocked the publication of the second part of Oviedo's *History.* In fact, Oviedo opens this chapter with a complaint about his inability to publish the second part of his history. Thus, as he writes for the king, he takes this opportunity to file a reply to Las Casas's complaint about Oviedo to the bishop of San Juan, Don Rodrigo de Bastidas.[34] Changing the inquiry-and-response pattern of the dialogue, Oviedo moves into monologue as he continues his harangue about the friar:

> The Bishop of San Juan . . . was happy that . . . everything I said and failed to say could be easily proven. . . . As the Bishop of San Juan is very noble and knows the truth and the lack of bias with which I write, the Bishop of Chiapas [Las Casas] was satisfied. But it is not my job to please either his palate nor anybody else's, but to do my duty, such as speaking with you, Sir, of what is true.[35]

As the penultimate utterance of the *alcaide* in this chapter, the passage serves to bring the purpose of the colloquy full circle. The *History* is often self-referential; it folds back onto itself and responds to earlier chapters as well as to Oviedo's critics. Yet Oviedo's efforts to persuade the reader—through both the chapter's content and the use of the dialogue form—that his account best represents historical reality are self-defeating. Half-truths and subjective statements permeate the text, undercutting his efforts to write an objective history. In this passage alone, for example, he exaggerates the number of languages into which his history had been translated, and he is blatantly sarcastic in his closing comment about Las Casas and the Dominican friars: "And so, with respect to the burden of the many friars, it truly seems to me that these lands sprout or even rain friars. . . . The whole thing seemed a pious farce; now they are starting out, and we do not know how it shall end."[36]

Oviedo's monologue ends with an abrupt change of tone: "But as [Las Casas and his friars] are going in the direction of those new volcanoes, tell me, Sir, what they are like, if you have seen them, and the nature of another one you have there in New Spain, which is called Guajocingo."[37] Cano responds with a long description of the aforementioned volcano, and the colloquy comes to a halt as he leaves for his ship. When viewed in the context of the chapter and the text as a whole, this ending may not be as arbitrary as it appears at first glance, since it serves as a link to the rest of the *History*. While the discussion about the truth of his work versus Las Casas's words follows the tone set by the chapter's introduction, the description of the volcano echoes narrative passages throughout the *History* that are devoted to the depiction of the natural wonders of the

New World. Whereas the former reveals Oviedo's concern for the historian's task, the latter eases the reader back into the flow of the narrative history.

CONCLUSIONS

Although the colloquy may be an integral part of Oviedo's process of continual revision, the examination of other histories and historical methods at the opening and closing of the chapter, as well as the manipulation of the dialogue and the nature of the material treated within the dialogue itself, demonstrates Oviedo's intention to do more than simply retract his earlier accounts and those of his critics and competitors. Ostensibly an interrogation aimed at establishing the truth about several significant events in the history of the Spanish Conquest of Mexico, the dialogue actually probes the issues with which all historians of the Indies must contend. Because of the unique nature of the European encounter with the New World, as well as the new demands placed on the sixteenth-century historiographer, Oviedo experiments with various theories and practices of historical representation in the *History,* and at times he shares his theories with the reader. The slowing of the narrative tempo enables the reader to appreciate not only the historian's task but also his attempt to ferret out the truth from conflicting testimony. The dialogue form brings the historical material one step closer to the reader and gives it an immediacy and importance that few parts of the *History* can claim.

The only other use of dialogued prose in the *History*—the transcription of interviews of Native Americans in Nicaragua—plays a similar role, pointing to a truth about the Conquest and evangelization process (bk. 42, chaps. 2, 3). Although lacking the naturalism of the Cano dialogue and Oviedo's presence, the passage records the Church's interviews of Native American leaders in Nicaragua about their religious beliefs. Through the Indians' words it becomes clear that the first conquerors failed to fulfill their evangelical obligation. One native leader after another replies that they had been baptized, but that they continue observing old customs and religious beliefs. The interviews took place in 1538 but were recorded by Oviedo in the 1540s, the critical years of the debate about the New Laws.

Although the question of whether the interview with Cano actually occurred in the way Oviedo records it is, to be sure, unanswerable, the use of the dialogue form reflects the author's awareness of the dialectical nature of historiography. The genre illustrates the historian's process of taking testimony and highlights the conflicting, multivoiced discourse that emerges.[38] In keeping with the original tenets of the dialogue form, Oviedo seeks to draw out a truth. Much as Juan de Valdés presents a linguistic truth in his *Diálogo de la lengua,* Antonio de Valdés portrays the ideal ruler in *Mercurio y Carón,* and Cervantes writes an artistic treatise in his "Coloquio de los perros," Oviedo, in his dialogue with Cano, advances criteria he believes are essential to the theory and practice of writing a "truthful" history. Furthermore, in keeping with the humanist use of the dialogue form to treat potentially dangerous material and debatable topics, Oviedo employs the genre in several ways. First, he criticizes the historical representations of the New World written by the Renaissance hero of the Conquest of Mexico, Hernán Cortés, and the man motivating the establishment of the New Laws, Las Casas. Second, he examines the ambiguous nature of truth, history, and historiography. By drawing out the historical truths of the events of the Conquest of Mexico in this chapter of the *History,* Oviedo points to the errors of other writers' accounts of the Conquest. He both asserts the reliability of his own history and suggests a methodology for historical discourse on the New World.

SEVEN

NATIVE AMERICANS IN OVIEDO'S *HISTORY*

(bk. 29, chap. 26)

No discussion of Oviedo's *General and Natural History of the Indies* would be complete without addressing his controversial representation of Native Americans. Oviedo depicts Native American cultures with the same zeal and detail that inform his portraits of nature and the conquest, often including extensive ethnographic information. But his outright condemnation of the Indians often contradicts his more culturally sensitive ethnographic portraits. Oviedo's strong opinions and extensive ethnographic material made him a key figure in the sixteenth-century controversy among Spaniards about the nature and proper treatment of Native Americans.

From the inaugural moment when Christopher Columbus displayed six Native Americans to the royal court in 1493 and the pope granted the Crown of Castile control of the Catholic Church in the Indies until well after the debate in 1550 at Valladolid between the "Defender of the Indians," Bartolomé de Las Casas, and the humanist Juan Ginés de Sepúlveda, Crown officials, ecclesiastics, and colonists ardently debated the "true nature" of American Indians. The basic issue focused on Spaniards' varied perceptions of Native Americans' capacity for adopting Christianity and European culture but often included strong economic interests. The positions taken on the question determined if "just war" (*guerra justa*) could be waged on Indians and if they could be virtually enslaved through the system of *repartimiento* and *encomienda.* At stake were issues about governance and ethics as well as power and money. Considered an expert on New World affairs because of his royal administrative roles and his on-site experience, Oviedo was one of many Spaniards asked to testify before the king and the Council of the Indies during the first fifty years of the conquest and colonization of America. While Oviedo remained a strong supporter of the *encomienda* system throughout his lifetime, his descriptions of Native Americans in his *History* evolved over time. As a result, the portraits are complex and at times appear inconsistent. By applying a critical framework that takes into account the compositional chronology of the text as well as the evolving economic and political imperial situation in which Oviedo was deeply enmeshed, we see that the historian's depictions of Native Americans at first reveal a bureaucrat whose primary interest focused on the administrative issues of the Indies, which in turn affected his own profits, but later a chronicler whose interest grew in the particular reality of the New World.

During Oviedo's initial trip to America in 1514, he became the first Spaniard to read the *requerimiento,* the document dictated to the Indians before war was waged on them. (Oviedo describes this scene in book 29, chapter 7. It is ironic because he read it to a deserted town.) In a short time he became an *encomendero,* a Spaniard who had the right to the labor and tribute of a certain number of Indians.[1] At one point, his job even included branding newly captured Indians. Oviedo's role as an advocate for the *encomienda* system clashed with the views of the Dominican Friar Bartolomé de Las Casas.[2] In 1519, both Oviedo and Las Casas petitioned the king for land grants in the Main Land of America (Tierra Firme) and for knights to help settle the region. While Oviedo requested one hundred aristocratic knights from an established order to pacify Indians, Las Casas petitioned for the right to create a new order of knights with farmers to protect the land from intrusion.[3] Neither man's petition was granted in full, but in 1520 Las Casas received the rights to establish an experimental community, known as Cumaná, in which the Dominicans attempted to help Native Americans live without being subjugated to the Spaniards. Within several years Oviedo was granted the governorship of Cartagena, with rights to an *encomienda.* However, both men failed to carry out their visions for forming new societies in America—the Spaniards in Cumaná were killed, and Oviedo declined the governorship because of native rebellions and lack of funding.[4] Nonetheless, on the theory that Indians were fallen Christians and unable to adopt civilized European customs, Oviedo continued to encourage the Crown to maintain the *encomienda* system. Las Casas strongly objected to this position. He argued that the Indians were not barbaric but eminently teachable human beings. As social experiments like Cumaná that tested Native Americans' ability to convert to Christianity failed, debates intensified in Spain. In 1525, Oviedo was called before the newly formed Council of the Indies to render an official opinion on the subject. He argued that the subjugation of the Indians was the only way to bring about peace. He was recalled to make further depositions in 1530–1531 and 1532.[5] In the 1540s he continued to advise the Crown via official correspondence. By the end of the decade, Sepúlveda, the spokesman for the *encomienda* system in the 1550 debate, based many of his arguments on Oviedo's published writings about the nature of the Indian.[6]

The Crown and its counselors struggled with the implementation of a new political-religious model in its newly acquired and ever-expanding territories. The *encomienda* system assigned Native Americans to Spaniards for profit, through either labor or tribute, but in return Spaniards were to instruct Indians in Christianity. As Lewis Hanke explains, until 1492 the model for dealing with non-Christians living in Spanish territories was based on the precedent set in dealing with the Muslim and Jewish populations of Spain. Generally this system granted encomenderos the right to tribute without the responsibility of religious instruction. In this sense, there existed a degree of religious tolerance, though perhaps only because the monarch was too weak to enforce conversion campaigns. Both Hanke and Silvio Zavala describe at length the rarely linear development of royal policy regarding its new Native American subjects.[7] The Papal Bull of 1493 immediately wedded Spain's sovereignty over the New World territories to the process of evangelizing its inhabitants.

By 1495 the Crown had begun a policy that over the next half century vacillated between treating the Native Americans as slaves and setting them free to develop their own Christian communities. In 1502, as efforts to establish a tribute system failed, Hispaniola's governor, Nicolás Ovando, began to institutionalize the practice of *encomienda* as a system of forced Indian labor. During this decade Ferdinand and Isabella would both approve the liberty of Indians (1500) and insist on limiting their service to Spaniards to a year or two (1509). At the beginning of the next decade, Dominican friars in Hispaniola initiated the first strong protests to the *encomienda* system (1511–1513). The Crown's response to these complaints was multifaceted. Several laws and legal documents codified the rights and treatment of Native Americans (the Laws of Burgos, 1512) and presented a theological justification and procedure for "pacifying" inhabitants, which often resulted in their enslavement (the *requerimiento,* 1513). When the monarchy changed, the new king, Charles, heard the first important public debate dealing with the topic. In 1519 the Franciscan bishop of Tierra Firme, Juan de Quevedo, basing his argument on Aristotelian categories in which some human beings were classified as natural slaves, argued against Las Casas, saying that Indians were natural slaves.[8] Within the year Charles had abolished the *encomienda* system and authorized a series of experiments to convert and peacefully colonize the region (1520). But by 1524–1525 new legislation religitimized the enslavement of Indians along the coast of Tierra Firme (the coast of modern-day Colombia, Venezuela, and Panama), where Oviedo had lived. The legality and justice of the *requerimiento* were not only revisited but reestablished and further codified. From 1529 until 1543 policy continued to vacillate, yet new legislation limiting or abolishing the *encomienda* and enslavement of Native Americans rarely lasted for more than a year. As debates intensified, the number of *encomiendas* increased, and the indigenous populations decreased. The antislavery edict of 1530 was revoked the same year; another in 1534 met a similar fate; and the comprehensive New Laws of 1542 were immediately revised and ultimately revoked after widespread rebellion among Spaniards living in the Indies. Finally, by midcentury, wishing to lay to rest the question of whether the Indian was an inferior human being and a natural slave or was capable of living as a Christian (and therefore as a rational being), the Crown inaugurated the debates between Sepúlveda and Las Casas. Although 1550 was the culmination of more than fifty years of debates and is generally seen as the point at which the position of the *encomendero* prevailed, the debates lessened but did not cease after this date.[9] In spite of decades of debate, no deep reform of the system took place in the first sixty years of conquest and colonization. Finally, in 1573 the Crown took control of the *encomienda,* but it was too late to undo the vast destruction of most of the indigenous cultures.[10]

Oviedo's discussion of the Indians in his writings from at least 1525 to 1549 must be understood in the context of the extensive policy debates going on around him.[11] In his first published description of the inhabitants of Tierra Firme, the author sketches with a tone of moral revulsion their "idolatries and errors" (idolatrías y errores); they practiced polygamy and abortion and ate human flesh (*Sumario* 1526). This barbaric behavior, he suggests, is linked to their physiology: the Indians had thick, bestial skulls, which revealed their inferior status as human beings and therefore entitled the Crown to employ the *encomienda* system. But at least a decade later, when writing the final draft on Tierra Firme for the *Historia general,* Oviedo presents a very different portrait: he documents in extensive detail the intricacies of some native social structures that promoted peace and cooperation (bk. 29, chap. 26), while maintaining nevertheless that these were "not rational beings" (gente sin razón) (bk. 29, chap. 28). These often conflicting descriptions of Native American societies have caused scholars to read Oviedo in different lights—usually reflecting their own critical agendas.

For centuries, critics following Las Casas's lead cast Oviedo in the role of "deadly enemy of the Indian." Álvaro Félix Bolaños notes in his study of the reception of Oviedo's work, "Panegírico y libelo," that two extremes of criticism tended to prevail through the eighteenth and nineteenth centuries: one condemned Oviedo, the other tried to vindicate him. Passages in the 1526 *Sumario* that condemned Native Americans, many of which were repeated in the 1535/1547 editions of the first part of the *History,* were extensively quoted by his detractors. In the mid–nineteenth century Amador de los Ríos combated the views of Oviedo as Indian-hater by writing a lengthy panegyric portrait of the historian in his introductory study to his edition of the *History.* Important twentieth-century works by scholars such as Antonello Gerbi, Pérez de Tudela, Enrique Otte, and Alberto M. Salas tend to be more historically rigorous, but they often continue to present Oviedo in either a completely positive or negative light. By the 1970s and 1980s both historians and literary scholars began to analyze more closely the textual representations of the conquest. As part of this approach, some scholars began to point out the contradictions in and evolution of Oviedo's representations of Native Americans. Stephanie Merrim (1989), for example, perceives in the *Sumario* a tension between Oviedo the ethnographer and Oviedo the Christian moralist. In the same year, Giuliano Soria published an entire book on the issue of Oviedo and "the problem of the Indian." He convincingly argues that Oviedo's characterizations of Native Americans are complex and evolving: the apparent incongruity of the portraits corresponds to the tension between conventional opinion and political expediency, on the one hand, and to Oviedo's ethnographic inclination on the other. Indeed, Soria points out cases in the later parts of the *History* in which Oviedo's and Las Casas's points of view are not so far apart. Alexandre Coello de la Rosa's recent book on Oviedo (2002) devotes several chapters to this question, examining what he calls the "binary dualism" of the representation of the Indian and its link to political agendas. He and other critics, too, conclude that before 1540 Oviedo saw only two types of Indians, the noble and the savage, and that his responses vacillated between fascination and repulsion. After 1540, Oviedo increasingly reproached Spaniards who committed grave atrocities against the native populations and began to give them a more sympathetic voice in his text (174).

Although critics like Soria and Coello mention the relationship between political changes in the Indies and Oviedo's portraits, they do not study closely compositional dates of specific narrative passages and strategies and the effect these had on the depiction of Native Americans. As we have seen before with Oviedo, the deeper one digs into the historical contexts and dates of composition of his decades-long writings about the

Indies, the more one sees the evolution of his historical project and its internal contradictions. A closer examination of Oviedo's representation of Native Americans at different stages of his writing career from 1525 to 1547 exposes the wide variety of mediating factors that influenced his descriptions. Ultimately, I suggest the good Indian/bad Indian dichotomy that scholars have generally seen is part of a much more complex narrative of colonized and colonizer, one which responds to a myriad of conflicting influences that deeply affect the portrait of both over time and in varying colonial situations. The chronological order and narrative placement of descriptions are key to establishing an interpretative critical framework for understanding the apparent inconsistencies in Oviedo's treatment of the Native American. These dates and strategies help uncover the connection between the author's representation of Native Americans and the concrete political-economic situation at the moment of writing as well as his evolving epistemological and philological concerns about writing a New World history.

To the extent possible, I will examine Oviedo's writings in the order of their composition, starting with the *Sumario,* moving on to the 1535/1547 edition of part I of the *History,* and finishing with parts II and III, as published in the mid–nineteenth century. In conjunction with composition dates and narrative strategies three central contextualizing historical considerations need to be taken into account: first, the author's official role and political situation in the courts at the time of writing, and how these related to imperial policy regarding the Indies; second, whether Oviedo bases his description on his own eyewitness accounts or on a secondary source; third, the extent to which the native group described had been conquered and whether Europeans viewed its culture as civilized. Within these three considerations, I examine Oviedo's evolving views about good government, the novelty of the New World, and what today we call ethnography. As we will see, the outwardly contradictory portraits in fact reflect Oviedo's concern for the proper administration of the Indies and his own fortune as well as his growing interest in the proper representation of the New World's difference from the Old.

THE *SUMARIO* (1526) AND THE *HISTORIA* (PART I, 1535)

While in Spain in 1525, Oviedo wrote his brief natural history of the West Indies, the *Sumario.* Destined first and foremost to be read by the new emperor, Charles V, the text provides a schematic view of the new territories. Writing in Spain after his first two sojourns to America, Oviedo focuses on exotic New World phenomena. Only one chapter details the inhabitants of Tierra Firme (chap. 10). The author's opening sketches mention the specific cosmography of the region and the inhabitants' social organization. With what appears to be a humanistic concern for including linguistic terms and names, the first paragraphs seem to be an objective report. The chronicler soon turns, however, to a listing of the inhabitants' "idolatrías y errores": they practice polygamy, divorce, abortion, premarital sex; they eat human flesh; and they bury people alive. These sins, argues Oviedo, are the "religion of the devil" and like those committed by pagans in ancient times:

> Returning to the function of the *tequina* the Indians have, which is to speak with the Devil, and by whose hand and counsel those diabolical sacrifices, rites and ceremonies of the Indians take place, I maintain that neither the ancient Romans, nor the Greeks, nor the Trojans, nor Alexander, nor Darius, nor other ancient princes, were exempt from these kinds of errors and superstitions because they were not Catholics.[12] (*Sumario,* 126–127)

God punishes the Native Americans' crimes by sending devastating hurricanes and, ultimately, the Spaniards who conquer them. The chronicler argues that although Spanish conquistadors committed grave crimes in Tierra Firme, it was part of the divine plan:

> Persons have come to these parts who, giving little thought to their conscience and fear of human and divine justice, have committed acts which seem not to be of men, but of dragons and infidels, for, without warning nor having any human respect, have been the reason why many Indians who might have been converted and saved, perished in different ways and manners. In the case of those Indians who died in this way and who might not be converted, were they alive they might [still] have been useful in Your Majesty's service, and been of use and benefit to Christians . . . and [they who] have been the cause of this call [a place] "peaceful" when it is deserted and I, rather than "peaceful" call it "destroyed." But in these lands God and the world are satisfied with Your Majesty's holy intention and acts up to the present, for with the aid of many theologians, legal experts, and persons of great knowledge, you have provided and remedied by means of your justice all that

has been possible to do, and even more with the new reform of your Royal Council of the Indies.[13] (*Sumario,* 125–126)

Having established a strongly negative moral interpretation of indigenous practices and the Spaniards' God-given obligation to conquest (in spite of the crimes against humanity), the author turns to a more detached description of native artifacts: houses, hammocks, and henequen. Yet these, too, are placed into a moral framework, albeit indirectly:

> It has just occurred to me that one thing I have seen very often in these Indians is that their skulls are four times as thick as those of Christians. And so, when you are engaged in warfare with them and you engage in hand-to-hand combat, you must be very careful not to give them knife thrusts to the head, as many swords have been seen to shatter.[14] (*Sumario,* 140)

This passage serves as a bridge to a description of how inhabitants paint their bodies and prepare for war. Whereas the "idolatrías y errores" emphasize the Native Americans' status as fallen Christians (given Oviedo's belief that they had been part of a first evangelization by early Christians), the comment about a more "bestial" skull and barbaric war practices underscores the Indians' place as natural slaves in Aristotelian natural order. Both depictions rationalize the *encomienda* system, precisely at a time when Oviedo stood to gain significantly from policy that supported it.

In between the brief condemnation of the Spanish pacification as "depopulation" and his characterization of the Indians as the worst pagans in history, Oviedo inserts a reference to the monarch's policy and "the new reform of your Royal Council of the Indies" (126).[15] The *Sumario* was written on the heels of Las Casas's failure in Cumaná (1522), Oviedo's loss of his house and lands in Darién (1524), and nearly contemporaneously with the 1524 law that allowed the enslavement of Indians in Tierra Firme and with Oviedo's 1525 deposition to the Council of the Indies. At the same time, Oviedo was offered the governorship of Cartagena. New policies were being tested, implemented, and revoked, and Oviedo worked ambitiously (and with some degree of success) to become an important royal official. He helped determine policy in the Indies and personally benefited from it. The *Sumario* was yet another tool of Oviedo's ambition.

In closing the short chapter on the inhabitants of Tierra Firme, the author cross-referenced this section to the *General History,* explaining that the *History* expounds on the material in the *Sumario*: "Abundantly pointed out in my *General History of the Indies*" (*Sumario,* 143).[16] Part II of the *History* describes in some detail indigenous practices and social organization in Tierra Firme (bks. 26–29), but we do not know if these books were drafted contemporaneously with the *Sumario.* Although some chapters within these books were begun as early as 1527, most evidence suggests that the ethnographic chapters were written at least a decade later. (Oviedo extensively revised the history in 1540–1542, and there are no early editions of parts II and III.) To fill in the chronological gap between the writing of the *Sumario* and part II of the *History,* I turn to the 1535 edition of part I, which chronicles Columbus's voyages and the "conquest and pacification" of the Antilles/Caribbean. The chronological-geographical organization of part I allowed Oviedo to detail early royal policy regarding inhabitants of the West Indies and to describe encounters with new peoples found in different parts of the new territories.

There is no systematic description of Native American Indians in part I; rather the author tends to disperse the information throughout the text. First, the opening books of the history typically deal with the philosophical, moral, and administrative issues concerning the native inhabitants and their place in the Crown of Castile's territories (bks. 2–4). It is apparent that the period 1493–1516 was one of intense debate and great fluctuation in policy toward Native Americans. The author expounds two theories that propose to legitimize Spanish rule of the Americas and label Indians as fallen Christians: First, that the Indies had been part of the legendary Hesperides, where the Visigoth monarchs of Hispania had ruled (bk. 2, chap. 3); second, that Christ's apostles had evangelized America (bk. 2, chap. 7). Having established the Indies as part of the monarch's original territories and its natives as lapsed Christian subjects, Oviedo says he will document the Indians' "criminal customs" (criminales costumbres), their warlike nature and inability to live in a civilized manner (bk. 2, chap. 8), but not until later in the history, "in its proper place" (en su lugar) (35). The Caribs are singled out as barbaric savages:

> [The islands] were populated by Indian archers called *Caribs,* which in their language means "brave" and "daring." They shoot with such a foul-smelling and irritating herb that it is incurable, and the men who are wounded with it die in a raging state. . . . The archers from these islands who shoot with this herb eat human flesh, except those from

> Boriquén [Puerto Rico]. But, besides the people of these islands, human flesh is eaten in many areas of Tierra Firme, as shall be stated in its proper place.[17] (bk. 2, chap. 8)

Nonetheless, a degree of ambivalence, if not sensitivity, to the ethnic variations among island natives emerges as the author differentiates the natives in Boriquén. He also recalls seeing the first Indians brought to the Spanish court in 1493: they were "domestic" (domésticos) and "peaceful Indians" (indios de paz). Indeed, one became a servant to Prince Don Juan (bk. 2, chap. 7). Others engaged in war only when threatened: "There never were conflicts or differences among the Indians of this island, nor would they ever take place, save for one of these three causes: territorial boundaries, fishing rights, or when Carib archers from the other islands would come to assault them" (bk. 3, chap. 4).[18] Oviedo thus further develops a dichotomy begun by Columbus which stipulated two types of Indians: warlike (Caribs) and peaceful (most others). Notably, in these opening books Oviedo describes the disappearance of the colonizers left by Columbus on his first voyage, but they lack the harshly castigating tone of the *Sumario*. He explains that the Spanish sailors were not men of great honor, inferring that perhaps they had provoked the Indians. This sets the stage for Oviedo's subsequent discussion of early policy launched by Queen Isabella and Cardinal Cisneros regarding the justice of enslaving Indians (bk. 4, chaps. 2, 3).[19]

Having discussed the governance of the Indies, the author develops a section with bountiful, vivid details of native customs on Hispaniola (bk. 5). It echoes the strong negative stereotyping found in the *Sumario* and thus continues to justify the waging of war on Indians and their enslavement:

> But finally, these Indians are a people far removed from wanting to understand the Catholic faith, and it is a case of hammering cold iron [that is, it is futile] to think that they will ever be Christians. This is how things have seemed to them in their cowls, or better yet, in their heads, as they don't wear cowls, nor were their heads like those of other folk, for they have such robust, thick skulls that the most important piece of advice which Christians have when they do battle with them is not to give them knife thrusts to the head, as their swords will shatter. Just as their skulls are thick, so is their reasoning bestial and ill-intentioned, as will be related further on with respect to those aspects

> of their rites, ceremonies, customs and other matters of the same ilk as may occur to me.[20] (bk. 5, *Proemio*)

While the preface condemns the Indians' "sinful" cultural practices and "bestial" anatomy, individual chapters illustrate specific "offenses" (delitos), "abominable customs" (abominables costumbres), "images of the Devil" (imágenes del diablo), and "idolatries" (idolatrías) that lead to God's "punishment" of the Indians (chaps. 1, 3). The author describes indigenous ceremonies, medicine doctors, and religious leaders. He lists native vices: many men practice sodomy, the "abominable sin" (pecado nefando) and "abominable against nature" (abominable contra natura); many women are lustful; many Indians paint their bodies and some are thieves (chap. 3). Even as Oviedo sternly condemns indigenous sexual and religious practices, he includes comparative ethnographic information. For example, he cites cases of European homosexual couples and married bigamists who later received papal dispensations (bk. 5, chap. 3). He also mentions Pliny and other classical authorities who describe people who ate human flesh (bk. 5, chap. 3). In yet another chapter, Oviedo again makes the practice more believable and culturally relative by noting that

> the historian proves that in other parts of the world there were, among the ancients, human sacrifices and offerings to their gods, and in many parts, likewise, there was eating of human flesh as at present there is in many parts of the main land of these Indies, as well as in some islands. (bk. 6, chap. 9)[21]

At times, Oviedo cannot resist an ethnographic impulse that temporarily sets aside the strong condemnation of Native Americans. He discusses the traditional song and dance (*areito*) and integrates it into European culture by comparing it to Old World cultural forms and by illustrating the musical instrument used (*tambor*). Elsewhere in the same book he develops his ethnographic project by describing and drawing tobacco leaves and hammocks (chap. 2). Indeed, when the author describes ethnographic objects, he tends to treat them as objective natural phenomena, an approach that does not require moral commentary.

A third narrative section about Indians in the 1535 *History* emerges in the exemplary story of the Indian cacique Don Enrique and the Spanish captain Francisco Barrionuevo during the natives' uprising on Hispaniola in 1519 (bk. 5, chaps. 4–11).[22] Unlike most Spanish–Native American encounters represented in part I, this one portrays Don Enrique as an undeniable hero who brought lasting peace to the island. Oviedo describes how the *cacique* responds honorably to Barrionuevo's efforts to pacify the island. Although, as we have seen, extensive sections of book 5 castigate most Hispaniola natives, Oviedo draws on the tradition of the novel of knight errantry and portrays their chief, Don Enrique, as a capable leader and a good Christian (chap. 11), even as the wisest man since Adam:

> With respect to the chieftain Don Enrique, it seems to me that he concluded the most honorable peace that any captain or prince from Adam onwards has ever made, and garnered more honor than the Duke of Bourbon in the defeat and imprisonment of the French King Francis in Pavia, keeping in mind the huge disparity and inequality which exists between the greatest Christian prince and Emperor of the Universe, and a man such as this Don Enrique. . . . Indeed, Don Enrique, if you could but know this and knew how to feel it, I esteem you as one of the most honorable and successful captains there has ever been on earth up until your own time.[23] (bk. 5, chap. 8)

Oviedo begs Charles to pardon the cacique and to honor him. Despite his pro-*encomienda* position, Oviedo appreciated many Native American artifacts and customs and even admired specific caciques—an inclination that will become more prominent in later parts of the history.

Book 6 on miscellany (*Depósitos*) is the last narrative section that includes information on Native Americans. It serves as a bridge between the general history (bks. 1–5) and the natural history (bks. 7–15). The *Depósitos* includes many ethnographic chapters on indigenous artifacts (canoes, fire drills, and houses), customs, and languages as well as depictions of mythical monsters (chap. 10).[24] Within this narrative frame of exotic curiosities, the descriptions of indigenous life in book 6 avoid the moral censure that accompanied this same material earlier in the history. In this new context, stories of such practices as cannibalism are added to a list of curious miscellany to pique the reader's interest. Similarly, book 6 contrasts sharply with the previous book by representing indigenous peoples as an extension of a land filled with exotic marvels. The dissimilarity in representation suggests that Oviedo's portrait of "savage" or "peaceful" Indians had a great deal to do with the interpretive context. In book 5, they are used as points of discussion, to get at the underlying challenges of the governance of a new territory, and are therefore seen as a threat to his own riches. By contrast, in book 6, the native subjects are independent "miscellany" and therefore required less moral or administrative framework. Moreover, Oviedo's impulse—and obvious delight—in accumulating such curiosities did not diminish over time, as some critics have argued. A comparison of the 1535 edition of book 6 with the final version of 1549 reveals that he added forty chapters to the original thirteen (chaps. 14–53).

After delving into the region's natural history (bks. 7–15), Oviedo returns to its general history and to a discussion of imperial policy. Once again, there is little ethnographic information, and native inhabitants tend to be framed as antagonists whose riches deserve to be confiscated.[25] In addition, however, Oviedo criticizes the role of Spaniards. Chronicling the Dominicans' attempt to evangelize and settle Tierra Firme, Oviedo vividly describes their brutal martyrdoms (chap. 3). But the historian blames Las Casas for the fiasco (chaps. 4, 5) and characterizes his 1519 proposal for evangelization as a fantasy with the "smell of promised cavalry and lies" (chap. 5).[26] (This is ironic given Oviedo's request for one hundred knights when he was offered a governorship.) The chronicler reveals that Las Casas's Cumaná experiment ended in the enslavement of the Indians (chap. 6). According to Oviedo, both the warlike nature of the Indians and the pretensions of some churchmen were to blame for a colonization that went awry. The author again points indirectly to his central concern with the administration of new lands and its effects on administrators like himself. This was the version of the *History* that was republished in 1547, just as Las Casas and Sepúlveda began their first debates.

The New World inhabitants played an integral role in Oviedo's representation of the natural and general history of the Indies. His interest in depicting ethnographic information may have been stimulated by the fact that he lived in Hispaniola for several years before publishing part I and by his concern that as natives died so did the possibility of recording the island's history. He remarks that many of his informants, the "elders" (viejos), had died by the time he was writing his final draft (bk. 5, chap. 4). In addition, Oviedo wrote from the perspective of the successful conquistador; by the 1530s most of the West Indies had been conquered, and native inhabitants were no longer a threat. The Spaniards had reached what Bolaños has termed a "desired status quo," that is, a state of affairs in which the rules of contact between colonizer and colonized reached a point that was stable enough for the Spaniards to pursue their business interests.[27] Indians were now sufficiently "safe" to treat as subjects of ethnographic interest and as a New World novelty within the larger scheme of the *Natural History*. In these same years, the debates over the *encomienda* system heated up: royal policy reversed itself three times (1529, 1530, 1534), and the recent conquests of the urban civilizations of the Mexicas and Incas once again challenged Spaniards' views of native populations. In general, then, Oviedo's condemnation of Indians as savages in the 1535 edition of part I coincides with his efforts to establish the rights to rule them and the administrative structure for accomplishing this. Curious ethnographic items are generally set apart from the discussion of indigenous populations as a whole, showing the tension between official policy and his interest in depicting Native Americans.

THE *HISTORY* (PARTS II AND III)

Nearly fifteen years elapsed between the first edition of part I and the completion of parts II and III of the *General and Natural History of the Indies*. During that time, as we have seen in previous chapters, Oviedo's historiographic methodology continued to evolve, as did the conquest itself. As a result, parts II and III have a more coherent narrative placement of information about Native Americans than part I, which was less organized. When Oviedo reports firsthand in books 26–29 on native populations in Tierra Firme, for example, most of the information is carefully divided into general history, encompassing the role of Native Americans in the conquest, and natural history, including the "individual features" (particularidades) of indigenous social and ethnographic practices and organizations. After depicting the general conquest and colonization of the area in book 29—along with the extensive litigation involved—Oviedo turns to ethnography and natural history. He announces that

> to avoid causing readers tedium by repeating that which was said before, here in this Book 29 some matters mentioned in previous books will be summarized, pointing out differences which might exist from that which was said in the first part from that which will be told in this second part about similar matters.[28] (bk. 29, chap. 26)

Of the thirty-four chapters in this book, Oviedo devotes five to various Native American groups in Tierra Firme (chaps. 26–28, 31, 32). Each native population and its distinct languages, customs, rites, and histories is far more particularly described than in the *Sumario* or the 1535 *History*.[29] The maturing of Oviedo's ethnographic impulse is evident.

Oviedo discusses dress (or lack of it), religious beliefs, housing, languages, bathing, food, social organization, marriage customs, and sexual practices. Even when these customs fly in the face of Christian norms, Oviedo provides extensive and detailed information that is sensitive to regional differences. Unlike the descriptions in the *Sumario,* here the sexual and religious practices are not a list of " idolatries and errors" (idolatrías y errores); the author refrains from condemning divorce, prostitution, polygamy, or abortion. For example:

> Among these women of Cueva, there are also some who publicly give themselves to whomever wants them, and these are called *irachas,* because to say "woman" they say *ira,* and one which belongs to many or is a concubine they call *iracha* (as a plural word, one which applies to many). There are others so enamored of libidinous behaviour that if they get pregnant they take a certain herb by means of which they induce and expel their pregnancy, for they say that old women can give birth, but they don't want to be so occupied as to have to give up their pleasures, nor get pregnant, so that on giving birth, their breasts would sag, for they are exceedingly proud of them, and have very fine ones.[30] (bk. 29, chap. 27)

On the whole there is less moralizing and politicking and more ethnographic documentation—although Oviedo never accepts the practice of sodomy. After talking about sexually active women who practice abortion, Oviedo lashes out: "In this province of Cueva there are also abominable sodomites, and keep young boys with whom they practice this vile offense" (bk. 29, chap. 27).[31] But he continues by furnishing information about how some cross-dressed men were integrated into the social structure:

> They dress them in petticoats, or in women's attire, and make use of them for all those activities which women do, from spinning to sweeping the house, and in all other things. They are not scorned or mistreated for this, and these long-suffering beings are called *camayoa.*[32] (bk. 29, chap. 27)

Only one chapter title includes a negative label ("sinful" [viciosas] and "idolatries" [idolatrías], chap. 26), while the others, titled "ceremonies and customs" (ceremonias e custumbres) and "individual features of the Indians" (particularidades de los indios), provide information intended to assist in knowing the province (*gobernación*) of Castilla del Oro. More complete information about the new subjects, argues Oviedo, should lead to better government of them, to integrating them into a new economic and political system. In this framework, ethnographic information is in support of good government.

Even the narrative passages on Tierra Firme cited verbatim from the *Sumario,* for example, the paragraph on the thickness of Indian skulls, lose some of their impact. Placed in a longer narrative without further discussion (chap. 28), wedged between a fairly objective description of warrior costumes and blood-letting practices, the observation still has the political implications it had in the *Sumario,* but it is couched in an extensive, complex description. There no longer seems to be an overriding emphasis on the barbarism of the Indians so prevalent in part I, book 5. Although Oviedo continues to state that the Native Americans were "not rational beings" (gente sin razón), he grants narrative space and interest to elaborating their customs—some of which undermine his negative statement about the rationality of the natives of Tierra Firme. Several important factors help account for this shift in the portrait. In the dozen or so years separating the composition of these two versions Oviedo's situation had changed. First, he no longer lived in Tierra Firme, and, second, he no longer was an aspiring governor but rather had been working in his role as official chronicler.

Oviedo announced in the *Sumario* that he had already written copiously about the natives of Tierra Firme in the *History,* but he admits later in the text that

> I recall referring to the present *General History,* which, though it was not yet carefully rendered from the notes and rough drafts which I had of these matters, I lacked neither the desire nor the hope of bringing this text to the state in which it is now. . . . I will now proceed step by step to clarify what I stated earlier. . . . I wish to advise [the reader] that here he will not find [these topics] presented as haphazardly as I did there, but they will be in their proper places.[33] (bk. 29, chap. 26)

The *Sumario* was the "herald or precursor" (mensajero o significado) of the history, yet he admits he treated the material as though it were a "criminal" (reo), forcing it into chapters. He claims the result was like a mixed fruit jam that has no distinct flavor, so one is left wanting to taste the fruits individually: "This is what I did in that summary: many things were jumbled together, making it impossible to understand where they are" (bk. 29, chap. 26).[34]

Given some of the internal dates in book 29, it is highly unlikely Oviedo wrote it first and selected passages from it to include in the *Sumario*.[35] Most probably the process was the reverse: he used selections from the *Sumario* for the *History* but expanded upon them. Understanding this method of composition helps one date this draft on the Indians of Tierra Firme to sometime after 1526 and helps to explain perhaps the fuller representation of native populations and their customs. Although some field notes for book 29 were begun as early as 1528 (see chapter 3 above), these chapters were drafted a good deal later, most likely in the 1540–1542 reorganization of the *History* (see chapter 5 above).

Elsewhere the author spells out the multiple purposes this information served. Both anticipating and apparently responding to criticism about the length of his description of Indians, Oviedo reprimands his readers and reminds them of his goals:

> Consider that these treatises are founded principally on the praise of God, as He is the Maker of so many new and diverse things . . . and second, because the mercy of the Emperor wishes that at his command all this be known and communicated to the entire world; and third, because it is a great joy for all men, of whichever rank they might be, to hear of new things.[36] (bk. 29, chap. 28)

Here Oviedo links information on Indians with the purpose of natural history, to depict natural phenomena. But in a chapter added in 1548 or 1549 he returns to the issue of good administration and who should govern. First he acknowledges that the vast divergences among indigenous groups made it difficult to know them: "The customs of these people are so many and so diverse, they cannot yet be understood or known, without time to make this happen, and more years to pass" (bk. 29, chap. 31).[37] While it was in the hands of the clergy to administer and evangelize the Indians, Oviedo accuses them of failing to produce good Christians: "Up to now I have seen a huge number of these Indians in the thirty-five years I have spent in these parts; I look at this generation and have found not one perfect Christian" (bk. 29, chap. 31).[38] More pointedly, he attacks the clergy, saying they did not complete the evangelization process but simply lined their own pockets:

> Most reverend Bishops and Prelates: examine your ministers well, for at times you are deluded in your choice and they deceive you. Do you wish to see this? Examine some of their purses and their private ventures, and the fortune with which they entered into their profits, and you will see how far removed they are from the profession of the priesthood.[39] (bk. 29, chap. 31)

According to Oviedo, the Indians may be continuing their own religious practices, but they are not to blame as much as the clerics, who were not doing their job.

Although the final drafts of this section of book 29 were composed in the same decade that the New Laws were put into effect and then repealed (1540s), there is little evidence of these policy changes in the chapters. As Oviedo spent more time in the Indies and as it became clear after 1532 that his most significant official role in the Spanish imperial project was that of documenting the conquest, rather than of governing new territories and Native Americans, he may have been freer to report the complexities of indigenous societies.[40] Although documents in the archives show that through the 1530s Oviedo continued to petition for *repartimientos* of Indians, it seems he had less at stake once he had lost his *encomienda* in Tierra Firme and had been appointed official chronicler and warden of the fort in Santo Domingo.[41] For a time, the author's deepest concern appears to have shifted to diligently creating a historical method and monitoring the reception of the *History*. As we have noted, he spent much of the early 1540s reorganizing the text and later attempting to publish it. But typically, he never settled completely into one niche: his early ambition to be appointed as governor in one of the territories in the Indies (recall his attempts in the 1520s) emerged again in 1546. Reacting to a political situation with the administration of a region, he petitioned for the governorship of Cartagena. He asked for terms similar to his contract from 1525 but added others that reveal his animosity toward certain Spanish groups: he asked that "lawyers, solicitors, and monks" (letrados, procuradores, and frailes) be prohibited from settling in Cartagena, saying they had destroyed the Indies.[42]

No doubt another key element factored into the shift in Oviedo's representation of the Native Americans. By the 1540s the conquistadors' greed had completely soured any of the original visions of establishing new societies in America. By then, whole populations in the Antilles and Central America had disappeared, and Spaniards had murdered each other at alarming rates in rebellions and civil wars extending from Tierra

Firme to Peru. As we saw in chapter 3, according to Oviedo, many royal officials and conquistadors had devastated the land and acted more barbarically than the Indians. Scathing portraits of most Spaniards contrast with largely sympathetic portrayals of caciques. As we have seen, in the 1535 edition of part I there was a lone laudatory sketch of a native chief, Don Enrique, accompanied by a praiseworthy description of the Spanish captain Barrionuevo (bk. 5, chaps. 6–8). By the 1540s, in part II, Oviedo depicted many wise Native American leaders who were betrayed time and again by treacherous Spaniards. Book 29 on Tierra Firme abounds with such stories. The caciques Paris and Bea are noble leaders who seek peace and the protection of their peoples (bk. 29, chaps. 9, 13). Yet conquistadors destroyed these social structures by raping women, torturing men, and unfairly attacking entire towns to enslave their inhabitants. Oviedo's portrayal of Spaniards as barbarians and of Indians as just rulers inverts the discourse of conquest and further underscores his overarching preoccupation with the administration of the Indies.[43] Those who impede good government, not the Indians, are now the problem. As the native populations were decimated Oviedo saw less need to portray them as enemies; he begins to portray partially lost cultures with some degree of sympathy.

Oviedo's increased awareness of cultural difference and his inversion in treatment of conquistadors and the conquered in Tierra Firme continue in his depictions of indigenous groups he had witnessed firsthand. Several chapters in the book about Nicaragua, for example, discuss marriage customs, sexual practices, religious beliefs, and *areitos* (bk. 42, chaps. 1–3, 11, 14–16).[44] They are combined with a report on the natural world, especially the *relación* about and drawings of the volcanoes, as well as a gruesome narrative describing Pedrarias Dávila feeding dead Indians to the dogs in the Plaza de León (chap. 11). Two things stand out in the book. First, Oviedo allows Native Americans to "talk"; they become an ethnographer's informants as he asks them questions and they respond ("With me asking the Indians what that signal meant," chap. 11).[45] He even includes in dialogue format an official inquiry into the Christian beliefs held by Indians after Spaniards had baptized them by the thousands years earlier (chaps. 2, 3). The dialogue is almost certainly not a verbatim recording of Native American responses, and it most certainly was highly mediated first by the original transcriber and later by Oviedo himself. But for the first time it carves out a narrative space that allows for the appearance of native speech. In addition, Oviedo continues to invert the discourse of the Indian as barbarian; he blames the Spaniards who failed to teach Catholic catechism. In another instance, when reporting Pedrarias Dávila's gruesome revenge on Indians by unleashing his dogs of war, the author deeply criticizes the Spaniards. However, once again we see Oviedo both depict the sins of Spaniards and yet never waver in his stance that cannibalistic practices were deserving of drastic penalties. This gruesome description of the massacre in León is preceded and followed by references that discuss indigenous cannibalism.

But what patterns emerge in the representation of Native Americans in regions that Oviedo never visited and in areas in which he never had a personal stake in their governance? Looking to the vastly disparate geographical territories and civilizations of the Mexicas and Incas (neither of which Oviedo had experienced) we see a very different set of concerns and, therefore, representations of Native Americans. Because the historian had to depend on a series of secondary sources for the histories of Mexico (Nueva España, bk. 33) and Peru (bk. 46), his focus more closely follows the concerns of his witnesses. Oviedo remained interested in documenting native customs, but in general his informants had less to say about this topic; most of them wrote *relaciones,* which focused on their own deeds in order to seek rewards for services rendered in the conquest. Because Oviedo's adherence to principles of trustworthiness did not allow him to invent material or to drastically alter his sources, there is comparatively sparse information and commentary about Mexica and Inca societies.[46] Unable to include extensive sections on natural history and native inhabitants in Mexico and Peru, Oviedo focused on establishing himself as a reliable historian by deftly monitoring the truth of his secondary accounts. He no longer had a personal stake in the conquest, nor firsthand experience, so his role as author comes to the fore.

The history of the conquest of New Spain illustrates Oviedo's shift from actor to author in his narrative approach to the Native Americans. Oviedo closely followed Cortés's *Carta de relación* in the first chapters of book 33, but he subdivided his informant's material into chapters in order to highlight topics that matched the historian's previous organizational schemas. Of particular interest is chapter 11. Its title, "Idolatries" (Idolatrías), signals one of Oviedo's favorite topics: "In which [book] we refer to the idolatrous practices and diabolical sacrifices of the Indians of New Spain" (bk. 33, chap. 11).[47] Yet the chapter fails to describe idolatries Oviedo-style. Allowing his source to tell the story, the author employs prose that closely mirrors Cortés's descriptive style and tone. In the few instances in which Oviedo mediates his source, he clearly demarcates his own narrative intervention. Later, when the historian expands his sources and revises Cortés's accounts, he follows this same historiographical method. For example, the title of chapter 46 announces titillating information about "sacrifices, rituals, and idolatry" (sacrificios e ritos e idolatría) from several soldiers present at the Conquest of Mexico. Although the report includes gruesome descriptions of a patio floor made out of layers of dried human blood, festivals in which human hearts were extracted, and children killing children, Oviedo does not intervene in the account to label these practices "errors" (errores) or "abominable acts" (abominables). The words "loathsome" (aborrescible), which describes the smell of the patio, and "idol" (ídolo), which refers to a Mexica god, apparently come from the original source.

A similar historiographical pattern emerges in book 46 on Peru, only now Oviedo's sources provide even less information about Native Americans. While Oviedo insists on calling attention to ethnographic material with select chapter titles promising material about native customs, the chapters actually include very little information. One chapter title, for example, announces Pizarro's march to Cajamarca and "some costumes and rites and damnable sacrifices" (chap. 4).[48] But in fact only one paragraph depicts indigenous customs. This pattern is repeated several times (chaps. 6, 9, 22). Such chapter titles certainly piqued readers' interest. More important, they reflected Oviedo's attempts to wed ethnographic information with the process of conquest and colonization. No doubt Europeans were fascinated by the intricate social organization and practices of the Mexica and Inca civilizations. But ultimately, Oviedo had scanty information to work with. In fact, the chronicler-bureaucrat may have encountered a further dilemma: the "civilized" societies of the Mexica and Inca did not fit his schema for an administrative paradigm: ungoverned savages who needed to be ruled. Because of the complexity of their societies and because he could not witness them firsthand, Oviedo instead meticulously compiled multiple reports and revised material as new accounts brought in additional, often contradictory, information.

CONCLUSIONS

The examination of Oviedo's representation of Native Americans—from the castigating *Sumario* to the more diverse 1535 edition of the *History* and the final, more nuanced treatment in parts of the 1540s *History*—reveals that Oviedo's immediate experience greatly affected the amount of information and its narrative placement. While firsthand experience had little influence on Oviedo's opinions of native populations, it had a good deal of influence on the extent to which he described them. He not only had more information, he usually had a personal stake in the description. On the other hand, the passage of time—and the great number of changes it brought in the conquest and in imperial policy as well as Oviedo's official positions and historiographic methodology—directly influenced his representation of Native Americans.

Not surprisingly, Oviedo's growing ethnographic interest in the "individual features" (particularidades) of distinct native groups parallels the increasing sophistication of his field drawings. As we saw in chapter 6, by the 1540s Oviedo's first schematic illustrations of flora had evolved into more detailed renditions of full plants. This representational change corresponded to a growing empirical concern: to render the full details of an object in a more naturalistic style in order to facilitate identification. But the tendency to depict the particular also coincides with Oviedo's grave concerns about the improper administration of the Indies. The first portraits of Native Americans as relatively savage corresponds to the author's perceived need to establish rule over them and to justify the *encomienda.* After the 1540–1542 reorganization and revision of the *History,* Oviedo increasingly saw his text as a systematic mapping of the newly formed provinces in the Indies, and thus he increasingly provides a fuller picture of the regions' inhabitants. This serves the dual purpose of helping good governance (knowledge is power) and of documenting the New World's novelties. As native populations decreased, the portraits of "barbaric" conquistadors and inept clerics set the stage for new discussions about good government. As the growing populations of Spanish colonists became more of a challenge to the king's administrative structure, Oviedo documents how often praiseworthy Native Americans were being destroyed, which threatened the economy and governance of the new territories. As Oviedo's ideas and experiences of America changed, so, too, did his representational practices.

Yet Oviedo's more diverse views of Native Americans never reached a broad reading public in the sixteenth century. Las Casas, surely reacting to the damage done to his cause by Oviedo's early editorial successes with the *Sumario* and the first part of the *History,* successfully blocked the publication of parts II and III in 1548. Almost a decade later, well after the 1550 debate had quieted down, these parts were set for publication, along with the revised version of part I. But the process was aborted because of the author's death the same year (1557). Soon after, under Philip II's reign, all material dealing with Native Americans would be severely censored and blocked from publication. Indeed, most readers were unable to see the evolution in Oviedo's representation of Native Americans until Amador de los Ríos published the complete history for the first time (1850s). Thus, the chronicler's reputation as "a deadly enemy of the Indians," as cast by Las Casas, continued for centuries.

Even now many readers read only the *Sumario* or part I of the *History* with their lively first-person accounts and strong moral tone. This may, however, limit readers' ability to see the complexities and apparent contradictions in Oviedo's depiction of Native Americans. Although he never wavered in his views about the *encomienda* system, the chronicler did modify his portrait of the Indians depending on imperial policy at the time, his own official role, and the degree to which indigenous cultures had been conquered. If in the *Sumario* Oviedo's logic is mostly consistent (the Indians are barbaric fallen Christians deserving enslavement), in later parts of the *History,* even as he is more systematic and clear about his description of Indians, he no longer links his support for the *encomienda* system with his moral and religious condemnation of the native populations. Instead, the descriptions become intimately connected with his views on the management (and mismanagement) of the new territories. The portrait of Native Americans is related to his treatment of Spanish conquistadors and clerics. The balance of condemnation and praise depends on the inherent quality of the civilization as well as on Oviedo's ideas of good governance and the concerns of an aristocratic administrator, as we witnessed also in chapter 3. The ethnographic impulse to document information in order to integrate new societies into a new economic-political system is coupled with Oviedo's increasingly strong impulse to document New World difference as a particular difference. The *History* reflects Oviedo's complex epistemological and philological concerns as well as his interests in economic and political issues. But Oviedo's contentious personality and ambitions within the system are never far from the surface of his narrative.

CONCLUSIONS

Whether Oviedo was writing about Native Americans, nature, or the conquest and colonization, his personal, political, and methodological concerns were never far from the surface of the narrative. The author's attempts to maintain the favor of the Crown and establish the truth of his account serve as the underpinnings to his historiographic writing. In the closing chapter of the *History,* he recalls more than fifty years of service to the Crown—from the time of the Catholic Kings and Columbus's first voyages (bk. 50, chap. 30). The historian records his travels, administrative duties, and writing as acts of service: information about the natural world and judgments about conquistadors, Spanish bureaucrats, and Indians provide knowledge with which to rule the new territories. Significantly, if Oviedo's accounts were successful he stood to gain power and fame through lucrative administrative posts.

Intimately linked to Oviedo's posture as a loyal servant was the establishment of his credibility as an author. Even as he closes his lengthy *History,* Oviedo harangues his detractors who asserted that a true history should be written in Latin. He counters their charges with an appeal to truth: "May the truth prevail above all else . . . for without elegance nor circumlocutions, nor embellishments nor rhetorical ornamentation, but in a straightforward manner have I allowed this *General and Natural History of the Indies* to reach this state, in accordance with the truth" (bk. 50, chap. 30).[1] He faced conflicting testimonies and representational quandaries as he wrote about an expanding new world in a period when the nature of truth and authority was being debated. As we have seen, Oviedo grappled with sixteenth-century epistemological, philosophical, historiographic, and canonical issues. Writing during an era in which representational practices were in flux, he unevenly (and at times uneasily) addresses these questions according to the material treated and the year written. In general, however, the author increasingly equated truth with experience and direct observation, and authoritative texts served as a point of departure to underscore the new. Unrecorded or partially recorded information and events required extensive detail and explanation. Oviedo frequently updates the natural world, detailing new species, information, and curiosities. And he provides courtroomlike multiple testimony about men's actions, hoping to facilitate justice and truth. Yet Oviedo's "truth" is often colored by his agenda.

Both his service to the Crown and his rhetorical dedication to truth highlight Oviedo's essential role as a player in Castile's project in the Indies. Whether comparing testimony or recording his own new observations, the historian carves out a space for himself in the narrative. He is the central mediator of information from the ancients to contemporary reports from the field. All sources come under scrutiny as he contested some and accepted others. Indeed, Oviedo emphasizes his personal role in the construction of the text by signing every copy of the 1535 edition and closing this same edition with a reproduction of his family coat of arms (fig. 78), which now included the New World constellation, the Southern Cross, as proof of his time in the Indies.

This is not to say that Oviedo's representational practices were static. The historian's first representations of the Indies, prior to about 1532, tended to be general and schematic when dealing with natural history and personal and political when dealing with general history. Early illustrations were depicted without much detail, and the first portraits of Native Americans were highly stereotyped and judgmental. In one case, he uses reports on indigenous women to support the Old World Amazonian myth. Oviedo's administrative posts and ambitions deeply influenced the narrative during his early years. He fought hard in the courts and in writing to gain new wealth, *repartimientos,* and bureaucratic titles. Some of these earlier sections abound with a juridical, autobiographical style that reflects his legal battles and petitions (for example, his bid for a governorship and interactions with Pedrarias Dávila). Overall, the author's stance in the early *History* is as an actor in the conquest and as a witness who experiences and records New World natural wonders without paying great attention to detail and perhaps veracity.

Beginning in the 1530s, soon after his appointment as official chronicler, and solidifying in the early 1540s when he reconfigured a large part of the *History,* Oviedo moves away from his role as participant-observer in the text and adapts the persona and methods of an official historian. The more schematic generalizations and frequent proclamations about his on-site presence give way to passages aimed at recording both specific

New World reality and a grander history. On the one hand, this results in extensive additions to and revisions of illustrations and descriptions as well as in more frequent moral judgements about Spaniards' actions. On the other hand, Oviedo offers more naturalism in his illustrations and more detail about species; he includes a broader picture of Native American cultures; he allows for the possibility of a New World reality in his revisions about republics of women; and he demotes Cortés from hero to liar in his new account of the Conquest of Mexico.

Oviedo's strong first-person presence does not disappear, however, in these later sections of the *History*. Rather, his voice becomes that of an official transcriber and historian. He has the knowledge and power—and thus authority—to access numerous testimonies and to control for truth. He increasingly collects and compares others' firsthand testimony. Oviedo's concept of writing history evolves into an idea of history as a series of accounts that need to be presented, and ultimately judged, in order to reveal the truth. This view, as we have seen, creates a central, nearly sanctified role for himself.

Perhaps with this partial understanding of the historian's complex text, roles, and representational processes, we can now revise our readings of the *History*. Its author is not just a hero of Spain's imperial project in the Indies, nor a villain whose text supported the enslavement of Native Americans, nor a contentious Castilian constantly protesting the words of others. He is a composite of these roles and many others—a man whose *History* offers insight into an early modern worldview, based on personal ambition but also grounded in the newly emerging intellectual framework of Europe's encounter with America. Oviedo began taking notes in the Central American jungle on his travels, surrounded by the violence, chaos, and greed that characterized the Conquest of the Tierra Firme. He continually sought personal justice and power through the courts and his writing. By the time he was finishing the *History,* Oviedo had lived for more than a dozen years in the relative stability of a salaried position as historian and garrison keeper, in the oldest Spanish town in the Americas. His complex legacy stands on the composite writings and revisions of the first three tomes.

APPENDIX A

Chronology of Fernández de Oviedo's Life and Works

1478	Born in Madrid
ca. 1490	*Mozo,* or page, in the household of the duke of Villahermosa
1493	*Mozo* for Prince Don Juan
1497	Prince Don Juan dies
ca. 1499	Italian sojourn begins
ca. 1502	Returns to Madrid
	Marries Margarita de Vergara
ca. 1503	In the service of the duke of Calabria, Ferdinand of Aragón
ca. 1505	Begins chronicling the Castilian monarchy
1505	Margarita dies
1509	Son Francisco González de Valdés born
150?	Marries Isabel de Aguilar
1512	Aborts expedition to Naples with the "Gran Capitán"
1513	Receives a variety of royal administrative posts in the Indies, including notary and overseer of the gold foundries (*veedor*)
1514	Sails for Central America (Darién, present-day Panama) with Pedrarias Dávila
1515	Returns to Spain
1516	Audiences with King Ferdinand and, later, Charles V
1519	Audience with Charles V; granted a governorship, which he declines
	Public encounter with Bartolomé de Las Casas
	Publishes chivalric novel, *Don Claribalte*
1520	Returns to Darién with his wife, Isabel, and their two children; all three die within two years
1522	Appointed lieutenant governor for Darién by Pedrarias Dávila, who moved the governing seat of Castilla del Oro to Panama; Oviedo steps down from the position within the year
	Attempt on his life
1523	Returns to Spain, marries Catalina de Ribafrecha en route in Santo Domingo
	First granted the governorship of Cartagena

1524 Audience with Charles V and further charges made against Pedrarias Dávila

1525 Secures the removal of Pedrarias Dávila as governor of Castilla del Oro
Under a more favorable contract, granted the governorship of Cartagena

1526 Publishes his first text about the Indies, the *Sumario,* in Toledo
Obtains license to publish a translation of Boccaccio's *Il corvaccio,* which was never published
Sails for Cartagena to take up the governorship but resigns before beginning

ca.1527–1529 Lives in León, Nicaragua, and works with its new governor, Pedrarias Dávila

ca. 1528 Writes the still-unpublished *Libro primero del Blasón,* a treatise on heraldry

1529 Returns to Panama

1530 Returns to Spain as an agent (*procurador*) to petition the court on behalf of the cities of Panama and Santo Domingo

1532 Named royal chronicler of the Indies, and later commander (*alcaide*) of the fort in Santo Domingo
Completes the first volume of the genealogy of the royal family, the *Catálogo Real*
Around this time, writes the *Relación . . . del rey Francisco de Francia,* an account of the king's Spanish captivity in 1525
Returns to the Indies and establishes his household in Santo Domingo

1534 Sails for Spain
Initiates petitions
Turns his manuscript history over to the Council of the Indies

1535 Publishes at his own expense the first part of the *Historia general y natural de las Indias* in Seville
Presents the *Epílogo Real, imperial y pontifical* to Charles V
Writes the first draft of a manual about the organization of Prince Don Juan's household, *Libro de la cámara,* for Prince Philip II
Completes the second and third parts of the *Catálogo Real*

1536 Returns to Santo Domingo
Repairs the fortress and continues work on the *Historia*
Son, Francisco, dies in Peru while performing his duties as *veedor*

1542 Trip to Spain to publish the rest of the *Historia* planned but canceled because of war with French in the Caribbean

1546 Sails for Spain

1547 Second edition of part I of the *Historia* published in Salamanca
Final draft of the *Libro de la cámara* complete
Work possibly begun on the *Batallas y quinquagenas,* a series of biographical-heraldic dialogues about noble Spanish gentlemen at the turn of the sixteenth century

1548 Translation of a popular Italian spiritual guide, *Reglas de la vida,* published in Seville

1549 Final version of the *Historia* deposited in a monastery in Seville after its publication had been blocked

Returns to Santo Domingo for the final time

1550 Last additions made to his still-incomplete *Batallas y quinquagenas*

1551 Marriage of his daughter, Juana

1555 The presentation of the still partially unpublished *Quinquagenas,* a three-volume work in prose and poetry with illustrations about Spanish nobility, to Prince Philip

1557 Third edition of part I of the *Historia* (this time including the first book of part II) published in Valladolid

Publication of entire part II of the *Historia* begins with book 20; the rest is cut short by Oviedo's death

June 27, 1557 Oviedo dies in Santo Domingo; his son-in-law inherits the position of *alcaide*

APPENDIX B

Map of Hispaniola and Tierra Firme, ca. 1540

APPENDIX C

Translations of passages from Fernández de Oviedo's Historia general y natural de las Indias

TRANSLATOR'S NOTE

Translating colonial texts is an exercise in masochism, and I often wonder why I enjoy doing it. I suppose it is because I love the colonial period, especially relations of the wonders of the Americas in the initial years, a project in which Fernando González de Oviedo participated as few others did. I also enjoy working with Kathleen Myers. We have collaborated before (*Neither Saints nor Sinners: Writing the Lives of Women in America*), and for her sake I agreed to take on Oviedo, one of the most challenging translations I have ever worked through.

Oviedo sets up many linguistic minefields in his voluminous and ever-evolving magnum opus. His sentences can be interminable (I bushwhacked my way through one that was twenty-nine lines long), so, to spare the contemporary reader, I inserted punctuation or simply broke them up into more manageable units. Conjunctions are frequently omitted. At times Oviedo's spelling is different from contemporary Spanish ("ternán" instead of "tendrán," for example). His use of relative and possessive pronouns can be whimsical, and the meaning of certain words obscure. The one which gave me the most trouble was "gisola," but more about that later.

Like many other early chroniclers of the Americas, Oviedo lacked a classical education and was thus slightly insecure as a writer. Again like other chroniclers, he underscored the authority he derived from experience to counterbalance his lack of Latin and Greek. He reiterates this point many times in the "Prologue" to the Emperor Charles V:

> At least that which I shall write will be a true history, deviating from all the fables which in the matter other writers, without seeing [these things], from Spain and without getting their feet wet, have presumed to write with elegant and uncommon prose, in Latin and in the vernacular, based on information from many different sources, and have produced histories more attuned to fine style than to the veracity of what is told, for just as a blind man cannot distinguish colors, so the man who is not there is unable to attest to things, [as compared to] him who sees them.

Oviedo's lack of classical training also made life harder for me. In spite of—or perhaps because of—his uncertainty in Latin, Oviedo at times threw in Latin phrases, some of which make no sense whatsoever (see the penultimate paragraph of the Prologue). He also made clear his debt to Pliny the Elder (23–79 CE) and his famous *Natural History* in the organization of his material on the Americas. While speaking of Pliny, Oviedo further referred to a saying by another Roman, one he called "Plancho." Who on earth could that be? Thank God for my contacts in local departments of Classics, as my own command of Latin is rudimentary at best. Whereas the phrase referred to above—*Nulla umquam in hispaniis victoria viator vel similis invenitur*—had stumped both George Ryan and Teresa Ramsby, from the mangled quote Oviedo associated with "Plancho" Teresa could piece together that he was referring to Lucius Munatius Plancus (87–15 BCE), one of Caesar's friends. A lot of spadework to clear up one identity.

As Kathleen Myers makes clear in this book, Oviedo was fully aware of his unique capabilities as a chronicler. In him serendipity combined a thirst for knowledge, ambition, and tenacity. As I was ruminating on the writing of this note, I realized that I, too, brought to bear some unique qualifications as his translator. Besides a strong background in colonial studies and fluency in both Spanish and English, I am an Episcopalian who sails. Let me explain.

In doing translations from the sixteenth and seventeenth centuries, cadence is a quality to which I give high priority. As a practicing Episcopalian, biblical cadences are ingrained in me, especially those of the stately King James Version of the Bible; this often helped me to keep my translations respectful of Oviedo's own interior rhythms. I am also an avid sailor and reader of maritime histories and novels, especially Samuel Eliot Morison, C. S. Forester's Hornblower series, and Patrick O'Brien's Aubrey/Maturin novels. Having cruised midcoast Maine with my husband for over forty years, I am familiar with nautical terms such as mizzens, spankers, sounding, beating, tacking, etc., which came in very handy in translating a number of Oviedo's chapters dealing with maritime exploration. In spite of this expertise I almost met my Waterloo when Oviedo spoke of his practical skill in navigation. Studying cosmology at a university was one thing, he said, but his expertise came from what he termed "la cátedra de la gisola" or "the lecture hall of the gisola." But what on earth was a gisola? All manner of dictionaries, both contemporary and historical, came up with no results. My husband and I talked this conundrum over and decided, since the term clearly had to do with navigation, translating it as "the quarterdeck," the place on a ship were navigational decisions were made, was probably a good compromise. But as a wordsmith I was not content. Enter two loyal and qualified graduate students. David Arbesú and Yamile Silva were tireless in their attempts to help me, and both finally came up with the definition: "the box in which the compass was housed." In nautical terminology, a binnacle. As this is not a word which is familiar to the general reader, I left it "the lecture hall of the quarterdeck," figuring it was metonymically accurate with respect to the binnacle. Arriving at this *mot juste* took at least three weeks, but what joy for the translator!

These are examples of the backstage work that needs to be done in order to translate responsibly. (Here I want to enter a word of thanks to my colleague and friend, Maria Tymoczko, whose insights into the process of translation have been invaluable to me.) Technology has made the job easier, but only to a degree, as was pointed out in an article on the translation project of the Oxyrhynchus Papiri at Oxford. The project director's remarks as to the qualifications of his translators resonated with me for obvious reasons: "You have to put [pool] all your knowledge of language and literature to put a story together and provide a context. There has been a boom in technology, but it doesn't replace the knowledge of the language and the eye that has to focus on the details" (quoted in Sarah Lyall, "Historical Discovery? Well, Yes and No," *New York Times,* May 30, 2005, B6.)

There is never a final translation, and this is no exception, but it's my best shot. Oviedo may have been an irascible, litigious curmudgeon, but he had access to incredible sources and the will to compile them. For that my hat is off to him. May my translations make these accessible to the English-speaking reader.

Nina M. Scott

1. PROLOGUE, PART I, BOOK I

This is the beginning of the first book of this volume. It consists of the preamble or introduction to this first part of the General and Natural History of the Indies, *directed to the Holy, Imperial, Catholic and Royal Majesty of the Emperor King, our Lord.*

Holy, Imperial, Catholic, Royal Majesty.

Albulensis, also known as El Tostado,[1] commented on the statement that the glorious doctor of the Church, Saint Jerome, made concerning Eusebius (*About the Times*), that the Ethiopians flourished by the banks of the Indus River. This [country of] Ethiopia is partly in Asia and partly in Africa. But the eastern Ethiopians are in India, which, according to Isidore (*Etymologies,* Book XIV, chap. III, "Regarding Asia"), got its name from the Indus River: *India vocata ab Indo flumine.* This same author, on a prior occasion, says that the Indus River flows into the Red Sea in the east: *Indus fluvius orientis qui rubro mari accipitur.* This is the eastern part of Ethiopia, but in modern and tested cosmography I see the Indus River not as the abovementioned authors wrote, but five hundred or more leagues removed from the Red and the Persian Seas; it flows into the ocean by the shores of the city called Lima, at the mouth of which is the kingdom of Cambaya; between this same Indus River and the Ganges is the greater or eastern part of India, which is, as I have said, very far from the Red Sea, and farther east than the Ethiopians, against whom it is said that Moses, as a captain of the Egyptians, was sent to fight. Yet later these Ethiopians were good Christians, and, as El Tostado says in the place cited above, were converted to the faith by Saint Matthew the Apostle. The beginning of the conversion was begun by the holy Eunuch, majordomo of Queen Candaçis, baptized and instructed by Saint Philip the Apostle.

I wish to point out and explain what I mean by true cosmography: that here I shall not refer to those Indies of which I have previously spoken, but to the Indies, islands and mainland of the Ocean Sea, which are presently under the dominion of the royal crown of Castile; in these your Indies are included innumerable and very large kingdoms, and provinces of such great wonder and riches as will be made known in the books of this *General and Natural History*.

Therefore, I beg Your Imperial Majesty to make my nightly labors worthwhile by concentrating your mind upon them, for naturally every man wishes to know, and rational understanding is what makes him superior to any other creature; in this superiority he is like God, such as in that part [of Genesis] where He said: "Let us create man in our image and likeness." For this reason neither our will nor our spirit are content with understanding and speculating on only a few things, nor with regarding those which are ordinary, close to or even within our native land. Rather, ([those men] who most share this sweet desire), by travelling through other far-flung provinces, and after many and varied dangers, never cease to inquire on land and sea about the marvelous and uncounted works which God Himself, the Lord of all, reveals to us, so that we should praise Him all the more [while] satisfying the delightful acquisitiveness of this our pilgrimage. And He declares to us, by what we see on earth, that He Who could create all is sufficient for all we do not comprehend of Him, due to His greatness and our lack of stature. [This is] principally because of the human limitation which is part of our mortal being, from which stem other causes and inconveniences which might impair such a praiseworthy occupation as seeing with our physical eyes what in this creation is visible to them (besides that which may be contemplated) of this universal sphere which the Greeks call *cosmos* and the Latins *mundo*.[2] Some cosmographers would have it that much less than a fifth thereof is inhabited; from which opinion I am very far removed, as a man who, apart from all that Ptolemy wrote, knows that in this empire of the Indies (which Your Imperial Majesty and the royal crown of Castile possess) there are such great kingdoms and provinces, and such very strange peoples, of different customs, rites and idolatries, far removed from anything which has been recorded, *ab initio* up to our own time, that the span of a man's life is hardly sufficient [either] to see it, to begin to comprehend, or [even] to conjecture upon it.

What mortal understanding can comprehend such diversity of languages, habits, [or] customs among the people of the Indies? Such variety of animals, from domestic to wild and savage? Such an unutterable multitude of trees, [some] laden with diverse kinds of fruit and others barren, both those which the Indians cultivate and those produced by Nature's own work without the aid of human hands? How many plants and herbs which are useful and beneficial to man? How many innumerable others unknown to him, whose flowers and sweet fragrances are so different from the ones he knows? Such diversity of birds of prey and other raptors? So many high and fertile mountains, with others so varied and harsh? How many plains and arable places suitable for agriculture, and with exceedingly useful access to rivers? How many mountains more astonishing and frightening than Etna or Mongibel, Vulcan and Estrogol, with one and all under your rule?

Ancient poets and historians might not have praised the ones I have [just] mentioned had they known of Masaya, Maribio and Guajocingo, and those which anon will be spoken of by this your writer and scribe.

How many even valleys and delightful flowers! How many coastlines with generous beaches and most excellent harbors! How many and such mighty navigable rivers! What numerous and great lakes! How many cold and hot springs, in close proximity to each other! So much tar and other materials and liquids! How many fish, both those we know in Spain, as well as many others which have been neither known nor seen there? How many mines of gold and silver and copper! What rich amounts of pearls and precious stones are found each day! Where was it ever known or heard of that in such a brief span of time, and in places so far removed from our own Europe, so many products and so much livestock, brought over such boundless wide seas, could be raised, and in such abundance as our eyes have seen in these Indies? And this domain has received these things not as a stepmother, but as a truer mother than the land which sent them, for some of them are more numerous and better than those produced in Spain, be it livestock which is useful to the service of man, or bread, vegetables, fruit, sugar and cañafístola;[3] the first of these items left Spain in my own time, and in a short while have multiplied to such a degree that ships laden with sugar, cañafístola, and cow hides return to provide these for Spain. And the same [trade] could be established with other items not mentioned here, [yet which] these Indies, before the Spaniards discovered them, produced and still produce: goods such as cotton, archil,[4] brazil wood, alum, and other products which are desired by many kingdoms of this world, and which would be very useful to them. Our merchants disdain them, preferring to load their ships solely with gold, silver and pearls, and the other things I mentioned previously.

As what might be written about this enormous new empire is so vast, and the reading thereof so admirable, the account itself will excuse me with Your Imperial Majesty if it is not told as fully as the material itself demands: it is sufficient that I, as a man who all these years has regarded these things, will use what life is left him in setting down this sweet and agreeable *General and Natural History of the Indies,* using all I have seen and may see, and that which has and may still come to my attention, from its first discovery, with all I may see and attain thereof, as long as my life shall last. But the mercy of Your Imperial Majesty towards a servant who serves you from these parts and perseveres with his natural inclination to inquire, as I have inquired into some of these things, has seen fit to ask me to write and send them to your Royal Council of the Indies, so that, as they are augmented and become better known, they may be included in its glorious *Spanish Chronicle*. By means of this treatise, Your Majesty, besides serving the Lord our God by publishing and making known to the rest of the world what is under your royal Castilian sceptre, you do a great favor to all Christian kingdoms by providing them with the opportunity of rendering infinite thanks to God for the expansion of their holy Catholic faith. This, with your holy and most Christian zeal, increases each day in these Indies. And this will be the glorious culmination of the immortality of your perpetual and unique fame, that not only will faithful Christians serve Your Imperial Majesty, who, [with] great kindness will instruct them to communicate this true and new history, but even the infidels and idolaters of the entire world, who may dwell far from these lands, on hearing of these miracles will see themselves obliged to do the same, praising the Creator thereof, being as how [the Indies] are so unknown to them, and far from their hemisphere and horizons.

This is a matter, most powerful Lord, in which my age and diligence, given the greatness of the objective and of its circumstances, cannot be sufficient for its perfect definition, granted my flawed style and the brevity of my days. But at least that which I shall write will be a true history, deviating from all the fables which in this matter other writers, without seeing [these things], from Spain and without getting their feet wet, have presumed to write with elegant and uncommon prose, in Latin and in the vernacular, based on information from many different sources, and have produced histories more attuned to fine style than to the veracity of what is told, for just as a blind man cannot distinguish colors, so the man who is not there is unable to attest to things, [as compared to] him who sees them.

I wish to assure Your Imperial Majesty that my lines will be stripped of an abundance of artificial words created to entice readers, but they will be most copious with the truth, and in accordance therewith, will say what does not contradict it, so that your sovereign kindness may send it [the book] to be polished and glossed. Given the care and truthfulness [I used in writing] what here is informing Your Magnificence, may he who takes charge of correcting [my text] not deviate from the intention and the work, retelling it in a better style; not least so that it will not offend my good wish, nor do I wish to be denied praise for a work which has taken me so long and with so many obstacles which I have suffered, compiling and inquiring in all the ways I was able to know the certainty of these subjects from the year 1513 of the birth of our Savior, when King Ferdinand the Catholic, of glorious memory, grandfather of Your Imperial Majesty, sent me as his inspector of the gold foundries to Panama, where I fulfilled that office the best I could, such as in the conquest and pacification of some parts of those lands by means of arms, serving God and Your Majesties as captain and vassal during those harsh beginnings in which a number of cities and towns were settled, which now are populated by Christians,[5] [and] where, with great glory for the royal sceptre of Spain, [our] holy religion has continued to be served.

In said conquest, those of us who came with Pedrarias Dávila, deputy and captain general of the Catholic King and later of Your Majesties, must have numbered about two thousand men, and there we encountered another five hundred or more Spaniards under the command of Vasco Núñez de Balboa in the city of Darién (which was also earlier called la Guardia and later Santa María de la Antigua); this same city was the seat of the bishopric of Castilla del Oro, today deserted, and not without grave fault of the one who caused this [Dávila], for it was located in the place which was most suitable for the conquest of the Indian archers of that region. And of these two thousand five hundred men I have mentioned, there are, I believe, today not forty left in or out of all of the Indies, for, to serve Your Majesties, and to assure the safety of the Christians who later went to those regions, it was best, or better said, essential, that this be accomplished. At the cost of our lives we endured the harsh nature of the territory, the climate, the dense vegetation and underbrush, the danger of the rivers there, great lizards and tigers, and testing water and food, in order to benefit the traders and settlers who, reaping what others sowed, now enjoy the fruits of other men's labors.

And while Your Imperial Majesty was in Toledo in the year of our Lord 1525, I wrote a summary of part of what is contained here, whose title was: OVIEDO, *Of the Natural History of the Indies,* whereas this [present] treatise will be entitled *General and Natural History of the Indies.* All that was contained in the summary can be found in this and in the other two parts, in the second and the third, better and more fully stated, because the [earlier version] was written in Spain, while my materials and sources were in the city of Santo Domingo on the island of Hispaniola (where my home is). In the ten years which have passed since I wrote the former I have seen much more than what I then knew of these topics, focusing far greater attention on those things which it was particularly important to see and understand. Furthermore, it should be noted that all which that [former] report or summary contains will be [included] in this treatise, its sections expanded, and with other amazing and completely new items, of which earlier I had no knowledge, having neither seen nor known of them.

And so, most powerful Lord, for the reasons explained above, it is right that these histories be made known in all the world's republics, so that all the world should realize the extent and greatness of these states which God retained for your royal Castilian crown for the good fortune and merits of Your Imperial Majesty, under whose favor and protection I offer the present work, and humbly beg, in recompense for the time I have worked thereon, and the length of time I have served your royal house of Castile, [for it has been] more than forty years that I have been among the number of servants thereof, that you will be pleased to accept my books; for, though the ones I here write do not entail much skill or ingenuity, nor are of such quality as to require long speeches and verbal adornment, they have not been created without much labor, nor with the ease with which other topics may be compiled and written down, but it is, at least, very pleasurable reading to hear about and understand so many secrets of Nature.

If one finds a number of strange and barbarous words here, the explanation therefore is the newness of what is being written about. I will not have my language skills questioned, for I was born in Madrid, grew up in the royal household, conversed with noble folk, and have read a thing or two, so that people might suspect that I do understand my own Castilian language, which among the spoken languages is held to be the best of all. Whatever is in this volume which might not sound right will be names or words I have put down of my own volition to explain the things the Indians mean by them.

May Your Majesty compensate for the failures of my pen with my good intentions. As Pliny said of his own [pen] in the prologue to his *Natural History*: it is hard to make old things new; to bestow authority on what is new; brilliance to what is out of the ordinary; clarity to the obscure; wit to the tedious, and authenticity to what is doubtful. It is sufficient that I have desired and desire to serve Your Imperial Majesty and please whomever may see my work, and if I have not known how to do this, let my intention be praised. May the reader be satisfied with what I have seen and lived with many dangers; may he enjoy it and suffer none of them, and may he be able to read it in his own country without undergoing such hunger and thirst, heat and cold, or innumerable other travails, without venturing into storms at sea, nor the misfortunes one suffers in those lands. For his benefit and leisure was I born and have adventured and seen these works of Nature, or, better said, the Master of Nature, [all of] which I have written down in twenty books which are contained in this first part or volume, as well as the second and third parts, on which I am at present occupied, [and] which will address matters pertaining to Tierra Firme.[6]

Actually, the last book, which here is placed as number twenty, will later on be put at the end of the third part, because it is suited to all three; this [part] is entitled *Of misfortunes and shipwrecks, of events which took place in the seas of these Indies.* All of these books are divided according to the nature and quality of the matters discussed therein; I have not culled them from two hundred thousand volumes I might have read, as Pliny wrote in the example discussed above, where it seems that he related what he had read, and in some cases he says that he augmented what the ancients had not understood or [when] life [experience] proved them to be wrong; I, however, compiled what I here write from two hundred thousand hardships, privations and dangers in the more than twenty-two years that I have personally witnessed and experienced these things, serving God and my king in these Indies, and having crossed the wide ocean eight times.

Furthermore, though I am in no way qualified to follow or imitate Pliny himself (neither in repeating what he said, [nor] as a model of the universal character of the *Natural History,* though I follow his way of organizing my books and their topics, as he did), I do agree with what he confirms in his introduction, where he says that it is an indication of a depraved character and of an unfortunate mind purposely to desire to be caught with the booty [rather] than to return what has been lent him, above all when profits are made by means of usury. So as not to incur in such a crime, nor to fail to acknowledge what is Pliny's (such as the organization and the title of the book), in this matter I do imitate him.

In one way my book will differ from Pliny's model: this will be to relate something of the conquest of these Indies, and, at the beginning, justify the reason for their discovery and other matters; though they are outside [my] *Natural History* they will be essential to it in order to understand the origin and foundation of it all, especially so that there will be a better understanding of what impelled the Catholic Kings Don Fernando and Doña Isabel, Your Imperial Majesty's grandparents, to search for these lands, or, better stated, what made God impel them.

All these matters, and what may pertain to particular accounts, will be clarified and put in their appropriate place, with the help of the Holy Spirit and His divine aid, with the express desire that all that this text may contain shall be under the correction and emendation of our Holy Mother and Apostolic Roman Church, whose servant and least creature I am, and in whose obedience I promise to live and die. But, because all those jealous of their honor and personal rectitude feared the criticism of their detractors, and not only Pliny, who was such a renowned author, but many others who cannot be enumerated, even holy King David himself when he begged God to free him from a devious tongue; with much greater reason I should fear the same, for the dead and the absent cannot answer for themselves. As Pliny repeated that saying by Plancho,[7] when he said that the dead do not fight or dispute except with masks, so I, besides all this, want to say to those who reprove me from Europe, Asia, or Africa: let them realize that I am not physically located in any of these three places (as can be surmised from what has been seen and discovered of the southern sea and the curvature which the earth takes around it to the North and the Cape of Labrador). As readers must listen to me from very far away, may they not judge me without seeing this land where I am and about which I write; may it suffice that I write from here, in a time of innumerable eye witnesses, and that my books are written for Your Imperial Majesty, whose empire this is, and that they are written at his command, that I earn my living as the chronicler of these matters, and that I am not so devoid of wit as to dare to relate the opposite of the truth before such august and Imperial Majesty so as to forfeit his grace and my honor. Besides, these are not matters which are discussed for specific persons' ambitious honors, [using] words and fictions in the hope of being gratified by anyone; rather, in accepting that true statement of the wise man who said "*the mouth that lies smites the soul,*" I trust in God that He will preserve my own from such danger, and that, as faithful scribe, I shall be rewarded by Him for the great liberality of His compassion and the royal command of Your Imperial Majesty, whose glorious person may Our Lord favor for many years and allow to enjoy his complete reign, as your exalted heart desires and we, your loyal and true subjects desire, of which the entire universal Christian republic has need, *Amen.*

For among all the princes who in this world call themselves faithful and Christian, only Your Imperial Majesty at present sustains the Catholic religion and Church of God, and protects it against the populous, wicked sect and great power of Mohammed, sending its principal chief, the Grand Turk, into exile, with such great shedding of Turkish blood, and such splendid victories at sea and on land, as happened earlier, in the years 1532 and 1533, when other Christian princes were silent, awaiting how these actions of yours would come out; our merciful and just God led events and actions to such an immortal triumph that it will not be forgotten as long as men live; and so it will be accepted and rewarded in the heavenly life, in which Your Imperial Majesty will be glorified along with the blessed King Recaredo, the first of this name, and his brother, Saint Hermenegildo the martyr, from whom stems the extensive branch and ancient origin of your royal lineage and Spanish throne; of whom el Burgensis[8] said that when sixty thousand French invaded Spain, King Recaredo sent his Captain General, Claudius, out from Toledo, who vanquished them, killing and capturing the majority; for which reason [el Burgensis] said, *Nulla umquam in hispaniis victoria viator vel similis invenitur.*[9] Archbishop Rodrigo, whom el Burgensis succeeded, writes in the same vein, and these excellent men could better describe [these matters] if they had seen what your captains and subjects achieved in the year 1525 against [the French] King Francis, his cavalry and his might, [which resulted in] the imprisonment of his person and that of many of the most illustrious men of his kingdom in the siege of Pavia, or were they to see that which we trust God will do to further your good fortune and triumphant name.

All of these [matters] are for your elegant chroniclers over there in Spain, who will enjoy seeing and writing about them; whereas here, in these very remote lands, those of us who cherish [being in] your royal service and who may not see what is said of Your Imperial Majesty's victories, receive such a share in this joy as all men feel who love their prince as they should, as loyal subjects and Christians; because in truth I do not think men could call themselves such who forget to give everlasting thanks to God for the increase of Your Imperial person and life, for in it are contained our own, and all the benefits of the Christian religion.

2. BOOK 29, CHAPTER 6

Concerning the trip made by the governor, Pedrarias Dávila, to Tierra Firme, called Castilla del Oro, where Vasco Núñez de Balboa was captain.

Because of the complaints which Bachelor Enciso had lodged with His Most Serene and Catholic Majesty, King Don Fernando, against Vasco Núñez, in which he always made mention of his unjust prison and exile, and of the cruelty he had shown against Diego de Nicuesa; and because of the report which later on was drawn up by the representatives of Darién—the overseer Juan de Quicedo and Captain Rodrigo de Colmenares—and the letters against him written by Bachelor Diego del Corral and Gonzalo de Badajoz, who was Diego de Nicuesa's lieutenant, and Luis de Mercado and Alonso Pérez de la Rúa, whom Vasco Núñez had imprisoned, the King decided to send Pedrarias Dávila with a splendid fleet in order to ascertain about Vasco Núñez de Balboa's guilt, and to govern Castilla del Oro in Tierra Firme.

For this [venture] at least three thousand men gathered in Seville, and there [also] went the officials which the King had sent for his financial matters: Alonso de la

Puente as treasurer, Diego Márquez as paymaster, Juan de Tabira as agent, Juan de Quicedo as overseer of the gold foundries (he died back in Seville, and I, the chronicler, Gonzalo Fernández de Oviedo y Valdés, was granted this office of overseer by [Ferdinand] the Catholic King). Pedrarias's principal magistrate was Bachelor Gaspar de Espinosa, who later on appropriated a Master's title, and hailed from Medina de Ríoseco, while the lieutenant of commander-in-chief Pedrarias was a nobleman from Córdoba, called Juan de Ayora, the brother of the chronicler Gonzalo de Ayora. The captains of groups of a hundred men were: Luis Carrillo; Francisco Dávila; Antonio Téllez de Guzmán; Diego de Bustamante; Contreras; Francisco Vázquez Coronado de Valdés; Juan de Zorita; Gamarra; Villafañe; Atienza; Gaspar de Morales, the governor's cousin; Pedrarias the younger, who was going for artillery captain, and was the governor's nephew; Gonzalo Fernández de Lago; and Captain Meneses. I have named them because from all of them, or most of them, and from others who were already over there, and others who subsequently called themselves captains and were such, things afterwards came to be that belong in this story and are important.

In terms of spiritual matters, the bishop Brother Don Juan de Quevedo, of the Order of Saint Francis, went, the first prelate to go to Tierra Firme, with the title of Bishop of Santa María de la Antigua and of Castilla del Oro. The seat of that bishopric was the town I called Santa María de la Antigua del Darién, which was taken by Vasco Núñez and those who remained of Captain Alonso de Hojeda's fleet. After the establishment of the bishopric, this [town], by order of the Pope and the Catholic King, was denominated a city and was metropolitan and seat, as was mentioned, of the bishopric of Castilla del Oro, because these were noble people.

In light of what happened later, I state that, among the orders and charges which the Catholic King resolved and sent on to Pedrarias, his governor, was that he was to be especially careful with the following four matters: first, that with great attention and vigilance he was to deal with the conversion and good treatment of the Indians; second, that no attorneys were to enter those lands, nor were there to be any lawyers or prosecutors in the land, for, as experience on this island and other places had proven, they were pernicious to the country, and, as masters of litigation and disputes, concoct more than there would be without them; court proceedings were to be decided speedily, simply and plainly, without allowing malicious ponderings, with justice meted out to all parties; third, that the Indians were to be read a certain notification (*requerimiento*) before declaring war on them, which will be mentioned later; fourth, that in all important matters the bishop and officials would be informed and their counsel sought. In all of these things the intention of the Prince who decided them is evident, holy and good, with the idea that governor and prelate would always be in agreement in the service of God and King, in the good governance and administration of the State, the pacification of the Indians and the colonization of the land. But it all came out the opposite, as from matters that were to be resolved for the common good there arose two factions and interest groups which turned out to be very harmful, one passionately in the service of the governor, the other of the bishop. In this way, officials who were to temper [the factions] and to try to reach agreement among them were embroiled in these same conflicts, as will be elaborated on later in its proper place.

After the fleet had been fitted out, there was a delay in departure because of the weather, and, because of new information which came from Tierra Firme, the King ordered half of the people to be dismissed, so that only fifteen hundred men were to go; after having put on a fine show in Seville, they were let go, and the governor, with the fifteen hundred, proceeded to Sanlúcar de Barrameda. But because of the great things which were told of those lands the number of people kept increasing to over two thousand or more, and these were some of the finest and best-selected people who ever went to the Indies. And had no more than five hundred gone, it would have been just fine for what happened later on.

And so, with twenty-two *naos* and caravels the fleet set sail, taking as principal pilot Juan Serrano (he who was subsequently killed with Captain Ferdinand Magellan in the discovery of the great Strait and the Spice voyage, as was told in Book XX, Chapter I). This fleet departed with very good weather from the port of Sanlúcar de Barrameda on Shrove Sunday in the year 1514. After the flagship had sailed some four or five leagues into the open sea, the weather suddenly changed and it had to turn back. The last ship to leave the harbor was the one I was on, and there was yet one more still at anchor, in which the treasurer Diego Márquez sailed, which refused to cast off because her pilot, named Pedro Miguel, had better knowledge of conditions than any other: he saw that the weather was unfavorable and stayed put. The weather turned into a gale—which some called a howling westerly—and was very severe. The river pilots had let the ships depart into the open sea and had returned to Sanlúcar in their boats, but as the sea was very rough, the weather obliged the fleet to return to the river. As the ship on which I sailed had been the last to leave, it was the first to return; on entering by the sandbar, we ran aground, and since we had no pilot were on the brink of foundering. God in His mercy chose to come to our aid, and with one side of the ship almost taking on water we anchored inside the Guadalquivir River from which we had departed. One by one the *naos* and caravels of the fleet did the same. We were in the harbor for two days without being able to go ashore because of the weather, nor were the ships safe in the river, with some dragging and others lying to, so that we were still feeling the effects of the storm. But at last the weather improved, and, so that the provisions should not be eaten up, the governor and all his people disembarked, in order to wait on land for better weather for our venture. Since so much time had gone by waiting to sail we were all worn out and in penury, and the ones who had persevered until the second departure even more so; many decided on other ventures and gave up the voyage, going home or wherever they wished, and these were luckier than others. We were in this situation all during Lent, doing voluntary penance, many pawning their cloaks in order to eat, and others their cloaks and coats and anything else, until it pleased God during Holy Week to bring us the weather for which we were waiting. On Holy Tuesday, the 11th of April of 1514, the fleet set sail again and followed its course with good weather.

Eight or nine days later it entered the harbor on the island of Gomera, where we spent twenty days taking on fresh stores of meat and fish, cheese, water and wood, and from there we proceeded on with very favorable weather. One Saturday, on the third of June, the eve of Pentecost, the fleet anchored by the island of Dominica, at a watering place where there is a good river; the people went ashore and were there for three days with the flagship anchored next to the river. The day after we arrived was Pentecost; solemn mass was said, with general rejoicing by all. Captain General Pedrarias ordered that the inlet be named the Bay of Fonseca, as though back then he had been the first to discover it.

This is a practice I mock and many laugh at; in some places in this history I reprove it, and will never praise anyone who does this, unless he be a sovereign and there be just cause to nullify a prior name. That particular bay was discovered years before, and many of our pilots and seamen who were there with us had seen it, known it, and entered it on other occasions. But it seems that governors and captains who are newly arrived in these lands feel it is fine to change the names of harbors, rivers, mountains and headlands in order to enhance their own deeds and relegate to oblivion those which their predecessors had accomplished; this is something I will not allow to happen in my histories, nor will I take away any man's merits. I know very well that the bishop of Palencia, Don Juan Rodríguez de Fonseca, who at that time was president of the Royal Council of the Indies, was the reason why this governor was selected for this office, and, in order to ingratiate himself with this man, it seemed good to Pedrarias to affix the name of Fonseca onto that bay. However, I will not refrain from telling the truth, and, as faithful chronicler, will make people aware of such names wherever I may encounter them and see that someone who has no right to do this is unjustly altering them. So, this cove or harbor is called the "Watering Place," and is on the island of Dominica, on the western side, fourteen degrees from this part of the equinoctial line.

That is where the governor reached his agreement with the bishop, officials, pilots and with Bachelor Enciso, who acted as principal magistrate of that settlement, and with Captain Rodrigo de Colmenares, as men who said they knew the coast of Tierra Firme, about the way in which the voyage should be conducted from there on. The King had commanded that Pedrarias, as far as he was able [and] without the obstacle of a defeat on his way to Darién, should reconnoiter certain islands and harbors belonging to the Caribs, such as Santa Cruz, La Guaira, Cartagena, Caramari, Codego, and the islands of Barú, St. Bernard, Arenas and Fuerte, which long ago had been declared territories where slaves could be taken, by reason of the fact that in all of these aforementioned islands and harbors the people eat human flesh, and also because of the harm they had done to Christians and to other Indians who were the King's vassals, as on many occasions they had killed Spaniards who had sailed into these places. They agreed that the fleet should reconnoiter Cape Aguja at Santa Marta, which is on the coast of Tierra Firme, to ascertain if eleven Christians were still alive, who, Captain Rodrigo Colmenares said, had been left there when the

[Indians] had killed over thirty of his men; they also wanted to explore the nature of the land and construct a fortress there, which was very necessary to protect the ships which might come later on. Afterwards the fleet would go from there to Cartagena and Codego, and to Barú and Fuerte islands (for they were directly in the path which the fleet would take to Darién), but refrain from going to Santa Cruz because that island was disproportionately out of the way in the voyage.

Many times later on, as time went by and there was discussion of the advice which we there took, I have seen it gossiped and laughed about with others of those who were then there, when we recalled such immense foolishness as to have given credence in that matter to such a man as Captain Rodrigo de Colmenares, for he had acknowledged that in La Guaira thirty of his men had been killed when he sailed by there in a ship, on his way from this city of Santo Domingo to Darién, and did not deny that he had left there so as to avoid offending the Indians, and more than just in passing had sought safety in the ship and had sailed away. We will see with what kind of safeconduct and under what assurance those eleven Christians had been left behind, which he presumed were still alive! . . . In Castile some men of scant knowledge have remarked on this and much other nonsense, for they see that those who listen to them do not understand them.

In the end, because of that agreement or proposal, on the following day by order of the general everyone embarked at the previously mentioned harbor on Dominica or the Watering Place, but as a number of our companions were missing, he ordered some of the lombard cannons fired, so that if anyone had gone inland, he would come back to be picked up. For this purpose Lieutenant Juan de Ayora remained ashore that night with a group of guards and the trumpets, which he had sounded from time to time. In this way several youths were picked up, and among the last there came one who had served the governor for many years, and whose name was St. Martin. Because he was so late, the lieutenant had harsh words for him, and St. Martin, now angry, said that he would not get aboard and wanted to stay there on the beach. One should not believe this was really his intention; rather, he was replying angrily for having received a tongue lashing. Juan de Ayora, respecting the fact that he was one of the governor's men, went to tell the latter what his servant was saying. Because of this, the angry Pedrarias, without listening further, sent Captain Gaspar de Morales, his cousin and servant, with orders not to listen to or mind a word but to hang him from a tree there on the mainland. Several of the guard's halberdiers went with the captain; the orders were carried out, and thus the sinner was hanged. It is true that about five or six months after this a suit was brought against [the governor] in Darién, accusing him of disobedience, but what many suspected and complained about in this speedy execution of justice, as well as the reward which the governor bestowed on that particular servant, was that it was a case of settling some old account or unpleasantness which had occurred [between them] some time ago.

An hour later, as I was with the governor on his ship, there came an honorable cleric on behalf of the bishop—his chaplain, named Cantado—and told the general that his lord the bishop requested that he permit this man to be buried, seeing as how he was a Christian, and should not be left hanging there for the Indians to eat, and the governor said that this should be done. This cleric himself and some others, escorted by several soldiers, went ashore and buried him at the foot of the tree, on the very beach of the bay. This cruel and hasty execution alarmed many, for they suspected that the governor we were accompanying was going to be extremely harsh and in fact would do other things without heeding law or process, and it would be prudent for each man to step carefully, as it was with his own servants that he began to show how he would punish others.

Returning to our voyage, we left the island of Dominica one day after Easter. On Monday, the twelfth of June, the fleet arrived at the port of Santa Marta, which is on the Garra coast in Castilla del Oro, and there began Pedrarias's governance. At ten in the morning all of the *naos* and ships were moored or at anchor in the harbor. On land numerous Indian bowmen were walking there on the beach, from one direction to another, with many feather tufts and painted with vermilion, very proud with their bows and quivers of arrows. The governor and the bishop decided to take counsel with the other captains, and it was determined that Lieutenant Juan de Ayora and other captains would go out in three small boats, filled with as many men as could fit in them, heavily armed, and demand that the Indians come to obey the Holy Mother Church, and in matters temporal recognize the King and Queen our lords, and the crown and scepter of Castile, as their sovereigns and natural lords. In order to carry out this injunction they were to take with them an Indian who had been to Spain and was from the province of Cueva, in Tierra Firme, and Captain Rodrigo de Colmenares as our speaker in that place (for he said that he understood some of the Caribs' language), as a kind of interpreter. They were to assure the Indians and tell them that this fleet was not going to do them any harm or injury, and that if they wanted peace, no war would be declared on them, and they would be treated as good vassals of the Kings our lords, and receive many good turns. If they chose the opposite, they would be treated as their deeds merited. The general ordered his lieutenant and those who accompanied him not to be the aggressors nor to do [the Indians] harm, to bear their shrieking as best they could so that there would be no breach with them, but only to the point that no Christians who went with him be offended or mistreated.

The governor ordered that I and certain other persons should go in the three boats, all of which left the flagship for the land. I commanded the one nearest the shore with up to twenty men; the one next to me, but farther at sea, was under the command of Lieutenant Juan de Ayora, with twenty-five men, and the third one, farthest off, was commanded by Captain Rodrigo de Colmenares with about fifteen men and the Indian interpreter. All three boats were lined up evenly, with little space between them. Then the [Indians] approached the boats, running along the shore to place themselves where they thought we might want to land. Up to a hundred Indians were there to meet us with great audacity, with handsome feather headdresses, their bodies and faces daubed with vermilion, all of them the color of blood, with their bows and arrows and tremendous boldness, indicating to us that they were going to resist our sortie. When we were so close to them that we could hear each other easily (had we been able to understand each other), the Indian and Colmenares loudly shouted many words at them and the Caribs quieted down a little, but the truth was that they did not understand any more than if a Vizcayan in his Basque tongue were speaking to a German or an Arab or other even more foreign tongue. Then the Indians paid no more attention to what they were saying, nor to the signs which Rodrigo de Colmenares and the Indian were vainly making. Rather, thinking to provoke us with great force and many yells, they rushed up to the water's edge, shooting many arrows which reached our boats. Some flew high and in front of us, and several of the Indians went into the water up to their waist in order to shoot at us. When Juan de Ayora saw this he began to protest and to tell the Spaniards that they were not to shoot with crossbows or harquebusses or anything else, but to cover themselves with their shields and wait; he asked for witnesses to the fact that neither he nor the Christians were the aggressors, that they had offered the Indians peace and they had refused it. It was they who began hostilities and tried to provoke and kill our people, notwithstanding the terms that had been offered to them, thereby acquitting the royal conscience of our Princes, their captains and soldiers. The harm that would follow was the Indians' responsibility, not that of the Christians.

When the lieutenant at last saw that his words and admonitions were rejected or not understood, that their arrows, made of extremely poisonous plants, descended on us like a heavy downpour, that we were in grave danger if we stayed there, yet to retreat was shameful, he sent back a skiff which had come along with us, to let the governor know what was happening. But as we had to hurry and at this point excessive patience seemed pusillanimous, we fired two small charges of the gunpowder which we had in the boats over their heads. The lieutenant ordered us to run the bows aground on the shore, which was done post haste, and all of us leaped into the shallows, but as quick as we were, the Indians' flight to safety was even quicker. The governor, with other boats and more people, was already coming around a bend on the coast, and we waited for him on the shore, as they had waved their cloaks as a signal to us to wait for them and not to pursue the Indians.

After the general had leaped ashore we got to a nearby thatched hut; then, with his naked sword in his hand, he began to cut branches from the trees which grew there as an act of taking possession, and continued to do so in the name of Their Highnesses as their captain general, and in the name of the royal crown and scepter of Castile. Thus he confirmed the right of royal possession which the sovereigns of Castile have in these Indies, islands and Tierra Firme of the Ocean Sea. If it were necessary they would take possession of them anew as lands of their realm and royal patrimony, affirming the good treatment, governance and justice which would be extended to those Indians and native inhabitants of these lands who wished to obey our Holy Catholic faith and would accept obedience to the royal crown of Castile and of the Monarchs our lords, with the same measure of justice and protection as all their other subjects. But those who chose the opposite he would punish for being rebellious, disobedient and obdurate; he would proceed against them according to law and statute, and by the order of Their Highnesses. All of his acts he ordered written down, and requested [the document] as proof.

Seeing the disobedience of the Indians, he ordered the lieutenant with three hundred men to march one or two leagues inland and attempt to capture some live Indians without doing them harm, and then come back, as he wanted to wait for him, as indeed he did wait, there on the coast. This was done, and two small settlements of some fifteen or twenty huts, which they reached from this same harbor at a distance of half a league or a bit more, were found uninhabited. On the beach and sandy ground of that harbor they took four or five dragnets and other nets which had been hung to dry, nicely made of twisted cotton (for fishing). Further inland they found a few hammocks, which are the beds in which the Indians sleep; they had left them among the brush and groves of trees in order to flee more readily and climb up into the mountains and ranges.

After four or five hours which the governor spent ashore, he ordered trumpets to be blown to get his people back to the boats; he also had a few gunshots fired so that the lieutenant and those who had gone with him would come back to the harbor, which they did, and everyone got aboard. On that day no Christian was wounded and no Indian killed or taken prisoner.

3. BOOK 7, CHAPTER 16

Concerning pinecones (pineapples),[10] *which is what Christians call them, because they look like them; this fruit the Indians call* yayama, *and a certain type of the same fruit they call* boniama, *and another kind they call* yayagua, *as shall be explained in this chapter, although in other places it has other names.*

On this island of Hispaniola there are some thistles, each of which produces a pineapple (or, better said, an artichoke), because it looks like what Spaniards call a pinecone, yet without being one. This is one of the most beautiful fruits I have seen in all the world in which I have travelled. At least neither in Spain, nor France, nor England, Germany, nor in Italy, Sicily, nor in the other countries of His Imperial Majesty, such as Burgundy, Flanders, Tirol, Artois, nor Holland, nor Zeeland, nor in the rest is there such a lovely fruit, even if we count milleruelos[11] from Sicily, or muscatel pears, or any of those excellent fruits which King Ferdinand I of Naples collected in his gardens in the Park, Paradise or Pujo Real, of which opinion had it that these [the gardens] held preeminence over all the orchards of the most excellent fruits belonging to any Christians: not in the Esquiva Noya of Ercole, Duke of Ferrara, located on that island of his in the Po River; nor in the portable orchard of the Lord Ludovico Sforza, Duke of Milan, where they used carts to bring the fruit-laden trees to his table and his chamber. None of these, nor many others I have seen, had fruits like this pineapple or artichoke, nor do I think that anywhere in the world there is one to equal it in the things I shall now recount. These are: beauty of aspect; sweetness of scent; an excellent taste. So, among the five bodily senses, three of which can be applied to fruits, and even a fourth, which is touch, [this fruit] partakes most excellently of these four things or senses, above all the fruits or delicacies which man's diligence in the exercise of agriculture produces. It has yet another great advantage, which is that it is maintained and grown without any trouble to the farmer. [With respect to] the fifth sense, that of hearing, the fruit can neither hear nor listen, but in its stead, the reader can listen attentively to what I write about this fruit, and can be certain that I am neither mistaken nor prolix in what I might say thereof. For, given that the fruit cannot possess the other four senses which above I wished to attribute to it, it must be understood that it is the person who eats it who exercises these senses, and not the fruit itself (which has no spirit but vegetative and sensitive drives, as it lacks reason, which man, along with all the others, possesses). The vegetative drive is the one by means of which plants and all similar creatures grow; the sensitive drive receives impulses of benefit or harm, just as when one waters, cleans or digs around trees and plants they feel this cultivation and attention by thriving and growing; but when one neglects, singes or cuts them, they dry up and are ruined. Let us leave these matters to the experts and return to what I wanted to relate.

Contemplating the beauty of this fruit, man takes pleasure in seeing the composition and adornment with which Nature has endowed it and made it so pleasurable to his sight, for the delight of this sense. Smelling it, the other sense enjoys a mixed scent of quince, peaches, very fine melons and other delightful sensations which all these fruits, together or alone, with no unpleasantness, possess; not only the table onto which they are put, but a large part of the house in which a pineapple is found, if it is ripe and in perfect condition, smells very good and, above all other fruits, comforts the sense of smell in a marvelous and surpassing manner. To taste it is something so appetizing and sweet that in this case words fail me properly to praise the object itself, for none of the other fruits which I have named can in any conceivable way compare to this one. To touch it, if truth be told, is not all that soft or gentle, for it seems that the fruit itself wants to be picked up respectfully, with a towel or handkerchief, but once in your hand, no other gives such contentment. And, weighing all these attributes and individual features, there is no [person of] middling judgment who would not give these pineapples or artichokes preeminence over all fruits. Neither the illustration of my pen nor my words can bestow on the original the accurate description or the glory of this fruit in a manner so wholly satisfactory as to be able to explain the matter without a brush or a drawing, and even with these it would be necessary to use colors to make it more like (if not entirely, at least in part), to make it easier to understand than by what I do and say, because in some manner the reader's sight would be able to share in this truth. All this notwithstanding, I will include it the best way I know, as badly drawn as described; yet, for those who may have seen this fruit, that will suffice, and they will fill in the rest. And for those who never have seen it but here, the picture cannot displease them if they listen to the reading, with such emendation and declaration that I assure them that if ever they do see it they will pardon me if I did not know or was unable justly to praise this fruit. In truth, he who might wish to fault me must respect and take note of the fact that this fruit has different types and goodness of taste (one is better than another), and even [differs] in other ways. And he who would judge must take into consideration what has been said, and what more I shall say in the process or extensive commentary on the differences among these pineapples. And if, because of a deficiency in the colors and in the drawing, I am unable to make people understand what I would like to say, blame my opinion, in which, to my eyes, it is the loveliest of all the fruits I have seen, the one which smells and tastes the best. With respect to its size and color, which is green, it is lit up and nuanced with a strong yellow color; as it ripens it loses the green and becomes more a deep gold, and simultaneously its scent, like that of the most perfect peaches with a good dose of quince, gets stronger. This is the scent which comes closest to that of this fruit; [but] its taste is better than peaches, and juicier.

One peels around the outside and makes round cuts or slices, as the cutter wishes, for in each part, lengthwise or crosswise, it has little hairs and is easy to cut. On all these islands this fruit is as I have described, and very common, for it can be found on all of them and in Tierra Firme as well; as the Indians have many and diverse tongues, they call it by different names. At least in Tierra Firme, in an area of twenty or thirty leagues, one can encounter four or five languages; this fruit is one of the principal reasons why the few Christians who live in these lands can survive among these barbarous peoples.

Let us leave that [topic] in its place and return to the pine-fruit or artichoke. The Christians [initially] named it "pinecone" because it somewhat resembles one, but these [fruits] are handsomer and do not have the rustic nature of the pinecones of the Castilian piñón. The latter are wood, or nearly so, whereas these others can be cut with a knife like a melon, or better yet into round slices, taking off the outer shell, which looks like raised scales and hence the similarity with pinecones. But the scales do not open nor divide at their joints as the piñón cones do.

Indeed, just as Nature took great care with the plumage with which she adorned our European peacocks, she was equally attentive in the composition and beauty of this fruit, more than with any others I have seen, without comparison, and I suspect that there is no other of such a delightful, pretty aspect. They have a fine fleshiness, appetizing and most satisfactory to the palate, the size of middling melons, with some larger and some much smaller than these; the reason for this is that not all pineapples (though they resemble each other) are of the same kind or flavor. Some are sour, either because they are coarse and badly cultivated, or because the soil is unsuitable, or because as with all fruits it happens that one melon is better than another, and thus one pineapple may be much better than another. But there is no comparison between a good [pineapple] and any of the other fruits I have seen, taking into consideration all the things I have said which deal with this subject.

I expect that there will be other men who will not agree with me, for in Spain and in other parts of the world some insist that figs are better than pears, while others say that a quince is better than a peach or pears or figs, and still others that grapes are better than melons and other [fruits] I have mentioned. And so, in this matter everyone is more inclined to his own taste, and thinks that he who says something else does not feel about the matter the way he ought. But, leaving aside their factions or enamored palates (which I think are as different as men's faces are, one from another), if this were to be judged without strong emotions, I would still believe that the majority of the judges would be of my opinion about this fruit, even though I eat less of it than others. I repeat that it is unique in all the following things: in beauty of aspect, in taste, in smell; for to possess all these qualities, [be it] in a subject or in a fruit, I have never seen in any other fruit.

Each pineapple sprouts from a very harsh and spiny thistle, most unruly, and with long fleshy leaves; from the center of this thistle comes a round stem which produces but a single pineapple which takes ten months to a year to ripen; once it is cut this thistle will produce no more fruit, and has no use but to burden the land.

A person could inquire why, since it is a thistle, is this fruit not called an artichoke? I maintain that it was the responsibility of the first Christians who saw it over here, to give it one name or another. It seems to me that the better name would have been to call it an artichoke, with respect to the thistle and spines among which it grows, although it does resemble a pinecone more than an artichoke. The truth is that it is not totally unlike an artichoke, or unlike the thistle and spines from which it comes, though it looks more like a pinecone than an artichoke because in the crown, above the pineapple, this fruit bears and has a spiny shoot which is very handsome to see. Some have another [shoot] in addition to this one, and some, two or more shoots around the stalk where the fruit is attached to the stem of the thistle and from whence it springs. In order to plant other thistles or pineapples, these shoots are the seeds or offspring of this plant, for, if you take the shoot on top of the pineapple (or any other shoot which is set on its stalk), and set it two or three fingers' breadth down into the ground, leaving half of the shoot uncovered, then it grows very well. In the length of time to which I referred, each shoot produces another thistle and another pineapple, just as I have described. The leaves of this thistle are somewhat akin to aloe, except that they are longer and spinier, and not as thick or fleshy. This fruit would be far more appreciated were it not so abundant.

I feel that the pineapples from Tierra Firme are better and larger than the ones from these islands.

After this fruit has ripened, it does not keep more than fifteen or twenty days, but in the meantime, before it has spoiled or rotted, it is excellent. Though some people condemn it as choleric, I do not know that with any certainty; I do know that it stimulates the appetite, and for many who out of surfeit are unable to eat, it restores the desire to do so, gives them encouragement and the will to attempt to eat, and restores taste. Its most exact taste, that which it most resembles, is of peach, and has a mingled smell of peach and quince, but in the pineapple this scent is mixed with muscatel, and thus has a better taste than peaches.

The one defect which some find therein, for which reason it does not appeal to all tastes, is that wine, and may it be the best in the world, does not taste good if drunk after [eating] pineapple; the pineapple would be a unique find to wine lovers if it tasted as good as [wine] does with baked pears, and other things which wine fanciers know from experience. I think this is the reason why some people here do not like this fruit. Water, too, does not taste good if you drink it after eating pineapple, but this, which to some seems a defect and a great objection, to me seems an excellent and great advantage: one can give it to insatiables and to those fond of imbibing.

I also want to mention that the fleshy texture of this fruit has subtle fibers, much like the leaves of the thistles [i.e., artichokes] eaten in Spain, but much more hidden to the palate, more digestible and less troublesome when eating them, but they are not good for gums and teeth if you continue to eat them very frequently.

In some parts of Tierra Firme the Indians make wine from these pineapples and think it very healthy; I have drunk it and it is nowhere near as good as ours because it is very sweet, and no Spaniard nor Indian would drink it if they had Castilian wine, though the wine of Spain is not among the most select.

I said above that these pineapples come in different species, and this is true, especially three kinds. Some are called *yayama,* others *boniama,* and others *yayagua.* This last type is somewhat sour and harsh, white on the inside and winey. The one called boniama is white inside, sweet, and a bit fibrous. In its dimension the one called yayama is somewhat elongated, like the one I have here drawn, while the other two species of which I have spoken are rounder. The so-called yayama is the best of all. Inside its color is dark yellow, it is very sweet and delicious to eat, and all that has been said in praise of this fruit applies to it. In some places this kind and others grow wild, seeding themselves in the soil in great numbers. But without comparison those which are tilled and cultivated are the best and most delicate, fully acknowledging the care of the grower.

Some have been taken to Spain [but] very few get there. And even if they get there, they cannot be perfect and good because they had to be cut green and ripen at sea, and in this way they lose their goodness.

I have attempted to transport them, but because of faulty navigation and a loss of many days, they all spoiled and rotted; I tried to bring the shoots and they also spoiled. It is not a fruit that belongs in this country or in any other which is at least as cold as Spain. However, I have seen very good corn, which is bred in these parts, in my country, in Madrid, on lands inherited by the commander Hernán Ramírez Galindo, next to the devotional hermitage of Our Lady of Atocha (which now is a monastery of Dominican friars). I have also seen it in the city of Avila, as I related in the first chapter of this seventh book; in many parts of Andalusia corn has been grown, and therefore I am of the opinion that these pineapples or thistles could grow, bearing the shoots I described, were they harvested after three or four months here [in America].

4. BOOK 6, CHAPTER 33

Concerning the women who in the Indies live in women's republics and govern themselves, in imitation of the Amazons; I will insert two accounts here, until in the Second Part of the General History *we will come to the particular places and provinces where such women live, and there [we will] elaborate more fully on what needs to be written about this.*

Plinos and Escolopythus were exiled from their homeland;[12] these men, taking with them a great multitude of youths, went to Cappadocia, by the river Thermodon, and took the Themiscyrian lands, where they were in the habit of robbing their neighbors, but later these people killed them. The women, finding themselves exiled and widowed, took up arms, first defending their lands and [then] making war, daring, as a marvelous example to all ages, to establish their republic without husbands, rejecting their neighbors so as not to marry, as it would not be called marriage but servitude, and thus they ruled themselves, scorning to take a husband. And so that one would not appear to have an advantage over another, they killed those men who had stayed home, avenging the dead husbands by the death of the live ones. Afterwards, peace having been achieved by force, they began to sleep with their neighbors so that their generation would not die out; if any male children were born they killed them, but the females were instructed in their customs, neither bringing them up in idleness nor training them in wool crafts [i.e., spinning and weaving], but in the ways of arms, horses and the hunt. When they were young their right breast was burned off, so that it would not impede them when they shot their bow, for which reason they were called Amazons.[13] They had two queens, Marpesia and Lampedo, etc. This was the origin of their being called Amazons (according to what Justin wrote at length in the *Summary of Pompeius Trogus*), and their nation came to be very large.

Another thing astonishes me more than what has already been said, for these Amazons preserved and maintained their republic by having intercourse with men at certain times. But to have a republic of men who did not engage in intercourse with women, to live in a chaste manner, to endure and to have their people ever increase in number, that would be far more admirable. A case such as this is very possible, according to what Pliny writes, who, in speaking of Lake Asphalites [the Dead Sea], says of it thus: "On the west bank are the people of the Essenes, who in all things flee from evil men. They are the most marvelous people in all the world; they live without women and without any lust or money. They do not decrease in number because from time to time men worn down by misfortune come to live with them and follow their customs, for which reason these people, among whom no one is born, have endured for many centuries. Thus what is tedium or vexation of life to others is productive for them!"[14] All of this is from the aforementioned author.

With respect to what is stated in both individual cases [i.e., female and male], I will tell, with reference to the two entries I presented earlier, of two noteworthy accounts of women. The first is that when Jerónimo Dortal was exploring Tierra

Firme, in many places he and other Spaniards found communities where the women are absolute queens, or cacicas and rulers; they are the ones who command and govern, and not their husbands, though they have them. There was especially one, called Orocomay, who was obeyed for thirty leagues in the vicinity of her village, and was a good friend to the Christians. She consulted only with women, and no men lived in her town or community, except for those she had summoned to command them to do something or to send them to war, as will be explained in more detail in Book XXIV, Chapter X.

When Captain Nuño de Guzmán and his soldiers conquered New Galicia [western Mexico], they received word of a community of women, and later on our Spaniards began to call them Amazons. One captain, named Cristóbal de Oñate, was the first to beg Captain Nuño de Guzmán, his general, to do him the favor of allowing him [Oñate] to take charge of that campaign and the pacification of those Amazons. The general granted his wish and he went off with his company in search of them. In one village along the way he was seriously wounded and other Spaniards fared badly at the hands of certain Indians who came out to meet them, because of which this captain and those who were with him refused to go any farther. When the general got there the field marshal, named Captain Gonzalo López, asked to take over this mission of going to the women's community, and was granted his request. Afterwards the general himself wished to see these women; having gotten there with no resistance they easily entered the town where they lived, called Ciguatán (it is called that because in the language of this province Ciguatán means "a town of women"). They gave the Spaniards good things to eat and all they needed from what the women possessed. That settlement has a thousand houses and is very well arranged. They found out from the women themselves that young men from the vicinity come to their city for four months a year to sleep with them, and during that time they marry provisionally but for no longer. The men are concerned with serving the women and pleasing them in all the women demand that they do during the day in the town or out in the fields, and at night the women give them their bodies and beds. During this time the men cultivate and plant the corn and vegetable plots; they harvest them and deposit them in the homes where they have been housed. And when the allotted time is up, all of the men leave and go back to the lands from which they come. If the women become pregnant, after childbirth they send the sons to their fathers to bring up or do whatever they want with them, but if they bear daughters these they keep and bring them up to swell the ranks of their community. They have turquoise and emeralds in great abundance, and of very fine quality. But the real name of this town is not Ciguatán, as was stated earlier, but Ciguatlam, which means "a town of women." Other particular details of theirs will be discussed more extensively in Book XXXIV, Chapter VIII.

Back in Spain I wanted to gather information from this same Nuño de Guzmán about these women, because he is a fine gentleman and worthy of being believed. He told me it was a hoax and they were not Amazons, though some similar things were said about them. He went out and came back through these places, and found them married and proud of it. I maintain that it could be that, finding them in a married state, he went there during the time of their relationships, but let us leave this matter and go on.

Now that I have presented the two accounts to which I referred, I want to speak about what people said of the Essenes, of whom Pliny wrote what was quoted. And so that you, reader, will not be surprised, I will have you remember other similar descendants of people which you and I and many others have seen, whose numbers increase and who have lived for a very long time without the company of women. And, in the same vein, I will remind you of other congregations of women who live without the company of men, and which live and persevere and are never wanting, which is why I mention them.

Besides that which Saint Isidore says in his *Etymologies,*[15] we already know that the convent is understood to be a place where many are assembled together; thus I gather that there are many convents and places made up entirely of religious men who live in a saintly way, without the company of women, and there are many women and their convents which are without men, and have maintained themselves for a long time, as attested to by the Benedictines, the Bernardines, the Carthusians and other holy orders of religious men and women, each by themselves. This or these Essene communities, which the cited author [Pliny] places in Judea, must have been like these. They must have been celibate Jews, but not of the sanctity or goodness of the communities or convents of Christian religious men and women, who, like they, fleeing from evil and wordly sinners, withdraw and shut themselves away to serve God; they live without women and the women without men, chastely and with all decorum. Their numbers do not decrease because from time to time those who are suffering from adverse fortune, who want to serve God and leave the world, profess with those who took the religious habit earlier. Because of this these people have endured for many years and centuries, without any children being born among either the men or the women. For them it is very productive and excellent to remain apart from the customs of secular people. And when, because of the cleverness and skill of the devil some lack of chastity or dark sin is perpetrated by a professed monk, there is no lack of repentance or penitence because of his transgression and for the healing of his soul. Let us go on to the other examples.

5. BOOK 33, CHAPTER 54

In which the author explains why he stopped his journey and voyage to Spain, and relates other matters and events of New Spain; he tells of some particular subjects which have come to his attention, which are of the sort which the history has told, for the greater verification and truthfulness of some passages which were written in another manner, as [the author] was not as accurately informed as will be told now. And other matters of this sort will be related, in this way correcting several topics noted earlier, thus making known and perfecting others of which the readers must be apprised.

[The chapter begins with a discusssion of the function of history and of Charles V's politics in Europe. Oviedo had received a letter from the emperor telling him not to travel to Spain because of the war with France, and as Charles's obedient servant and *alcaide* (keeper) he said he would look after the fortress and port of Santo Domingo.]

Let us return to the narration of this western empire of our Indies, for as long as Our Lord sees fit to encourage my sight and my pen, for in truth it appears that Our Lord permits my eyes not to close and indeed gain greater clarity with respect to the history which I hold in my hands, as information and news have come to me to enable me to polish and perfect some important passages which were written previously, in accordance with what I was told then, and which in part were not well understood until now, having been neither perfect nor heedful, considering those who gave me reports about them. I, continuing the history, put them in this volume in good faith, assuming that they were true, as the witnesses affirmed they were. However, as men's understanding may be much better in some [persons] than in others, it is no wonder that they differ in their utterances and even in their deeds, especially in such cases in which intention, partiality, and individual interest causes these differences in the information which some have given me about things I myself have not seen. As only God is the One who knows and can understand all people, as a man I could be deceived or not as well informed as was advisable, but if I listen to many I will begin to comprehend at least partially some of these errors, and thus I will correct wherever it may be necessary to point out that which might be doubtful or off the right path.

God willed that on September 8, 1544, there arrived in this city of Santo Domingo a noble and illustrious man named Juan Cano, who lives in the City of Mexico and was born in the city of Cáceres, on his way back from Spain where he had gone on personal business. He is married to one of Montezuma's legitimate daughters, and came to New Spain with Captain Pánfilo de Narváez. He was fighting at the latter's side when he was taken prisoner, for this nobleman was [then] a youth of sixteen or seventeen, and later on he was present at all subsequent events in New Spain. I got in touch with him here, not only because I might wish him to be here, but because as an intelligent man and eyewitness he might satisfy my questions. For this reason he was in this fortress several times until his departure, which was on Thursday the twenty-fifth of the abovementioned month, in two ships which were going to New Spain. Because, as I have said in other places, it has been my custom to give the context and the names of the witnesses of what I wrote down wherever I happened to be, this present chapter will be continued as a dialogue, so as to agree in part with the [descriptive] title of this chapter LIV. So that I may not weary the reader with the names of the speakers, where you see the letters ALC. it means *alcaide* (keeper), and where you see CA. it means Juan Cano, with me asking and Juan Cano answering. I will relate the things of which we spoke, as there was no time for more because we only got to know each other and become friends shortly before his departure. And so I say:

Dialogue between the keeper of the fortress of the city and harbor of Santo Domingo on the island of Hispaniola, author and chronicler of these histories on the one hand, and on the other a gentleman resident in the great city of Mexico, by the name of Juan Cano.

ALC. Sir, yesterday I learned that your Grace lived in the the great city of Mexico and that your name was Juan Cano. Because I was friends with a gentleman named Diego Cano, who was a servant of His Serene Highness Prince Don Juan, my lord, of glorious memory, I want to know if he is alive, and where you, Sir, were born, and how you came to be in these parts. I will be happy if you do not find my questions troublesome, because I need to know some things about New Spain and in order to ascertain these it is necessary for me to find out about such persons and customs which merit credence. And so, Sir, you will do me a good turn in this matter.

CA. Señor Alcaide, I am the one who profits by getting to know you, for it has been a while that I have wanted to see you personally, as I am partial to you and very much wanted you to accept me for as good a friend and servant as I shall be to you. Answering what Your Grace wishes to know of me, I say that Diego Cano, scribe in Prince Don Juan's royal chamber and chamberlain of His Highness's tapestries, was my uncle, who recently died in the city of Cáceres, where he lived and where I was born. In terms of all else, Sir, I crossed from the island of Cuba to New Spain with Captain Pánfilo de Narváez, and though I was a very young man, I was at his side when he was taken prisoner by Hernán Cortés in his usual way. In the process his eye was ruptured, for he was fighting as a most valiant man, but as his people did not come to his aid and there were very few of his men around, he was wounded and taken prisoner. Cortés emerged the victor on the battlefield and persuaded the people who had come with Pánfilo to side with him. I was involved in all of the skirmishes and hand-to-hand combat in Mexico, and in everything which happened later on.

You asked me to tell how I came to be in these parts, and that I should not find your questions troublesome. In terms of why I am here, Sir, I say that I married Montezuma's legitimate daughter, called Doña Isabel, such a person, who, should she have been raised in Spain could not be better taught or instructed or Catholic, so well-spoken that her manner of being and fine graces would please you. She is very useful and beneficial to the peacefulness and contentment of the natives of these lands, as she is a lady in all respects and a friend to the Christians; because of her respect and example, even greater calm and tranquillity are impressed on the minds of the Mexicans. As for the rest which you might ask me, and which I remember, I, Sir, will tell what I know very truthfully.

ALC. I accept the favor which I shall receive thereby. I want to begin by saying that which comes to mind, and recall that I was told that Montezuma, her father, had over one hundred and fifty sons and daughters, and at one time had impregnated fifty women, which is what I recounted, along with other matters relating to this, in chapter XLVI. If this were indeed the case, I would like to find out how you know that Doña Isabel is Montezuma's legitimate daughter, and what system your father-in-law had so that one could tell the bastard or illegitimate children from the legitimate ones, and the legitimate wives from the concubines.

CA. The custom which was used and retained among the Mexicans when they took a legitimate wife was this, which will now be described. When a man and a woman agreed to enter into matrimony, relatives from both sides gathered in order to effect this, and celebrated a song festival (*areito*) after they had eaten or dined. When the time came for the bridal couple to go to bed and sleep as one, they took hold of the front skirt of the bride's shift and tied it to the cotton blanket which covered the bridegroom. Joined in this way, the principal relatives on both sides took their hands and led them to a chamber, where they left them alone and in the dark for three consecutive days; neither he nor she left the chamber, and the only one who entered it was an Indian woman who provided them with food or whatever they might need. During this time of confinement there was constant dancing and singing, which they call *mitote,* and after the three days are up there is no more feasting. If they marry without this ceremony, it is not seen as a [true] marriage, nor are the children which they have legitimate, nor do they inherit.

Thus, when Montezuma died, as legitimate children only my wife and her brother were left to him, both very young. Because of this a brother of Montezuma's was elected ruler, whose name was Cuitlavací, lord of Iztapalapa; he lived only sixty days after his election and died of smallpox. Then Montezuma's nephew, who was a *papa,* or important priest among the Indians, [and] whose name was Guatemucín, killed his cousin, the legitimate son of Montezuma, named Asupacací, Doña Isabel's blood brother, made himself the ruler and was very brave. He was the one who lost Mexico, was captured and later unjustly killed, along with other important lords and Indians. Then when Cortés and the Christians were established as rulers of Mexico, there was no legitimate offspring of Montezuma left, only bastards, except my wife, who was left a widow, as Guatemucín, lord of Mexico, the better to safeguard his position, took her to wife when she was very young, with the ceremony I described earlier, tying the shift to the blanket; they did not have any children, nor time to beget them. She converted to our holy Catholic faith and married an upright man named Pedro Gallego from among the first conquistadors; he had a son by her, named Juan Gallego Montezuma. Said Pedro Gallego died, and I married the aforementioned Doña Isabel, with whom God has given me three sons and two daughters, named Pedro Cano, Gonzalo Cano de Saavedra, Juan Cano, Doña Isabel and Doña Catalina.

ALC. Señor Juan Cano, I beg you to tell me: why did Hernán Cortés kill Guatemucín? Did he rebel later on, or what did he do so that he had to die?

CA. You must know that just as Captain Hernán Cortés cruelly tortured Guatimucín, [he did the same] to the king of Tacuba, who was called Tetepanquezal, and the lord of Tezcoco, burning their feet, smearing them with oil and holding them close to the live embers, and other diverse things so that they would give them their treasure. And while he had subjected them to constant hardship, he found out that Captain Cristóbal de Olid had rebelled in Puerto de Caballos in Honduras, in the province the Indians call Guaimura. He decided to pursue and punish the said Cristóbal de Olid, and left Mexico by land, with many Spaniards and natives, bringing these three aforementioned principal lords with him; later he hung them on the way there. And thus Doña Isabel became a widow and later married, in the way I have described, Pedro Gallego, and afterwards me.

ALC. Well, in a certain account which was sent to the Emperor our Lord, Hernán Cortés said that Guatemucín had succeeded to the rule of Mexico after Montezuma, because Montezuma's son and heir had died on the bridges, and that of two other sons left alive one was crazy or a simpleton, and the other paralyzed and incompetent because of his ailments. And I wrote this down in Chapter XVI, believing it to be true.

CA. Well, Your Grace may write what he likes, as the Marquis Hernán Cortés [may say] what he wishes, but I tell the truth before God and my conscience, and this is very well known.

ALC. Your Grace, Señor Juan Cano, tell me: why did the Indians of Mexico rise up as soon as Hernán Cortés left that city to find Pánfilo de Narváez, and left Montezuma a prisoner in the power of Pedro de Alvarado? I have heard much about these things, and I would like to write the truth, may God save my soul.

CA. Señor Alcaide, what you are asking is a question which few who dwell on earth will be able to explain, although the matter was most notorious and the injustice done the Indians obvious. From then on they felt such hatred towards the Christians that they never trusted them again; all subsequent misfortunes followed it, [such as] the rebellion in Mexico, and it happened in this way. Among other idolatrous practices these Mexicans had certain annual celebrations during which they gathered for their rites and ceremonies. When the time had come for one of these, Alvarado was guarding Montezuma and Cortés had gone to where you said. Many important Indians assembled and asked Capain Alvarado's permission to hold their ceremonies in the courtyards of their mosques or principal temples, adjacent to the Spaniards' quarters, so that the latter would not think that this gathering was for any other purpose, and the said captain gave them permission. Thus more than six hundred Indians, all of them lords, naked, adorned with much gold jewelry, beautiful plumes and precious stones, men as handsomely adorned and gallant as they could be, bearing neither offensive nor defensive weapons, danced and sang and celebrated their areito and festival according to their custom. At the precise moment when they were most absorbed in their rejoicing, Alvarado, impelled by greed, had fifteen men occupy each of the five entrances to the courtyard. Then he entered with the rest of the Spaniards, and they began to knife and kill the Indians, not pardoning even one, until in under an hour they finished them all. And this was the reason why the Mexicans, having seen those men killed and robbed with no risk [to the Spaniards], without deserving such cruelty as was meted out, rose up and waged war against said Alvarado and the Christians who with him were guarding Montezuma, as they had more than enough cause to do this.

ALC. How did Montezuma die? Because I have heard differing accounts and thus I have written different versions of it.

CA. Montezuma died of a stone people on the outside threw at him, which would never have happened if there had not been a guard with a shield in front of him, for if they had seen him, no one would have thrown a stone. And so, because of protecting him with the shield and not believing Montezuma was there, they hit him with a stone, from which he died. But I want you to know, Señor Alcaide, that from the time of the first Indian uprising until after Narváez was taken prisoner, notwithstanding the usual battles they had with the Christians, Montezuma always had them bring us food. After the Marquis [Cortés] came back, there was a large reception for him, and they gave the Spaniards a great deal to eat. You should know that Captain Alvarado, though his conscience pricked him, yet he did not repent his fault; but, wanting to gloss over the matter and placate Montezuma's spirit, told Hernán Cortés to pretend to arrest and punish him [Alvarado] because Montezuma had demanded his person and his death in exchange for those he had killed. Hernán Cortés refused to do this; instead, very angry, he said [the Indians] were dogs, that there was no need for what Alvarado asked him to do, and sent an Indian nobleman to set up the *tiánguis* or market. This nobleman, angry at seeing Cortés's wrath, the poor opinion he had of the surviving Indians, and the little he cared about the dead, feeling scorned and determined to seek vengeance, was the first to renew hostilities against the Spaniards within the hour.

ALC. I have always heard it said that moderation is good, mercy is holy, and arrogance is abominable. It is said that the treasure which Hernán Cortés shared out among all his soldiers was immense, when he decided to leave the city on the advice of a man named Botello, who prided himself on predicting what lay ahead.

CA. I know well who he was, and it is true that he was of the opinion that Cortés and the Christians should leave the city. When the time came to effect this, he did not let this be known to all, but only to those who were with him during this conversation; the rest, those who were in their rooms or their quarters, remained behind. There were two-hundred-and-seventy men, who fought for several days to defend themselves, until because of hunger they surrendered to the Indians; the latter kept their word the same way Alvarado had kept his to the ones we told about. And so, when they surrendered, all two-hundred-and-seventy Christians, not counting those who had died fighting, were cruelly sacrificed. But you should know, Sir, with respect to the generosity which Hernán Cortés, as you mentioned, showed his soldiers, those who took the most and loaded themselves down with gold and jewels were the soonest killed; to save the saddle the jackass perished, [as the saying goes], especially the one with the heaviest load. But those who refused [the booty] and took only their swords and weapons, got through more easily, opening their way with their swords.

ALC. It was a great pity so much treasure was lost, as well as one hundred and fifty-four Spaniards, forty-five mares and more than two thousand Indians, among them Montezuma's son and daughters, and all the other lords they had taken prisoner. I have it written thus in Chapter XIV in this history.

CA. In truth, Señor Alcaide, the person who told you that either did not see [what happened], or know the truth, or wanted to conceal it. I guarantee that the Spaniards who were killed in this action (counting those who, as I said before, remained in the city and those who were lost along the way, following Cortés and continuing our flight) numbered more than one thousand one hundred and seventy, as a review of the troops showed. With respect to the Indians, you refer to two thousand of our Tlaxcalan allies, but doubtless there were more than eight thousand.

ALC. I am amazed that after Cortés and those who escaped took refuge in the lands of Tlaxcala, that they did not kill him and the Christians, having left their [Tlaxcalan] allies dead back there; it is said that the people of Guaulipa, which is the boundary of Tlaxcala, fed them only if they were paid, and the only payment they wanted was gold.

CA. Hold all that to be false, Sir, for in their own homes the Christians could not have found a warmer welcome; everything they wanted, without even having to ask for it, was given to them freely and with good will.

ALC. The Marquis is quite a man, and is worthy of all he has and much more. I am sorry to see such a valiant gentleman maimed, missing two fingers on his left hand—as I wrote down and got from his account, and put in Chapter XV—but that is how war is: the honors and the palm of victory are not acquired by sleeping.

CA. Without a doubt, Sir, Cortés has been a successful and astute captain, and princes tend to bestow favors on those who serve them. It would be good if they did the same to all who are employed in their royal service, but I have seen some who work and serve and never get ahead, while others who have not done nearly as much are rewarded and furthered. Would that all would be rewarded as the Marquis has been for his two fingers, because of which you are sorry for him. God did not have to work hard to heal him, and you can forget about your concern: the fingers which he brought with him out of Castile when he first came here he still has now in Spain, as he never lost them nor are they missing. He never needed either a surgeon or a miracle to recover from this trial.

ALC. Señor Juan Cano, is the brutality true which they say the Marquis employed in Cholula, a city through which he passed the first time he went to Mexico?

CA. That is very true indeed, but I did not see it because I had not yet come to this country, but I found out about it later from many who saw it and were involved in this cruel deed.

ALC. How did you hear what happened?

CA. What I heard as a well-known fact was that in that city Hernán Cortés asked for three thousand Indians to carry burdens for him and they gave them to him; he put them all to death, with no escape for any.

ALC. The Emperor our lord is right to order Indians taken away from all Christians.

CA. Let that which His Majesty might command or need be done, for that is best, but I would not want just men to suffer because of transgressors. He who commits cruelties, let him pay them out, but why should he who commits no offense be punished? This is a matter which deserves more discussion, but I have to embark tonight and it is already almost time for the Ave María. Look, Señor Alcaide, if I can be of help to you in Mexico I will do it with all good will and commitment. As far as the freedom of the Indians is concerned, no doubt some should be asked if they want to be ruled and governed and instructed in matters of our holy Catholic faith while others should be exempted, but here you have the Bishop of Chiapas, Fray Bartolomé de Las Casas, who has been the promoter of these changes. He has come with many young monks of his order, and with him, Señor Alcaide, you can take up this matter of the Indians. I do not want to spend any more time nor speak further of this, although I could add my piece.

ALC. No doubt, Señor Juan Cano, Your Grace speaks as a prudent man; these things should be ordained by God, and one might think that this reverend bishop of Ciudad Real in the province of Chiapas has undertaken these pilgrimages in which he is involved as a zealous service to God and His Majesty, and may it please God that he and his friars will be successful in this service. But he is not all that favorably disposed towards me as you might think: he has even complained about me because of what I wrote about the peasants that he wanted to have knighted when he went to Cubagua and Cumaná, wanting to do so with crosses that resembled those of the order of Calatrava, though the people were peasants and members of the humble classes. He told this to the Bishop of San Juan, Don Rodrigo de Bastidas, so that he would tell me, which he did. What I replied to his complaint I did not do to gratify the Bishop of Chiapas, but the authority, kindness and holy intention of the Bishop of San Juan, whom I begged to tell [Las Casas] that when I wrote that I had no intention of causing him either pleasure or pain, but simply to tell what happened. He should go and look at a book, the first part of this *History of the Indies* which was published in the year 1535, that there was what I had written and there was no reason to dwell on it, for everything I said and failed to say could be easily proven. He should also know that the book had already appeared in Tuscan, French, German, Latin and Greek, though I had written it in Castilian. And just as he was going about with his enterprises I was not about to stop writing about the Indies as long as this was of use to Their Majesties; I trust in God that he will have better success in the future than in the past, and then he will think better of my pen. As the Bishop of San Juan is very noble and knows the truth and the lack of bias with which I write, the Bishop of Chiapas was satisfied. But it is not my job to please either his palate or any other's, but to do my duty, such as speaking with you, Sir, of what is true.

And so, with respect to the burden of the many friars, it truly seems to me that these lands sprout or even rain friars, but as all of them are without gray hair and under thirty, may it please God that all of them will be successful in serving Him. I have already seen them enter this city two by two, about thirty of them, all of them with their staffs, tunics, scapularies and hats, yet no cloaks, with the bishop following them. The whole thing seemed a pious farce; now they are starting out, and we do not know how it shall end. Time will tell, and may Our Lord use it to His good service. But as they are going in the direction of those new volcanoes, tell me, Sir, what they are like, if you have seen them, and the nature of another one you have there in New Spain, which is called Guajocingo.

CA. The Chalco or Guajocingo volcano is quite something: it lit up the night for three or four leagues or more, and by day emitted continuous smoke and at times tongues of fire. It is on a ridge in the Sierra Nevada which is perpetually covered with snow, located nine leagues from the city of Mexico. This fire and smoke of which I spoke lasted up to seven years after Hernán Cortés came to these parts, but now it no longer emits any fire. A great deal of high quality sulphur remained, which has been taken out to make gunpowder, and there is a great deal more to be had. In Guatemala there are two very frightening volcanoes or fiery mountains like these, that cast out huge incinerated stones and emit much smoke out of their craters. It is a most horrible sight, especially as it appeared when that sinful woman Doña Beatriz de la Cueva, the wife of governor Pedro de Alvarado, died. I beg Our Lord to be with Your Grace, Señor Alcaide, and give me your leave, for the boat which will take me to the ship is waiting.

ALC. Señor Juan Cano, may the Holy Spirit go with Your Grace, and give you such a successful crossing and voyage, that you will get home safely and in short order, and will find Doña Isabel and your sons and daughters in the state of health which Your Grace and they desire for each other.

6. BOOK 29, CHAPTER 26

Concerning the customs and depraved lifestyles of the Indians in the province of Cueva, their idolatries and other particulars of the governance of Castilla del Oro and its provinces.

To avoid causing the readers tedium by repeating that which was said before, here in this Book 29 some matters mentioned in previous books will be summarized, pointing out differences which might exist from that which was said in the first part from that which will be told in this second part about similar matters. And thus I say with respect to the religious practices or ways of idolatry in the province of Cueva, that among the Indians of Castilla del Oro it is very common to worship the sun and the moon, and to venerate the devil and hold him in high esteem; and so, for their idolatries and sacrifices they have men who are chosen and revered [for this], usually their physicians, who knew and used many herbs which were appropriate for treating a variety of ailments. From long use they know some of them; others are not completely effective but rest on the authority which their physician or teacher, called a *tequina,* would like to ascribe to them, for in fact in some cases they tell the truth and [the herbs] are excellent.

As to the nature of the persons of these Cueva Indians, most of them are somewhat larger than those of these our islands, more manly, and of the same color. They go about naked, and on their male member wear a shell or a wooden tube, with their testicles out, and the shell or tube is fastened or tied on by means of a string threaded through two little holes. The women wear petticoats made of little cotton blankets from the waist to the knee or shorter, which are wrapped around the body. Ladies and noblewomen (*espaves*) wear these petticoats down to the ankle. On their heads neither men nor women wear anything at all, and nothing else on their bodies but what has been described. Actually, some men, including the chiefest thereof, instead of a shell wore a gold tube, either twisted or plain, of very fine gold, and the most illustrious women wore a gold bar as an ornament horizontally under their breasts (of which they are very proud), so as to push up their breasts and keep them high and firm and keep them from sagging; [these bars] sometimes had birds or other decorations in relief on them and were of very fine gold; one of these bars was worth at least one hundred and fifty or even two hundred pesos.

This use of the gold bars to push up the breasts is a practice which only the illustrious women of the Gulf of Urabá enjoy. These women go into battle with their husbands, just as they also rule and lead their people when they are landowners. Besides the gold bars both women and men wear many gold medals and medallions, and handsome crests.

When the illustrious women and also the lords of these people go abroad, as they have neither horses nor large animals nor carts to transport them, they use another form of mount, in the form I shall now describe. The lord, cacique, *saco* or leader always has one or two dozen of the strongest Indians, selected to [bear] his litter, in which he travels lying down in a hammock strung horizontally along a naturally very light pole; the ends of the pole are placed across the shoulders of these Indians who go running, or half trotting, bearing the lord on their backs. When the two who are carrying him tire, without stopping two others, who are there for this purpose but bear no burden, take their place and continue on their way; if the land is flat, they can cover fifteen or twenty leagues in a day, using relays of these Indians at certain stops in order to replace each other. The Indians which they have for this purpose are mostly slaves or domestic servants, who are practically slaves and obliged to serve; and for the Indians who serve in this business of the hammocks, they look for ones who are *carates*. In order to understand what a carate is, I say that an Indian who is called a carate has scabs all over his body, or the major part thereof, with bumps on his skin as though he had ringworm. They look ugly, but for the most part they are ro bust and extremely strong; they appear scarred, and these scars are a result of the affliction which ends [only] when this itch or condition has covered their whole body and they have completely replaced their skin.

In some parts of this country the Indians are warlike, but in others not as much. They are not archers, but fight with war clubs, long lances, and spears they throw like darts, with *estóricas* (which are somewhat like pitchforks), made of well-carved canes, as I have drawn here (Plate 9, figures 2 and 3), with which they hurl the lances, always holding on to the estórica; they line up the tip of the estórica and the tip of the lance and hurl it very strongly and straight, either near or far, and well aimed, like good marksmen. Some of these lances whistle in the air, because near one end they carve a hollow or an orb, and because of the hollow and some holes therein, as soon as they hurl it and the air gets at it, when it flies high it makes a whistling noise. They use these whistling lances in their festivals when they fight for sport, but not in war, as this sound or whistle would warn the enemy; [however,] during warfare they throw them from one camp to another, or at night, as a way of expressing scorn for their enemies.

The Indians call on the men I have mentioned [tequinas], the ones they hold in high esteem, in order to ask their advice when they want to begin their wars, and for all other important matters. There are many shades of meaning in this term tequina, for a man is called tequina if he is more skilled or expert in some task, such as being the best hunter or fisherman, or better at making a net or a canoe, or other things, and it means the same as teacher. Thus, he who is a teacher in relations and information pertaining to the devil, is called a tequina for this ability, as it is he who directs the idolatries and ceremonies and sacrifices, and, according to the [Indians], speaks with the devil, who gives him his reply. He tells the others what to do, and what will happen tomorrow and for many days thereafter, because, as Satan is a former astrologer he knows the natural movements of time, the heavens, the planets, the zodiac, and influences from above; he sees where things go that are guided naturally, and so, because [he knows] the effects to which they are ultimately related, he can predict what will happen in the future. He makes them understand that because of his divinity, as lord and mover and arranger of all that is and shall be, he knows the things that are to come; he tells them when he will make it thunder and rain, and has control over the weather; he gives or takes away the fruits of the plants, grasses, and trees, and all that sustains [the earth's] creatures. And as they often see things happen which were foretold a few days earlier, they give him credit for everything else, and sacrifice to him in many different ways: in some places with blood and human life, in others with aromatic and good, and also evil-smelling incense. When God makes the opposite happen from that which the devil has told the tequina and the tequina the others, he lies to them, giving them to understand that the results have been changed because of some apparent slight or failing [on their part], just like the one who is an adept master of deceptions, especially with people who are very poor and unprepared in their defenses against such a great adversary, to whom they give the name *tuira*. In the language of Cueva they apply the same name to Christians, whom they hold to be astute and devil-like, and think that by calling them tuiras they honor and praise them greatly.

I am not surprised that these people govern themselves by attributing some kind of divinity and authority to their tequinas, because this mediator walks among them like the devil. Great was the prudence and rule of the ancient Romans and Carthaginians among all nations, but listen to Titus Livy and you will learn from him what great authority they gave to their soothsayers and seers, to whose mistakes, falsehoods, conjectures and mad sacrifices they were subject. When the devil intervened in these acts sometimes the [soothsayers] were right and foretold some things in which time and end results proved them right, without knowing anything about it, or with any more certainty than the common adversary of human nature [the devil] revealed to them, in order to lead them to their perdition and death, both physical and spiritual. As a result, when they failed to sacrifice or the sacrifice turned out badly, they thought up excuses or cautious, ambiguous answers, saying that the gods they worshiped were angry, just as the tequina tells the Indians by means of the tuira which they take for their god.

Listen to Valerius Maximus and you will see what keenness of religion and special care these ancients lavished on all things which they undertook and felt to be important, by means of their oracles or soothsayers. Many are the people of this universe who are under such diabolical misconceptions that they have wasted much time and thousands of years, yet there will never be a lack of those who were not enlightened or aided by Our Lord God. So much the greater is the obligation of Christians to recognize the mercy which the Redeemer used to teach them of His passion and to save them; the punishment of those ungrateful ones who do not acknowledge this and whose souls are forgetful of the love of God is thus most just.

In the Summary I wrote in 1526, which was published by the Emperor's order in the most royal city of Toledo, I treated a variety of topics, not in as orderly a fashion as I might have wished, nor as unencumbered of other matters because of many other pressing duties I had at that time. I lacked the necessary tranquillity for the kinds of things I discussed [in that text], and besides, I had neither my books nor my personal notes, and back then had not fully understood particular features and other matters new to me about which, in time, I have come to learn. I recall referring to the present *General History,* which, though it was not yet carefully rendered from the notes and rough drafts which I had of these matters, I lacked neither the desire nor the hope of bringing this text to the state in which it is now, and it is good that that which I promised should come to be. As to what I wrote before, I will now proceed step by step to clarify what I stated earlier. Should anyone wish to spy on these things, in order to accuse me of negligence (should it appear that I forget this or that), I wish to advise him that here he will not find them presented as haphazardly as I did there, but they will be in their proper places. The truth is that that summary was shorter than its title, as I called it: OVIEDO: *Of the Natural History of the Indies,* which treats much less than what it ought to contain with such a title. But that treatise was a kind of herald or precursor of the topics which I now discuss in this *General History* of these lands, somewhat like a compote, which is what people who make preserves out of sugar and a variety of fruits call it, when they mix all different kinds in one receptacle. Mostly some [of the fruits] get in each other's way and impede each other, so that one cannot or the fruits will not allow themselves to be tasted as distinctly as they might be, were each one immersed in its own syrup and put in its own container or jar. This is what I did in that summary: many things were jumbled together, making it impossible to understand where they are.

As earlier I began to talk about the arms with which they fight, and told of the spears they threw with the estóricas, it must be understood that these are the kinds of weapons used in this province of Cueva and in other particular provinces. They are [made with] poles from black palms and other trees with very fine woods, the tips slim and pointed so that they can go right through a man if they hit the soft parts of the body. Some are made with canes from certain ditch reeds, which are very straight and without any knots, about as thick as your little finger or even thinner, light and smooth, at the tip of which, instead of iron, they set another cane of black palm, one and a half or two spans long, beautifully carved and with many tongues. Some of them have animal or fish bones instead of iron, and are cone-shaped. The long lances which some of these Indians use, they also make of palm, *xagua* or other fine wood. They have one or double-sided war clubs, and in some provinces, such as Esquegua, Urraca, Borica and Paris, they have lances as long or longer than a pike, made of very strong and beautiful palm wood, as black as jet.

Their guazábaras or skirmishes often have no purpose, but the devil incites them; although one lord may have differences with or strong emotions towards another, they are people who only infrequently are impelled by reason. Most of them are irrational and induced by the devil and his tequina, giving them to understand that the war they are counselled to wage is divinely intended. Among the people of the same *tiba,* or lord, there are few quarrels or armed conflicts, nor is obedience to their elders [as] fickle as it may be among other peoples, for the chief or lord or tiba can dispose of the lives of his Indians as Christians dispose of the things they least esteem. There is no quarrel or dispute among them in which contentiousness lasts more than three days, especially if the lord is aware of it and orders what should be done in this controversy; just or unjust, whatever he commands is carried out *immediately.* In fact, as they consider stealing the gravest crime which can be committed, every man has the right to cut off both hands and string them around the neck of any thief he might catch in his cornfield or on his property, even if he has cut but one stalk without the permission of its owner.

The most common cause for war, for which these peoples fight and go into battle, is about who will have more lands and power, and also because of other conflicts. Those whom they are able to kill, they do, and those whom they take prisoner they brand and use as slaves; every lord has his own brand, and some extract a front tooth from the one who is now their slave. That is the sign, and the slave is called *paco.*

The principal lord is called *queví* and in some places *saco;* the term cacique is not from Tierra Firme, but is actually from this island of Hispaniola. As this was the first place the Christians conquered and settled, they have applied the term cacique to lords of other lands in these Indies where they have roamed. In the Cueva tongue, of which we are speaking here, the name for a lord is queví, and in some provinces of Castilla del Oro he is called tiba; in others *jura* and still others *guaxiro,* but this term guaxiro they have taken from the Caribs, for it is not native but appended and foreign to Cueva. In the same vein in Cueva, an important man, a lord of vassals, if he be subject to another greater man, is called *saco,* and [if] this saco has other Indians in subjection to him, who own lands and property, they are called *cabras*. They are like gentlemen and nobles, separated from the common people, and are more important than others of the people, and command them. But the cacique or saco and the cabra each has his name, just as the provinces, rivers, valleys, places and settlements do, as well as the trees, birds and fish have their own particular names; however, just as we use the general term "fish," they say *haboga*.

The way that an Indian, who is from the common, low or plebeian people, can rise to be a cabra and attain this name and rank to go before other commoners, is that when one lord distinguishes himself by fighting another in a battle and, fighting valiantly, is wounded; this blood is the charter of privilege and title and the inception of his nobility. Then the lord to whom he belongs calls him cabra, gives him people to command, and land or a woman, or gives him some other important gift for what he did that day in the lord's presence, because if the lord is not there, the honor is not bestowed. And from then on he is held in higher honor than other men, and is separated or removed from the plebeian and the common people. His sons succeed to this same nobility and call themselves cabras; they are obligated to follow a military career and military arts of warfare. The cabra's wife, besides her own name, is known as an *espave,* which means lady or illustrious woman, [not] a common or plebeian woman. She inherits this title as soon as her husband becomes a cabra and in the same vein the wives of the quevís or sacos or cabras are called espaves.

When they go to war, they take their chieftains or captains. These are sacos or cabras, and are already experienced men in matters of the arms they bear; they go out with their plumes, painted with vermilion or genipap juice, and bear insignias so as to be known in battle, like gold jewels or a plume or other device. They have a particular trait or custom which is inviolable among them, which is that although they capture spies and dismember them by torture, these will confess no other truth or lie than that which their captain, tiba or lord who sent them, ordered them to reveal, nor anything which might hurt their people. For the most part their campaigns begin with a drinking session or an areito [singing ceremony]; as soon as they are agreed on what to do, they sing about it either on the same day or the next one, and then everything which has been chanted in the areito is put into action. This [ceremony] is like a witnessing or a consultation with the common people, after the lord and his closest followers and the tequina have discussed the goal they want to accomplish. In voluntary conflicts the aggressors have to follow this protocol, because the defenders might have to act as necessity dictates.

In matters of justice they have executioners, who are like constables; these arrest and kill the common man whom the lord has ordered to be put to death. However, if the man who is to perish is a saco or cabra, no common or plebeian man may put his hands on him, but the lord who rules them all kills him with his own hands, with a war club, or with one or two lances he hurls at him first to wound him. If these preliminary blows do not kill him he gives the victim over to the executioner, because commencing the execution of justice is a kind of degradation and taking away of his status as a cabra or a noble.

APPENDIX D

Table. Historia general y natural *Manuscript Locations and Illustrations/Woodcuts*

Book	*Autograph Ms. Monserrate Ms.@RAH & HEH*	*16th-century copy Gascó/Trujillo @ BC & PR* (ca. 1570 copy of bks 17–50)	*18th-century copy Muñoz @ RAH (copy of extensive sections of the* HG*)*	*1535/47/57 edition, woodcuts*
I Preface	missing by 1780			
II Columbus's Voyages	missing by 1780			chap. 7 Columbus's coat of Arms, 10r chap. 11 Southern Cross, 16v
III Hispaniola	RAH 9/551 only last chaps.			
IV Hispaniola	HEH, *HM-177*			
V Indigenous customs	RAH *9/551* *tambores,* 14r pipe, 14v hammock, 16r			chap. 1 *tambores,* 46v chap. 2 pipe, 47r chap. 2 hammock, 47v
VI Miscellanea	HEH, *HM-177* *caney* (2), 3v,			chap. 1 *caney* (2 views), 58v, 59r

Book	*Autograph Ms. Monserrate Ms.@RAH & HEH*	*16th-century copy Gascó/Trujillo @ BC & PR* (ca. 1570 copy of bks 17–50)	*18th-century copy Muñoz @ RAH (copy of extensive sections of the* HG)	*1535/47/57 edition, woodcuts*
VI	4r *pampilla,* 5v axe, 7vcanoe, 8r fire drill, 9r Asturian gold collar, 12v gold panning scene, 18v St. Isidro's geometrical cylinder, 36r legendary bird, 45r			chap. 4 axe, 61r chap. 4 canoe, 61r chap. 5 fire drill, 61v chap. 8 gold panning scene, 66r
VII Agriculture	HEH, *HM-177* yucca leaves (2), 37r Taino native carrying baskets, 42v maguey plant, 43v pineapple, 46r			chap. 2 yucca leaves, 73r chap. 13 pineapple, 77v
VIII Cultivated Trees	missing by 1780		chap. 29 managua (missing) chap. 30 cacoa	chap. 1 plaintain leaf, 79r chap. 4 *higuero* leaf, 81r chap. 13 *guiabara* leaf, 83r chap. 14 *copey* leaf, 83v chap. 18 *guanábana / anón,* 84r chap. 20 *mamey* leaf, 84v

(*continued*)

Book	*Autograph Ms. Monserrate Ms.@RAH & HEH*	*16th-century copy Gascó/Trujillo @ BC & PR* (ca. 1570 copy of bks 17–50)	*18th-century copy Muñoz @ RAH (copy of extensive sections of the* HG)	*1535/47/57 edition, woodcuts*
VIII (*continued*)				chap. 23 *pitahaya,* 85v chap. 24 *cardos altos,* 86r chap. 25 *tunas,* 86v
IX Wild Trees	HEH *HM-177* cluster of coconuts, 53v *capera,* 66v fruit of cinnamon tree (2), 68r			
X Medicinal Trees	missing by 1780			chap. 1 cactus, 92r
XI Herbs, Seeds	HEH, *HM-177* morning glory, 73r *goacomax* leaf (balsam), 74r perebecenuc leaf, 76v lily, 78r *perorica* plant, 78v *coigaraca* plant, 80r			chap. 4 bálsamo leaf, 97v chap. 5 perebecenucleaf, 98r
XII Land Animals	missing by 1928 (through bk. 17, chap. 9)		Muñoz copy *A/34* chap. 10 tiger chap. 11 danta chap. 21 anteater	

Book	*Autograph Ms. Monserrate Ms.@RAH & HEH*	*16th-century copy Gascó/Trujillo @ BC & PR* (ca. 1570 copy of bks 17–50)	*18th-century copy Muñoz @ RAH (copy of extensive sections of the* HG)	*1535/47/57 edition, woodcuts*
XII				chap. 23 armadillo, chap. 24 perico ligero (sloth) chap. 27 churcha (opossum) chap. 29 bivana chap. 30 llama
XIII Sea Animals	missing by 1780			chap. 3 iguana, 103v chap. 10 manatee, 106r
XIV Birds	missing by 1780			
XV Insects	missing by 1780			
XVI Puerto Rico	missing by 1780			
XVII Cuba	missing	PR II/3041 chaps. 21-27		
XVIII Jamaica	missing			
XIX Cubagun	missing			chap. 9 *nacarón* shell. 159r
XX Strait of Magellan	missing by 1780	PR *II/3041* Patagonian windbreak, 35v fire tower, 62r Malucan coin, 89v		1557 edition chap. 6 Patagonian windbreak, 24r chap. 22 fire tower, 43r chap. 33 Moluccan coin (2 views), 59v

(*continued*)

Book	*Autograph Ms. Monserrate Ms.@RAH & HEH*	*16th-century copy Gascó/Trujillo @ BC & PR* (ca. 1570 copy of bks 17–50)	*18th-century copy Muñoz @ RAH (copy of extensive sections of the* HG)	*1535/47/57 edition, woodcuts*
XXI Tierra Firme (*continued*)	missing by 1780	PR *II/3041* curve of coastline, 155r		
XXII Austral Exploration	missing by 1780			
XXIII Paraná River/ River Plate	missing by 1780	PR *II/3041* map of Tierra Firme, 236–37		
XXIV Trinidad	missing by 1780			
XXV Venezuela	missing by 1780	PR *II/3041* map of Lake Maracaibo, 241–42		
XXVI Sta Marta	missing by 1780			
XXVII Cartagena	missing by 1780	PR *II/3041*		
XXVIII Veragua	missing by 1780	RAH *Fondos de Jesuitas,* v. 108		
XXIX Castilla del Oro	RAH *9/553* missing first 24 ff Gulf of Nicoya 76r *estoricas* (2), 92v, 93r house, 97v	BC *57-5-43* enlarged and colored copies of the Gulf, 126r spear, 148v and house, 154–55	RAH *9-401-8* copy of bks. 29–32 includes illustrations	
XXX Cartago	RAH *9/553*			

Book	*Autograph Ms. Monserrate Ms.@RAH & HEH*	*16th-century copy Gascó/Trujillo @ BC & PR* (ca. 1570 copy of bks 17–50*)*	*18th-century copy Muñoz @ RAH (copy of extensive sections of the* HG*)*	*1535/47/57 edition, woodcuts*
XXXI Honduras	RAH *9/553*			
XXXII Yucatán	HEH *HM-177* metal knocker on the Giralda in Sevilla, 94r horse ferry 95–96	BC *57-5-43* copy contains no knocker or horse ferry		
XXXIII New Spain	RAH *9/555* missing chaps. 34–42 volcano 157r	BC *57-5-43* volcano		
XXXIV New Galicia	RAH *9/554,* missing chaps. 6–9?			
XXXV Florida	RAH *9/554*			
XXXVI Florida government	missing by 1780			
XXXVII Also Florida	HEH *HM-177*			
XXXVIII Land mass	missing by 1780			
XXXIX Southern/ Austral seas	missing most of bks. 39 to 45 (1930)	PR *II/3042* snake, 12r		
XL Southern Passage Pacific Shore	missing			

(*continued*)

Book	*Autograph Ms. Monserrate Ms.@RAH & HEH*	*16th-century copy Gascó/Trujillo @ BC & PR* (ca. 1570 copy of bks 17–50)	*18th-century copy Muñoz @ RAH (copy of extensive sections of the* HG)	*1535/47/57 edition, woodcuts*
(*continued*)				
XLI Guatemala	missing			
XLII Nicaragua	RAH *9/557* contains chaps. 7–10 no illustrations	PR *II/3042* island of Ometepet, 56v Volcano of Mamea, 60v Alos llanos de los maribios@ 61v volcano of Masaya, 62–63 Masaya crater, 65r *voladores,* 84v Plaza of Tecoatega, 101–2 whirlabout, 104v		
XLIII Castilla del Oro	missing (1930)	PR *II/3042* map of Panama coast, 109r		
XLIV Peru	missing (1930)			
XLV Popayan	missing (1930)			
XLVI Nueva Castilla	RAH *9/556* chaps. 1, 14, 21–22; rest is missing	PR *II/3042* Inca weapon, 226v Inca head & hat, 231r		

Book	*Autograph Ms. Monserrate Ms.@RAH & HEH*	*16th-century copy Gascó/Trujillo @ BC & PR* (ca. 1570 copy of bks 17–50*)*	*18th-century copy Muñoz @ RAH (copy of extensive sections of the* HG*)*	*1535/47/57 edition, woodcuts*
XLVII New Toledo	RAH *9/556* missing chap. 23			
XLVIII Pizarro	RAH *9/557* missing ff. 1–35			
XLIX Quito	RAH *9/557* missing chaps. 1–9, 11–16			
L Shipwrecks	RAH *9/557* missing chaps. 22–30			Oviedo's coat of arms, f. 193v

APPENDIX E

Illustrations

La historia general delas Indias.

Con priuilegio imperial.

FIGURE 1.
Title page, Historia general y natural de las Indias, 1535 edition

Segundo. Fo x.

licos hizieron ſeñaladas mercedes: y en eſpecial le confirmaron ſu preuilegio enla dicha Barcelona. a. xxviij. de Mayo de mil y cccc.xciij. y entre otras de mas de le hazer noble ⁊ dar titulo de almirante perpetuo deſtas Indias a el ⁊ a ſus ſuceſſores / por via de mayoradgo. y que todos los que del dependieſſen: ⁊ avn ſus hermanos ſe llamaſſen don: le dieron las miſmas armas reales de Caſtilla y de Leon mezcladas ⁊ repartidas con otras que aſſi meſmo le concedieron de nueuo: aprouando ⁊ confirmando de ſu auctoridad real las otras armas antiguas de ſu linaje. E delas vnas ⁊ las otras formaron vn nueuo y hermoſo Eſcudo de armas con ſu Timbre ⁊ deuiſa / enla manera ⁊ forma que aqui ſe contiene: y ſe vee patente.

Vn eſcudo cõ vn caſtillo de oro en cãpo de goles o ſanguino cõ las puertas ⁊ vẽtanas azules: ⁊ vn leõ de purpura / o morado ẽ cãpo de plata cõ vna corona de oro: la lengua ſacada ⁊ rãpãte / aſſi como los reyes de caſtilla ⁊ de leõ los traen. Y aqſte caſtillo ⁊ leõ hã deſtar enel chieph o cabeça del eſcudo: el caſtillo enla parte derecha. y el Leõ enla ſinieſtra. Y de alli abaxo las dos partes reſtãtes del eſcudo todo / hã de eſtar partidas en mãtel: y enla parte derecha vna mar en memoria del grande mar oceano: las aguas al natural azules y blancas: ⁊ pueſta la tierra firme delas indias / que tome quaſi la circunferencia deſte quarto / dexãdola parte ſuperior ⁊ alta del abierta / de manera que las puntas deſta tierra grande mueſtran ocupar las partes del medio dia ⁊ tramontana. E la parte inferior que ſignifica

b ij

FIGURE 2.

Columbus's Coat of Arms (1535) Bk. 2, chap. 7

alos que enella no se ocupan. Pero quanto ala dificultad que dixe que padescē las agujas/o mejor diziendo el entendimiento ālos hōbres (pues ellas nos enseñan lo q̄ agora dixe) cree se quel diametro ⁊ mitad del mundo/o linea que atrauiessa de polo a polo cruzando la equinocial: passa por las yslas delos açores: porque nunca las agujas estan derechamente ⁊ de todo punto fixas en perficion de medio a medio del polo Artico: sino quando las naos ⁊ carauelas estan en aquel paraje ⁊ altura. Y quando de alli passan hazia estas partes ocidentales noruestean bien vna quarta quando mas se desuian de alli. E passando ala buelta para leuante desde las dichas yslas delos açores nordestean otra quarta q̄nto mas se alerā. Assi q̄ aquesto es lo que quise dezir quando toq̄ esta dificultad delas agujas para nuestro proposito. ¶ Quiero dezir otra cosa muy notable/q̄ los que no han nauegado por estas indias no la pueden auer visto: saluo los q̄ fuerē en ōmāda dela equinocial/o estuuierē alomenos en veynte ⁊ dos grados poco mas o menos della: y es que mirando ala parte del sur veran que se alçan sobre el orizonte quatro estrellas en cruz ✱ que andan al der

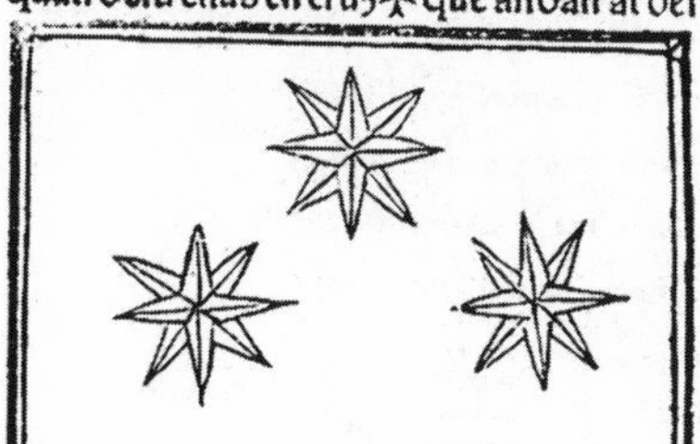

redor del circulo delas guardas del polo antartico/dela forma q̄ estā enesta figura puestas: las quales la cesarea. M. me dio por mejoramiento de mis armas: para que yo ⁊ mis sucessores las pusiessemos juntamente cōlas nr̄as antiguas de valdes/auiendo respecto alo q̄ yo he seruido en̄stas partes ⁊ indias ⁊ primero enla casa real de castilla: desde q̄ oue treze años: porq̄ en tal hedad comēce a seruir enla camara al serenissimo principe dō Juā mi señor ō gloriosa memoria: tio dela cesarea. M. ⁊ despues de sus dias alos reyes catholicos dō fernādo ⁊ doña ysabel de immortal recordacion: ⁊ ōspues a sus magestades: las q̄les armas estaran en fin ōste tractado pues q̄ es escripto en̄stas p̄tes dōde tātos trabajos padecē los hōbres q̄ veē estas estrellas: ⁊ dōde yo he gastado lo mejor de mi vida. toq̄ esta particularidad ōstas estrellas porq̄ son muy notable figura en̄l cielo. Enel q̄l ay otras innumerables q̄ se veē poco ātes dellas al parecer hazia el artico: y de alli discurriēdo la vista ala parte austral verā el cielo tan lleno de estrellas como esta sobre españa en diferentes interualos o figuras: q̄ no se veē ningūas dellas desde España/ni desde parte de toda la europa: ni enla mayor p̄te de asia ni africa/sino fuere passādo delos veynte ⁊ dos grados del polo artico: abaxādo el numero ōllos ala parte ōl polo antartico/yendo hazia la equinocial: ni se puedē ver en todo el tropico ō cācer. ¶ Tornādo ala historia tiēpo es q̄ se diga porque causa los indios ⁊ gente del rey goacanagari matarō enesta ysla española alos xp̄ianos q̄ el primero viaje dexo enella el Almirante don christoual colom: ⁊ que gentes fallo en esta tierra/hasta que adelante se continuen las otras cosas q̄ ala historia cōuienē: pa q̄ despues cō mas atēcion se escriuā los animales ⁊ aues ⁊ arboles ⁊ frutas ⁊ mātenimientos q̄ los idios teniā pa su sustētaciō: ⁊ las otras cosas q̄ hizierē al caso ōla historia.

¶ Capi. xij. delo que hizo el almirāte dō xp̄oual colō despues q̄ supo q̄ los idios auiā muerto los xp̄ianos q̄ dxo en esta ysla española el primero viaje/⁊ como fundo la cibdad dela ysabela ⁊ la fortaleza de sancto thomas: ⁊ como descubrio la ysla de jamayca: ⁊ vido mas particularmente la ysla ⁊ costa de cuba: ⁊ delas primeras muestras ō oro ō minas q̄ se lleuaron a españa.

FIGURE 3.
Southern Cross (1535) Bk. 2, chap. 11

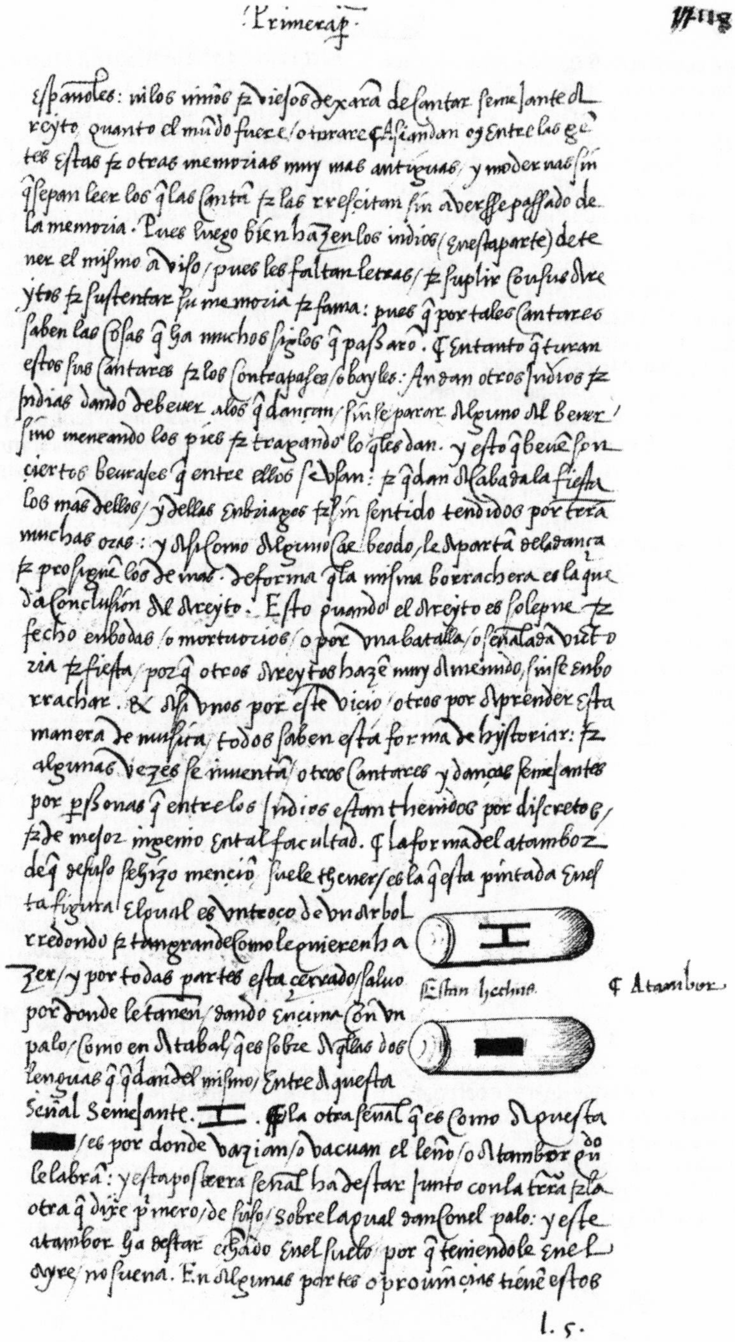

Primera p. 118

españoles: ni los niños y viejos dexarã de cantar semejante al
areyto quanto el mũdo fuere / o turare. Assi andan oy entre las gẽ
tes estas y otras memorias muy mas antiguas, y modernas sin
q sepan leer los q las cantã y las rresciten sin averse passado de
la memoria. Pues luego bien hazen los indios (en esta parte) de te
ner el mismo aviso / pues les faltan letras, y suplir con sus arey
tos y sustentar su memoria y fama: pues q por tales cantares
saben las cosas q ha muchos siglos q passarõ. ¶ En tanto q turan
estos sus cantares y los contrapasses / o bayles: andan otros indios y
indias dando de bever alos q dançan / sin se parar alguno al bever
sino meneando los pies y tragando lo q les dan. y esto q beuẽ son
ciertos beurajes q entre ellos se usan: y q dan al cabada la fiesta
los mas dellos / y dellas embriagos y sin sentido tendidos por tierra
muchas oras: y assi como alguno cae beodo, le apartã de la dança
y prosiguẽ los demas. de forma q la misma borrachera es la que
da conclusion al areyto. Esto quando el areyto es solepne y
fecho en bodas / o mortuorios / o por una batalla / o señalada vict o
ria y fiesta, porq otros areytos hazẽ muy al menudo, sin se enbo
rrachar. & assi unos por este vicio / otros por aprender esta
manera de musica, todos saben esta forma de hystoriar: y
algunas vezes se inventã otros cantares y danças semejantes
por psonas q entre los indios estan thenidos por discretos,
y de mejor ingenio en tal facultad. ¶ La forma del atambor
de q de susso se hizo mẽciõ suele thener / es la q esta pintada en es
ta figura. El qual es un troço de un arbol
rredondo y tan grande como le quieren ha
zer / y por todas partes esta cerrado / saluo
por donde le tanen / dando encima con un
palo, como en atabal, q es sobre aquellas dos
lenguas q q dan del mismo, entre aquesta
señal semejante. . ¶ la otra señal q es como aquesta
/ es por donde vaziam / o vacuan el leño / o atambor
en le labrã: y esta postrera señal ha de estar junto con la tierra y la
otra q dixe p̃mero, de susso / sobre la qual dan con el palo: y este
atambor ha destar echado en el suelo por q teniendole en el
ayre, no suena. En algunas partes o provincias tienẽ estos

Estan hechos ¶ Atambor

l. 5.

FIGURE 4.
Tambores *(RAH, 9/551, 14r) Bk. 5, chap. 2*

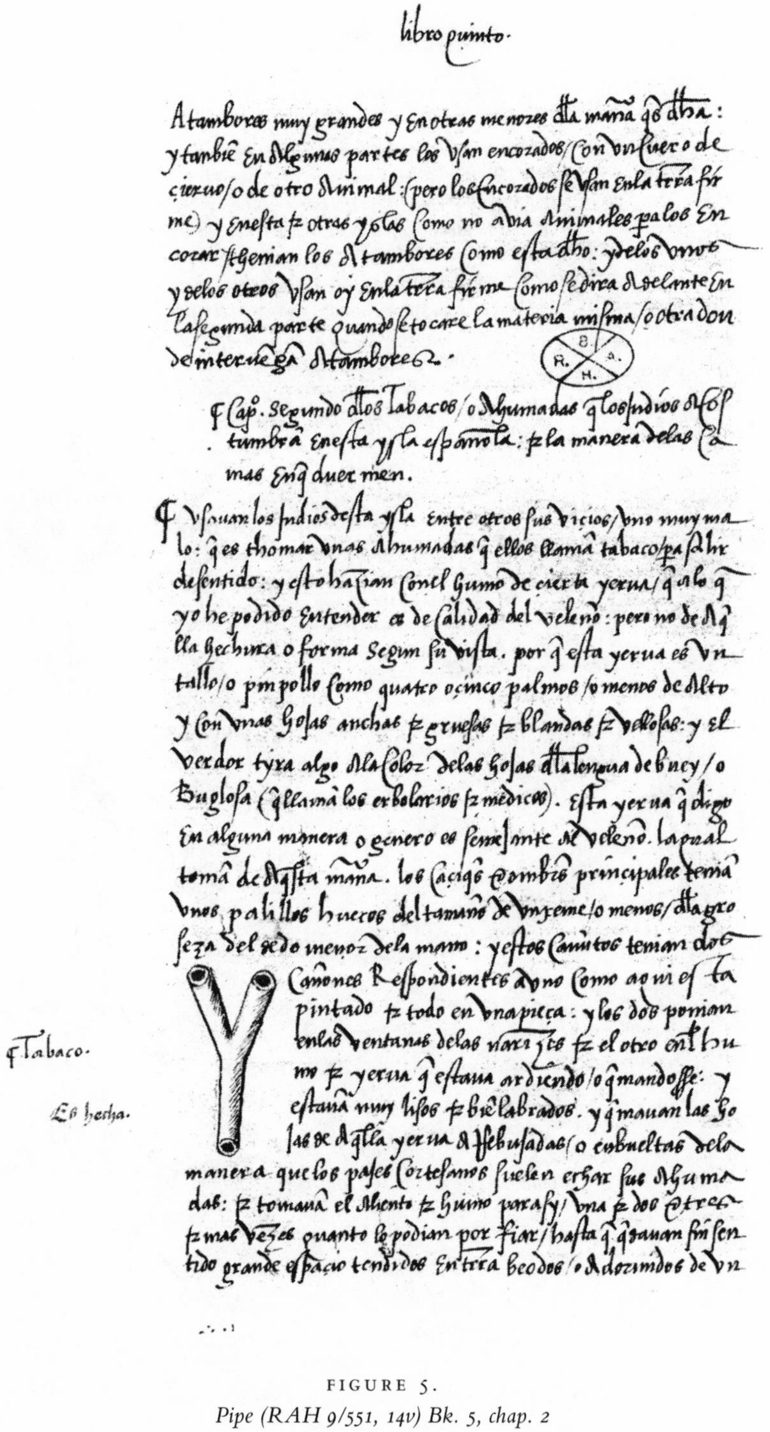
libro quinto.

Atambores muy grandes y en otras menores de la manera que es dicha: y tambien en algunas partes los usan encorados / con un cuero de cieruo / o de otro animal: (pero los encorados se usan en la tierra firme) y en esta e otras yslas (como no avia animales para los encorar) tenian los atambores como esta dicho: y de los unos y de los otros usan oy en la tierra firme (como se dira adelante en la segunda parte quando se tocare la materia misma / o otra donde intervenga atambores.

¶ Cap.º segundo de los tabacos / o ahumadas que los indios acostumbran en esta ysla española: e la manera de las camas en que duermen.

¶ Usavan los indios desta ysla entre otros sus vicios / uno muy malo: que es thomar unas ahumadas que ellos llaman tabaco / para salir de sentido: y esto hazian con el humo de cierta yerva / que a lo que yo he podido entender es de calidad del veleño: pero no de aquella hechura o forma segun su vista. por que esta yerva es un tallo / o pimpollo como quatro o cinco palmos / o menos de alto y con unas hojas anchas e gruesas e blandas e vellosas: y el verdor tyra algo a la color de las hojas de la lengua de buey / o buglosa (que llaman los erbolarios e medicos). esta yerva que digo en alguna manera o genero es semejante al veleño. la qual toman de aquesta manera. los caciques e hombres principales tenian unos palillos huecos del tamaño de un xeme / o menos / de la grosesa del dedo menor de la mano: y estos cañutos tenian dos cañones respondientes a uno como aqui esta pintado e todo en una pieça: y los dos ponian en las ventanas de las narizes e el otro en el humo e yerva que estava ardiendo / o quemandose: y estavan muy lisos e bien labrados. y quemavan las hojas de aquella yerva arrebujadas / o embueltas de la manera que los pajes cortesanos suelen echar sus ahumadas: e tomavan el aliento e humo para sy / una e dos e tres e mas vezes quanto lo podian porfiar / hasta que quedavan sin sentido grande espacio tendidos en tierra beodos / o adormidos de un

¶ Tabaco.

Es hecha.

FIGURE 5.
Pipe (RAH 9/551, 14v) Bk. 5, chap. 2

FIGURE 6.
Hammock (RAH 9/155, 16r) Bk. 5, chap. 2

FIGURE 7.
Caney *(HEH,* HM-177, *3v) Bk. 6, chap. 1*

+ 4

son las casas, o bohios o eracras desta ysla, & de otras yslas, q los indios hazen en pueblos y comunidades y tanbié en caserias apartados enel campo: y tanbié de otras diferencias das maneras como se dira en la segunda p.te desta natural y gñal hystoria quando se tratte delas casas dela tierra firme. Por q alla en algunas prouincias son de otra forma: y avn algunas dellas nunca oydas ni vistas, sino en aqlla tierra. Pero pues se debuxo la forma del caney/o casa redonda quiero assi mismo poner aqui la segunda manera de casas que he dicho. la qual es como aquesta q esta aqui patente para que mejor se entienda lo que en la una y en la otra tengo dicho. y puedesse thener por cierto que los dos otros dichos p.meros, la cubierta de paja, si es buena y bien puesta, q son de menos goteras q las casas de teja en españa: pero passado el tpo que digo ya la paja va pudriendosse & es nescessario renouar la cubierta & avn tanbié los estantes o postes excepto si son de algunas maderas delas q ay en estas partes q no se pudren debaxo de tierra assi como la corbana en esta ysla: y el guayacan me dize q en la prouincia de venençuela hazé estantes dlas casas con ello & q no se pudre, por ningñ tpo: y en la tierra firme ay otra madera q la llaman los xpianos madera prieta q tanpoco no se pudre debaxo de la tierra. pero por q en otras partes se ha de tractar delas maderas y se especificara mas las calidades dellas no ay nescessidad de dezir aqui mas delo q toca a estos edificios o maneras de casas:-

Cap. ij. del juego del Batey delos indios, q es el mismo q el dla pelota: avnq se juega de otra manera como aqui se dira. y la pelota es de otra especie o materia: q las pelotas que entre los xpianos se usan:-

Pues enel cap. de suso se dixo dla forma delos pueblos & delas casas delos indios: y q en cada pueblo avia lugar diputado enlas placas

otra manera de casa

Esta hecha.

NO
maderas q no se pudren debaxo de tierra.

FIGURE 8.
Caney *(HEH,* HM-177, *4r) Bk. 6, chap. 1*

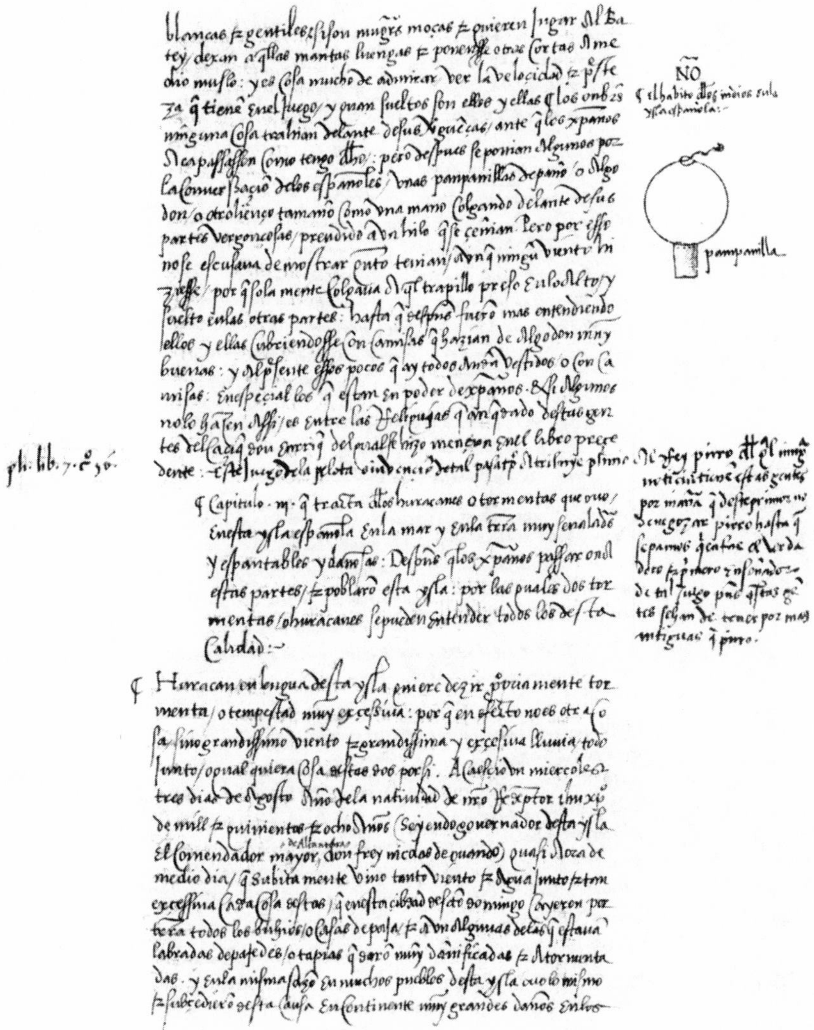

FIGURE 9.
Pampanillas *(HEH,* HM-177, *5v) Bk. 6, chap. 2*

FIGURE 10.

Axe (HEH, HM-177, *7v) Bk. 6, chap. 4*

8

barca quasi de talle de artesa / o dornajo: pero honda y luenga y estrecha: tan grande y gruesa como lo sufre la longitud y latitud del arbol de que la hazen: y por debaxo es llana y no le dexan quilla co mo a nuestras barcas y navios. Estas he visto de porte de quarenta y cinquenta ombres / y tan anchas que podria estar de traves una pipa holgadamente / entre los indios flecheros: porque destos usan estas canoas tan grandes / o mayores como lo que he dicho y llamanlas los caribes piraguas: y navegan con velas de algodon / y al remo asi mismo con sus nahes / (que assi llaman a los remos) y van algunas vezes bogando de pies / y a vezes asentados / y quando quieren de rodillas. Son estos nahes como palas luengas / y las caberas como una muleta de un coxo / o tollido. segun aqui esta pintado el nahe o remo y canoa. Ay algunas destas canoas tan pequeñas que no caben sino dos o tres indios: y otras seys y otras diez y de ay adelante segun su grandeza. Pero las unas y las otras son muy ligeras y mas peligrosas: por que se trastornan muchas vezes: pero no se

hunden aunque se hinchan de agua. Y como estos indios son grandes nadadores tornanlas a enderesçar / y danse muy buena maña a las vaziar. No son navios que se aparten mucho de la tierra por que como son baxos no pueden sufrir grande mar: y si haze un poco de temporal luego se anegan. y aunque no se hundan / no es buen passatiempo / andar asido (dentro del agua) a la canoa / en especial el que no sabe nadar / como ha acaescido muchas vezes [illegible] an ahogado. y con todo esso son mas seguras estas canoas que otras barcas (en caso del hundirse) por que aunque las barcas se hunden menos vezes / por ser mas alterosas y de mas sosten / las que una vez se hunden vanse al suelo. y las canoas aunque se aneguen

FIGURE II.
Canoe (HEH, HM-177, 8r) Bk. 6, chap. 4

FIGURE 12.
Fire drill (HEH, HM-177, 9r) Bk. 6, chap. 5

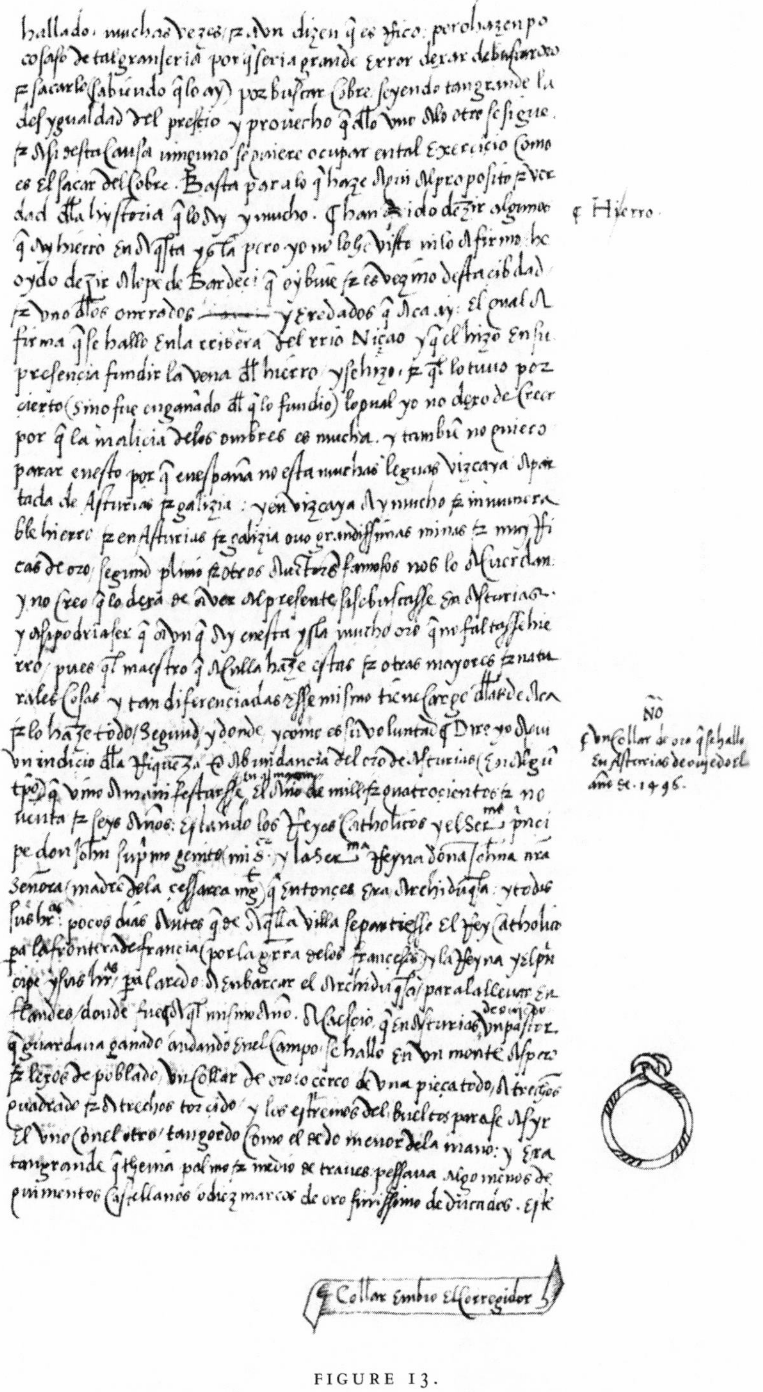
hallado muchas vezes & aun dizen q es rrico. pero no hazen po
co caso de tal granjeria por q seria grande error dexar de buscar oro
& sacarlo sabiendo q lo ay por buscar cobre seyendo tan grande la
desygualdad del precio y provecho q de lo uno a lo otro se sigue.
& asi desta causa ninguno se quiere ocupar en tal exercicio como
es el sacar del cobre. Basta para lo q haze aqui al proposito & ver
dad de la hystoria q lo ay y mucho. ¶ han querido dezir algunos
q ay hierro en aquesta ysla pero yo no lo he visto ni lo afirmo. he
oydo dezir a lope de bardeci q oy bive & es vezino desta cibdad
& uno de los onrrados y eredados q aca ay: el qual a
firma q se hallo en la ribera del rrio Niçao y q el hizo en su
presencia fundir la vena de hierro y se hizo. & q lo tuvo por
cierto (si no fue engañado de q lo fundio) lo qual yo no dexo de creer
por q la malicia de los ombres es mucha. y tambien no quiero
parar en esto por q en españa no esta muchas leguas Vizcaya apar
tada de Asturias & galizia: y en vizcaya ay mucho & innumera
ble hierro & en Asturias & galizia ovo grandissimas minas & muy ri
cas de oro segund plinio & otros auctores famosos nos lo acuerdan.
y no creo q lo dexa de aver al presente si se buscasse en asturias.
y asi podria ser q aun q ay en esta ysla mucho oro q no faltasse hie
rro pues el maestro q aquella haze estas & otras mayores & natu
rales cosas y tan diferenciadas esse mismo tiene cargo de [illegible] de aca
& lo haze todo segund y donde y como es su voluntad. Dire yo aqui
un indicio de la riqueza e abundancia del oro de asturias en algun
tiempo q vino a manifestarse el año de mill & quatrocientos & no
venta & seys años: estando los Reyes Catholicos y el Serenisimo princi
pe don Johan su primo genito (mi señor) y la Serenisima Reyna doña Johana nra
señora madre de la cessarea magestad q entonces era archiduquesa: y todos
sus hermanos pocos dias antes q de aquella villa se partiesse el Rey catholico
pa la frontera de francia (por la guerra delos franceses) y la Reyna y el prin
cipe y sus hermanas pa Laredo a enbarcar el archiduquesa para la llevar en
flandes donde fue aquel mismo año. Acaescio q en Asturias de oviedo un pastor
q guardava ganado andando en el campo se hallo en un monte apar
& lexos de poblado un collar de oro: o cerco de una pieça todo a trechos
quadrado & a trechos torcido y los estremos del bueltos para se asyr
el uno con el otro tan gordo como el dedo menor de la mano: y era
tan grande q tenia palmo & medio de traves pessava algo menos de
quinientos castellanos o diez marcos de oro finissimo de durados. este

¶ Hierro

No
¶ Un collar de oro q se hallo en Asturias de oviedo el año de 1496.

¶ Collar embio el corregidor

FIGURE 13.

Asturian gold collar (HEH, HM-177, 12v) Bk. 6, chap. 8

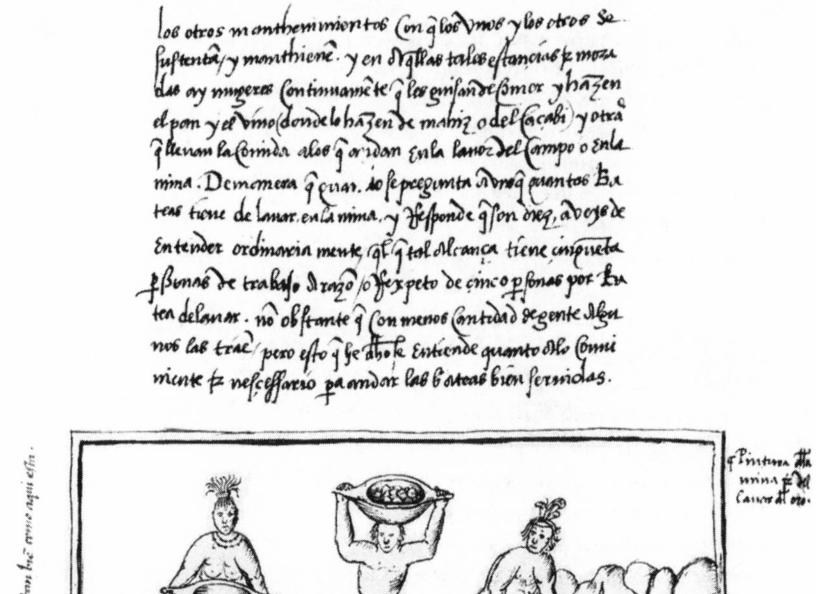

los otros mantenimientos con que los unos y los otros se
sustentan y mantienen. y en aquellas tales estancias e moradas ay mugeres continuamente que les guisan de comer y hazen
el pan y el vino (donde lo hazen de mahiz o del caçabi) y otras
que llevan la comida a los que andan en la labor del campo o en la
mina. De manera que quando se pregunta a alguno quantos bateas tiene de lavar en la mina. y responde que son diez, ase de
entender ordinariamente que el que tal alcança tiene cinquenta
personas de trabajo a razon o respeto de cinco personas por batea de lavar. no obstante que con menos cantidad de gente algunos las trae, pero esto que he dicho se entiende quanto a lo conviniente e nescessario para andar las bateas bien servidas.
Sacasse oro de otra manera en los rios e arroyos o lagunas de
agua: y es desta forma. Si es laguna procuran de la agotar siendo pequeña y que se pueda hazer: y despues labran y lavan aquella tierra del suelo y cogen el oro que en ella hallan segun se dixo de
suso. Pero si es rio o arroyo el que se ha de labrar sacan el agua
de su curso e despues que esta seco en medio de la madre por donde
primero yva el agua assi como la han samurado (que en lengua o
estilo de los que son mineros platicos quiere dezir agotado: porque
xamurar es agotar) hallan oro entre las piedras y oquedades

FIGURE 14.

Gold panning scene (HEH, HM-177, *18v) Bk. 6, chap. 8*

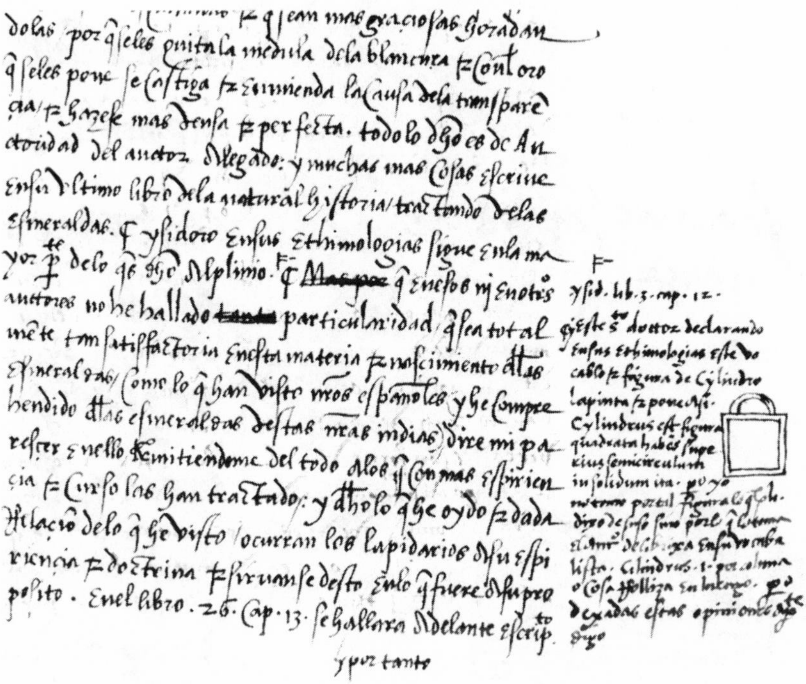

FIGURE 15.
San Isidro's geometric cylinder (HEH, HM-177, *36r, detail) Bk. 6, chap. 27*

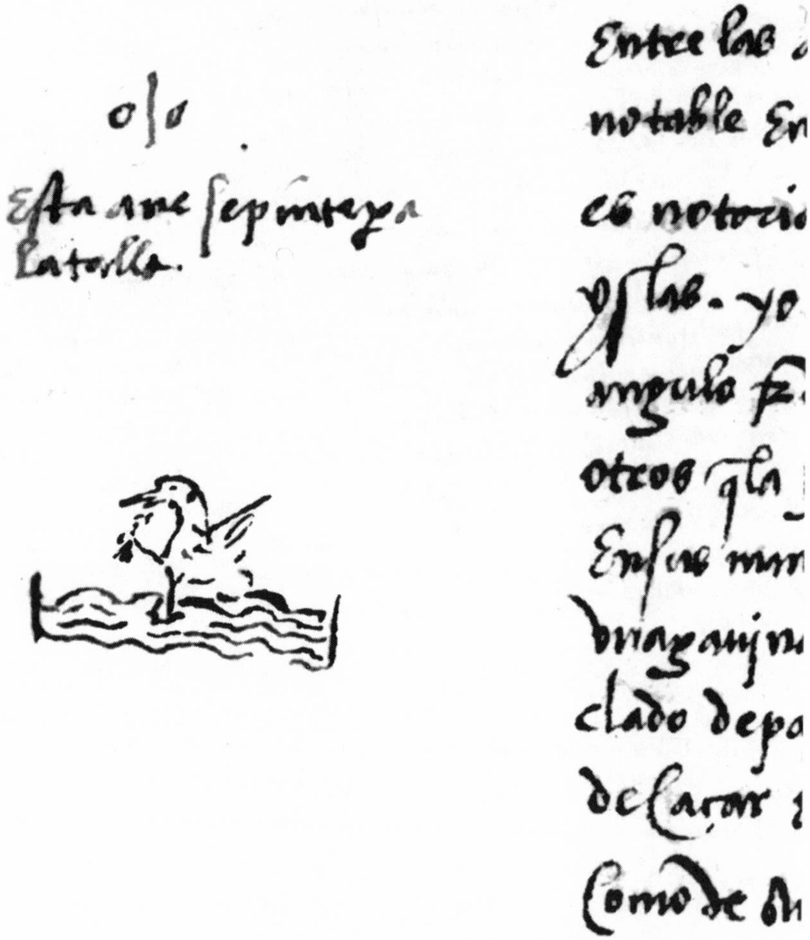

FIGURE 16.
Fanciful bird (HEH, HM-177, *45r) Bk. 6, chap. 36*

37

das de xpianos: y aun en algunas partes della tierra firme. ¶ La planta que
se llama yuca, son unas varas nudosas algo mas altas que un ombre
y otras mucho menores, gruesas como dos dedos y algunas mas
y otras menos. porque en esto del grossor y de la altura, es segun la
tierra es fertil o flaca: y aun tambien haze al caso que la planta es de di
uersos generos. quiere alguna yuca parescer en la hoja al cañamo
o como una palma de una mano del ombre abiertos los dedos ten
didos salvo que aquesta hoja es mayor e mas gruesa que la del cañamo e
cada hoja es de siete o de nueve puntas o departimientos. la vara
es muy nudosa como he dicho, y la tez della es como pardo blanquisco / y algunas quasi morada
e la hoja muy verde e paresce muy bien en el campo desque esta
criada e bien limpia la eredad en que esta.
¶ Ay otra generacion de yuca que las Ra
mas ni el fructo no es diferente della
que es dicho de suso: salvo en la hoja porque
aunque es assi mesmo de siete o de nueve
departiciones cada hoja, es de otra he
chura: e por tanto puse la forma de
la una e de la otra aqui debuxadas.
non obstante que en las mismas mane
ras de hojas, ay particulares y diferencia
das suertes o generaciones de yuca. y unas tienen mas ver
dor que otras e otras mas espezia Rama e otras mas o menos
blancor en el bastago o asta e otras diferencias en la corte
za que aqui hazen poco al caso dezirse. ¶ Para sembrar esta
planta (qual quiera dellas que he
dicho) hazen unos montones de
tierra redondos, por orden e limos
como en el reyno de toledo ponen
las viñas, y en especial en Ma
drid que se ponen las cepas a compas.
Cada monton tiene ocho o nueve
pies en redondo e las haldas del
uno tocan con poco intervalo
cerca del otro: e lo alto del monton no es
puntiagudo sino quasi llano e lo mas alto del
sera a la rodilla o algo mas e en cada monton ponen de ye /

Esta hecha mas no como esta.

n. 5.

FIGURE 17.
Yucca leaves (HEH, HM-177, *37r) Bk. 7, chap. 2*

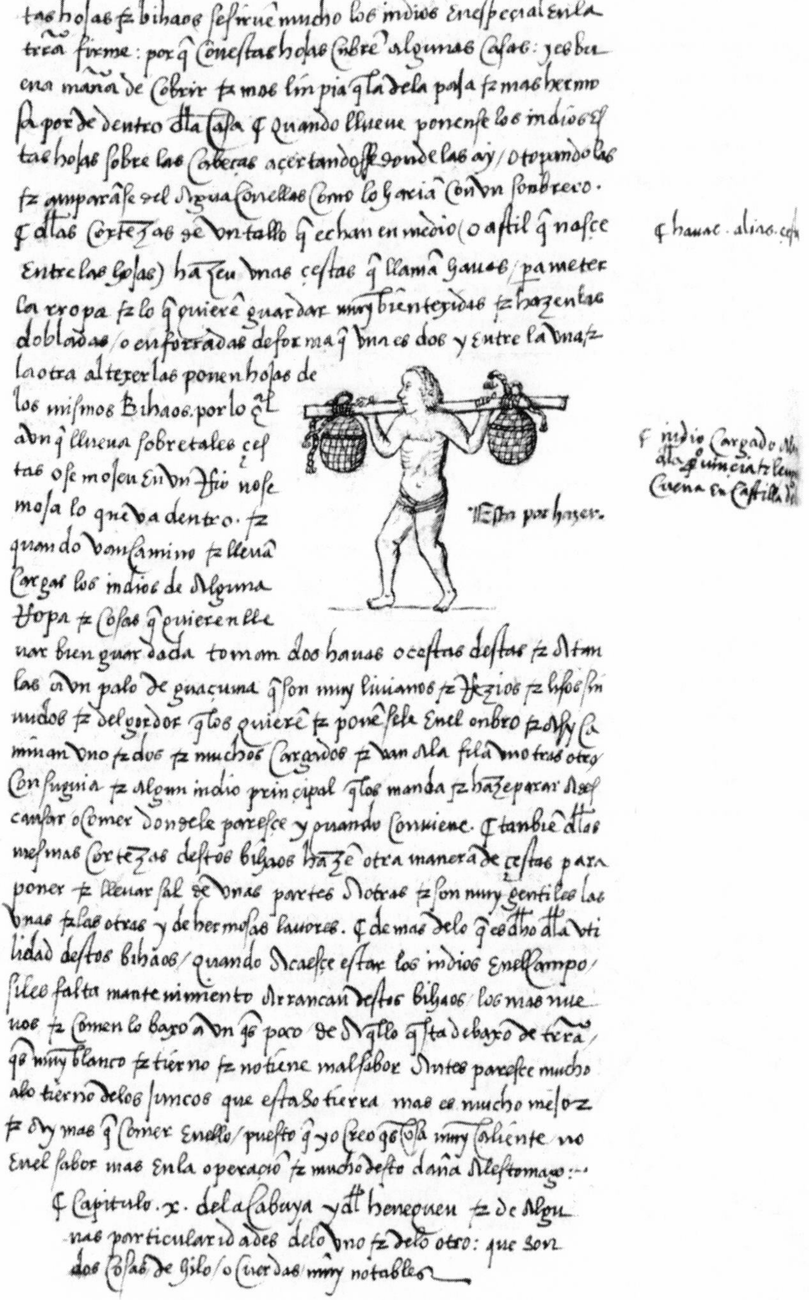
tas hojas & bihaos se sirue mucho los indios en especial en la
tierra firme: porq̃ con estas hojas cubre algunas casas: y es buena mañera de cobrir & mas limpia q̃ la dela paja & mas hermo
sa por de dentro dela casa ¶ Quando llueue ponense los indios es
tas hojas sobre las cabeças acertandose donde las ay / o topando las
& amparanse del agua con ellas como lo haria con vn sombrero.
¶ delas cortezas de vn tallo q̃ echan en medio (o astil q̃ nasce
entre las hojas) hazen vnas cestas q̃ llaman hauas pa meter
la ropa & lo q̃ quieren guardar muy bien texidas & hazen las
dobladas / o enforradas de forma q̃ vna es dos y entre la vna &
la otra al texer las ponen hojas de
los mismos bihaos. por lo q̃l
avnq̃ llueua sobre tales ces
tas o se mojen en vn rrio no se
moja lo que va dentro. &
quando van camino & lleuan
cargas los indios de alguna
ropa & cosas q̃ quieren lle
uar bien guardada toman dos hauas o cestas destas & atan
las a vn palo de guaçuma q̃ son muy liuianos & rezios & lisos sin
nudos & del gordor q̃ los quieren & ponen sele en el onbro & assy ca
minan vno & dos & muchos cargados & van a la fila vno tras otro
con su guia & algun indio principal q̃ los manda & haze parar a des
cansar o comer donde le paresce y quando conuiene. ¶ tanbien delas
mesmas cortezas destos bihaos haze otra manera de cestas para
poner & lleuar sal de vnas partes a otras & son muy gentiles las
vnas & las otras y de hermosas lauores. ¶ demas delo q̃ es dho dela vti
lidad destos bihaos / quando acaesce estar los indios en el campo /
si les falta mantenimiento arrancan destos bihaos los mas nue
uos & comen lo baxo a vn geme poco de aquello q̃ sta debaxo de tierra
q̃ es muy blanco & tierno & no tiene mal sabor antes paresce mucho
alo tierno delos juncos que esta so tierra mas es mucho mejor
& ay mas q̃ comer en ello / puesto q̃ yo creo q̃ es cosa muy caliente no
en el sabor mas en la operaçion & mucho desto daña al estomago:—
¶ Capitulo. x. dela cabuya y del henequen & de algunas particularidades delo vno & delo otro: que son
dos cosas de hilo / o cuerdas muy notables

¶ hauas. alias. cestas

Esta por hazer.

¶ indio cargado

FIGURE 18.

Indian carrying baskets (HEH, HM-177, 42v) Bk. 7, chap. 9

forma siegan vn hierro por gruesso q̃ sea, z lo cortan como si fuesse vna cosa tierna / o muy facil de cortar. ¶ En tierra firme he yo visto esçido cortar d'trocas los indios ancoras de navios d'la manera q̃ esta dicho. ¶ Quando se tracte d'la segunda parte d'esta general hyst.ª de indias y de la tierra firme se diran mas particularidades d'estas cuerdas d'l henequen e de la cabuya, por q̃ alla se sirven mucho dellas: assi en lo q̃ esta dicho como en otras maneras :–

¶ Cap.º xj. d'l maguey. que es otra yerva en algo semejante d'la cabuya: puede servir de mantenimiento: en tp̃o de nesçessidad z el principal efecto suyo es para hilos: y d'estos cordeles o sogas muy buenas e para otras cosas :–

¶ En la impressiõ primera d'estas cosas de indias no se hizo mençiõ de vna yerva muy vtil z nesçessaria en estas partes la qual se llama Maguey z tiene mucha semejança con la yuca assi en algunos efettos z provechos como en la vista. la hoja della vna e de la otra son anchas en los estremos z vienense ensangostando hasta su nasçimiento: pero nasçen en vn tronco o d'la manera q̃ nasçe vna lechuga z es por ençima se d'aq̃l tronco assi q̃ toma vn campo redondo / o compas de vna braça / segund son grandes o pequeñas. este maguey echa en la mitad vna vara / o tallo liso e derecho / mas alto q̃ vn ombre biẽ alto: y en el fin d'este bastago vnas flores en el estremo amarillas z hechas en vna cantidad de vn palmo en lo mas alto q̃ paresçen vna maçorca (o talle della). d'la manera que se hazen en españa los gamones. Esta es muy vtil z buena yerva por q̃ se hazen d'lla muchas cosas. lo vno hazese hilo / z cuerdas z sogas como de la cabuya z d'l henequen. lo otro d'la corteza de aq̃lla vara q̃ nasçe en la mitad se hazen çestas z atan con ella lo q̃ quierẽ. y de mas desto en tp̃o de nesçessidad a falta de mahiz z caçabi z de otros manthenimientos / es manjar para suplir la hambre z no de mal sabor. por q̃ de aq̃lla cepa / o rayz en q̃ nasçe se asa z lo comẽ los ombres / no por dulçe pasto / mas no teniendo otros manjares este no es dañoso ni empacha z basta a sostener la gente. En la vista es muy hermosa de ver esta yerva / o planta, las hojas de la qual son mayores q̃ desde el cobdo de vn ombre hasta en fin

FIGURE 19.

Maguey plant (HEH, HM-177, *43v) Bk. 7, chap. 11*

FIGURE 20.

Pineapple (HEH, HM-177, *46r) Bk. 7, chap. 13 (14)*

eneſta cibdad. El primero arbol que ouo eneſta yſla de eſtos fue enel moneſterio de ſant franciſco dela ciudad dela vega: ⁊ por enxẽplo de aqͥl ſe puſierõ otros ⁊ ſe hizierõ eſtos eredamiẽtos ⁊ grãjeria q̃ es muy buena ⁊ prouechoſa ⁊ rica: ⁊ las naues que tornan a eſpaña ſiempre lleuan muchas pipas llenas deſta cañafiſtola.

¶.viij. Hãſe pueſto ⁊ ay eñſta cibdad muchas parras delas d̃ caſtilla ⁊ lleuã buenas vuas ⁊ aſſi creo q̃ ſe hariã en grãde abundãcia ſi ſe dieſſen a ellas: y entendieſſen biẽ lo que han meneſter: porque como la tierra es humeda luego que ha dado el fruto la parra / ſi luego la podan / luego torna a brotar: ⁊ aſſi ſe eſquilman mucho ⁊ ſe enuejecẽ preſto. Eſtas ſe truxeron de caſtilla: pero ſin eſtas deſta cibdad ay muchas parras de las miſmas enlos eredamiẽtos ⁊ poblaciones deſtas yſlas traydas como he dicho de eſpaña: no obſtante lo qual digo que aſſi eneſta yſla como en otras y en muchas partes dela tierra firme ay muchas parras ſaluajes ⁊ de muy buenas vuas: ⁊ de muchas dellas he yo comido enla tierra firme: y es coſa muy comun: ⁊ aſſi creo que fueron todas las d̃l mũdo en ſu p̃ncipio: ⁊ d̃las tales ſe tomo el origẽ pa las cultiuar ⁊ hazer mejores.

¶.ix. Ay eneſta cibdad algunos oliuos grãdes ⁊ hermoſos arboles que aſſi miſmo fueron traydos de eſpaña: pero ſon eſteriles ⁊ no lleuan fructo ſino hojas. Y tambien los ay en algunos eredamiẽtos ⁊ otras partes deſta yſla: pero como he dicho ſin fruto. Y es gran notable que todas las frutas d̃ cueſco que ſe han traydo de eſpaña / o de otras partes a eſta yſla / por marauilla prenden: ⁊ ſi prenden no lleuan fruto alguno ſino hojas. Por cierto yo he traydo cueſcos d̃ duraznos: ⁊ melocotones / ⁊ aluerchigas d̃ toledo / ⁊ ciruelas de frayle: ⁊ de guindas ⁊ cerezas ⁊ piñones: ⁊ todos eſtos cueſcos he hecho ſembrar en diuerſas partes y eredades ⁊ ninguna de todas ha prendido. Plinio: lib. doze: capitu. ſeſto / dize que los oliuos enla india ſon eſteriles ⁊ que no produzen otro fruto del que haze el oliuo ſaluaje. De manera que eſtos nueſtros deſta yſla ſon mas eſteriles que los que Plinio dize dela india: porque ſi aquellos como el dize dã el fruto que los oliuos ſaluajes / o azebuches: los d̃ aca no lleuã ſino ſolamẽte hojas.

¶.x. Ay vna fruta q̃ aca llaman platanos /

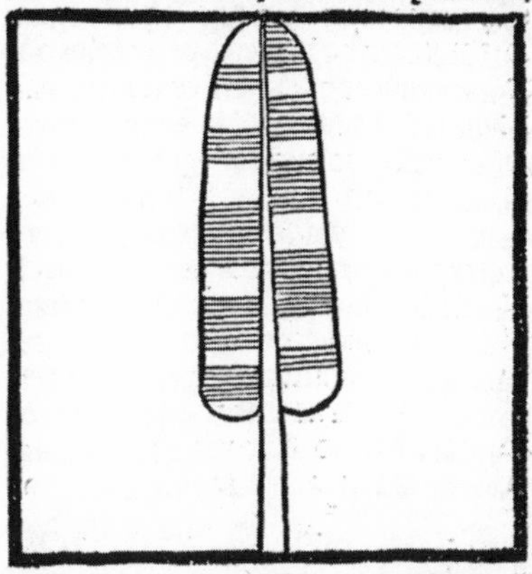

pero enla verdad / ni eſte es arbol / ni platano: ſaluo vna planta. Eſtos no los auia eneſtas indias ⁊ fueron traydos a ellas: po aca aſſi ſe quedaran con eſte inpropꝛio nombre de platanos. Siẽbran ſe vna vez ⁊ no mas porque de vno ſe multiplican muchos ⁊ va enellos aumentandoſe vna ſubceſſion ẽ grãdiſſima abundancia: porque como el platano mas antiguo ha procreado tres o q̃tro ⁊ ſeys ⁊ mas hijos al rededor de ſi: lleua vn razimo ⁊ fruto que ellos hazen: ⁊ aquel cortado ſecaſe la plãta que lo echo o produzio: ⁊ porque no embarace ni tarde en ſe ſecar / aſſi como cortan el fruto cortan el tronco d̃ſta planta porque no es de prouecho ni lleua mas: ⁊ luego pierde ſu virtud: ⁊ queda ẽ los hijos ⁊ ſubceſſores que auiã nacido al rededor. Dixe de ſuſo que eſtos no ſon platanos: porque la forma del platano ſegũ lo que del eſcriuẽ es muy diferente ⁊ d̃ otra manera. Eſtos de aca tienen las hojas muy grandes ⁊ muy anchas: ⁊ ſon altos como arboles: ⁊ hazenſe algunos tan grueſſos enel trõco como vn hombre por la cintura: ⁊ como el muſlo otros: ⁊ aſſi algunos algo mas

FIGURE 21.
Plantain leaf (1535) Bk. 8, chap. 1

hombres exercitan: ⁊ hasta q̄ vn medico acierta a curar/haze mas excessos que ha ley do renglones en su oficio ni en otros. Podrase con verdad dezir deste arbol otra propiedad vista y esperimētada cada dia que lo quisieren hazer o la necessidad lo permita que quando enel campo no se halla agua por la qual necessidad suelen perecer los hōbres/comoquier que el agua es tan p̄ncipal parte de la sustentacion dela vida: si ouiere destos arboles cauē en las rayzes dellos/⁊ cortando vn troço de la rayz ⁊ aquel poniēdo enla boca: y por el otro estremo / o cabo dl tal raygon tener le alto leuantado con el puño/ el dara tāta agua que baste a quitar de trabajo a qualquier sediēto / porque luego gotea ⁊ despues a chorro cae el hilo del agua dlas tales rayzes: esto he yo prouado conla misma sed ⁊ necessidad / ⁊ otros muchos: y esto se aprendio delos indios.

Capitu.iij. Del arbol llamado Caymito/⁊ d su fruta ⁊ diferēcia da hoja de todos los arboles.

Caymito es vn arbol dlos mas conocidos que puede auer enel mundo/porque sus hojas tiene quasi redondas / ⁊ dela vna parte estan verdes ⁊ de la otra son de vna color que parece que estan secas o como chamuscadas. E assi aū que este entre mucha espessura de arboles se conoce y es muy diferēciado entre todos ellos: echa vna fruta morada prolongada ⁊ tamaña como el trecho q̄ ay ē vn dedo d coyūtura a coyūtura po no tan gruessa como el dedo/de dentro es blanca como leche ⁊ çumosa: ⁊ q̄ndo se come es aquello d dentro como leche pegajosa y espessa. Estos arboles eñsta ysla lleuan esta fruta como he dicho y enestas otras yslas assi mismo: pero enla tierra firme es la fruta redōda ⁊ tamaña como pelotas de jugar ala pelota chica/o poco menores. Y esta es la diferencia que ay delos de aqui alos dela tierra firme: enlo demas el arbol ⁊ la hoja/ ⁊ todo lo que he dicho es de vna misma manera. Esta fruta es sana y de buena digestion. Y enesta plaça de sctō domingo se vēde harta della enel tiēpo que la ay. La madera deste arbol es rezia ⁊ buena para labrar si la dexan algun tpo curar ⁊ q̄ no se labre verde segun dizen carpinteros ⁊ los maestros de tal arte.

Capitu.iiij. Del arbol llamado Higuero: el acento de la.u. ha de ser luēgo: o de espacio dicho d manera que no se pronuncien breuemente ni juntas estas tres letras.gue.sino que se detenga poquita cosa ētre la.u.y la.e.⁊ diga.hi gu ero. Digo esto porque el lector no entienda/higuero/o higuera de higos.

Higuero es arbol grande como los morales de castilla ⁊ mas y menos. La fruta que lleuā son vnas calabaças redondas ⁊ algunas prolongadas: ⁊ las re-

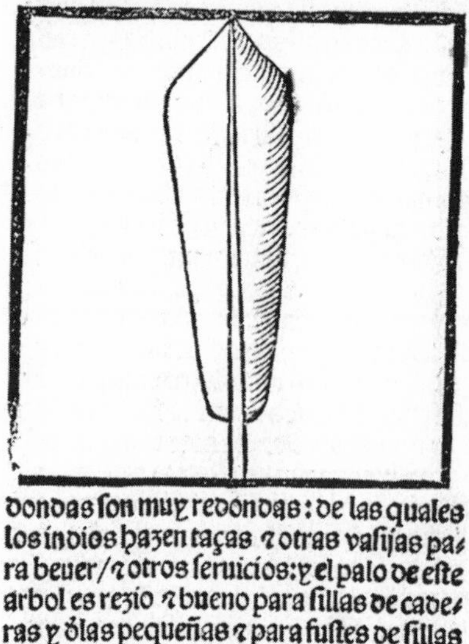

dondas son muy redondas: de las quales los indios hazen taças ⁊ otras vasijas para beuer/⁊ otros seruicios: y el palo de este arbol es rezio ⁊ bueno para sillas de caderas y dlas pequeñas ⁊ para fustes de sillas ginetas ⁊ otras cosas. Es correoso ⁊ fuerte ⁊ parece enel pelo despues de labrado/ granado/o espino: la hoja deste arbol es luenga y estrecha/⁊ lo mas ancho della es enel estremo o enla punta: y desde ella va disminuyendo para abaxo al peçon d do esta assi

l

FIGURE 22.
Higuero *(fig leaf) (1535) Bk. 8, chap. 4*

para la comer han d' echar la fruta ẽ agua ⁊ alli estrujarla ẽtre los dedos pa q̃ no se pegue alos labrios. Y es esta leche como la q̃ les sale alos higos verdes por los peçones ⁊ aũ mas enojosa. Y echandose como he dicho ẽ agua y estrujando el fruto / o exprimiẽdole / luego aq̃lla leche se d'spide ⁊ se cae enel agua. Estos arboles son grandes y es vna d'las mejores maderas q̃ ay ẽnsta ysla española ⁊ mas rezia ⁊ fuerte.

Capitulo. xiij. d'l arbol llamado Guiabara que los christianos llaman Uuero: porque echa por fruta vna manera de vuas: ⁊ de su madera y otras particularidades deste arbol.

L arbol Guiabara es buẽ arbol ⁊ de gẽtil madera ẽ especial para hazer caruõ: porq̃ como son arboles copados y estẽdidos ẽ ramas aunq̃ son gruessos no son para fabricas sino para tajones d' carnicerias y cepos ⁊ otras cosas: porq̃ vigas ni alfarxias no se puedẽ sacar d'stos arboles es la madera algo colorada q̃ parece madroño / po es mas rezia. La fruta son vnos razimos d' vnas vuas raras ⁊ desuiadas vnas de otras: ⁊ como rosadas o moradas ⁊ buenas de comer: aũ q̃ tienẽ poco de comer: porq̃ el cuesco q̃ tienẽ es mucho / segũ el tamaño delas vuas / o granos. Porq̃ los mas

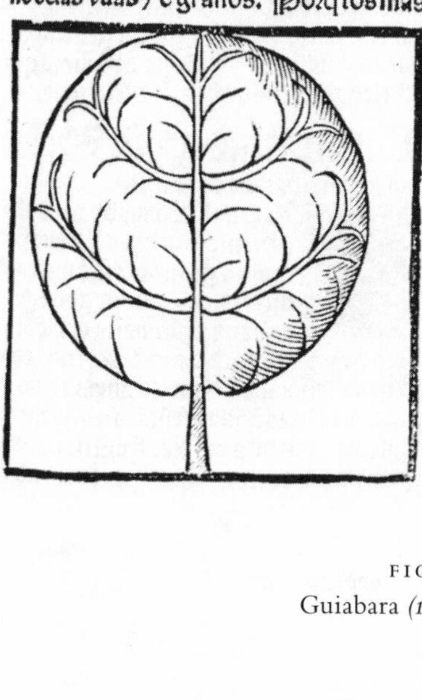

gordos destos granos o vuas son como pelotas de escopetas o algo mayores o como auellanas cõ cascara algunas. Tienẽ la hoja dela manera q̃ esta aqui debuxada. La q̃l por ser tan diferente ⁊ señalada hoja entre todas las otras la puse aq̃. Es la mayor hoja como d' vn palmo d' ancho / o algo mas ⁊ desde aq̃sta grandeza para abaxo. Enel tiẽpo q̃ enesta ysla ⁊ sus comarcanas / ⁊ aũ enla tierra firme se cõtinuaua la guerra como no trayan los christianos ala mano el papel ⁊ tinta seruiã se destas hojas como lo hizierã de papel ⁊ tinta. Esta hoja es v'de ⁊ gruessa ⁊ tan gorda como dos hojas de yedra q̃ estuuiessen jũtas: ⁊ las venas son coloradas ⁊ con vn alfiler o vn cabo de agujeta escriuẽ lo q̃ quierẽ enestas hojas del vn cabo ⁊ del otro: estando verdes o reziẽ cortadas d' aq̃l dia: y las letras parecen blancas rascuñadas / o tã diferẽtes d'la tez de la hoja que q̃da entre las letras q̃ es en fin muy legible y clara letra la q̃ enestas hojas se haze. E assi escriptas las hojas embiã las cõ vn indio donde quierẽ: ⁊ va biẽ escripto sin q̃ se borra de la hoja: dela vna ⁊ de la otra parte ⁊ aq̃llas venas / aunq̃ el lomo de ẽ medio es algo grossezuelo las otras ramas d'las venas son d'lgadas ⁊ no enpachã o estoruã al escreuir.

Capitulo. xiiij. Del arbol llamado Copey: en las hojas del qual pueden assi mismo escriuir.

Opey es vn arbol muy bueno y de gẽtil madera ⁊ tiene la hoja assi como se dixo de suso del arbol guiabara / o vuero: pero el Copey es mayor arbol mucho: ⁊ la hoja menor q̃ la d'l guiabara / po es mas gruessa dobladamẽte ⁊ mejor / o mas abta para escreuir enella de la manera que se dixo enel capitulo antes deste con vn alfiler o cabo de vna agujeta: ⁊ las venas destas hojas son mas delgadas ⁊ no empachã tanto al escreuir como las de suso / y en aq̃llos primeros tiẽpos de la conquista desta ⁊ delas otras yslas: hazian los christianos naypes destas hojas del Copey paraju-

l iij

FIGURE 23.
Guiabara *(1535) Bk. 8, chap. 13*

gar a cartas/τ se jugauã hartos dineros cõ
ellos por no tener otros mejores: y enestas

hojas deburauã los reyes τ cauallos/τ so-
tas τ pũtos τ todas las otras figuras τ va
lores q̃ suele auer enlos naypes: τ como son
gruessas estas hojas sufriã muy biẽ lo q̃ en
ellas assi se pintaua y el barajarlas đspues đ
hechas naypes. la fruta đste arbol no la he
visto aũ q̃ he visto muchas vezes las hojas.

¶ Capitulo. xv. del arbol llamado Haguey τ de su fruta.

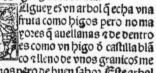

HAguey es vn arbol q̃ echa vna
fruta como higos pero no ma
yores q̃ auellanas τ de dentro
es como vn higo đ castilla blã
co τ lleno de vnos granicos me
nudissimos pero de buen sabor. Este arbol
aun que su madera no es delas buenas no
es inutil porque delas cortezas del se haziã
enel tiempo passado sogas / τ cuerdas por
los indios/ τ aun por los christianos. E assi
mismo alpargates quando les faltauan los
de cañamo / o no venian de castilla / τ aun
que viniessen eran harto buenos los que se
hazian de las cortezas de estos arboles / τ
turauan assaz.

¶ Capitulo. xvj. Del arbol q̃ llaman Cibucan τ de su fruta.

CIbucã es vn arbol đ los bue
nos q̃ ay enesta ysla española. El qual tiene la hoja como salze y echa vna fruta como auellanas blancas: τ đ dẽ
tro della tiene menudissimos granitos q̃ pa
recẽ liendres: pero aunq̃ la cõparacion sea tal
o estos granitos seã como sal tã menuda co
mo he dicho/la fruta es dulce: τ si la cõpara
ciõ parece fea: dixelo assi porq̃ muchos le lla
mã a este manjar la fruta/o el arbol de las
liẽdres. La madera đstos arboles es assaz
buena τ son arboles frescos τ q̃ parecẽ biẽ.
No ha de entẽder el letor por este nombre
Cibucã: q̃ es aq̃lla talega o prensa en q̃ se
esprime el pã caçabi/ este arbol ni hecha đl.
Porq̃ como estos indios erã cortos τ lo sõ
de vocablos/de vna misma manera llamã
diuersas cosas. Veo enesto q̃ tiene q̃ hazer
la talega o prensa en q̃ se purga el Caçabi/
con este arbol: o q̃ tiene q̃ hazer aq̃l animal
maldito τ menor q̃ pulga que se entra ẽ los
pies llamado nigua con el rio llamado Nigua: pero no es de marauillar si entre estas
gentes saluajes ay tales faltas en la lengua.
Pues que el portugues al cuchillo llama fa
ca: τ a vna hacanea assi mismo la llama fa-
ca. Y el castellano por honrrar a vna due-
ña τ dezir q̃ es sabia/la llama cuerda: τ tam
biẽ llama cuerda a vna đ vn arco o vallesta/
o otra cuerda comũ. Y aun si q̃sieremos bus
car esto entre otras lenguas τ gentes se ha
llarã los mismos đfetos/ no obstãte lo qual
esta lengua đlos indios es breuissima.

¶ Capitulo. xvij. Del arbol Guanabano τ de su fruta.

EL arbol Guanabano es alto
y hermoso arbol τ su fruta her
mosa τ grande como melones
medianos / τ aun alguna guanabana ay tamaña como la ca
beça de vn muchacho: es verde τ por desu
so tiene señaladas vnas escamas como la
piña/mas lisas aq̃llas señales τ no leuanta
das como las dela piña: es fruta fria τ para
quando haze calor/ τ aun q̃ se coma vn hõ-

FIGURE 24.
Copey *(1535) Bk. 8, chap. 14*

bre vna Guanabana entera no le hara daño. El cuero o corteza es delgado como el d

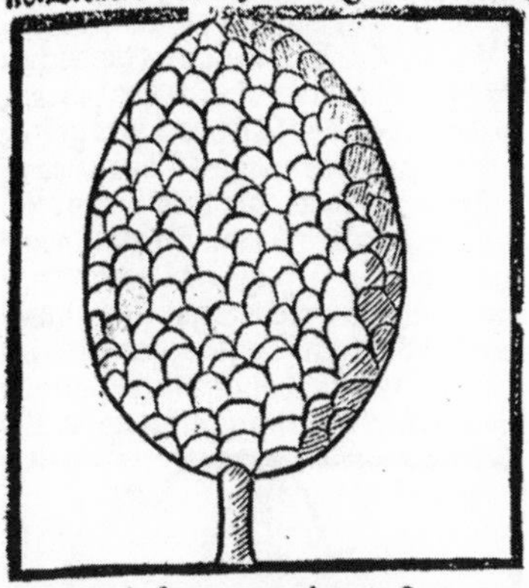

vna pera ⁊ la fruta ⁊ manjar de dẽtro es como natas o manjar blãco/ porq̃ haze alguna correa. Y es blãquissima esta comida/o
manjar/⁊ deshazese luego enla boca como
agua cõ vn dulçor bueno:y entre aq̃lla carnosidad ay assaz pepitas grãdes como las
dlas calabaças:po mas grossezuelas ⁊ leo
nadas escuras. Son como he dicho altos/
⁊ grãdes y hermosos arboles ⁊ muy frescas
⁊ verdes las hojas ⁊ quasi d la hechura de
la hoja dela lima/la madera es razonable/
pero no rezia.

Capitulo.xviij. Del arbol llamado Anon/⁊ de su fructa/el qual ⁊ la fruta es muy semejante ala Guanabana de que se trato enel capitulo de suso.

Anon es vn arbol/el qual ⁊ su
fruta tienẽ mucha semejãça cõ
el Guanabano de q̃ se trato en
el capitulo antes deste. En grã
deza del arbol y enla hoja y en
el talle ⁊ faciõ dela fruta assi enel parecer co
mo enla carnosidad ⁊ pepitas saluo en dos
cosas. La vna q̃l Anon es la fruta muy me
nor:⁊ la otra en q̃ es de muy mejor sabor el
Anon ami gusto/aun q̃ a algunos oygo cõ
tradezirme/o porq̃ tienẽ mas abiuado el gu
sto q̃ yo ⁊ lo gustã con mas apetito/o por vẽ
tura tienẽ mas aspero el gusto q̃ yo le tẽgo.
Biẽ es la verdad q̃ yo mas amistad he teni
do cõla fruta q̃ cõla carne ni otros mãjares.
No la pĩto esta fruta porq̃ tiene el mismo d
buxo q̃ la Guanabana d suso/excepto q̃ la
guanabana es vde:y el Anon es amarillo:
y assi tiene las escamas y el mãjar d dẽtro/
aunq̃ ami parecer no tã aguanoso como la
guanabana sino algo mas espesso es lo q̃ se
come ⁊ de mejor gusto como he dicho sino
me engaño:la madera deste arbol es como
la del desuso/po del vno ⁊ dl otro haziã mu
cha estimacion ⁊ hazen los Indios en sus
asientos y eredades ⁊ los precian.

Capitulo.xix. dl arbol dicho Guayabo ⁊ de su fruta:

El guayabo es arbol muy comũ enesta ysla y enlas otras y
enla tierra firme/y es preciado ⁊
de buena fruta ⁊ madera/⁊ ay
innumerables arboles destos
saluajes: pero sõ menores que los q̃ se cul-
tiuã:enlo q̃l tienen mucho cuydado los Indios. son tã grãdes arboles estos como los
naranjos:pero mas raras y dsparzidas las
ramas ⁊ la hoja no tan verde ⁊ dela hechu
ra dela del laurel:po algo mas ancha ⁊ mas
gruessa/⁊ mas leuãtadas las venas: son de
dos especies mas todos los guayabos lleuan vna manera de mãçanas o pomas pro
lõgadas algũas ⁊ otras redõdas:mas vnos
arboles echan esta fruta colorada rosada
por de dẽtro/⁊ otras son blãcas:pero dfue
ra/las vnas y las otras son verdes/o amarillas si las dexã mucho madurar:pero por
que estando muy maduras/no son de tan
buen sabor ⁊ aun hinchense de gusanos/
cojẽ las algo verdes:son algunas tã gruessas como camuesas ⁊ menores tãbiẽ: y aunq̃
esten verdes por defuera/ ay algunas d tal
genero q̃ no dexã de estar maduras por esso. Sõ de dẽtro maciças ⁊ diuididas ẽ qua
tro quartos o apartamiẽtos atajados dela
carnosidad q̃ es la q̃ esta enel circuyto dela
misma fruta:po en aq̃llos quarterones esta
la carnosidad dsta fruta q̃ ay dẽtro dllos lle

l iiij

El Anon no es amarillo, sino Verde obscuro y la corteza tiene las escamas blandas, y es mejor q̃ la Guanauana.

FIGURE 25.
Guanábana/añon *(1535) Bk. 8, chap. 18*

na ď vnos granillos durissimos: po tragan se y es buena fruta ⁊ de buena digestiõ: ⁊ tã biẽ son buenas pa el fluxo del viẽtre ⁊ res triñen quãdo se comẽ no ďl todo maduras: ⁊ q̃ antes estẽ algo duras pa q̃ cesse el fluxo del viẽtre. Entre aq̃llos granos q̃ he dicho ⁊ la corteza tienẽ la carnosidad tan guessa como vn cañon ď vn ansar ⁊ menos / segun son grãdes o pequeñas. Llamase esta mã çana o poma Guayaba y al arbol Guaya bo como he dicho: ⁊ tiene cada Guayaba vna coronilla ď vnas hogicas pequeñas q̃ facilmẽte se le caẽ: la corteza ďsta fruta es ďl gada como ď vna pera o Cermeña / ⁊ assi se mõda: es arbol ď buẽa sombra ⁊ de gẽtil ma dera para muchas cosas menudas ⁊ no pa ra vigas ni estãtes o postes: porq̃ las ramas y el trõco son ďsuiados ⁊ torcidos: po la fru ta se tiene aca por buena y es comũ ẽ todas las indias o ẽ la mayor parte ďllas: po auen tajã se mucho enel natio o genero ẽ ser muy mejores vnas guayabas q̃ otras: puesto q̃ por los mõtes ⁊ boscajes se hallã estos ar boles / po los q̃ ďllos son saluajes son peq̃ ños ⁊ tãbiẽ es la fruta mediana. Ay algũos arboles ďstos q̃ huele la flor ďllos como jaz mines o mejor: ⁊ q̃ere parescer la flor ala ďl azahar po no tã gruessa. Los idios ponẽ es tos arboles ẽ sus eredamiẽtos / ⁊ lo mismo hazẽ los xp̃ianos: mas quiẽ no ha comido es ta fruta no se agradara ďlla hasta q̃ la con tinue por causa ďlos granillos hasta q̃ se be zẽ a tragallos cõ los otros trabajos ď estas partes: po este no lo es sino buena fruta / sõ arboles q̃ p̃sto enuejecen: ⁊ como passan de cinco o seys años son viejos ⁊ la fruta lo en seña: porque siempre es menor cada año / ⁊ se va disminuyendo enla grandeza / ⁊ aun el sabor siempre se empeora ⁊ haze mas as pero: ⁊ por tanto son de reponer / o plantar otros nueuos Guayabos y en buen terri torio / porque es el arbol del mundo q̃ me jor reconoce la buena tierra: ⁊ pocas vezes se hazen bien enlas tierras delgadas.

¶ Capi. xx. del arbol Mamey ⁊ ď su fruta llamada assi mismo mamey

En la nu.a España huele esta guayava a chinces, y solo q̃ la acostumbran a comer, lo haze sin asco.

EL mamey / es vno de los mas hermosos arboles q̃ pue de auer enel mũdo / porq̃ son grãdes arboles ⁊ de muchas ramas ⁊ hermosas hojas / ⁊ copados ⁊ verdes ⁊ frescos: ⁊ son tã grãdes como los grandes nogales ď españa: aun q̃ no tã esparzidas las ramas sino mas reco gidos. La hoja es ďl tamaño ď la ďl nogal o mas y de la faciõ q̃ aqui esta debuxada / y es mas verde ď vna parte que ď otra ⁊ mas gruessa q̃ ďl nogal: y tan luẽga como vn pal mo de lõgitud: ⁊ a proporciõ la latitud o an chura po ďl talle q̃ esta aqui figurada. La

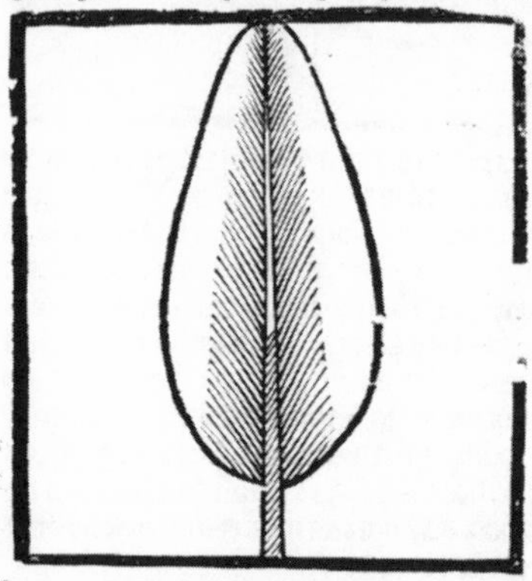

fruta deste arbol es la mejor q̃ ay enesta ys la española: es ď muy buen sabor y echa es tos frutos redõdos / muy redõdos ⁊ otros no tanto: po todos tirã al redõdo / ay los tã gruessos como puño ⁊ medio / ⁊ como vn puño ⁊ algo menores / ⁊ tiene vna corteza q̃ tira a color leonada aspera algo ⁊ semejãte ala corteza ďlas perazas / pero mas dura ⁊ mas espessa. Algunos tienẽ vn cuesco ⁊ o tros dos ⁊ algunos tres jũtos po distintos enel medio del pomo o fruto a manera ď pe pitas cubiertas cõ vna telilla delgada ⁊ aq̃ llas pepitas de la color ⁊ tez de vna castaña mõdada: ⁊ aun cortando las son assi mismo como castañas enla carnosidad ďstas pepi tas o cuescos ⁊ tã semejãtes alas castañas q̃ no les falta sino el sabor / para ser la misma

FIGURE 26.
Mamey *(1535) Bk. 8, chap. 20*

Libro

Pitahaya es vna fruta tamaña como vn puño cerrado/ poco mas/ ⁊ poco menos algunas: esto es su comũ grandeza. Nace en vnos cardos muy espinosos y estremados ala vista por q̃ no tienen hoja/ saluo vnas ramas o braços luẽgos: q̃ siruẽ en lugar de rama ⁊ de hoja los quales son de quatro esquinas ⁊ mas luẽga cada rama/o braço destos/q̃ vna braçada d̃ vn hõbre: y entre esquina y esquina vna canal ⁊ por todas las esquinas ⁊ canales atrechos sembradas o nacidas vnas espinas fieras y enconadas tan luẽgas como la mitad de vn dedo mayor dela mano o mayores: d̃ tres ẽ tres o q̃tro ẽ q̃tro espinas: y ẽtre estas hojas o ramas q̃ sõ como he dicho nace esta

fruta llamada Pitahaya: la q̃l es coloradissima como vn carmesi rosado/ ⁊ q̃ere significar escamas enla corteza aun q̃ no lo son/ ⁊ tiene vn cuero gruesso: ⁊ aq̃l cortado con vn cuchillo q̃ facilmente se corta/ esta por d̃ dẽtro llena de granillos como vn higo mezclados cõ vna pasta o carnosidad/ q̃ ella y ellos son d̃ color de vn fino carmesi: ⁊ toda aq̃lla mistiõ delos granillos ⁊ lo de mas todo se come: y lo q̃ toca lo para tã colorado/ como lo suelẽ hazer las moras o mas. Essa na fruta ⁊ a muchos les sabe biẽ: po yo escojeria otras muchas antes q̃ a ella/ haze ẽla orina lo q̃ las tunas/ aunq̃ no tã p̃sto: po d̃s de a dos oras q̃ se comẽ dos o tres dellas si orina el q̃ las comio parece q̃ echa verdadera sangre. No es mala fruta ni dañosa y es de buẽ parecer ala vista: pero los cardones dõde nacẽ es cosa fiera ⁊ de mucha saluajez su forma d̃llos: los quales son verdes ⁊ las espinas pardas o blãquiscas y la fruta colorada como he dicho/ ⁊ segũ aqui la he debuxado: ⁊ para sacar vna Pitahaya de dõde esta nascida/ no ha de ser a priessa ni sin buen tiento porque aq̃llos cardos son muchos ⁊ juntos ⁊ muy armados.

¶ Capitu. xxiiij. de vnos cardos altos ⁊ derechos mayores que lanças darmas/ ⁊ aun como picas luẽgas quadrados y espinosos: alos quales llamã los x̃pianos Cirios: porque parescen cirios o hachas de cera/ excepto enlas espinas.

Los cardones o cirios q̃ llaman los christianos enesta ysla son vna manera de cardos muy espinosos ⁊ saluajes que no ay enellos parte de dõde se puedã tocar sin muy fieras espinas no obstante q̃ la natura selas pone por ordẽ ⁊ atrechos vnas de otras cõ mucha ordẽ ⁊ compas en su compusicion. Ellos son muy verdes ⁊ tan altos como vna lança de armas/ ⁊ algunos como vna pica ⁊ otros muy menores ⁊ tan gruessos como la pantorrilla d̃ vna pierna de vn hombre que ni sea gruessa ni delgada. Nascen juntos ⁊ muy derechos como aqui eñ sta hoja los he querido significar eneste debuxo ⁊ pintura dellos. Estos lleuan vna fruta colorada como vn carmesi: del tamaño d̃ vna nuez dulce ⁊ buena de comer/ pero llena de innumerables granillos ⁊ muy coloradissima/ ⁊ tiñe los labrios ⁊ las manos lo que alcança el çumo de ella/ no es fruta para dessear pero no es de mal gusto/ ni se dexa de comer quando esta madura/ ⁊ bien sazonada. Estos cardos despues que han crescido todo lo que han de crecer se enuegecen ⁊ secan y echan

estas Ramas no pueden estar sin Arbol, y assi las pitahayas se crian en aquellas pencas, y estas se enredan en qualq̃ arbol, y las ay muy blancas por dentro y son las mejores.

FIGURE 27.
Pitahaya *(1535) Bk. 8, chap. 23 (26)*

otros apar delos secos. De manera q̃ los nueuos estã verdes ⁊ las espinas pardas/⁊

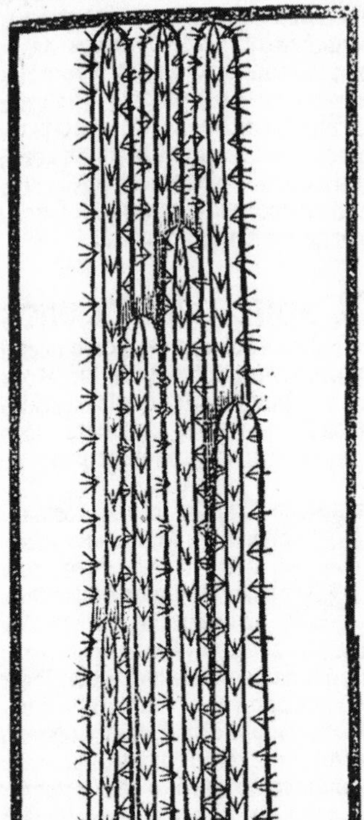

los mas antiguos ⁊ viejos estã secos ẽ vn esquadrõ. No he podido alcançar a saber de q̃ se seruiã los indios destos cardones: pero alomenos enla tierra firme en la prouincia de Nicaragua no estan estos cardones fuera delos eredamientos delos indios. Y para solamẽte la fruta me parece q̃ no es cosa para curar mucho dlla. Y por esto sospecho q̃ a mayor efecto o por alguna especial propriedad los conseruã aculla: ⁊ assi deuierã hazerlo aca q̃ndo esta ysla estaua pobla-da de indios. Puesto q̃ enlos mõtes ⁊ arcabucos o bosques ay muchos destos cardones enesta ysla: pero lo q̃ agora esta hecho monte, era enel tpõ passado muy habitado donde esta fruta ⁊ cardones se hallã. Lo q̃ yo he podido comprehender enesto no es mas delo q̃ he dicho: ⁊ por ventura esta fruta q̃ ami paresce no substãcial ni d suaue sabor deue tener otro gusto enel paladar destos indios/ ⁊ seria para otros efectos q̃ no alcançan los christianos hasta agora. Alo menos enesta ysla yo no he podido inquirir mas de lo que tengo dicho eneste caso.

¶ Capitu. xxv. delos cardos delas Tunas ⁊ su fruta.

Pues se ha dicho delos cardones o cirios enel capitulo d suso ⁊ primero dire de otros cardos delas pitahayas: pareceme q̃ como en lugar apropriado es bien que diga aqui de otros cardos q̃ llaman Tunas/ ⁊ la fruta que echan tiene el mismo nombre. Y porq̃ adelante enel libro dezeno se dira del arbol delas soldaduras tenga memoria el letor deste capitulo d las Tunas porq̃ tienẽ mucha semejãça las hojas destos cardos con las del arbol q̃ digo: ni estoy fuera de opiniõ q̃ estos mismos cardos se cõuierten en aq̃llos arboles: ⁊ ya q̃ aq̃sto no sea porq̃ enla verdad en la fruta son muy apartados: alomenos ẽla vista dã a entẽder q̃ han algũ deudo/ por la semejãça delas hojas ⁊ delas espinas. Estos cardos o Tunas lleuã vnos muy donosos higos q̃ es su fruta: largos ⁊ verdes ⁊ algo en parte colorados por defuera el cuero dllos ⁊ tienen vnas coronillas como las nispolas de Castilla: ⁊ de dentro son coloradas mucho q̃ tirã a rosado llenas de granillos como los vdaderos higos/ ⁊ assi es la corteza d aq̃sta fruta como la del higo/ o poco mas gruessa. Sõ de buẽ gusto y de buena digestion/ ⁊ cada dia los vendẽ enla plaça desta cibdad por buena fruta. Los cardos ẽ q̃ nacẽ tienẽ las hojas algo redõdas ⁊ muy gruessas y espinosas: ⁊ por los cantos y ẽlo llano

estos Cardones sirven los Indios tambien para tener cercados y defendidos sus heredades y Corrales de sus Casas.

Muchas frutas a dexado de Referir que ay en las Yslas de Barlovento = Papaya: Catas. Mamon: guindas, Cereças, y Varias species de Siruelas, y otras frutas que son proprias

FIGURE 28.

Cardos altos *(1535) Bk. 8, chap. 24 (27)*

Libro

dellas a trechos estan sus fieras y enconadas espinas tres o q̃tro o mas juntas: y es
tan gruessa la hoja como la mitad o tercera
parte del gordor de vn dedo de la mano de
vn hõbre/ ⁊ cada hoja es tan grande como
vna mano abiertos ⁊ tendidos los dedos ⁊
algunas menores: porq̃ van creciẽdo/ ⁊ de
vna hoja nacẽ otras ẽlos cantos ⁊ d̃ la otra
otras: ⁊ assi se van arborando ⁊ leuantãdo
estos cardos o tunas hasta ser tan altos co
mo hasta la rodilla o tres palmos de altura
poco mas o menos. Y enesta manera de se
yr aumẽtando enla forma del crecer y enlas
mismas hojas y espinas paresçẽ al arbol de
las soldaduras q̃ dire de suso. Llame do-
nosa esta fruta por que comiendo cinco/ o
seys destos higos / es tal burla para quien
nunca los ha comido para le poner en mucho cuydado ⁊ temor dela muerte: sin auer
otro peligro alguno. E como hombre que
lo he prouado dire lo que me acaecio la pri
mera vez que comi estas tunas. Que ẽ verdad yo diera quãto tenia por hallarme dõ
de me pudiera consejar con el medico ⁊ bus
car remedio para la vida: ⁊ fue desta mane
ra. El año de. M.d.xv. viniendo de la tier
ra firme a esta cibdad de sancto Domingo
despues que me desembarque enel fin d̃sta
ysla española viniendo por la prouincia de
xaragua : venian en mi compañia el piloto
andres niño ⁊ otros compañeros. Y como
algunos dellos eran mas platicos enla trr̃a
⁊ conocian esta fruta comian la d̃ buena ga
na/ porq̃ enel campo hallauamos mucha de
lla/ ⁊ yo comẽce a les hazer compañia enel
manjar ⁊ comi algunas dellas ⁊ supieron-
me bien. Y q̃ndo fue ora de parar a comer
apeamonos de los cauallos enel campo a
par d̃ vn rio. E yo aparteme a verter aguas
⁊ orine vna gran cãtidad de verdadera san
gre (alo que ami me parescia) ⁊ aun no ose
verter tanta quanta pudiera/ o me pedia la
necessidad: pensando que se me podria aca
bar la vida de aquella manera. Por que
sin dubda crey que tenia todas las venas
del cuerpo rompidas/ ⁊ que se me auia ydo
la sangre ala vexiga. Como hombre que
yo no tenia esperiencia dela fruta/ ni tampo
co alcançaua a entender la composicion de
la orden delas venas: ni la propriedad destas tunas que auia comido: ⁊ como q̃de es
pantado ⁊ se me mudo la color por mi mie-
do: llegose ami el andres niño. El q̃l era a-
quel piloto que se perdio despues enla mar
del sur enel descubrimiento del capitan gil
gonçalez Dauila/ como se dira adelante en
su lugar: el qual era hõbre de biẽ ⁊ mi amigo: ⁊ q̃riẽdo burlar dixome. Señor parece
me q̃ teneys mala color/ q̃ tal os sentis/ due
leos algo: y esto dezialo el tã sereno ⁊ sin al
teraciõ / q̃ yo crey q̃ condoliẽdose d̃ mi mal
dezia verdad: respondile. Ami no me duele
nada/ mas daria yo mi cauallo y otros q̃tro
por estar cerca de santo domingo o del licẽ
ciado Barreda q̃ es gran medico/ porq̃ sin
dubda yo deuo de tener rotas quantas ve
nas tẽgo enel cuerpo. E dicho esto el no pu
do mas ẽcubrir la risa. Y porq̃ me vido en
congoxa (⁊ ala verdad no era poca) replico
riyendose. Señor no temays q̃ las Tunas
hazen que penseys esso. Y quãdo torneys
a orinar sera menos turbia la orina con mu
cha parte: y ala segunda o tercera vez no a-
ura nada desso: ni aureys menester al licẽcia
do barreda que dezis/ ni aura causa q̃ deys
los cauallos que agora prometiades. Yo
quede consolado / y en parte curado/ pero
no del todo/ hasta que entre los de la com-

Estas Tunas q̃ a referido son las silvestres, las que se cultivan en esta nueva España son blancas por dentro, y encarnadas, y amarillas y de sal sabor, y licor que estan reputadas por la mejor fruta aunq̃ compita la piña, y no tienen las espinas que estas, y las pencas son mayores, y en ellas se cria la grana, y son mas altas que un hombre puesto a cavallo. y se llama la planta Nopal.

FIGURE 29.
Tunas *(prickly pear) (1535) Bk. 8, chap. 25 (28)*

FIGURE 30.
Managua *(RAH, Muñoz, A/34, no image available) Bk. 8, chap. 29*

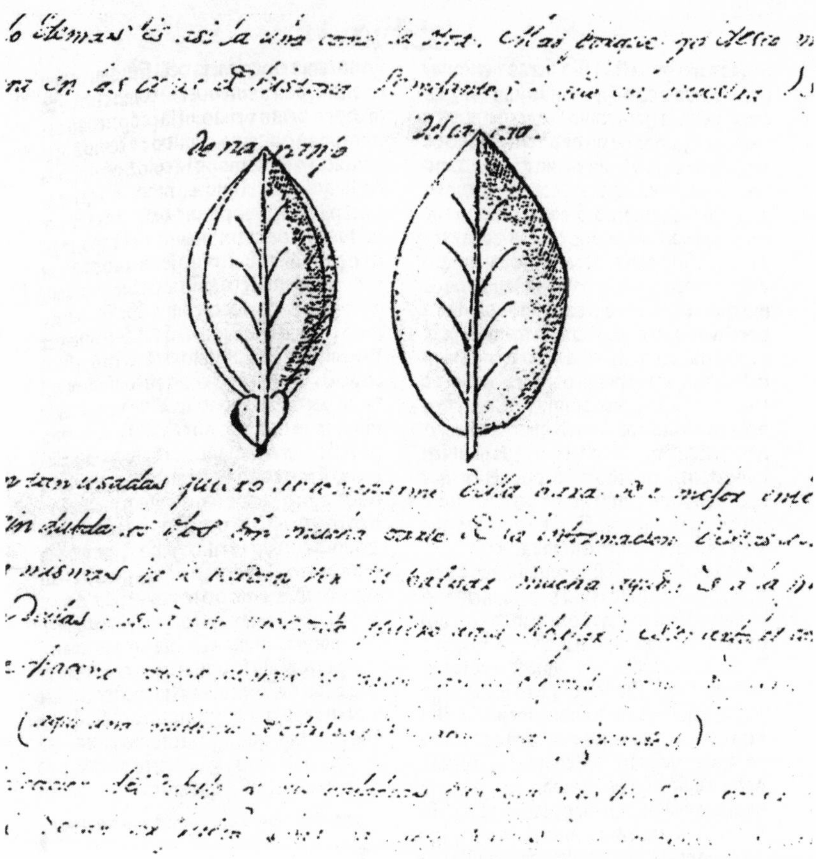

FIGURE 31.
Cacoa *(RAH, Muñoz, A/34) Bk. 8, chap. 30*

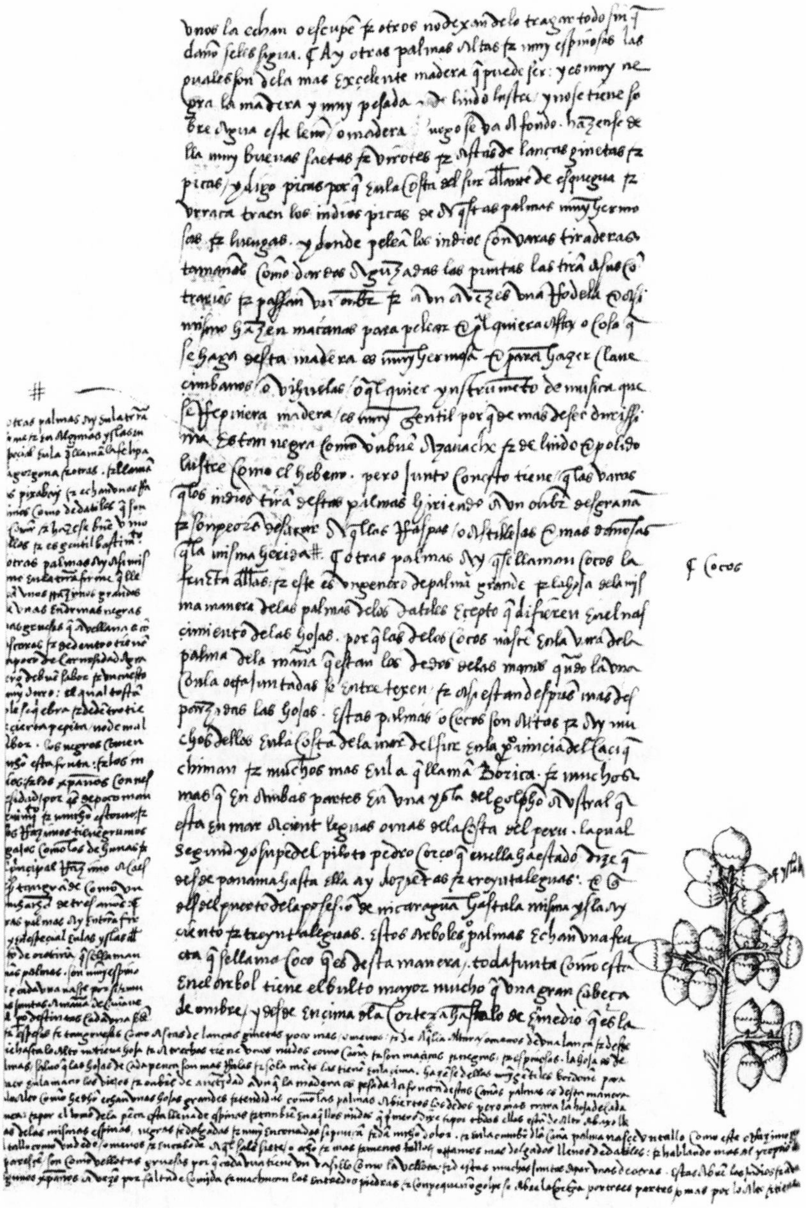

FIGURE 32.
Cluster of coconuts (HEH, HM-177, *53v) Bk. 9, chap. 4*

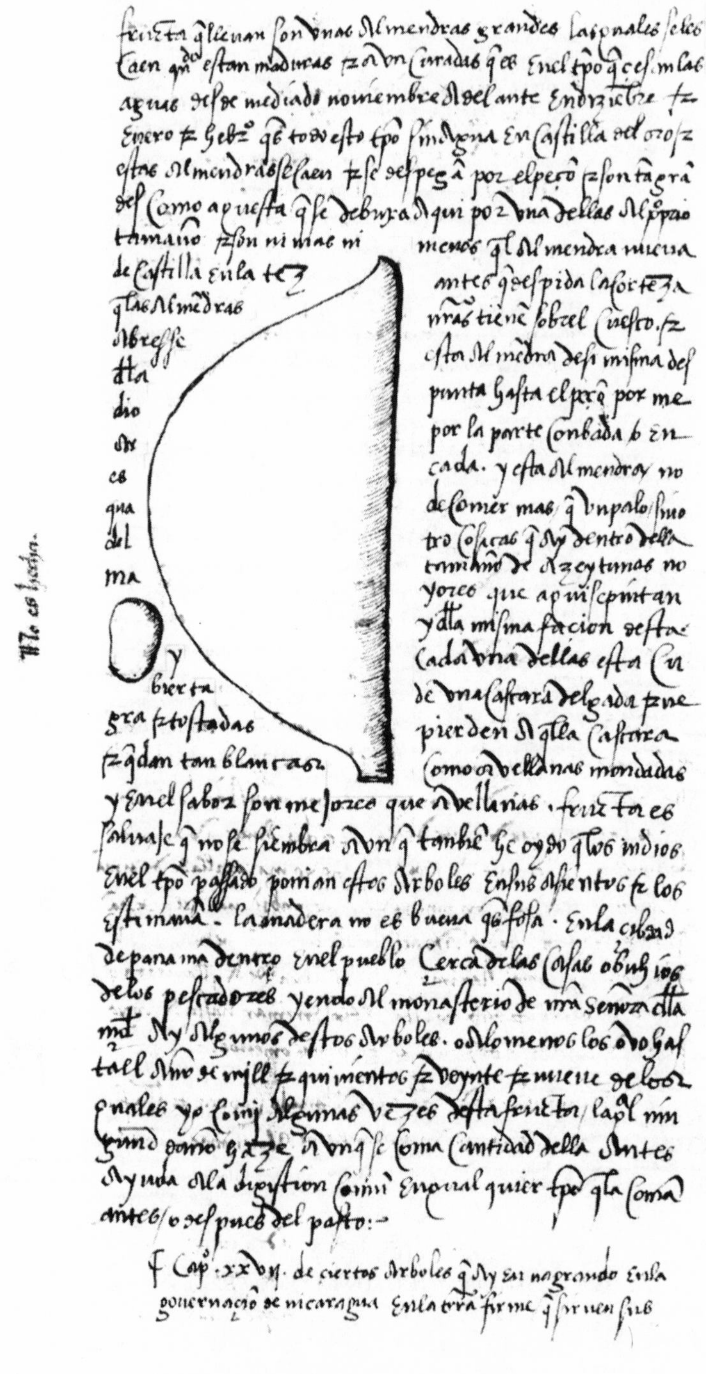

fenєta q lleuan son vnas almendras grandes las quales se les
caen quando estan maduras y avn çerradas q es en el tpo q cessan las
aguas desde mediado novienbre adelante en diziembre y
enero y hebrero q es todo esto tpo sin agua en castilla del oro y
estas almendras se les caen y se despegan por el peçon y son tan gran
des como aquesta q se debuxa aqui por vna dellas al propio
tamaño y son ni mas ni menos q el almendra nueva
de castilla en la tez antes q se espida la corteza
... vras tiene sobre el cuesco y
esta almendra de si misma des
punta hasta el peçon por me
por la parte conbada b en
cada. y esta almendra no
de comer mas q vn palo sino
tro cascaras q ay dentro della
tamaño de azeytunas no
yores que aqui se pintan
y de la misma facion desta
cada vna dellas esta cu
de vna cascara delgada y se
pierden de q la cascara
como avellanas mondadas
y en el sabor son mejores que avellanas. fenєta es
salvaje q no se siembra avnq tambien he oydo q los indios
en el tpo passado ponian estos arboles en sus asientos y los
estimavan. la madera no es buena q es fofa. en la cibdad
de panama dentro en el pueblo çerca de las casas obispales
de los pescadores yendo al monasterio de nra señora dela
md ay algunos destos arboles. o al lo menos los avia hasta
el año de mill y quinientos y veynte y nueve de los or
ginales yo comi algunas vezes desta fenєta la ql mu
cho daño haze avnq se coma cantidad della antes
ayuda ala digestion comun en qualquier tpo q la coman
antes o despues del pasto:-

¶ Cap.° xxvij. de ciertos arboles q ay en nagrando en la
governaçio de nicaragua en la tra firme q siruen sus

FIGURE 33.
Capera *(HEH, HM-177, 66v) Bk. 9, chap. 26*

FIGURE 34.
Fruit of cinnamon tree in Quito (HEH, HM-177, 68r) Bk. 9, chap. 31

ceſſario pintarle ḋ mano de tal pintoꝛ/ ⁊ de
tan apꝛopꝛiadas coloꝛes q̄ poꝛ la viſta ſe cō
pꝛehēdieſſe lo q̄ poꝛ las palabꝛas no creo q̄
es poſſible entēder ningū abſente/ tā al pꝛo
pꝛio como de otros arboles ſe entiēde/ poꝛ
ſer tan deſſemejāte de todos / q̄ otro nōbꝛe
me pareſce q̄ no ay tā al pꝛopoſito ḋ ſu ſalua
jez/ y eſtremos nūca oydos ni viſtos (en o⸗
tras partes) ſino moſtruo del genero delos
arboles. Machacadas las pencas ḋſte ar
bol q̄tadas las eſpinas p̄mero/ ⁊ tēdido lo
q̄ aſſi ſe machacare en vn paño de lienço a
manera de emplaſto: ⁊ ligada con ello vna
pierna o bꝛaço q̄bꝛado deſpues q̄ p̄mero ſe
ayā concertado los hueſſos rompidos / lo
ſuelda ⁊ jūta ⁊ afixa tan p̄fectamēte como ſi
nunca ſe q̄bꝛarā/ ſi bien ſe conciertā pꝛime⸗
ro los hueſſos delas tales q̄bꝛaduras: ⁊ ha
ſta q̄ ha hecho ſu operaciō eſta tan aſido el
emplaſto o medicina ya dicha con la carne
q̄ es muy dificultoſo ⁊ penoſo deſpegarlo/
p̄o aſſi como ha curado / ⁊ hecho ſu buena
operaciō/ luego poꝛ ſi miſmo ſe aparta ⁊ de
ſecha el emplaſto de aq̄l lugar dōde lo auiā
pueſto. Deſtos miſmos arboles ay muchos
enla pꝛouincia de nicaragua en la tierra fir⸗
me: y echā vna fruta coloꝛada bꝛeſcada/ ta
maña como vna azeytuna grueſſa de coloꝛ
de vn muy fino carmeſi: ⁊ tiene vnas eſpi⸗
nas poꝛ encima toda ella como vello quaſi
inueſibles poꝛ ſu ſotileza ⁊ delgadez: y en⸗
tranſe poꝛ los dedos quādo hombꝛe las to
ma en las manos. E ḋſta fruta en aq̄lla trr̄a
las indias hazē cierta paſta ⁊ coꝛtā la en pe
daços quadꝛados tan delgados como vna
alcoꝛça ⁊ tamaños como vna vña del dedo
y embueltas en algodō/ poꝛq̄ no ſe q̄bꝛen
las ſacā alas plaças y a ſus mercados a vē⸗
der/ y es coſa eſtimada para ſe pītar cō eſta
coloꝛ los indios ⁊ indias. Y es excelēte co⸗
loꝛ de carmeſi muy bueno: ⁊ alguno ḋllo de
clina a coloꝛ roſado: y es mejoꝛ coloꝛ para ſe
afeytar las mugeres: q̄ la q̄ en Italia ⁊ va⸗
lēcia o eſpaña y otras partes vſan las que
q̄erē emēdar/ o mejoꝛ diziēdo remēdar y eſ
tragar la ymagē o figura q̄ dios les dio: deſ
tas pieças o paſtillas deſta coloꝛ he yo eſ⸗
perimētado muchas en ḋbuxos ⁊ pinturas
poꝛ mi plazer: ⁊ poꝛ ver ſi es coloꝛ durable/
⁊ hallo q̄ es excelēte pintura: poꝛq̄ en algu⸗
nas coſas pintadas en papel yo la tēgo pue
ſta mas ha de ſeys años / y eſta oy mejoꝛ ⁊
mas biua la coloꝛ q̄ el p̄mero dia q̄ ſe aſſen⸗
to. Y tengo lo poꝛ mucho poꝛq̄ ſe tēplo con
agua clara ⁊ ſin goma ni alguna otra dili⸗
gēcia delas q̄ los pintoꝛes ſuelē vſar para tē
plar ſus coloꝛes ātes q̄ las labꝛē. Es muy ſe

mejāte eſte arbol ē las hojas alos cardos cō
q̄ eneſta cibdad vardā las paredes ḋlos coꝛ
rales delas caſas o como las hojas ḋ las tu
nas q̄ ſon los miſmos cardos de quiē ſe di⸗
xo enel libꝛo octauo: enel capitulo. xxv. Eſ⸗
tos arboles no creſce el mayoꝛ dellos mas
alto q̄ dos eſtados o poca coſa mas dela eſ⸗
tatura de vn hombꝛe: la coloꝛ del tronco es
pardo aſpero ⁊ los bꝛaços o ramas aſſi miſ
mo/ ⁊ los eſtremos dellas q̄ ſon las hojas eſ
tan algo verdes. E algunas nacē poꝛ el tra
ues donde q̄ere de nueuo pꝛincipiarſe otra
rama enla miſma hoja: p̄o todas las hojas
como he dicho ſon muy eſpinoſas como las
tunas: ⁊ aſſi miſmo las ramas. Pero cō mi
mal debuxo poꝛne aq̄ la foꝛma q̄ tiene eſte
arbol ſi lo ſupiere hazer: para q̄ juntamēte
con lo q̄ del tengo dicho mejoꝛ ſe pueda en⸗
tēder ⁊ conſiderar. E ſi eſto no baſtare di⸗
go que q̄en deſde eſta cibdad de ſanto do⸗
mingo deſta yſla eſpañola fuere ala villa ḋ

FIGURE 35.
Cactus (1535) Bk. 10, chap. 1

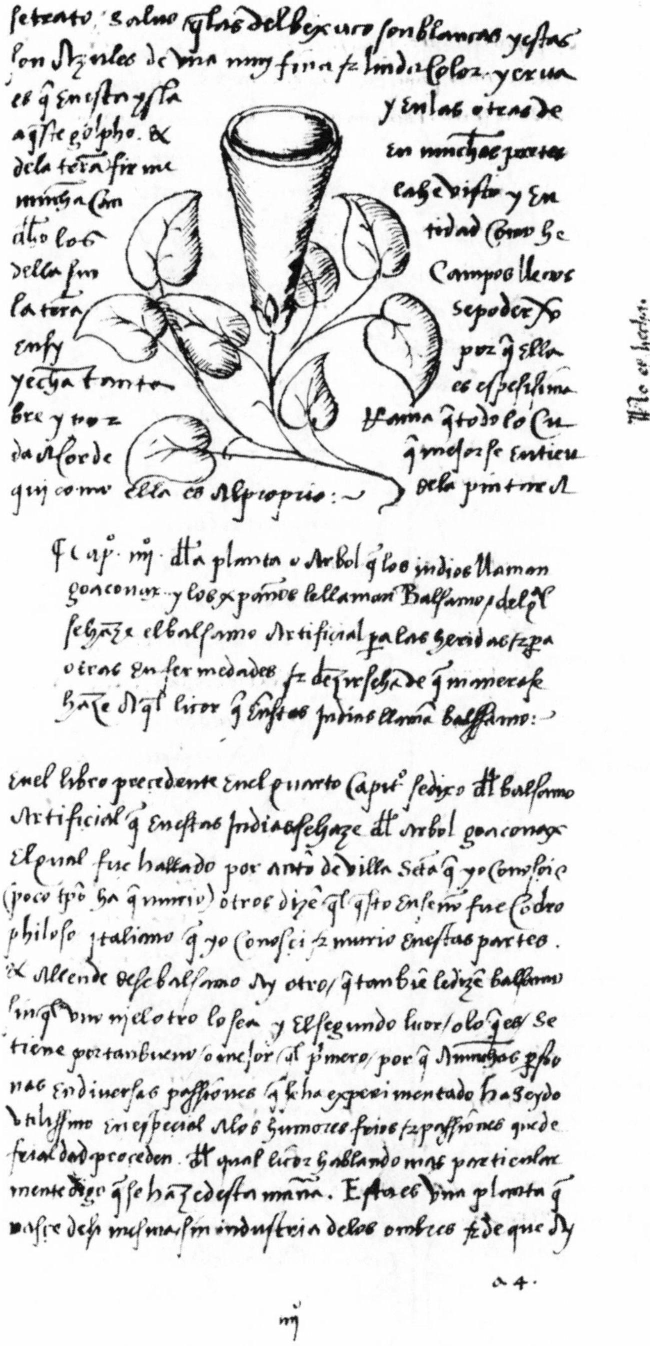

FIGURE 36.
Morning glory (HEH, HM-177, 73r) Bk. 11, chap. 3

FIGURE 37.
Goaconax *leaf (balsam) (HEH,* HM-177, *74r) Bk. 11, chap. 4*

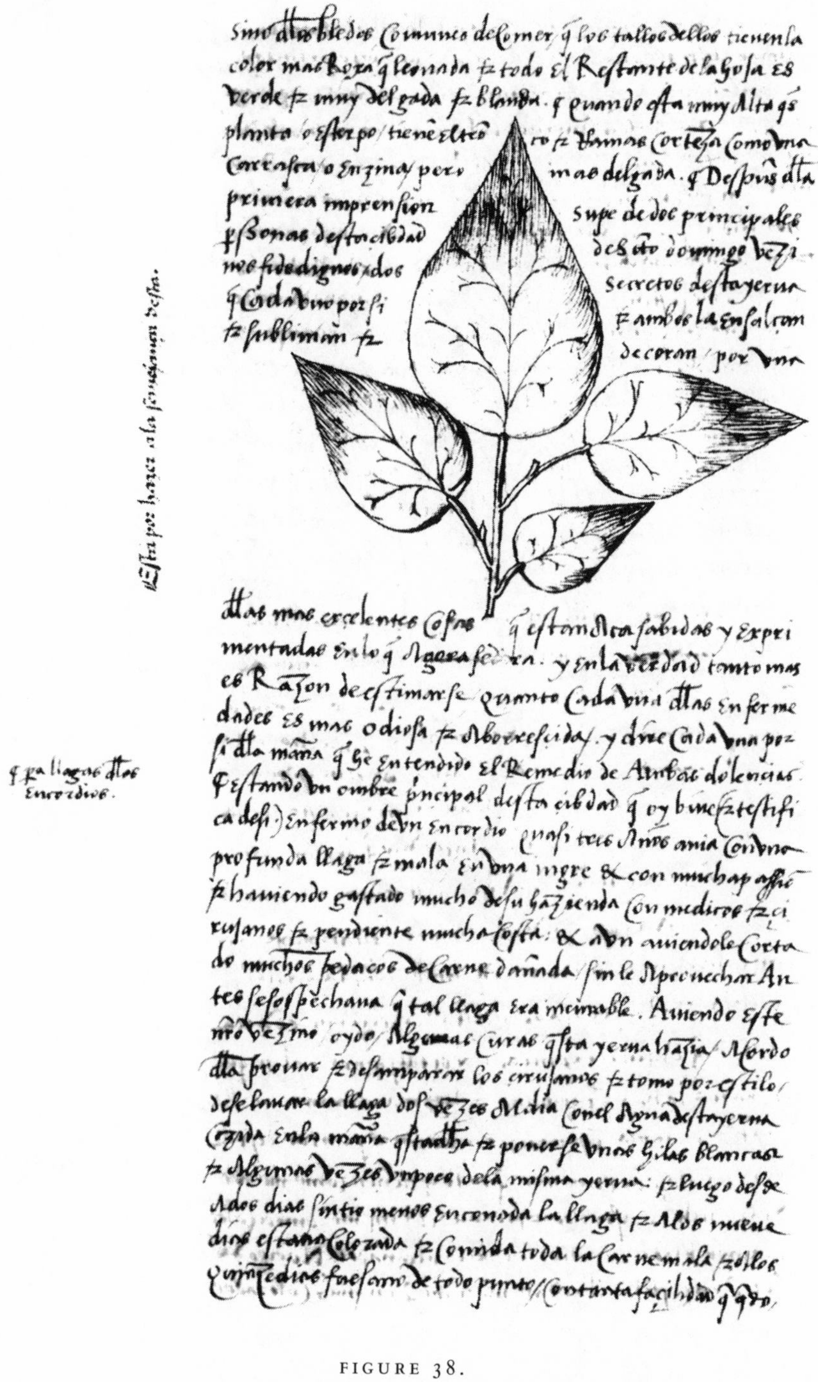

FIGURE 38.
Perebecnuc *leaf (HEH,* HM-177, *76v) Bk. 11, chap. 5*

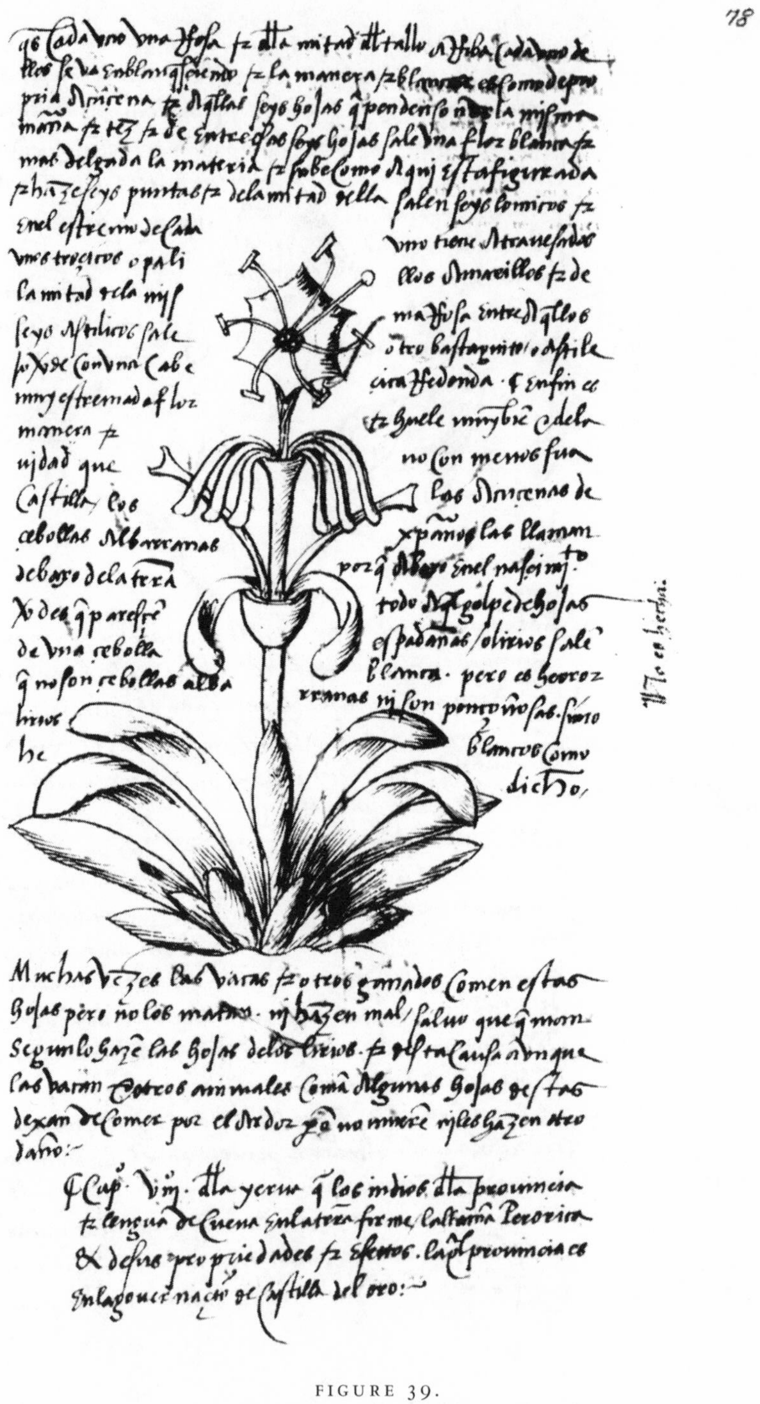

FIGURE 39.
Lily (HEH, HM-177, 78r) Bk. 11, chap. 7

FIGURE 40.
Perorica *plant (HEH,* HM-177, *78v) Bk. 11, chap. 7*

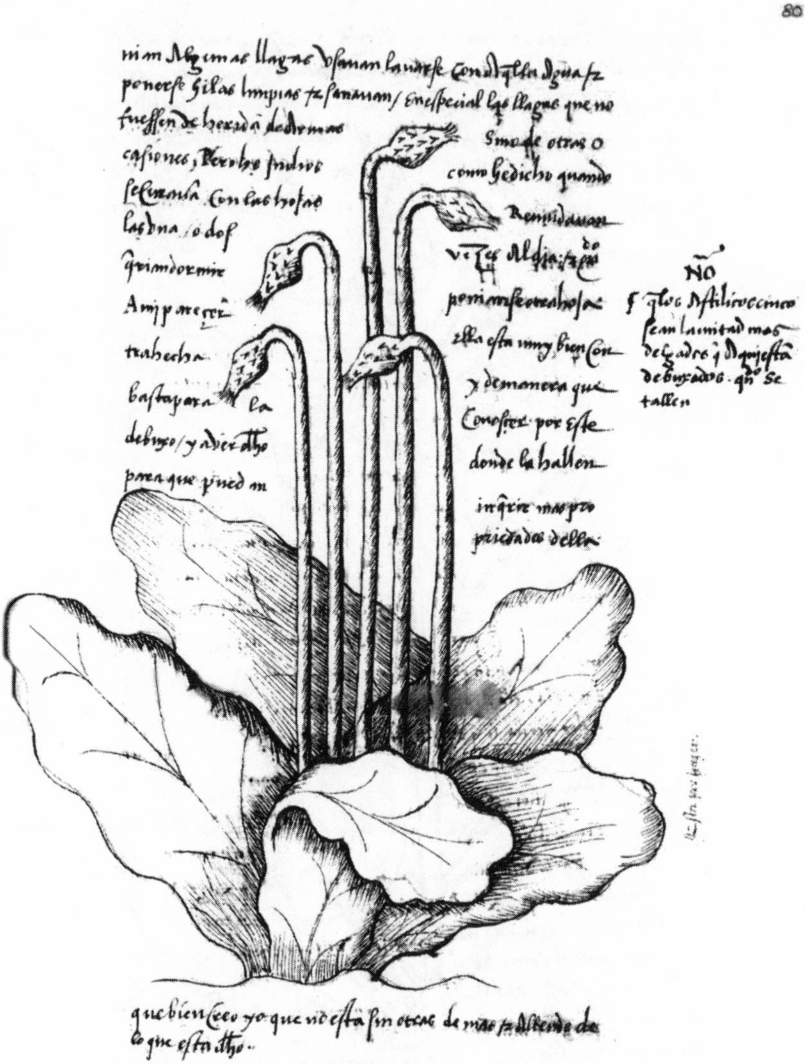

FIGURE 41.
Coigaraca *plant (daisy family) (HEH,* HM-177, *80r) Bk. 11, chap. 9*

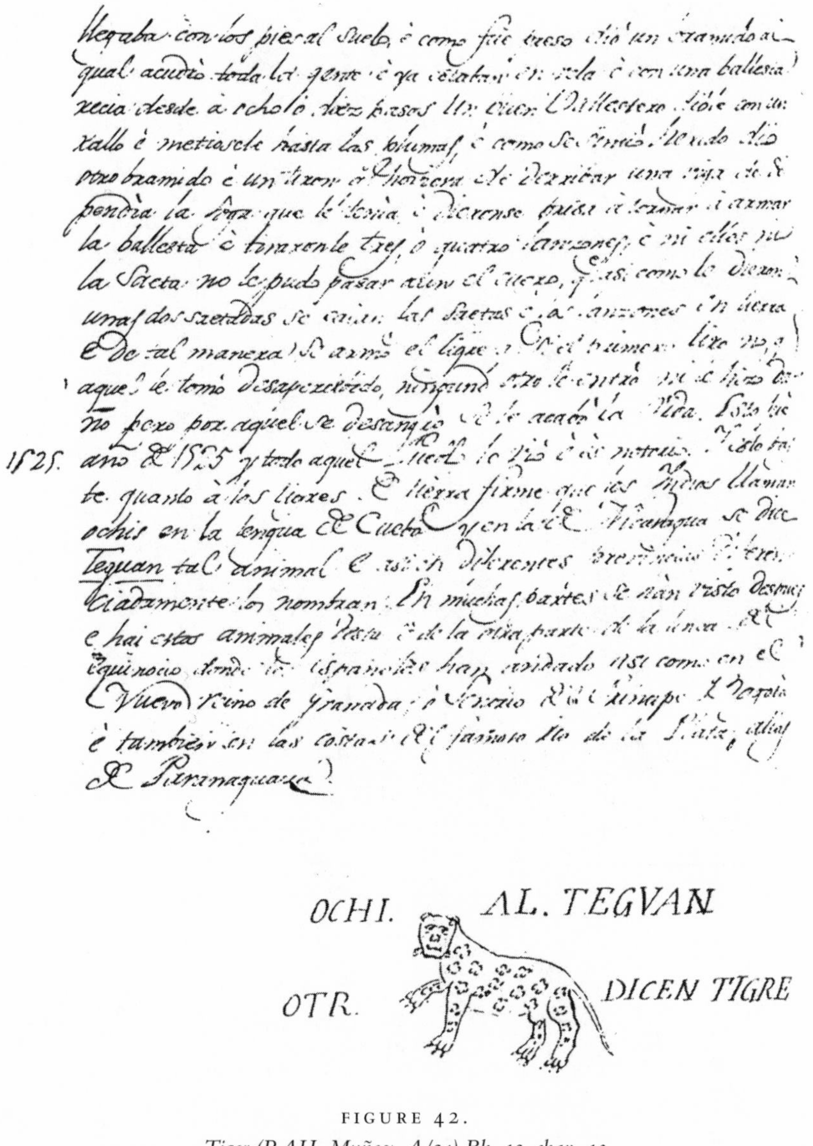

llegaba con los pies al suelo, é como fue preso dió un bramido al qual acudió toda la gente é ya estaban en vela é con una ballesta recia desde á ocho ó diez pasos un buen ballestero le dió con un rallo é metiosele hasta las plumas, é como se sintió herido dió otro bramido é un tiron de [illegible] de derribar una viga de [illegible] pendía la [illegible] que le tenía é dierense priesa á tornar á armar la ballesta é tiraronle tres ó quatro [illegible] é [illegible] la saeta no le pudo pasar aun el cuero, é así como le dieron unas dos saetadas se caian las saetas é [illegible] en tierra é de tal manera se armó el tigre [illegible] el primero tiro [illegible] aquel le tomó desapercibido, ninguno otro le entró [illegible] no pero por aquel se desangró [illegible] le acabó la vida. Esto fue
1525. año de 1525 y todo aquel [illegible] lo vió é [illegible] Digo [illegible] te quanto á los tigres de tierra firme que los indios llaman ochis en la lengua de Cueba y en la de Nicaragua se dice Teguan tal animal é [illegible] diferentes [illegible] ciadamente los nombran. En muchas partes se han visto despues é hai estos animales desta é de la otra parte de la linea del equinocio donde los españoles han andado asi como en el Nuevo Reino de Granada, é [illegible] é tambien en las costas del famoso rio de la Plata, [illegible] de Paranaguazu.

FIGURE 42.
Tiger (RAH, Muñoz, A/34) Bk. 12, chap. 10

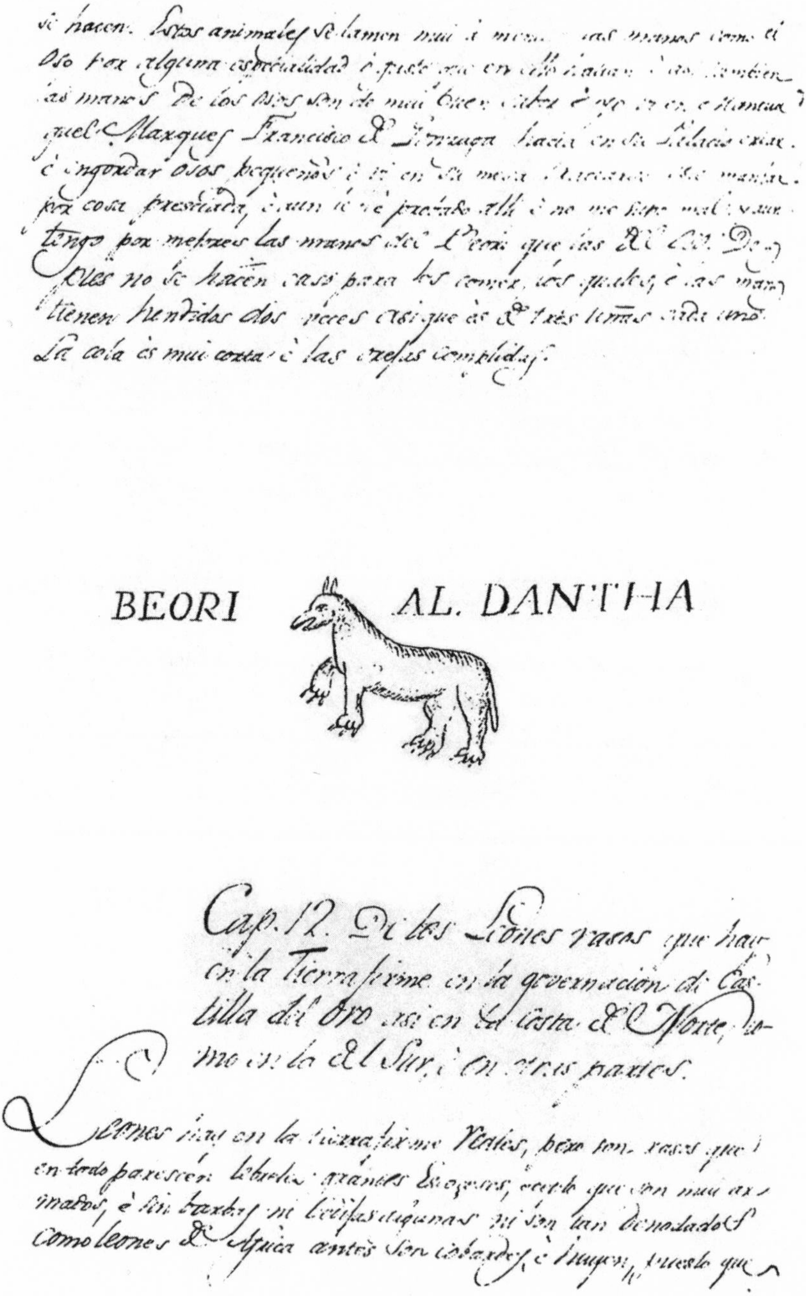

FIGURE 43.

Danta (RAH, Muñoz, A/34) Bk. 12, chap. 11

FIGURE 44.
Anteater (RAH, Muñoz, A/34) Bk. 12, chap. 21

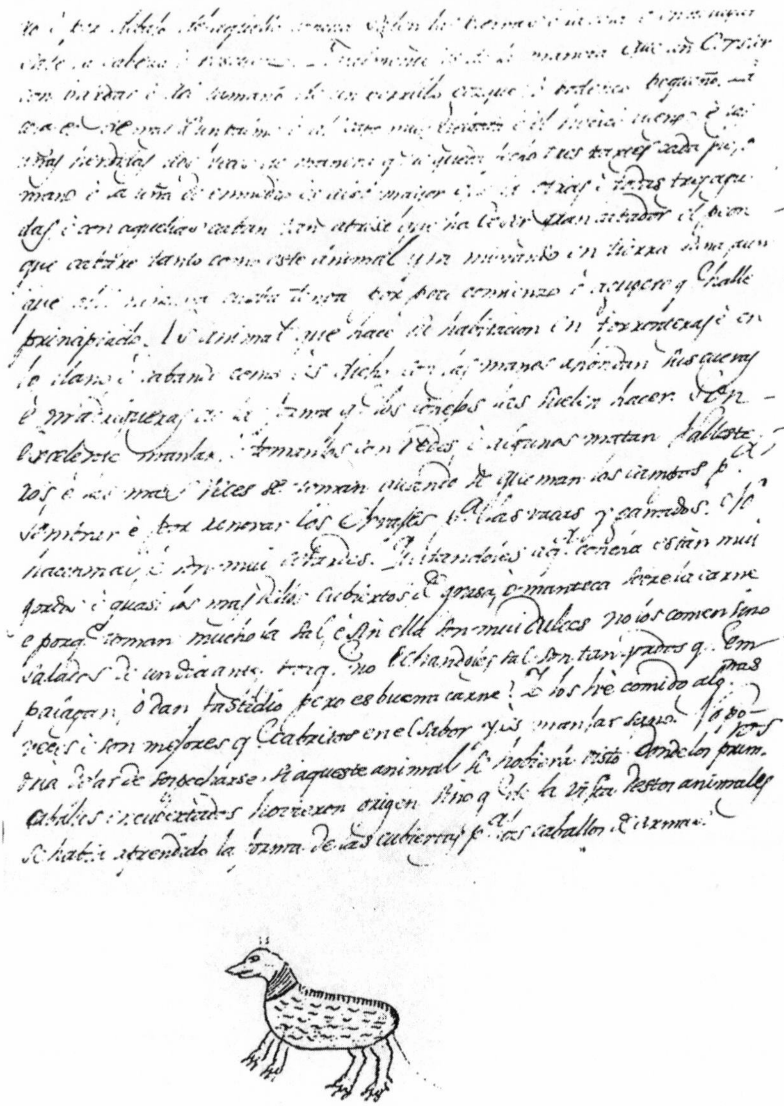

FIGURE 45.
Armadillo (RAH, Muñoz, A/34) Bk. 12, chap. 23

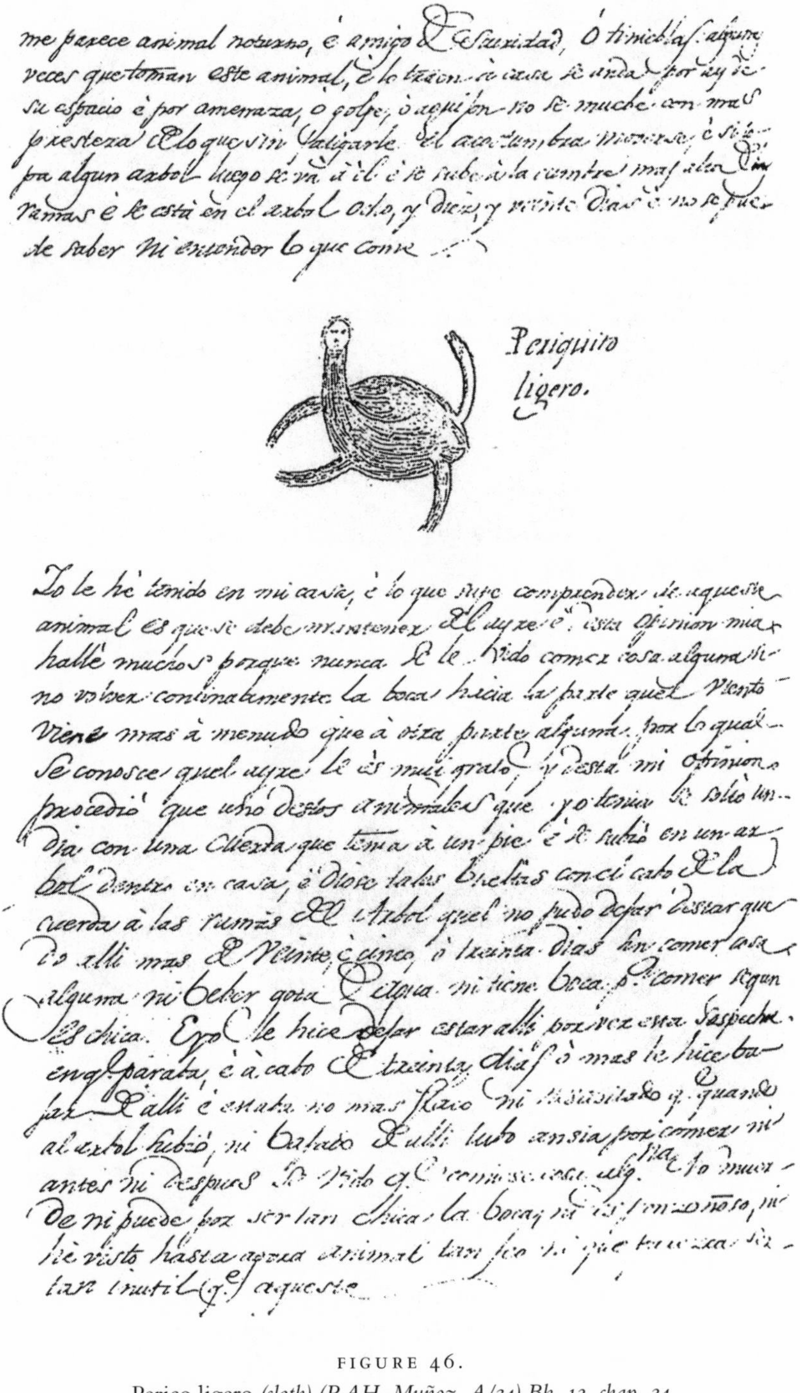

me parece animal noturno, é amigo de escuridad, ó tinieblas. algunas veces que toman este animal, é lo traen á casa se anda por ay de su espacio é por amenaza, ó golpe, ó aguijon no se mueve con mas presteza de lo que sin fatigarle él acostumbra moverse; é si topa algun arbol luego se va á él é se sube á la cumbre mas alta de las ramas é se está en el arbol ocho, y diez, y veinte dias é no se puede saber ni entender lo que come.

Periquito ligero.

Yo le he tenido en mi casa, é lo que supe comprender de aqueste animal es que se debe mantener del ayre; é desta opinion mia hallé muchos porque nunca se le ha visto comer cosa alguna sino volver continuamente la boca hacia la parte quel viento viene mas á menudo que á otra parte alguna, por lo qual se conosce quel ayre le es mui grato, y desta mi opinion procedió que uno destos animales que yo tenia se salió un dia con una cuerda que tenia á un pie é se subió en un arbol dentro en casa, é diose tales bueltas con el cabo de la cuerda á las ramas del arbol quel no pudo dexar de estar que estuvo alli mas de veinte é cinco, ó treinta dias sin comer cosa alguna ni beber gota de agua, ni tiene boca para comer segun es chica. Yo le hice dexar estar alli por ver esta sospecha en que para ta, é á cabo de treinta dias ó mas le hice baxar de alli é estaba no mas flaco ni desustanciado que quando al arbol subió, ni baxado de alli tuvo ansia por comer ni antes ni despues se ha visto que comiese cosa alguna. No muerde ni puede por ser tan chica la boca, ni es ponzoñoso, ni hé visto hasta agora animal tan feo ni que tenga ser tan inutil (q.e) aqueste.

FIGURE 46.
Perico ligero *(sloth) (RAH, Muñoz, A/34) Bk. 12, chap. 24*

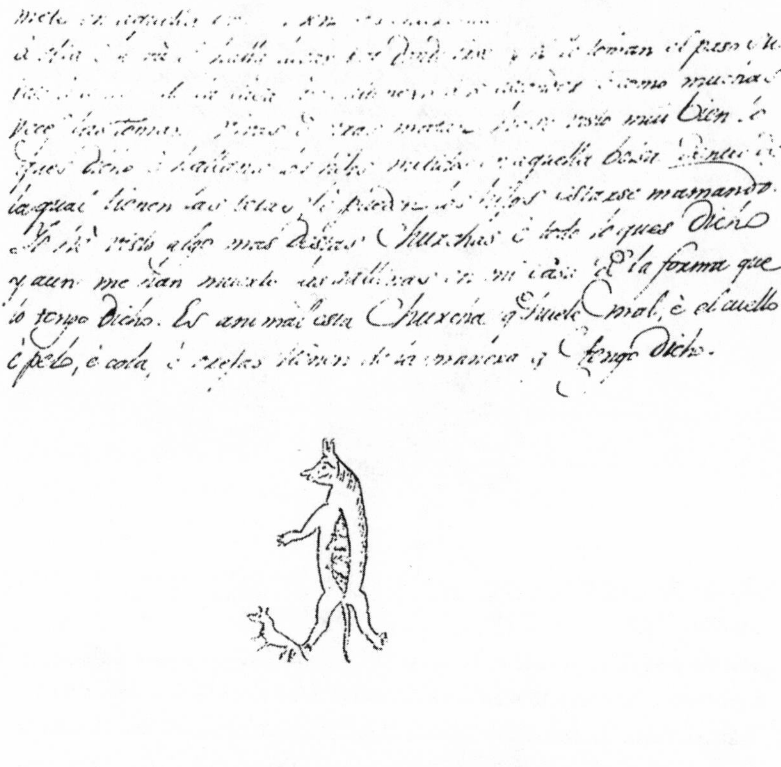
[illegible]
[illegible] tenian el peso [illegible]
[illegible] como muchas
[illegible] muy bien è
[illegible] aquella bolsa [illegible]
la qual tienen las tetas [illegible] hijos estarse mamando.
[illegible] algo mas destas Churchas è todo lo ques dicho
y aun me dan mucho [illegible] en mi casa de la forma que
lo tengo dicho. Es animal esta Churcha q̃ suele [illegible] mal, è el cuello
è pelo, è cola, è [illegible] de la manera q̃ tengo dicho.

Cap. 28. De las hardas que hay
en la tierra firme è en especial en la governacion de Castilla del Oro è en las
provincias de la lengua de Cueva

Hardas hay en tierra firme algo mayores que las de España
è no tan peludas ni tan bermejas porque tienen estas el pelo
mas llano, è mas escuro en los lomos, è la cola de la mesma
hechura, pero mas gruesa la cabeza que las de Castilla. Es ay

FIGURE 47.
Churcha *(opossum) (RAH, Muñoz, A/34) Bk.* 12, *chap.* 27

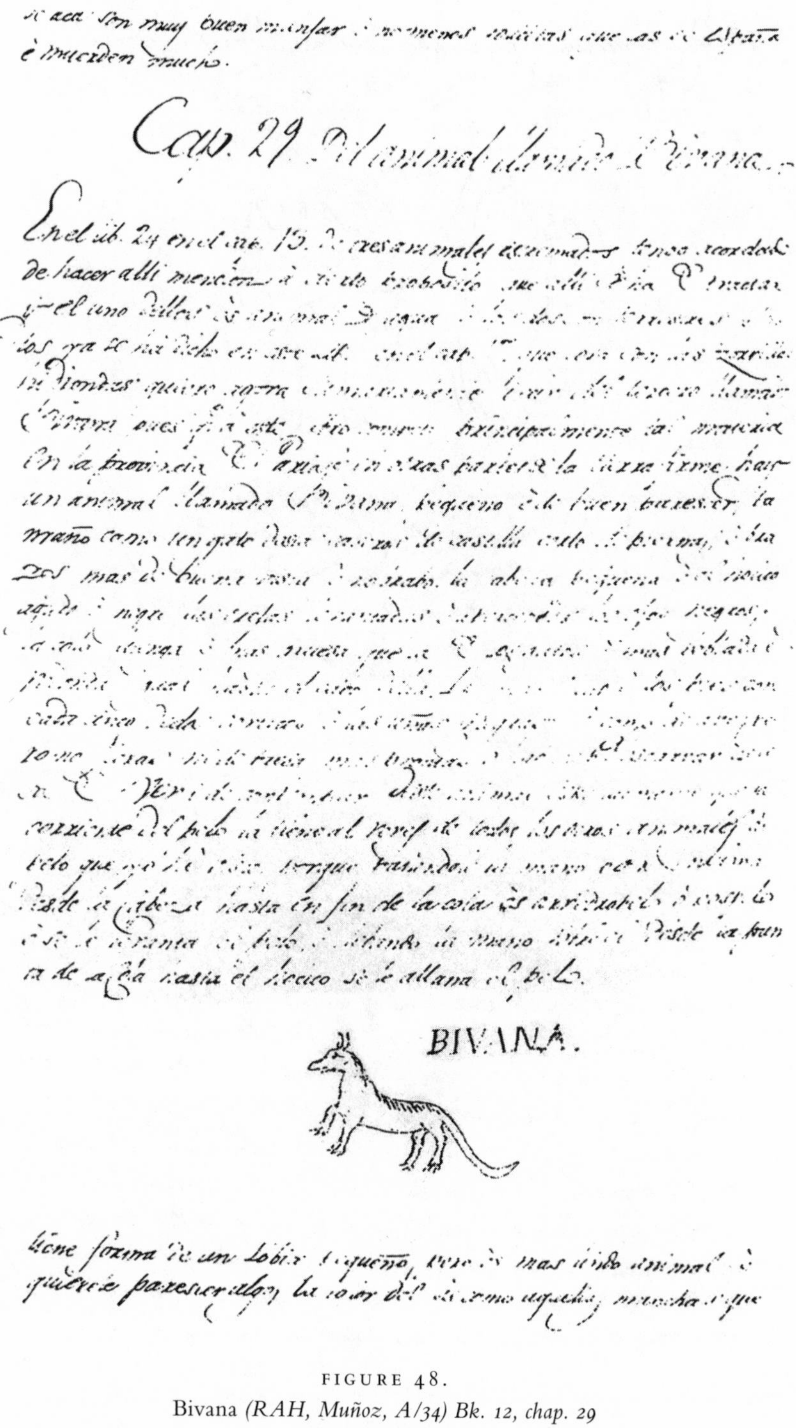

FIGURE 48.
Bivana *(RAH, Muñoz, A/34) Bk. 12, chap. 29*

FIGURE 49.

Llama (RAH, Muñoz, A/34) Bk. 12, chap. 30

lagartos que he dicho erã cocodrilos. Pe
ro enla ṽdad la/y v ana/ muy diferente ani
mal es del cocodrilo: y en ninguna cosa a el
semejãte. Esta que aqui yo pinte quiere al-

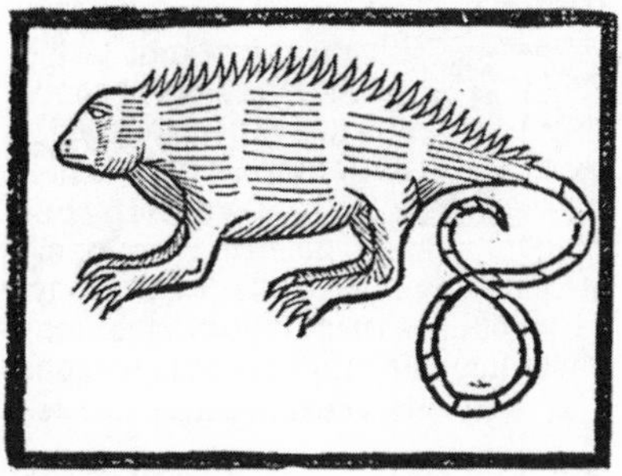

go semejar ala/y v ana/ y a la verdad esta
forma tienen/cõla protestacion o auiso que
al principio deste capitulo se toco: que aque
ste animal es como neutral/ ⁊ q̃ no se deter-
minan los hombres si es terrestre o ð agua
porq̃ enla vna y enla otra estimaciõ se puede sospechar que tiene mucha parte.

¶ Capitu.iiij. del pexe llamado Vihuela ⁊ de sus armas.

El pexe o pescado llamado vi
huela es grande animal / ⁊ la
mandibula o hocico alto/o superior ðl es vna espada orlada
de vnos colmillos/o nauajas
de vna parte ⁊ de otra/tan luenga como vn
braço de vn hombre ⁊ algunos mayores ⁊
menores segun la grandeza ⁊ cuerpo deste
animal/que tales armas tiene. Yo le he vi
sto enel darien en la tierra firme tan grande
q̃ vn carro con vn par de bueyes tenia har
ta carga ⁊ peso que traer enel desde el agua
hasta el publo. Estas espadas que digo estan llenas de vnas puntas de huesso maciças ⁊ rezias ⁊ muy agudas/ o punçantes ð
vna parte ⁊ otra dela espada conla qual no
sele para pescado delante sin que le mate. Y
tambien ay estos pescados enlas costas de
sta ⁊ delas otras yslas ðstas partes. Estos
pescados me dizen ami los hombres de la
mar que los ay en españa pero sin estas pũ
tas o puas enlas espadas/no se si lo crea por
q̃ en algunos templos en españa las he visto colgadas pero no se de donde las han lle
uado/ o si las ay enel mar de españa assi fieras: mas aca enestas mares delas indias ⁊
tierra firme muchas destas he visto ð la ma
nera q̃ tengo dicho. Son buenos pescados
de comer/ po no tales como los pequeños
dellos mismos/⁊ de otros de los menores
ð otras especies / porque por la mayor par
te los pescados muy grandes no son sanos
aca alo que yo he entendido ⁊ las mas vezes se comẽ por necessidad/excepto el Ma
nati que aun que son muy grãdes son muy
buenos ⁊ sanos: del qual Manati se dira
mas adelante en su lugar.

¶ Capitulo. v. Delos pexes boladores que se hallan en el grande golpho del mar oceano/ viniendo de España a estas indias.

Alguno preguntara la causa
porque digo que estos pesca
dos boladores se hallan a la
venida a estas ptes enel grãde mar ⁊ golpho del oceano:
⁊ no dire ala buelta desde aquestas indias
a españa/o Europa. Y por sacar desta dub
da al lector/digo que aun que ala buelta se
hallan los mismos pescados / assi como ala
venida no son tantos en mucha manera/ni
los nauios bueluen por el mismo rumbo/o
derrota que aca vinieron/ ⁊ ala vanda del
norte no ay tantos como por estotra via ha
zia el sur o parte ðla tierra firme. Hallan se
desde tan pequeños como vn Abejoncico
hasta tamaños como grandes Sardinas.
Estos quando las naues van corriendo en
su viage ⁊ ala vela se leuantan de vna parte y de otra a manadas grandes ⁊ peque-
ñas/pero enellos es grandissimo ⁊ incon-
table el numero destos peces boladores: y
de vn buelo acaesce yr a caer espacio de do-
zientos passos/⁊ mas/⁊ menos: ⁊ acaece al
gunas vezes caer dẽtro ẽlas naos: ⁊ yo los
he tenido biuos en las manos ⁊ los he comido. Y son muy buen pescado al sabor/

FIGURE 50.
Iguana (1535) Bk. 13, chap. 3 (Bk. 12, chap. 7)

ça o vestigio: y en topandola trastornanla con vn palo/y dexala estar assi de espaldas porque no se puede mas mouer despues q̃ esta trastornada por su grandissima pesadũbre: ⁊ vã a buscar mas. E assi acaece tomar muchas quando ellas salen a desouar ẽ tierra como he dicho. ¶ Los que no las han visto o no han leydo pensaran que en estas y otras cosas yo me alargo: y en la verdad antes me tengo atras porque soy amigo d̃ no perder mi credito y de conseruarle en todo quanto pudiere. Y para este efecto busco testigos algunas vezes en los auctores antiguos para que me crean como a autor moderno ⁊ que hablo de vista contando estas cosas a los que estan apartados destas nuestras indias/porque aca quãtos no fueren ciegos las veen. Y para este efecto q̃en dubdare lo que he dicho destos animales informese de plinio: libro nono: capitulo. x. y dezir le ha que en el mar d̃ india son tamañas las tortugas que el huesso o cobertura de vna basta para cobrir vna habitable casa. E dize mas que entre las yslas del mar roxo nauegan con tales conchas en lugar de barcas. Y el que fuere informado deste y otros auctores vera q̃ yo no digo sa q̃ tanto como ellos escriuen/mas puedo lo testificar mejor que Plinio/ pues que el no dize auer las visto: ⁊ yo digo que estas otras las he comido muchas vezes/ y es cosa tan comũ ⁊ notoria q̃ no ay aca cosa mas espe rimentada ni mas continuamente vista. ¶ Son muy buen manjar ⁊ sano/⁊ no tan enojoso al gusto como los otros pescados aũ q̃ se cõtinue. ¶ Las hicoteas o menores tortugas d̃ q̃ se hizo d̃ suso mẽciõ/la mayor d̃llas sera de dos palmos de luengo ⁊ d̃ alli abaxo menores. Estas se hallan en los lagos y en muchas partes de aquesta ysla española. Y cada dia se venden por essas calles ⁊ plaças de esta cibdad de sancto Domingo/⁊ son sano manjar. E son vna cierta especie d̃ tortugas/⁊ niguña diferẽcia ay en la forma d̃llas/sino en el tamaño ⁊ grandeza: a estas pequeñas llaman los indios Hicoteas.

Los huevos de las tortugas tienen su clara como todos; y las hicoteas son de mayor manera.

¶ Capitulo. x. del Manati y de su grandeza ⁊ forma: ⁊ de la manera que algunas vezes los indios tomauan este grãde animal con el pexe reuerso: ⁊ otras particularidades.

Manati es vn pescado de los mas notables ⁊ no oydos de quantos yo he leydo o visto. Destos ni plinio hablo/ni el Alberto magno ẽ su propietatibus rerum escriuio: ni en españa los ay. Ni jamas oy a hõbre dela mar ni dela tierra que dixesse auer los visto ni oydo: sino ẽ estas yslas ⁊ tierra firme de estas indias de

españa. Este es vn grande pescado de la mar/aun que muy continuamente los matan enlos rios grandes en esta ysla y en las otras destas partes. Son mayores mucho que los tiburones ⁊ marraxos de quien se dixo de suso enlos capitulos precedentes/ assi de longitud como de latitud. Los que son grandes son feos: ⁊ paresce mucho el Manati a vna odrina de aquellas en que se acarrea ⁊ lleua el mosto en Medina del campo y areualo ⁊ por aquella tierra. La cabeça de aqueste pescado es como de vn buey ⁊ mayor. Tiene los ojos pequeños segun su grandeza. Tiene dos tocones con que nada gruessos en lugar de braços/⁊ altos cerca dela cabeça. Y es pescado de cuero y no de escama mansissimo ⁊ sube se por los rios ⁊ llegase a las orillas ⁊ pasce en tierra sin salir del rio/si puede desde el agua alcançar la yerua. En tierra firme matan los

o ij

FIGURE 51.
Manatee (1535) Bk. 13, chap. 10 (9)

enesta materia delas perlas. Digo que yo tengo por impossible lo que dizen quanto al engendrarse del rocio: y ser turbias o claras ni tampoco amarillas por los truenos: por que en vna mesma ostia no son todas las perlas que tiene de vna bondad ⁊ redondez / ni de vna perficion de color / ni de vn tamaño sino en diferente manera algunas. Lo otro como se puede prouar lo que dizen: pues que muchas dellas se sacan de diez y de doze braças de agua en hondo: donde muy pegadas ⁊ asidas conlas peñas en algunas partes estan. Quien las vido claras antes que atronasse: ⁊ despues vio que las mismas se auiã tornado obscuras y delos defectos ya dichos. Deremos esto creer alos que no sabran contradezir lo: porque yo las he visto ⁊ tenido tã negras como azauache: ⁊ otras leonadas / ⁊ otras muy amarillas y resplandescientes como oro: ⁊ otras quajadas y espessas ⁊ sin resplandor: ⁊ otras quasi azules: ⁊ otras como azogadas: ⁊ otras que tiran sobre color verde: ⁊ otras a diuersas colores declinando. E assi quanto mas diferentes y enfermas enla vista / o para menos estimar estan / tanto mas y de mayor estimacion son las perfectas. E muy raras vezes se hallan las que son dinas de se poner en estima o regla de quilates para la vencion dellas. Pero en quãto ala forma de su creacion acuerde se quien esto lee d lo que se dixo enel capitulo segundo deste libro diez y nueue: ⁊ aquello puede tener por muy cierto. Y tambien podria ser que enestas partes se formassen ⁊ criassen de vna manera: y enel oriente ⁊ donde dizen plinio ⁊ otros auctores que las ay se engendrassen de otra forma / o por el rocio que ellos dizẽ. Porque natura en algunas partes haze en diferentes modos sus operaciones en vn mismo genero de criaturas: contentese pues el lector con lo dicho y passemos a otra manera de plas que se hazen y nascen enlos Nacarones / de quien hize mencion enel prohemio: porque de aquestos nunca lo ley ni lo he visto por algũ auctor escripto: ⁊ yo los he lleuado a España / ⁊ ay muchos dellos enla costa austral dela tierra firme enla puĩcia q̃ llamã de nicaragua: y enlas yslas de chara ⁊ chira ⁊ pocosi: ⁊ otras yslas del golfo de orotiña.

Capitulo nueue delos nacarones en que se hallan perlas enla prouincia de nicaragua ⁊ golfo de orotiña ⁊ otras partes.

En el golfo de orotiña ⁊ yslas q̃ ay enel: assi como Chira ⁊ chara ⁊ Pocosi: ⁊ otras que son dẽtro del cabo blanco enla costa d nicaragua ẽla mar dl sur he yo visto muchos dstos nacarones: y d alli erã los q̃ dixe d suso q̃ auia lleuado a españa: estos son

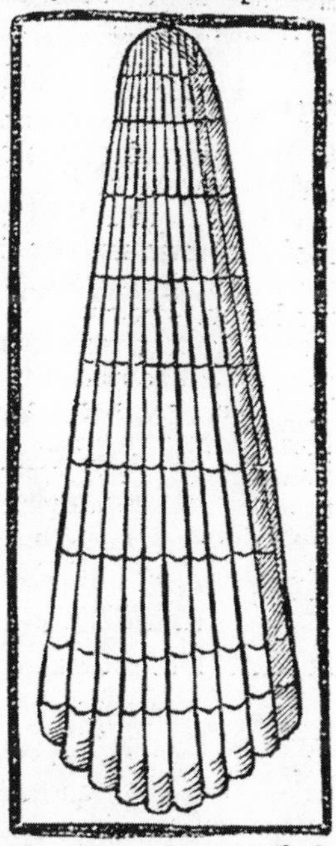

vna mañra d cõchas dl talle q̃ aq̃ esta dbuxado: ⁊ sõ dos pegados assi como las ostias lo estã: ⁊ asidos por las pũtas ⁊ algo mas / d mañra q̃ lo ãcho es lo q̃ se abre ⁊ cierra por si mismos: estos nacarones sõ grãdes y medianos ⁊ menores: los mayores rã luẽgos como vn codo hasta ẽ fin dlos dedos: y el ãcho dela pala de

FIGURE 52.

Nacarón *shell (1535) Bk. 19, chap. 9*

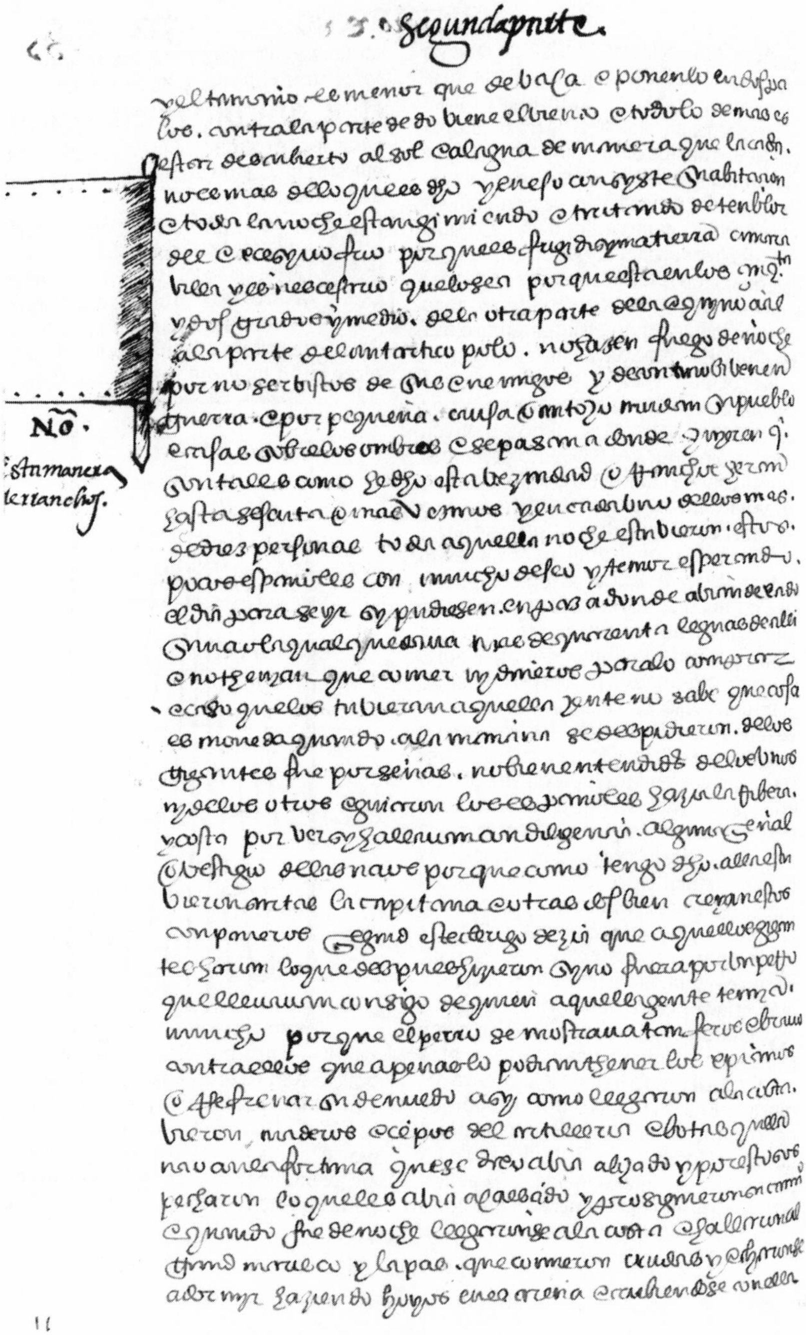

FIGURE 53.

Patagonian windbreak (PR II/3041, 35v) Bk. 20, chap. 6 (7)

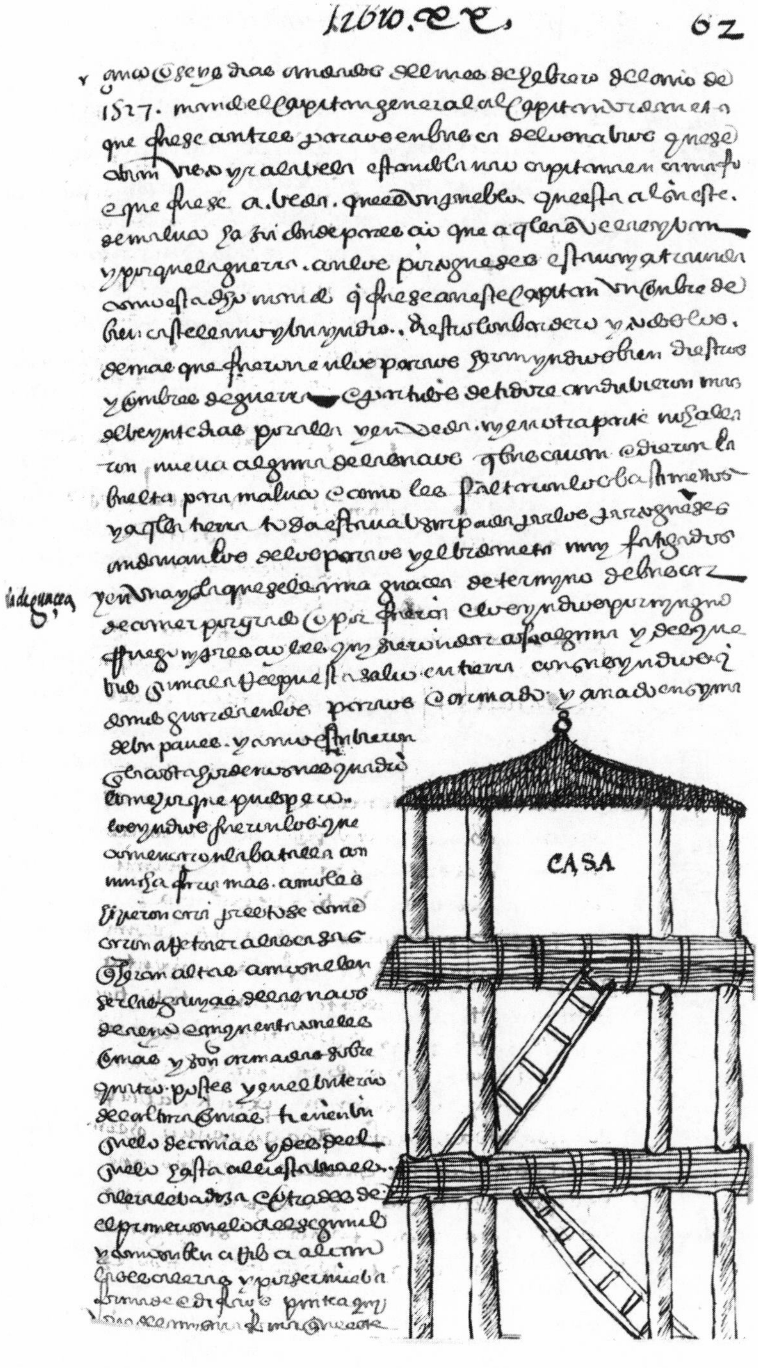

FIGURE 54.
Fire tower (PR II/3041, 62r) Bk. 20, chap. 22 (23)

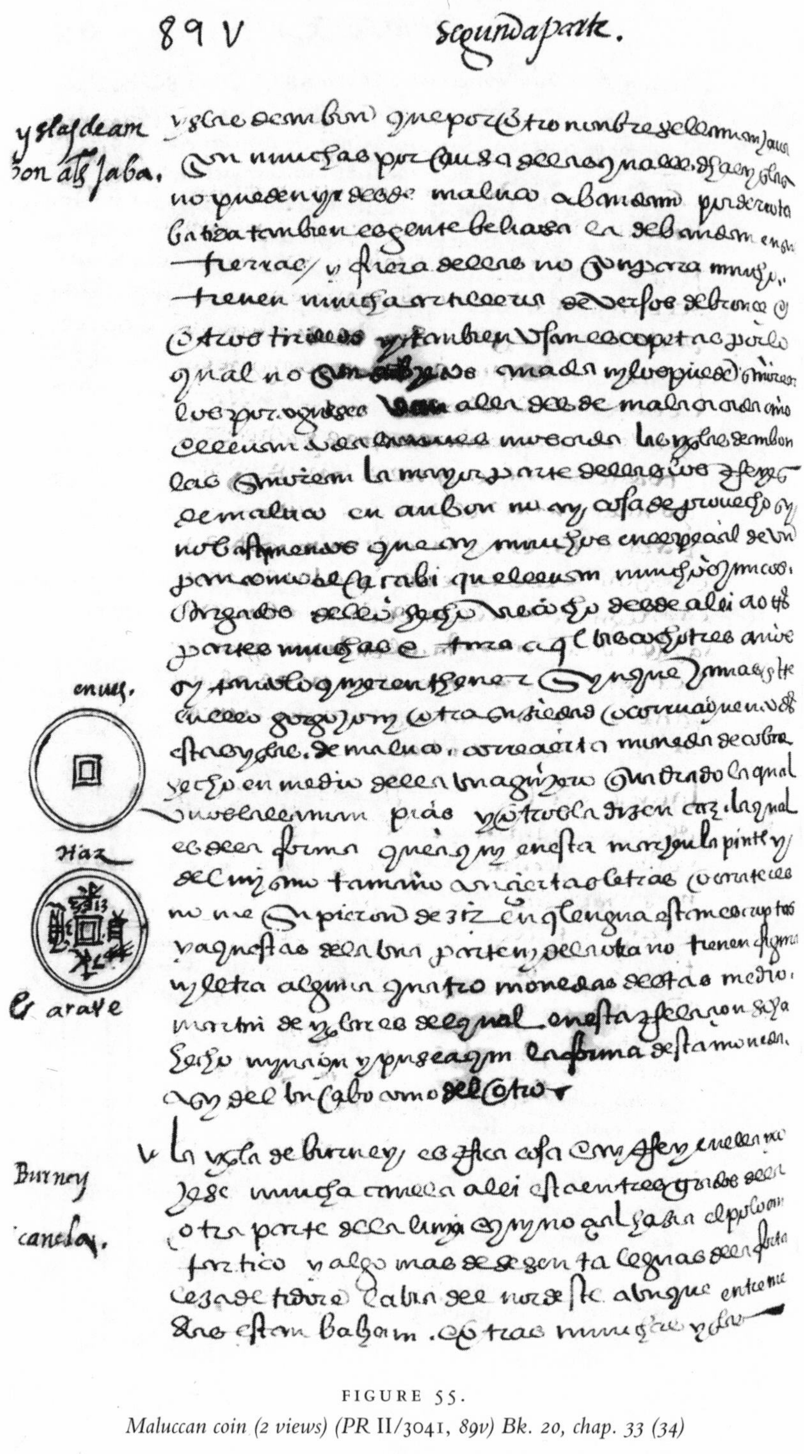

FIGURE 55.

Maluccan coin (2 views) (PR II/3041, 89v) Bk. 20, chap. 33 (34)

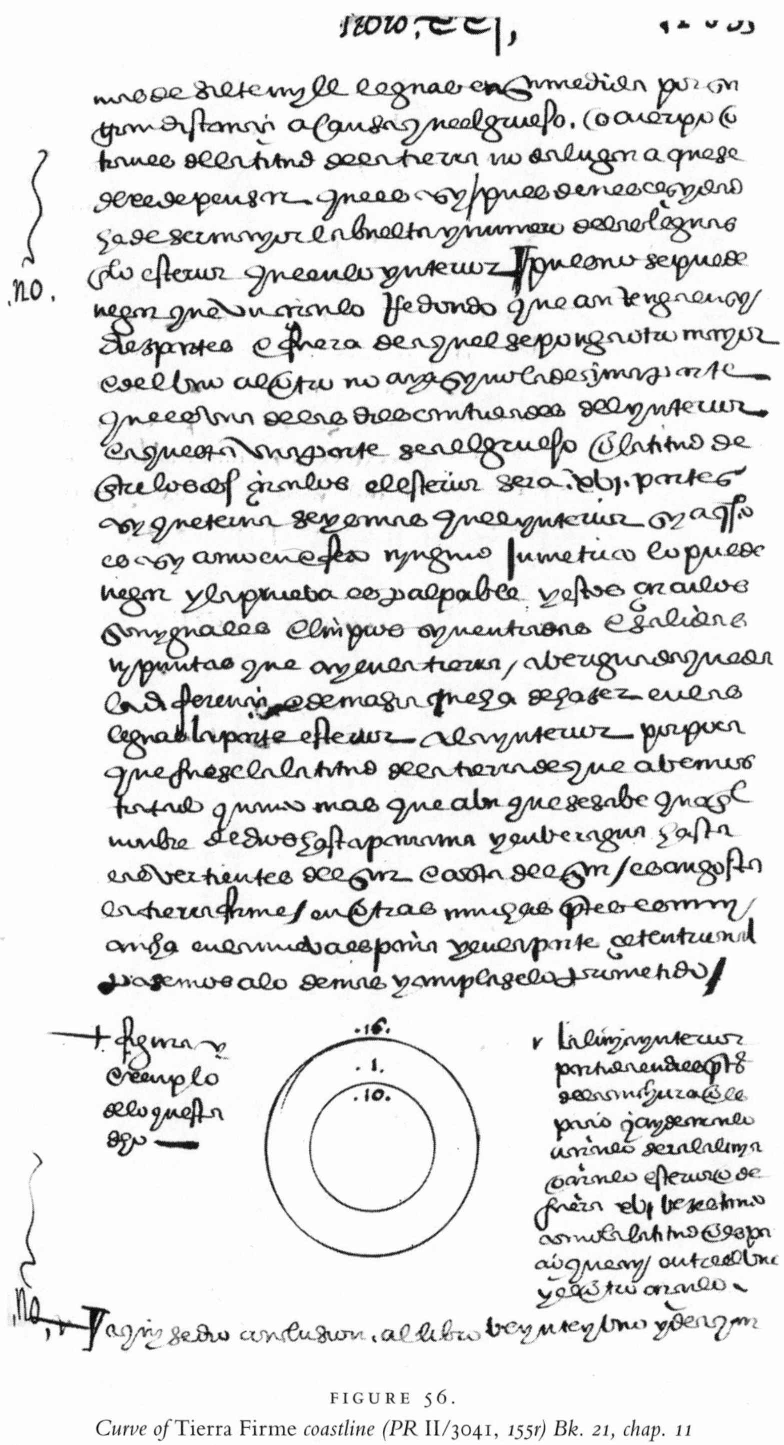

FIGURE 56.
Curve of Tierra Firme *coastline (PR* II/3041, *155r) Bk. 21, chap. 11*

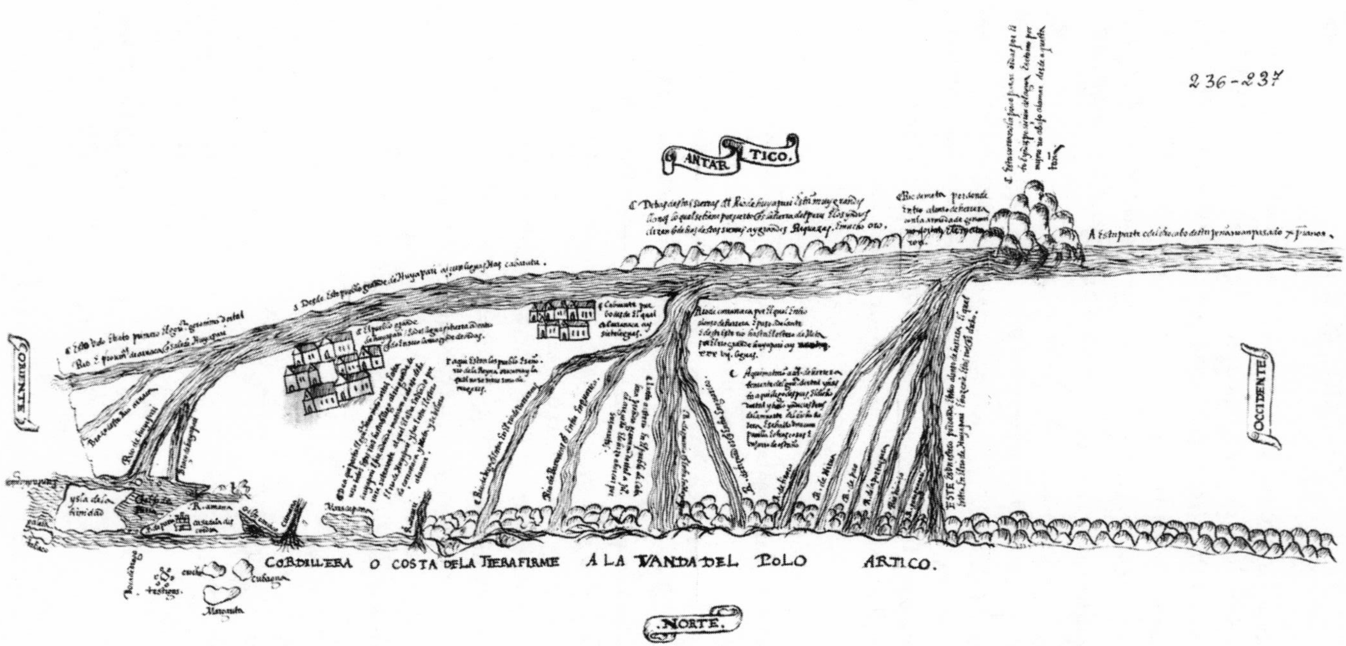

FIGURE 57.

Map of Tierra Firme *(PR* II/3041, *236–237) Bk. 24, chap. 15*

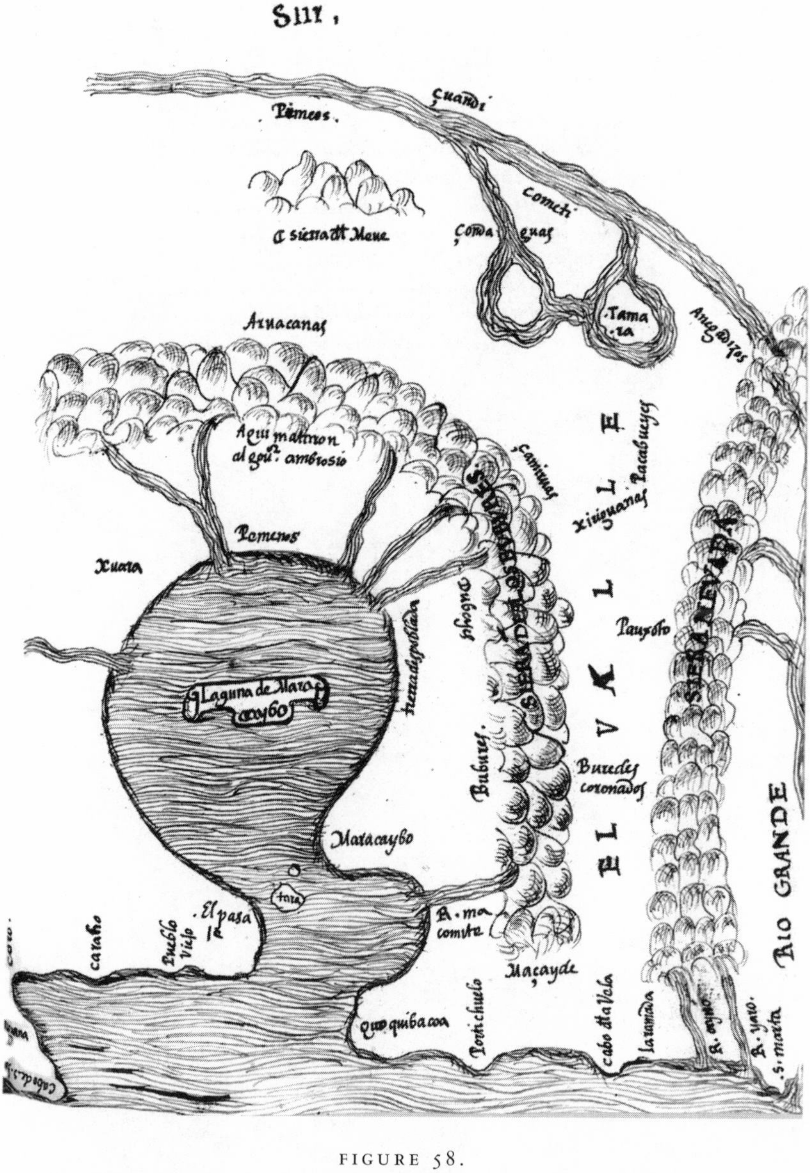

FIGURE 58.

Map of the Lake of Maracaibo (PR II/3041, *241–242) Bk. 25, chap. 1*

FIGURE 59.
Gulf of Nicoya (RAH 9/553, 76r) Bk. 29, chap. 21

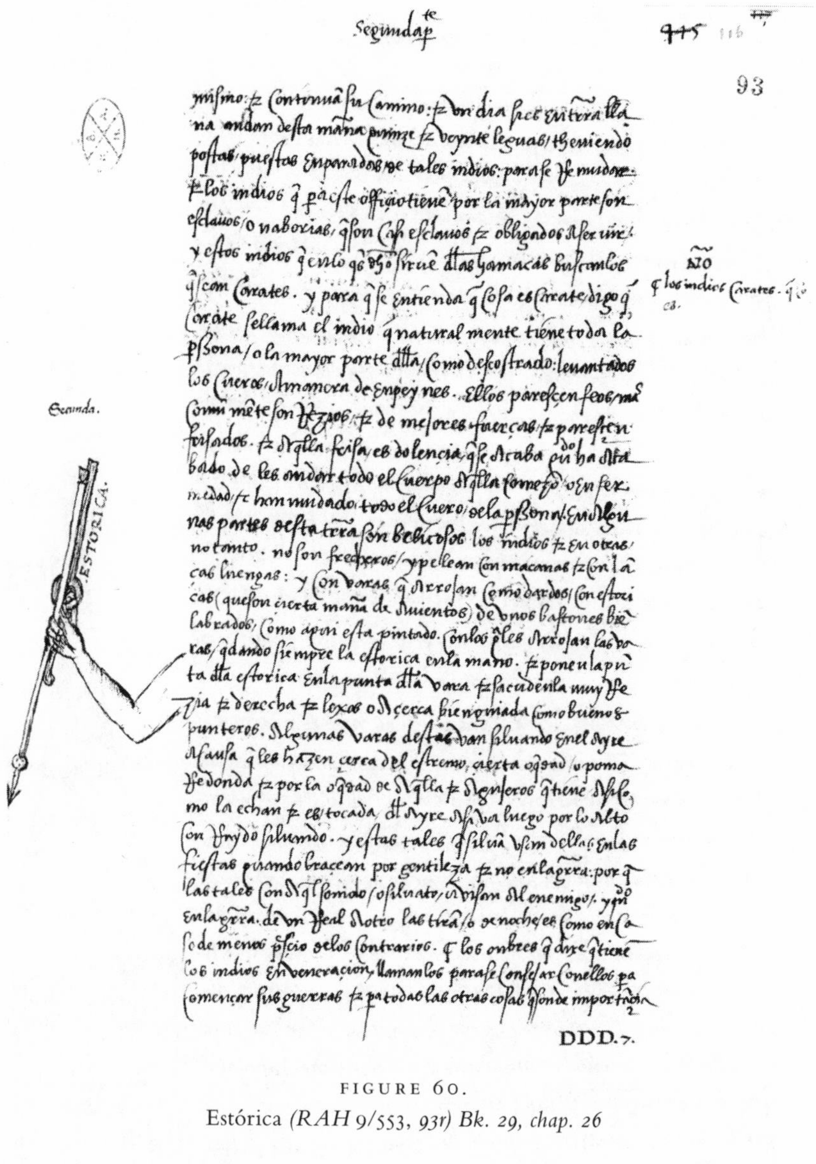

FIGURE 60.
Estórica *(RAH 9/553, 93r) Bk. 29, chap. 26*

libro. ~~xxvi~~. xxix.
por tierra llana / por ciertos escalones hechos de bexucos /
nascidos e rebueltos e atados al arbol / e el terreno
de abaxo cubierto de agua e paludes baxos e partes
hondos / e de alli salen en canoas a la tierra enxuta donde ha
zen sus labranças e conucos. esta manera de pueblos hazen
por estar seguros del fuego e de sus enemigos e de las bes
tias fieras e por que estan mas fuertes. En las otras parte
donde los indios pueblan / por la mayor parte es desparzi
dos en valles e laderas e costas de rrios / o donde les pa
resce: e tambien en las sierras (a la manera de estas monta
ñas de españa e en vizcaya e galizia) pueblan como en
barrios unas casas desviadas de otras / pero muchas de
llas e gran territorio debaxo de la obidiençia de un caciq
o tiba / o saco / o quij / o señor principal / por que estos nonbres
como tengo dicho usan los señores en diferentes provinçias.
Este nonbre quij. quiere dezir en dragungo grande. y asi
al que en la lengua de cueva llaman quij es mas señor e de mas es
tado e gente quel tiba / ni el saco. Ay otra manera de buhi
os / o casas en nata redondos con unos chapiteles muy altos
e son de mucho aposento e seguros por quel viento de la brisa
que alli corre muchas vezes del año / con mucho impeto / no los puede
assi coser como a los que son quadrados / o de otra forma: son de
rezia e buena madera e mas hermosos de dentro que to
das las maneras de casas que se ha dicho / e ponen en la punta del
chapitel una cosa de barro cozido a manera de candelero e
el cuello alto: y en la forma que esta aqui pintado. la paja con
que se cubre es muy buena e las cañas de las paredes gruesas e
por de fuera e de dentro forradas las paredes de caña delga
da muy bien puesta e con muchos apartamientos. El assi
ento deste pueblo es muy gentil e de hermosas vegas e muy
llano e dispuesto para ganados e todas granjerias e ay mu
chas vacas e puercos e yeguas e es tierra de mucha caça e
·EN·
·NA

FIGURE 61.
Nata house (RAH 9/553, 97v) Bk. 29, chap. 27

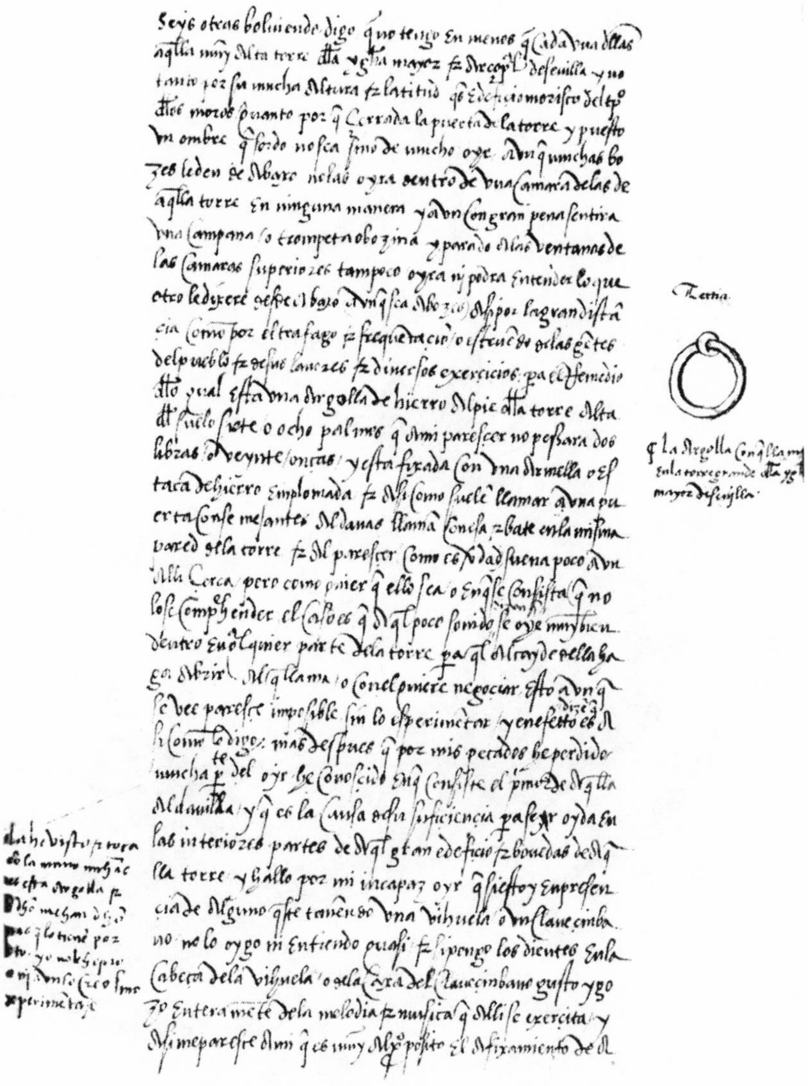

FIGURE 62.
Metal knocker on the Giralda, Sevilla (HEH, HM-177, 94r) Bk. 32, chap. 4

FIGURE 63.
Horse ferry (HEH, HM-177, *95–96) Bk. 32, chap. 4*

tomar la governacion de la tierra por diego velazquez. y que
era poder q el tenia ordenado de hazer cap.n y alcalde mayor
y q el avia de ser alguazil mayor y le avia de prender / o
matar. y q en esto eran muchas personas q el tenia puestas
en una copia / la qual se hallo en su posada / aunq fecha pe
daços / con algunas personas q declaro q avie platicado lo su
sodicho: y q no solamente esto se avia ordenado alli en the
payeco pero q tambien lo avia comunicado y puesto en plati
ca estando en la gora de la provincia de tepeaca. y vista su
confision deste delinquente / q se llamava antonio de villa
fañe natural de la cibdad de çamora y como se ratifico
en ella / un alcalde y el mismo hernando cortes le condenaron a mu
erte y fue executada en su persona / y puesto q en este cri
men avia otros muy culpados disimulose con ellos haziendo
doles obras de amigos / por q el caso era suyo propio (& aun
mas q proprio) la qual disimulacion no fue de provecho
por otras causas q cortes dize en su relacion endereçadas
a las passiones de entre el y diego velazquez / q son mas
pa los processos y libelos en q ellos anduvieron sobre la gover
nacion de aquella tierra q no para nra historia. ¶ despues
q fue presa la cibdad de temixtitan y do el general a la de cuyoacan
fallescio alli aquel don fernando q la historia ha dicho q era
señor de thezcuco / cuya muerte peso mucho a los españo
les / por q era muy buen vasallo y servidor de sus mag. y gran
amigo verdadero de los xpianos: y comparescer de los señores y
principales de aquella su cibdad y provincia se dio aquel señorio
en nombre de sus mag. de a otro hermano suyo: el qual pidio el
baptismo y llamaronle don carlos: buen mancebo y de gentil
conversacion. ¶ En algunas partes destas
historias se ha hecho memoria de las provinci
as de Tascalteal y guaxocingo y por q
alli ovo una montaña q quiere ymi tar y
parescer mucho al monte de vul can ys
la (cerra de secilia) q tan discanta do
es de muchos historiales y po etas
sera bien q aqueste otro no quede en olvido pues dize el general

¶ Como murio don fern.do señor de tezcuco y se dio en el estado su hr.o don Carlos.

Nota

¶ guaxocingo. Como subieron ciertos españoles a aquel monte a ver q cosa era por mandado del Cap. Hr.do Cortes.

Quinta.

FIGURE 64.
Volcano (Guajocingo) *(RAH 9/555, 157r) Bk. 33, chap. 33*

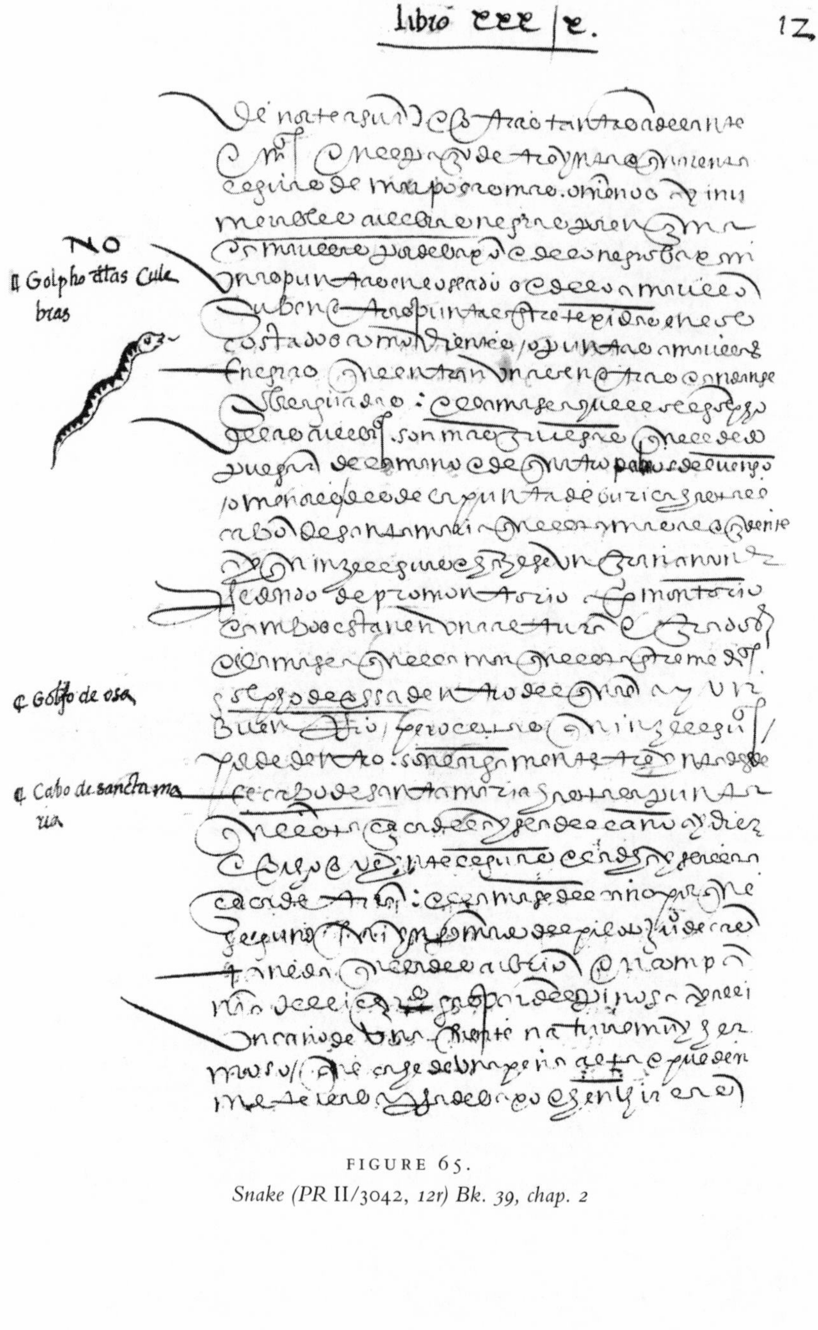

FIGURE 65.
Snake (PR II/3042, 12r) Bk. 39, chap. 2

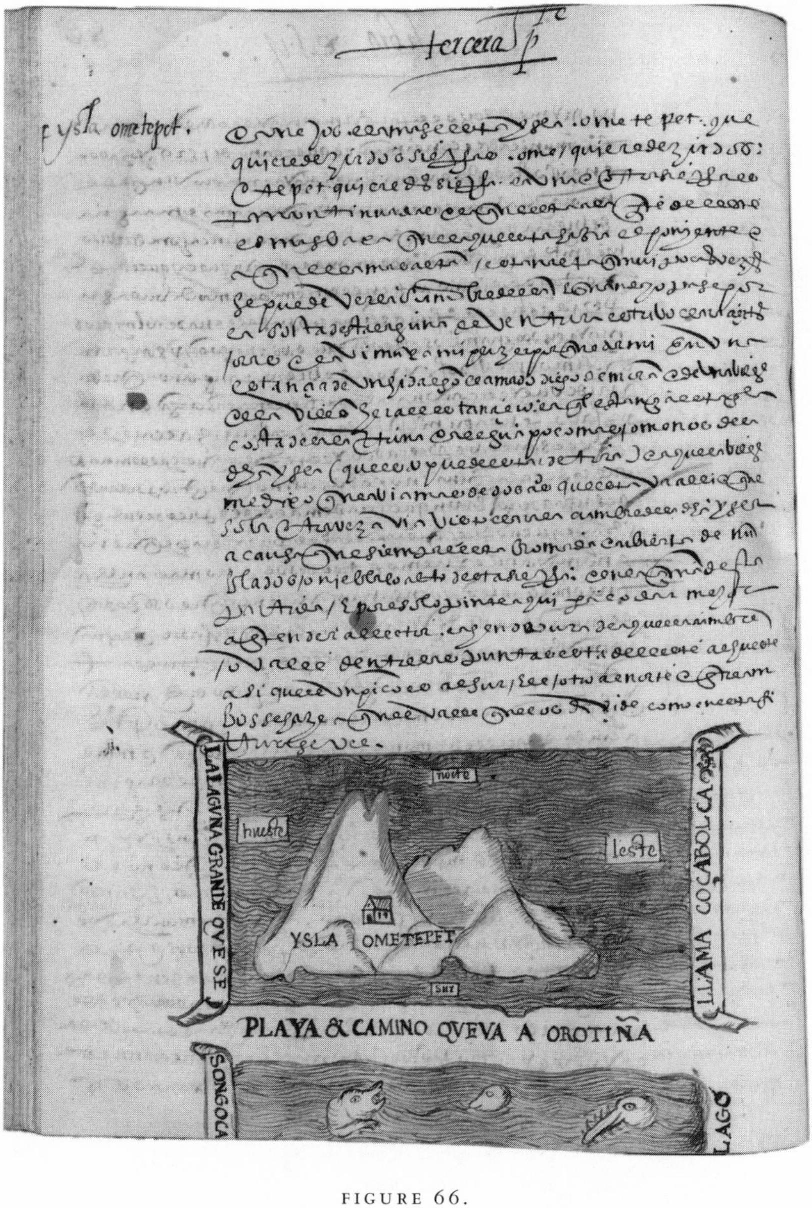

FIGURE 66.

Island of Ometepet (PR II/3042, 56v) Bk. 42, chap. 4

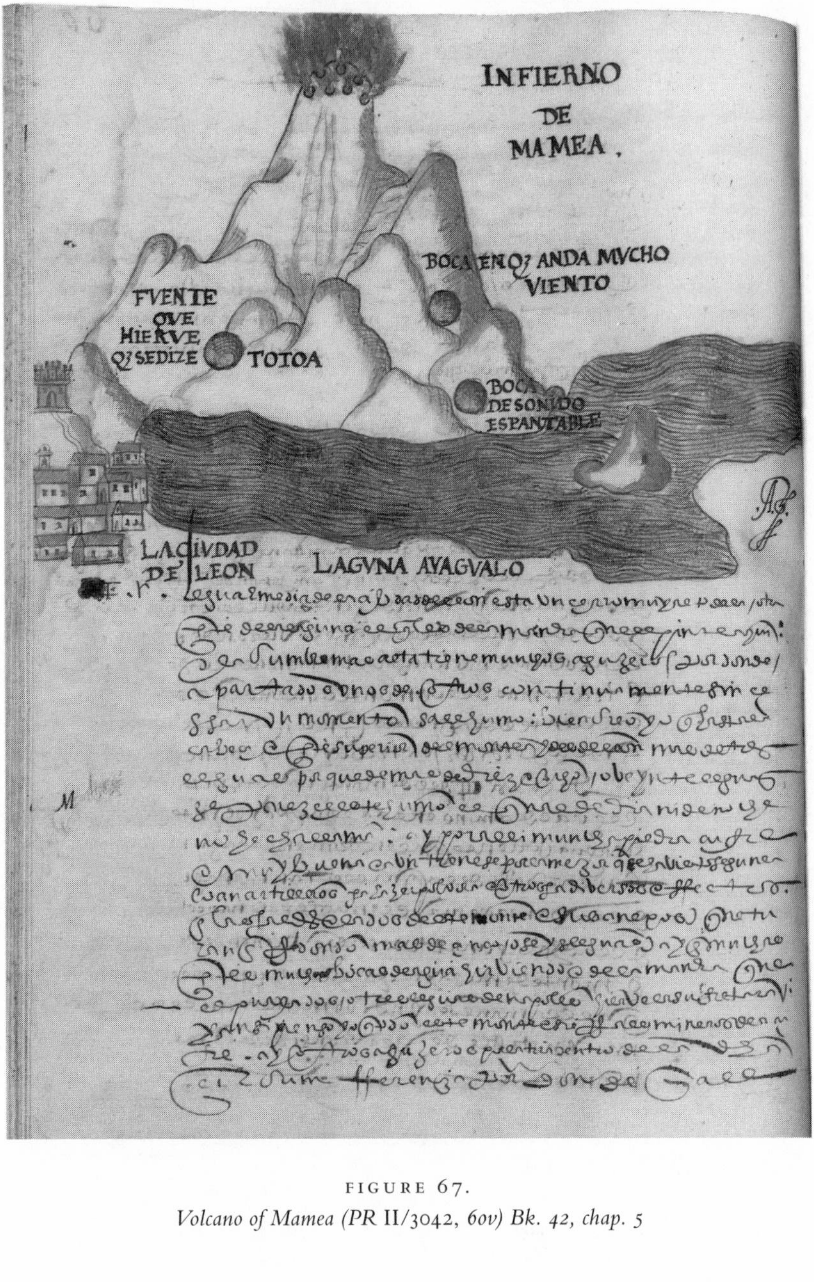

FIGURE 67.
Volcano of Mamea (PR II/3042, 60v) Bk. 42, chap. 5

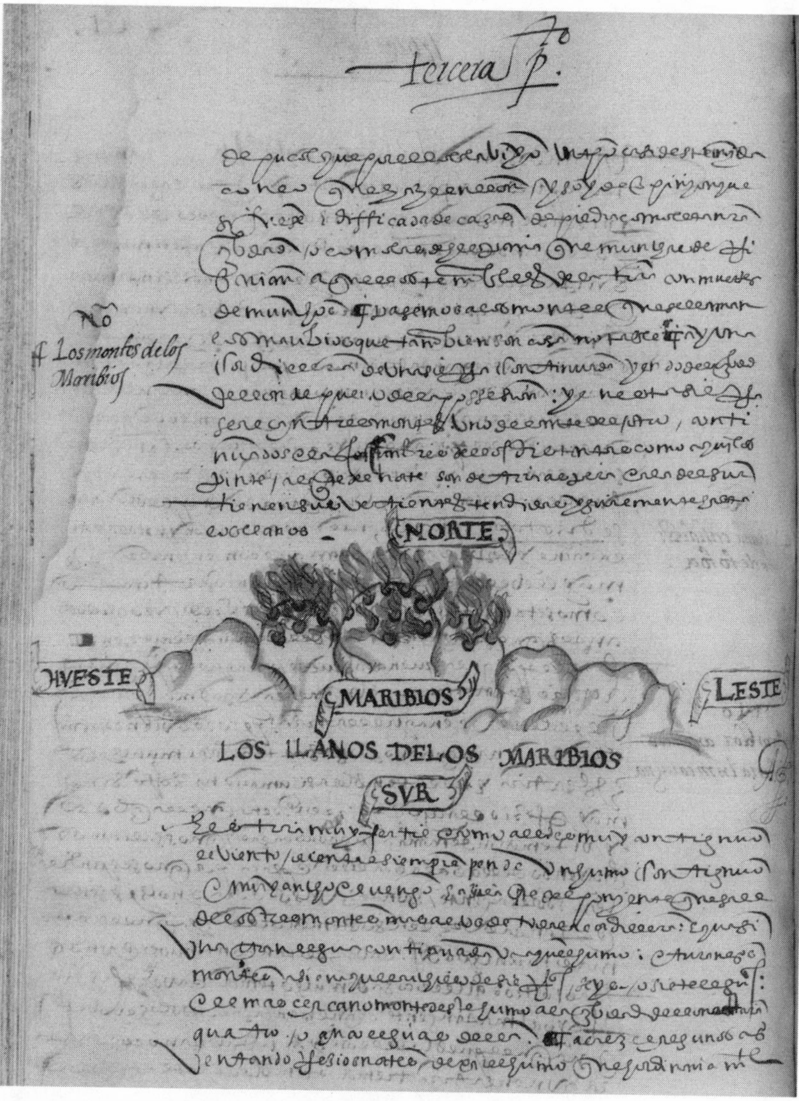

FIGURE 68.

"Los llanos de los maribios" (PR II/3042, 61v) Bk. 42, chap. 5

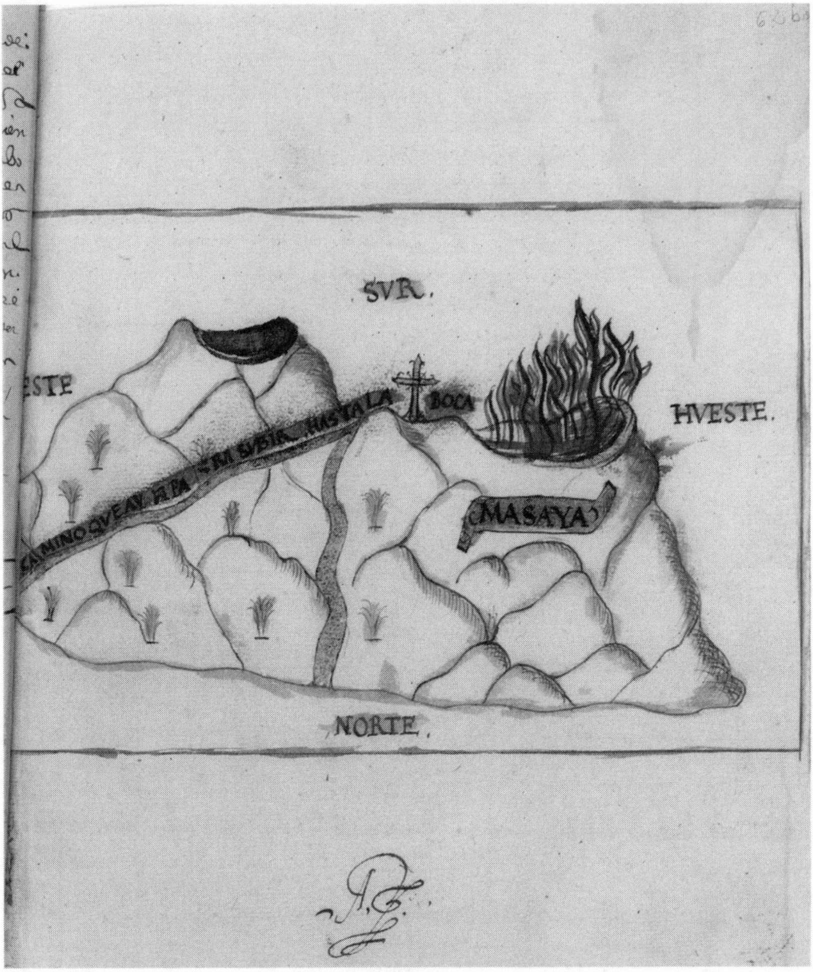

FIGURE 69.
Road to the Volcano Masaya (PR II/3042, *62–63) Bk. 42, chap. 6 (5)*

FIGURE 70.

Diagram of the crater of Masaya (PR II/3042, 65r) Bk. 42, chap. 6 (5)

FIGURE 71.
Voladores *(PR* II/3042, *84v) Bk. 42, chap. 11*

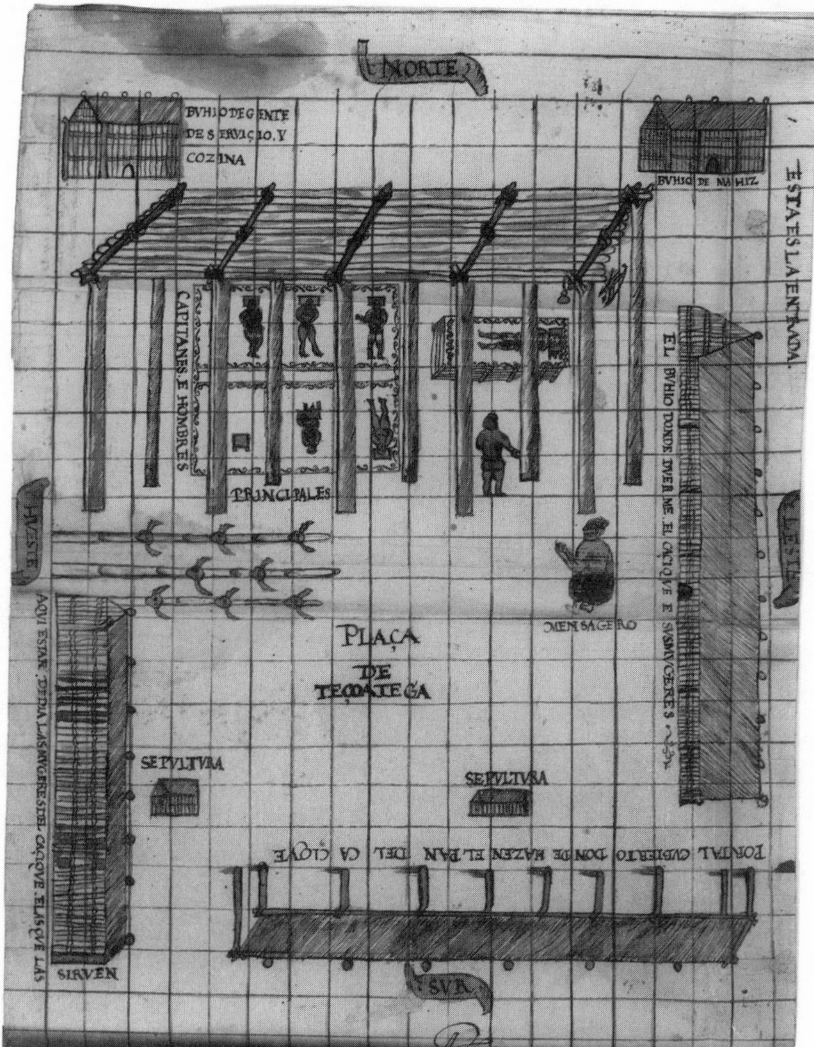

FIGURE 72.

Plaza of Tecoatega (PR II/3042, 101–102) Bk. 42, chap. 13

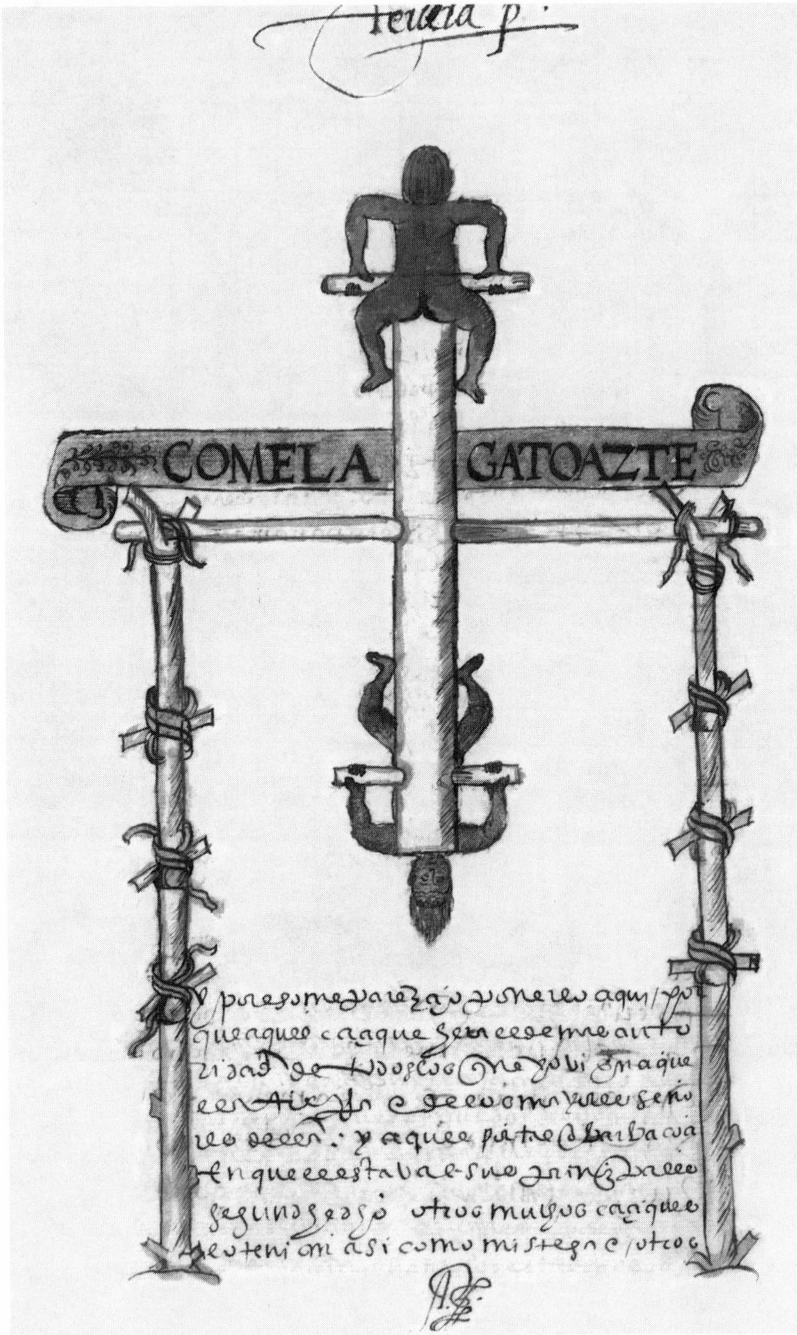

FIGURE 73.
Whirlabout (PR II/3042, *104v) Bk. 42, chap. 13*

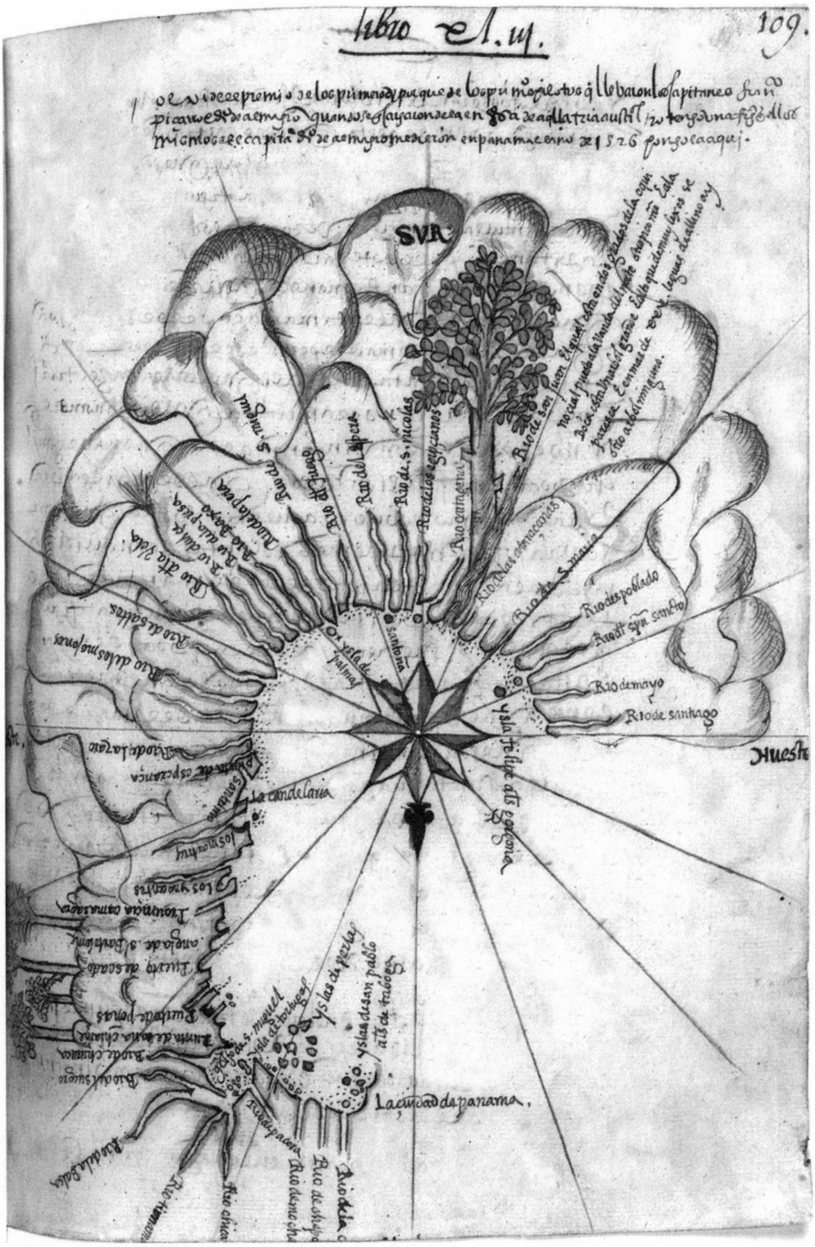

FIGURE 74.
Map of Panama coast (PR II/3042, 109r) Bk. 43, chap. 1

FIGURE 75.
Inca weapon (PR II/3042, 226v) Bk. 46, chap. 17

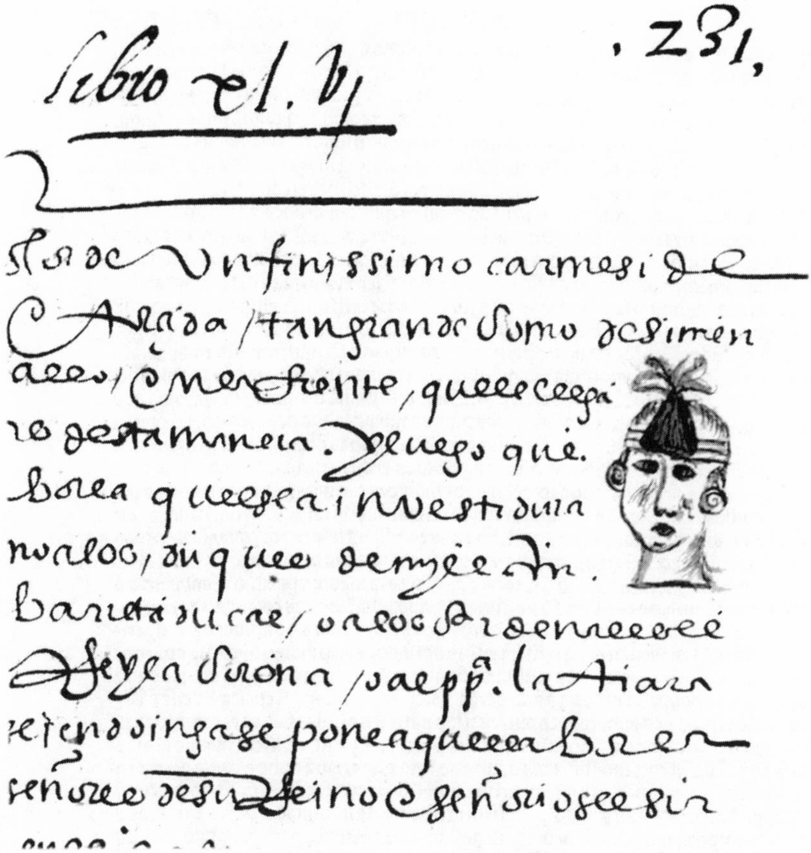

FIGURE 76.
Inca head and hat (detail) (PR II/3042, 231r) Bk. 46, chap. 17

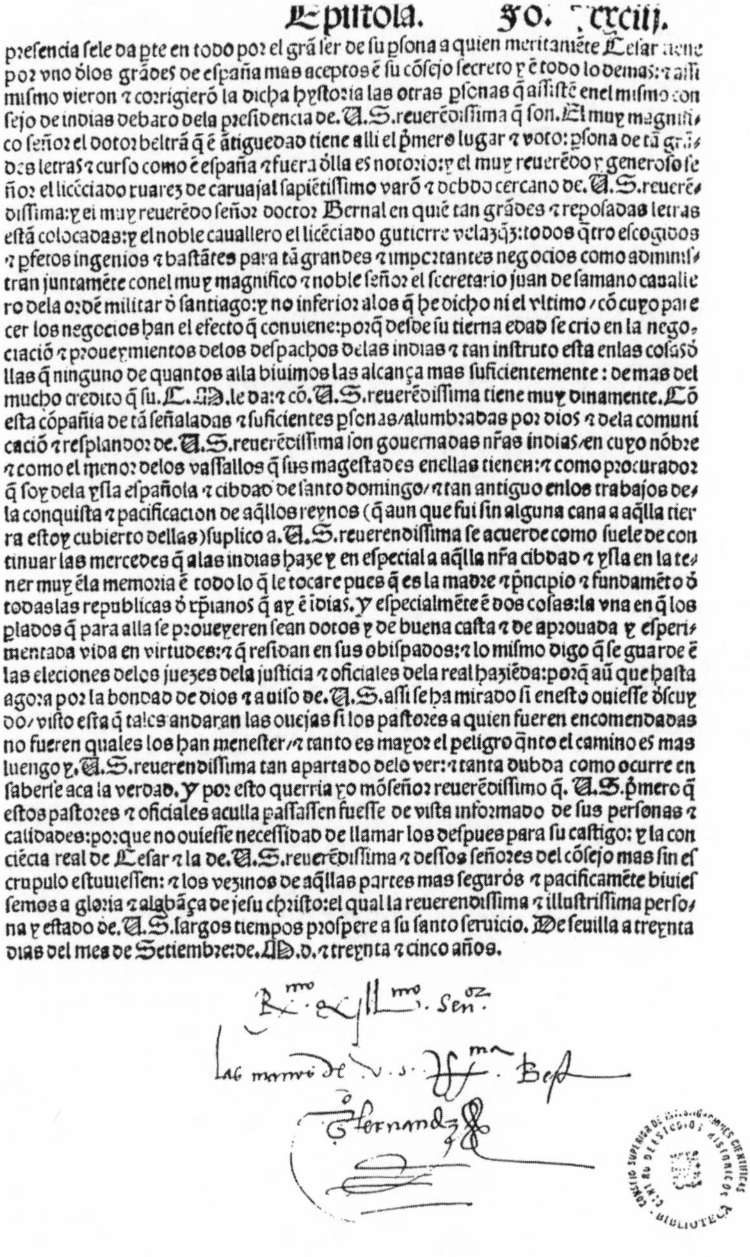

Epistola. Fo. ccciij.

presencia se le da pte en todo por el grã ser de su psona a quien meritamẽte Cesar tiene por vno dlos grãdes de españa mas aceptos ẽ su cõsejo secreto y ẽ todo lo demas: ⁊ assi mismo vieron ⁊ corrigierõ la dicha hystoria las otras psonas q̃ assistẽ enel mismo consejo de indias debaxo dela presidencia de. V. S. reuerẽdissima q̃ son. El muy magnifico señor el doctor beltrã q̃ ẽ ãtiguedad tiene alli el pmero lugar ⁊ voto: psona de tã grãdes letras ⁊ curso como ẽ españa ⁊ fuera della es notorio: y el muy reuerẽdo y generoso señor el licẽciado xuarez de caruajal sapiẽtissimo varõ ⁊ deudo cercano de. V. S. reuerẽdissima: y el muy reuerẽdo señor doctor Bernal en quiẽ tan grãdes ⁊ reposadas letras estã colocadas: y el noble cauallero el licẽciado gutierre velazq̃z: todos q̃tro escogidos ⁊ pfetos ingenios ⁊ bastãtes para tã grandes ⁊ importantes negocios como administran juntamẽte conel muy magnifico ⁊ noble señor el secretario juan de samano cauallero dela ordẽ militar d santiago: y no inferior alos q̃ he dicho ni el vltimo / cõ cuyo parecer los negocios han el efecto q̃ conuiene: porq̃ desde su tierna edad se crio en la negociaciõ ⁊ proueymientos delos despachos delas indias ⁊ tan instruto esta enlas cosas dllas q̃ ninguno de quantos alla biuimos las alcança mas suficientemente: demas del mucho credito q̃ su. C. M. le da: ⁊ cõ. V. S. reuerẽdissima tiene muy dinamente. Cõ esta cõpañia de tã señaladas ⁊ suficientes psonas / alumbradas por dios ⁊ dela comunicaciõ ⁊ resplandor de. V. S. reuerẽdissima son gouernadas nr̃as indias / en cuyo nõbre ⁊ como el menor delos vassallos q̃ sus magestades enellas tienen: ⁊ como procurador q̃ soy dela ysla española ⁊ cibdad de santo domingo / ⁊ tan antiguo enlos trabajos dela conquista ⁊ pacificacion de aq̃llos reynos (q̃ aun que fui sin alguna cana a aq̃lla tierra estoy cubierto dellas) suplico a. V. S. reuerendissima se acuerde como suele de continuar las mercedes q̃ alas indias haze y en especial a aq̃lla nr̃a cibdad ⁊ ysla en la tener muy ẽla memoria ẽ todo lo q̃ le tocare pues q̃ es la madre ⁊ pncipio ⁊ fundamẽto d todas las republicas d xpianos q̃ ay ẽ idias. Y especialmẽte ẽ dos cosas: la vna en q̃ los plados q̃ para alla se proueyeren sean doctos y de buena casta ⁊ de aprouada y esperimentada vida en virtudes: ⁊ q̃ residan en sus obispados: ⁊ lo mismo digo q̃ se guarde ẽ las eleciones delos juezes dela justicia ⁊ oficiales dela real haziẽda: porq̃ aũ que hasta agora por la bondad de dios ⁊ auiso de. V. S. assi se ha mirado si enesto ouiesse dscuydo / visto esta q̃ tales andaran las ouejas si los pastores a quien fueren encomendadas no fueren quales los han menester / ⁊ tanto es mayor el peligro q̃nto el camino es mas luengo y. V. S. reuerendissima tan apartado delo ver: ⁊ tanta dubda como ocurre en saberse aca la verdad. Y por esto querria yo mõseñor reuerẽdissimo q̃. V. S. pmero q̃ estos pastores ⁊ oficiales aculla passassen fuesse de vista informado de sus personas ⁊ calidades: porque no ouiesse necessidad de llamar los despues para su castigo: y la conciẽcia real de Cesar ⁊ la de. V. S. reuerẽdissima ⁊ dessos señores del cõsejo mas sin escrupulo estuuiessen: ⁊ los vezinos de aq̃llas partes mas segurõs ⁊ pacificamẽte biuiessemos a gloria ⁊ alabãça de jesu christo: el qual la reuerendissima ⁊ illustrissima persona y estado de. V. S. largos tiempos prospere a su santo seruicio. De seuilla a treynta dias del mes de Setiembre: de. M. d. ⁊ treynta ⁊ cinco años.

FIGURE 77

Oviedo's signature, f. 193r (Seville, 1535)

FIGURE 78.
Oviedo's Coat of Arms, f. 193 (1535, 193v)

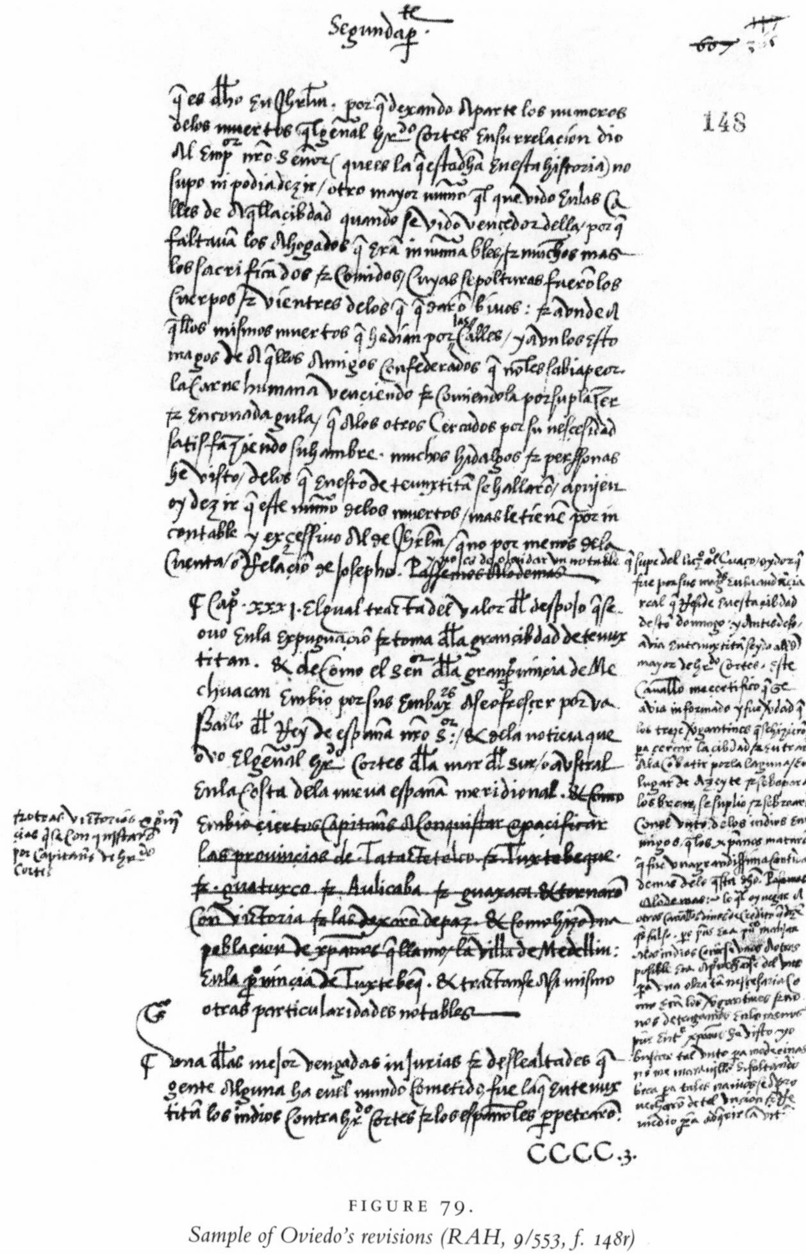

FIGURE 79.
Sample of Oviedo's revisions (RAH, 9/553, f. 148r)

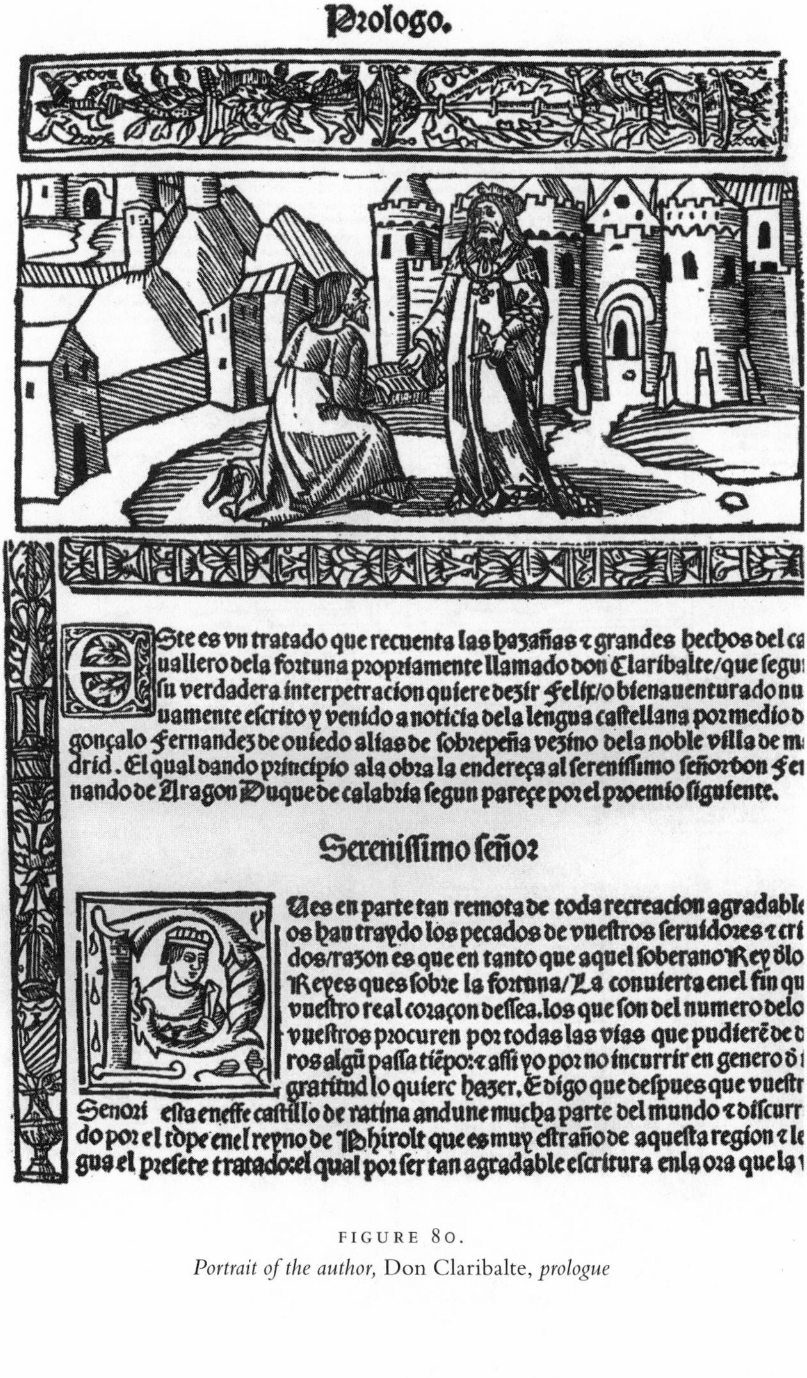

Prologo.

Este es vn tratado que recuenta las hazañas ⁊ grandes hechos del ca
uallero dela fortuna propriamente llamado don Claribalte/que segu
su verdadera interpetracion quiere dezir Felix/o bienauenturado nu
uamente escrito y venido a noticia dela lengua castellana por medio d
gonçalo Fernandez de ouiedo alias de sobrepeña vezino dela noble villa de ma
drid. El qual dando principio ala obra la endereça al serenissimo señor don Fer
nando de Aragon Duque de calabria segun pareçe por el proemio siguiente.

Serenissimo señor

Pues en parte tan remota de toda recreacion agradabl
os han traydo los pecados de vuestros seruidores ⁊ cri
dos/razon es que en tanto que aquel soberano Rey dlo
Reyes que sobre la fortuna/La conuierta enel fin qu
vuestro real coraçon dessea. los que son del numero delo
vuestros procuren por todas las vias que pudierē de d
ros algũ passa tiēpo: ⁊ assi yo por no incurrir en genero d i
gratitud lo quiere hazer. E digo que despues que vuestr
Señor i esta enesse castillo de ratina anduue mucha parte del mundo ⁊ discurr
do por el tōpe enel reyno de Phirolt que es muy estraño de aquesta region ⁊ le
gus el presete tratado: el qual por ser tan agradable escritura enla ora que la v

FIGURE 80.
Portrait of the author, Don Claribalte, *prologue*

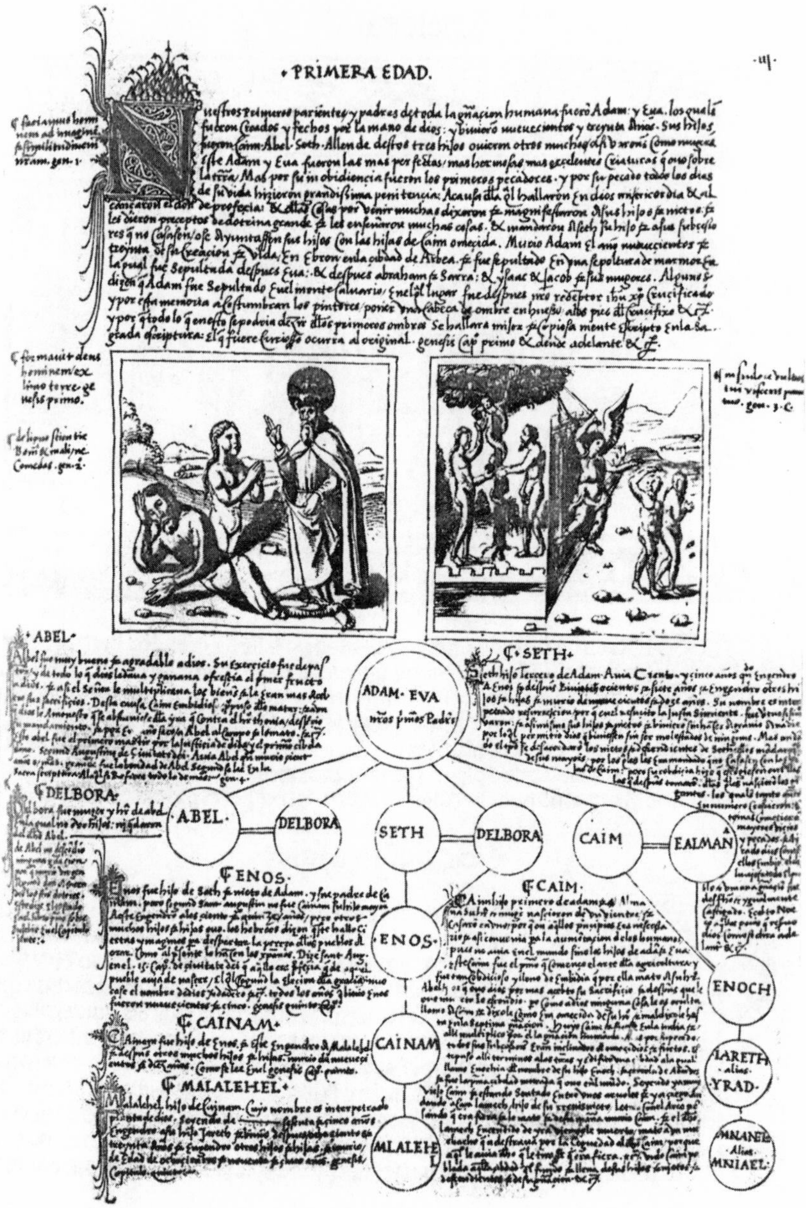

FIGURE 81.

Sample genealogy, Catálogo Real *(BE hIf, f. 11r, 1532)*

FIGURE 82.
Sample Coat of Arms, Batallas y Quinquagenas *(BUS 359, f. 304r)*

LÁMINA IV.

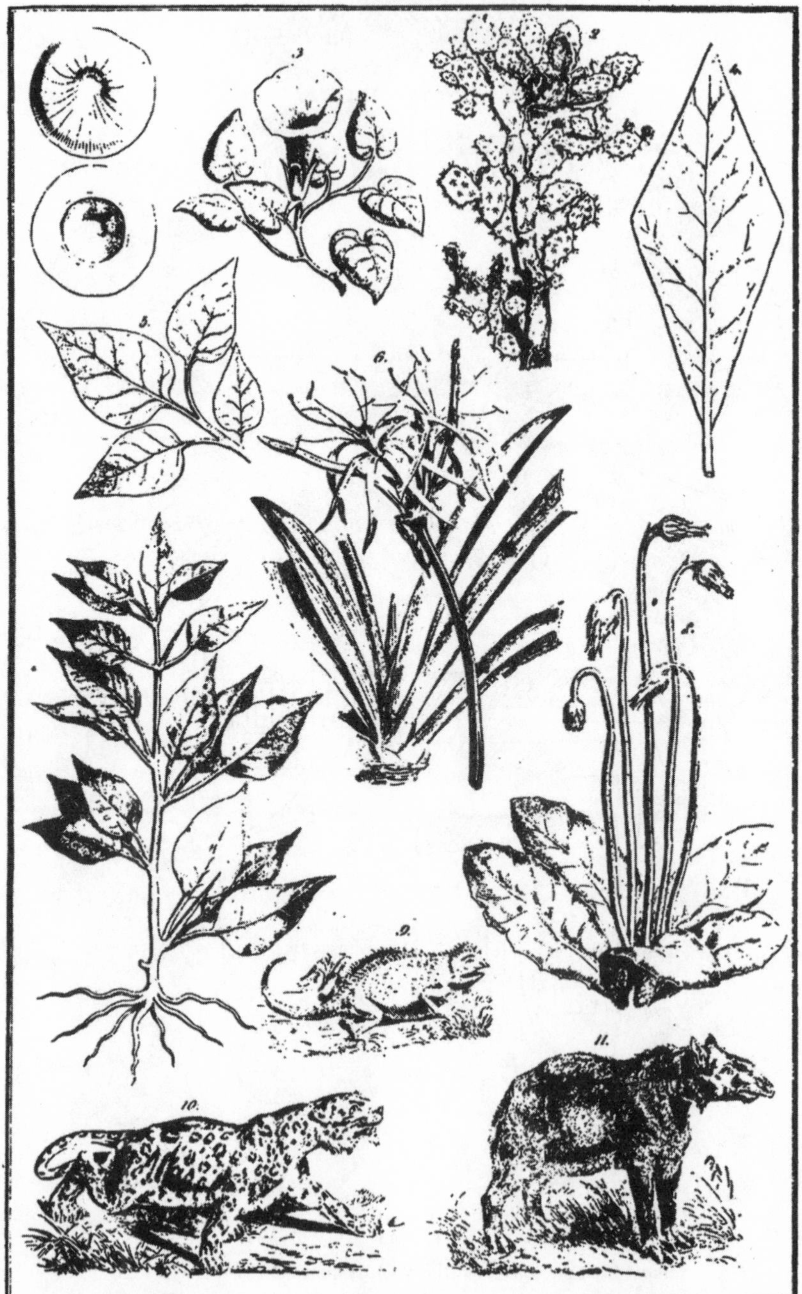

FIGURE 83.
Sample of Oviedo's illustrations as reproduced in Amador de los Ríos, *Plate 4 (1850–1855)*

NOTES

INTRODUCTION

1. See Daymond Turner, *Gonzalo Fernández de Oviedo: An Annotated Bibliography,* for a complete list of these early editions and translations.

2. See Félix Bolaños, *Panegírico y libelo* (23–65) and Antonello Gerbi, *Nature* (130–135), for thorough studies of the reception of Oviedo's work.

3. For a more complete publishing history and information on Oviedo's text, see Jesús Carrillo's recent introduction to *Oviedo on Columbus.*

4. See also the work by Enrique Otte, "Aspiraciones," and Peña y Cámara, "Contribuciones," for example.

5. See, for example, Rolena Adorno and Patrick Pautz's *Alvar Núñez Cabeza de Vaca,* 13–44. Indeed, this important aspect of Oviedo's historiographical methodology could have been yet another chapter/case in my book. I have not included it here as a separate chapter because chapters 5 and 6 deal with some aspects of Oviedo's use of sources, and scholars such as Adorno and Patricia Galloway have studied Oviedo's use of sources in detail.

6. Curiously, however, there are spaces left for drawings in Amador de los Ríos's manuscript copy of the *History,* indicating that he at first thought to leave the illustrations in the narrative as they are in the original. (The manuscript copy is at the Hispanic Society in New York City.) Perhaps an editor insisted on removing them to an appendix in order to reduce costs.

7. Oviedo left a complete version of the *History,* known as the Monserrate manuscript, in Seville around 1549, as Daymond Turner notes in his article "Forgotten Treasures." In 1563 the inquisitor and *maestre* of the Cathedral of Seville, Andrés Gascó, began copying the manuscript, which was finished sometime around 1566 by his nephew, Antonio Gascó. This manuscript copy is known as the Trujillos manuscript. By the late eighteenth century, the Royal Academy of History purchased the extant portions of the Monserrate manuscript (RAH, Salazar Collection 9/551–9/556). The historian Juan Bautista Muñoz meticulously listed the surviving sections of the manuscript, noting that entire books and chapters were already missing by 1780. As part of this project, Muñoz compared the Monserrate manuscript with the

Trujillos copy, recording in great detail the additions and revisions of books 1–19 made in the 1535 edition (RAH, Muñoz Collection, A/34). Sometime in the early twentieth century a section of the extant portion of the Monserrate manuscript was removed from the Royal Academy and later sold to the Huntington Library in San Marino, California (HM 177, books 4, 6, 32, and 37); around this time other sections of the *History* were lost. Thus today the bulk of the extant Monserrate manuscript is housed at the Royal Academy, but four books are at the Huntington. The Seville Trujillos sixteenth-century copy of the *History* is now dispersed among three archives: the Biblioteca Colombina in Seville (MS 83-6-15), which contains books 29–32; the library of the Royal Palace in Madrid (Mss II/3041 and II/3042), containing book 17, chapters 21–27, and books 39–50; the Royal Academy of History (Jesuit Collection, vol. 108), houses book 28. Amador de los Ríos's manuscript for his 1850s publication of the *History,* which Pérez de Tudela used for his 1950s edition, is housed at the Hispanic Society in New York City (HC: NS5/604/1). For a complete listing of the manuscript status of each of the fifty books in the *History,* consult the table in appendix D. For a lengthier discussion of the manuscript history, see Jesús Carrillo, "Introduction," *Oviedo on Columbus,* 28–29.

8. For excellent readings of Oviedo's role in the clash and violent accommodations between Spaniards and Native Americans, see Jose Rabasa, *Writing Violence,* and Álvaro Félix Bolaños, *Barbarie y canibalismo en la retórica colonial.*

ONE

1. Oviedo was linked with the Crown of Castile most of his life, and during this period Spain was not a unified state but rather an association of provinces with one king. Furthermore, Castile had three-fourths of the population in Spain and ruled directly over the Indies.

2. The first of these households was that of Ferdinand's illegitimate half-brother, Alonso of Aragon, duke of Villahermosa. There are many biographical sketches of Oviedo, each with its own particular slant. Some of the most notable biographical accounts of Oviedo's life include José Amador de los Ríos, "Vida y escritos," Enrique Otte, "Aspiraciones," José de la Peña y Cámara, "Contribuciones documentales," Juan Pérez de Tudela Bueso, "Vida y escritos," Alberto Salas, *Tres cronistas,* and Daymond Turner, *Gonzalo Fernández de Oviedo y Valdés.* There is only one full-length biography, Manuel Ballesteros, *Gonzalo Fernández de Oviedo,* but Gerbi's *Nature* has a lengthy section on Oviedo and contributes important information to our understanding of the chronicler's life. For an overview of the contributions of these diverse biographical accounts, consult Álvaro Félix Bolaños, "Panegírico y libelo." Perhaps the most significant archival source for biographical information about Oviedo's life in the Indies is the General Archives of the Indies in Seville. Nearly two hundred royal licenses and legal documents describe his travels, bureaucratic positions, and lawsuits.

3. Oviedo describes this post and his subsequent one as keeper of the keys to the household in his manual about the organization of the prince's household, *Libro de la cámara real del príncipe don Juan.*

4. See Daymond Turner, *Gonzalo Fernández de Oviedo,* x–xi.

5. For a thorough account of Oviedo's years in Italy, see Antonello Gerbi, *Nature,* 145–200.

6. Ibid., 165.

7. In an appendix, Gerbi reproduces the contract between Oviedo, Battista Ramusio, and Antonio Priuli. *Ibid.,* 411–414.

8. Discurrí por toda Italia, donde me di todo lo que yo pude a saber e leer y entender la lengua toscana y buscando libro en ella, de los cuales tengo algunos que ha más de 55 años que están en mi compañía.

9. See Daymond Turner's important study, "Los libros del alcaide."

10. Ibid., 151.

11. *Historia,* bk. 6, chap. 39.

12. I cite individual documents below from the AGI; the majority are in the collections known as *Indiferente, Panamá,* and *Patronato,* but *Contaduría, Justicia,* and *Santo Domingo* also have documents dealing with Oviedo's life and writings.

13. AGI Panama 233, L. 1, ff. 86v–87v, 1519 ("los oficios de escribano mayor de minas, de crimen y juzgado, del hierro de los indios, marcador y fundidor por poder de Lope Conchillos"); ff. 115–123v ("veedor del oro y demás metales y se funden en las provincias del Darién . . . salario de 70,000 maravedíes anuales").

14. There are dozens of documents in the AGI that date from this period. One of particular importance is the "Relación autógrafa de Oviedo exponiendo el mal estado en que se hallaban las cosas en Tierra Firme, atribuyéndolo a la mucha edad, a la codicia y la constancia del gobernador Pedrarias Dávila" (Patronato 193, R. 9, 1523). The majority of others revolve around instructions given to Oviedo in 1519 to collect from Pedrarias the wealth left by the execution of Núñez de Balboa and his men (e.g., Panama 233, L. 1, f. 254, 1519) and a series of cases that generally emerged as a result of Oviedo's 1524 *residencia,* the formal process of hearing cases against a Crown employee before he left the position (Panama 233, L. 1, ff. 348–349, 1524). The most frequent ongoing litigation deals with the collection of Núñez's wealth (e.g., Panama 233, L. 2, ff. 64r and 105, 1525); monies owed to Lope Conchillos's widow (e.g., Panama 233, L. 1, f. 368, 1524); justice sought by Pedrarias's right-hand man, the Bachiller Corral, upon his banishment by Oviedo (Panama 233, L. 2, f. 99v, 1526); and cases of other residents of Santa María (such as Maria Mexía, Panama 233, L. 1, f. 370, 1524). Oviedo discusses much of this litigation when he writes about his years in Santa María del Antigua; I discuss these in more depth in chapter 3, a discussion of book 29. For more information about cases dealing with Pedrarias Dávila, consult the Muñoz Collection at the Royal Academy of History ("Extractos de juicios de residencia 1517–1553" and "Pedrarias Dávila y sus tenientes y oficiales"). Also see the study by Pablo Alvarez Rubiano, *Pedrarias Dávila.*

15. AGI, Panama 233, L. 1, ff. 235r.

16. Documents in the AGI list servants, *plata labrada,* and other items from Oviedo's household that he was allowed to transport to the Indies (Indiferente 420, L. 9, f. 62, 1519; Panama 233, L. 1, ff. 244, 261–276, 1519).

17. Yo hice una casa en la cibdad de Sancta María del Antigua del Darién . . . que me costó quince mil pesos de buen oro en la qual se pudiera aposentar un príncipe, con buenos aposentos altos y baxos e con un hermoso huerto de muchos naranjos e otros árboles, sobre la ribera de un gentil río que pasa por aquella cibdad.

18. Some of these are listed in note 14 above.

19. See Turner, *Gonzalo Fernández de Oviedo,* xiii.

20. There is a great deal of documentation about this position and its responsibilities. The first source is from 1523, "Asiento y capitulación tomados con Oviedo para hacer una fortaleza en la isla de Codgo, el puerto de Cartagena" (Indiferente 415, L. 1, f. 51v–52v). The one from 1525 delineates Oviedo's duties as governor, "Capitulaciones tomadas con Gonzalo Fernández de Oviedo para la pacificación y población del puerto de Cartagena," and others spell out the title, privileges, and organization of the post (Panama 233, L. 2, ff. 17r–20r and ff. 31r–34v, 1525).

21. We see, for example, Oviedo asking for the right to not pay duty *(almojarifazgo)* on the mines in Panama (Panama 233, L. 5, f. 104, 1532) and to reduce the royal fifth for the gold extracted in Hispaniola to a tenth (Patronato 275, r. 42, 1541). Oviedo was also given the title of *regidor* of Panama (Panama 233, L. 2, f. 15r).

22. The council's recommendation is telling and may shed light on Oviedo's insistence on the role of his experience in documenting history. "Gonzalo Hernández de Oviedo . . . ha tenido cuidado e inclinación de escribir las cosas de las Indias y hase ofrecido aquí que siendo Vuestra Majestad servido recogera todo lo que en esto tiene escrito y más escrivirá todo lo que queda, poniendo particularmente las propiedades de cada tierra e isla y extrañezas que en ella ha habido y hubiere y las condiciones de los moradores y animales de ella . . . al Consejo muy poderoso señor paresce que será cosa conveniente que hubiese memoria del tiempo en las que las Indias se descubrieron y desde aquel principio acá todo lo que en ellas había y ha pasado, para que se ponga en la crónica de España y no se pierda memoria y tan bien nos paresce que Oviedo tiene más habilidad y experiencia que ninguno otro de los que allí están, para ello siendo Vuestra Majestad servido al Consejo paresce que a éste se le mandase que juntase todo lo que tiene escrito y discurriese por aquellas tierras donde no ha andado para ver lo que no tiene visto, de todo hiciese memoriales y los enviase a este Consejo para que aquí se ordenase y se pusiese en la crónica, y que Vuestra Majestad hiciese merced a Oviedo de alguna ayuda de costa cada año, por el trabajo que en ello ha de poner y para ayuda a un scriviente que consigo ha de traer (*Petición al consejo,* 1532, as quoted in Muñoz's copy, RAH, A/102, f. 78v).

23. Bien es lo que decís que se escriban las cosas de las Indias para que haya memoria della, y pues os parece que Gonzalo Hernández de Oviedo lo hará bien, por haber estado tanto tiempo en aquellas partes, por la experiencia y noticia que tiene de las cosas dellas, dadle cargo dello, con tanto que antes se imprima ni publique lo que escribiere, presente ante Nos una copia dello para que lo mandemos ver . . . proveedlo

así y que pues se le ha de dar este salario [30,000 maravedíes] escriba las cosas de las dichas Indias complidamente e por buen estilo (Archivo General de Simancas, Secretaria de Estado, leg. 636, f. 101).

24. AGI Santo Domingo 868, L. 1, ff. 14v–15r and ff. 25r–26r, 1536.

25. For a more complete list, see Alberto M. Salas, *Tres cronistas,* 74.

26. After seeing the first part of the *History,* the queen granted Oviedo the rights to continue work on it (AGI Indiferente 422, L. 16, ff 206, 1535).

27. See example noted for Hispaniola in note 21; other documents from this period are in the Muñoz Collection at the RAH.

28. See Turner, *Gonzalo Fernández de Oviedo,* xv.

29. There is no extant copy of this text; we only have Oviedo's petition to publish the work, see Turner, *Gonzalez Fernández de Oviedo,* xv.

30. There is an eighteenth-century copy of this in the Muñoz Collection at the Real Academia de la Historia.

31. *Historia general y natural de las Indias* (bk. 20, ca. 1556). A copy of this book is held in the Ayer Collection at the Newberry Library; a contemporary handwritten note in it says the publication was suspended because of the author's death.

32. Gerbi, *Nature,* 143.

33. By 1570 Philip sought a systematic compilation of information about his American possessions and subjects. In addition to appointing a royal chronicler of the Indies, Philip asked his physician, Francisco Hernández, to compile an extensive illustrated herbal of New World flora. He also began the administrative process of collecting *Relaciones geográficas,* based on a fifty-point questionnaire for every province in Spanish America.

34. Evelia Romano de Thuesen, "Transcripción y edición del *Catálogo Real de Castilla.*"

35. See the bibliography and list of Oviedo's work for specific details about these editions.

36. Although there is some evidence he planned and may have even continued to write a fourth part after 1549. See the outline included in the Muñoz Collection at the Real Academia de Historia (A/30, A/81).

37. See Gerbi, *Nature,* 25.

38. See Daymond Turner, "La Biblioteca de Gonzalo Fernández de Oviedo."

39. The autograph manuscript includes many Latin quotes in the text that are crossed out and have the Spanish translation inserted above them.

40. See, for example, Manuel Ballesteros, *Gonzalo Fernández de Oviedo,* 49.

TWO

[Spanish version of chapter epigraph: Esto que he dicho no se puede aprender en Salamanca, ni en Boloña, ni en París, sino en la cátedra de la gísola . . . ni porque uno estudie la Cosmografía e la sepa muy mejor que el Tholomeo, no sabrá, con cuantas palabras están escriptas, navegar hasta que lo use. Ni el que lee medicina curará como debe al enfermo, hasta que experimentado, sea para catar el pulso, e por él entienda los paroxismos e términos que se deben porveer en la dolencia . . . Con esto consuena un proverbio cortesano que suelen decir los curiosos: el que no fue paje, siempre huele a acemilero.]

Note: All citations in this book are taken from Juan Pérez de Tudela Bueso's edition of the *History,* which follows Amador de los Ríos's 1850s edition. I use it because it is the most accessible of the Spanish editions. In quoting passages from the text I refer only to the book and chapter numbers. Chapters tend to be short in most of the *History,* and, having book and chapter information, the reader can easily find the reference in any edition of the text. In addition, readers who are familiar with Oviedo's text will be able to easily place the citation in the overall organization of the *History.* See the chart in appendix D for a list of the content of each of the fifty books.

1. Pues dijo Plinio de la suya [pluma], en el proemio de la *Natural Historia,* que es cosa difícil hacer las cosas viejas nuevas; e a las nuevas dar auctoridad . . . e a las dudosas, fe.

2. Also see Gerbi, *Nature,* 156–166.

3. See *ibid.,* 392.

4. Narraciones de verdades por hombre sabio para enseñar vivir bien.

5. Compañera de la eloquencia, maestra de la ignorancia.

6. I translate Oviedo's *Proemio* as "preface."

7. For a fuller discussion of this debate, see Edmundo O'Gorman, *The Invention of America,* chaps. 1–2.

8. Mercaderías que en muchos reinos del mundo lo desean.

9. Los unos y los otros [están] debajo de vuestra monarquía.

10. Para que en todo él [mundo] se sepa la amplitud e grandeza de estos Estados que guardaba Dios a vuestra real corona de Castilla en ventura y méritos de Vuestra Cesárea Majestad.

11. Ha 22 años . . . veo y experimento . . . sirviendo a Dios e a mi rey.

12. Aplacible lección de oir y entender tantos secretos de Natura.

13. My thanks to Félix Bolaños for this observation.

14. Godos son y españoles los que estas nuestras Indias hallaron.

15. E pues dijo Plinio que de cinco partes del mundo no se habitaban sino las tres, siguese que lo menos de él supieron, e fue mucho más aquello de que no tovieron noticias los pasados . . . E eso de la tórrida zona . . . es error por cierto al presente muy averiguado, pues que cada día nuestros españoles pasan del trópico de Cáncer al de Capricornio e de aquel tornan a estotro. E ved que, tan en contra está la verdad.

THREE

1. The names for this area are confusing because they shifted during the early part of the sixteenth century. Tierra Firme referred to the entire mainland south

and west of Hispaniola. In 1509 it was divided into two parts, Nueva Andalucía and Castilla del Oro, which, as Oviedo explains, was later subdivided by Charles V into three provinces: Santa Marta, Cartagena, and Castilla del Oro. The base of operations for Tierra Firme/Castilla del Oro was a town in Panama called Darién, also known as Santa María del Antigua del Darién, where Oviedo first lived in the early 1520s. The government seat was moved to the town of Panama by Pedrarias Dávila. The three provinces of Castilla del Oro were later divided into Darién (east), Panama (center), and Veragua (West). G. F. Dille's *Writing from the Edge of the World* (published after my book went to press) provides a good introductory study of Oviedo's years in Darién and a translation of book 29, chapters 6–24.

2. This part of the history contains book 25, the role of the Germans in Tierra Firme; book 26, Santa Marta; book 27, Cartagena; book 28, Veragua (just north of Castilla del Oro); book 29, Castilla del Oro; book 30, more on Cartagena; book 31, Honduras; book 32, Yucatán; book 33, Mexico.

3. I focus on the first eighteen chapters of book 26 because subsequent chapters were appended in 1548, when the Nuevo Reino de Granada was added to the province of Santa Marta.

4. El tesorero Alonso de la Puente ordenaba las instruciones e capítulos que llevaba cada capitán, e una de las primeras cláusulas que ponía, era que se le diesen al gobernador dos partes en el oro y en los indios que se tomasen . . . e así se proveían muchos capitanes que después, cuando tornaban, aunque hubiesen fecho mill desatinos e crueldades, eran defendidos con el favor de los mismos oficiales (bk. 29, chap. 10).

5. Oviedo describes how the system began early with Bartolomé Hurtado's conquest: "E éstas fueron las primeras partes [de indios] que el gobernador e obispo e oficiales e alcalde mayor llevaron sin las ganar ni haber causa para que se les diesen. Y en tal hora lo comenzaron, que se quedaron en costumbre de las llevar de allí adelante (a lo menos el gobernador e oficiales). . . . Así como el gobernador e obispo . . . hobieron rescibido aquel presente o parte de los indios, [Bartolomé Hurtado] venido a dar cuenta particular del viaje, e de cómo había fecho las diligencias que y el Requerimiento que el Rey mandaba hacer a los tristes indios, antes que fuesen presos ni se les moviese a guerra, paresció que habían seído salteados, e que primero fueron atados que les dijesen ni supiesen que había Papa, ni Iglesia, ni cosa de cuantas el Requerimiento decía . . . e después de estar metidos en cadena . . . tiraban con ellos aprisionados adelante, e no dejando de dar palos a quien poco andaba, y haciéndoles otros muchos ultrajes, y fuerzas y adulterios con mujeres extrañas y apartadas de la fe. Y tampoco hobo castigo ni reprensión en esto, sino tan larga disimulación, que fué principio para tantos males, que nunca se acabarían de escribir" (bk. 29, chap. 9).

6. "I arrived at one of these places with about fifty men who accompanied me, and found it deserted, the people having fled to the mountains. By chance I entered one of those houses or *buhíos* (it must have been the arsenal of this state or of its chief) in which there were many bows and innumerable handfuls of arrows, as well as balls made of grass the color of waxy pitch. As I was angry at them for having wounded

one of my men, I had one of the musketeers set fire to the house with a match. There was little wind, for which reason in the space of half an hour it and all the other houses in the village, of which there were more than forty, had burned down." [Yo entré en un lugar destos con hasta cincuenta hombres que conmigo iban, y halléle despoblado y la gente ida al monte; y acaso entré en una casa o buhío de aquellos (que debiera ser casa de munición de la república o de su cacique), en que había muchos arcos e innumerables manojos de flechas, y muchas pelotas de hierba de color de cera pez. Y como yo iba enojado del hombre que me habían herido, y hice a un escopetero que con la mecha pusiese fuego a quel buhío; y el aire duro poco, mas fue tan a propósito, que en espacio de media hora estaba quemado aquel y todos los otros buhíos de aquel pueblo, que eran más de cuarenta.]

7. In another passages he boasts again: "I came as his majesty's collector of the assets of the adelantado (Núñez de Balboa). . . . Not only that I held the chief clerkship for Secretary Lope Conchillos, the office of the assayer as well as the inspectorship of mines and as such would have a hand in everything. . . . What made me most dangerous in Pedrarias's opinion were my distrust and the appointments which I had negotiated as perpetual aldermen of the city of Darién for myself. . . . All these appointments I procured as much to honor these people as to serve God and king by stopping Pedrarias" (bk. 29, chap. 14).

8. For example: "This gold brought by the licentiate together with that mined in Panama, Capir, and Juanaga by the settlers . . . amounted to seventy thousand pesos" (bk. 29, chap. 14).

9. "I was not accustomed to the mistresses which my neighbors had (some had more than one). . . . I wanted to live in a state of matrimony." [No era acostumbrado a las mancebas que mis vexcinos tenían (e aun algunos duplicadas) . . . deseaba vivir en el estado matrimonial.]

10. See Pérez de Tudela, "Introducción," *Historia general y natural de las Indias.*

11. For an excellent study of Oviedo's ideas on leadership, see Álvaro Félix Bolaños, "El líder ideal."

12. Tuve tanto intento a desarmar a aquellos indios flecheros como procurar oro.

13. E así hice otras cosas, en que yo pensaba que servía a Dios e al Rey, e que eran en pro e utilidad del común.

14. Mi condición de hombre libre no pudo comportar cosas feas e torpes, pues querer hacer justicia entre gentes acostumbradas a estar sin ella e a mal vivir, no podía ser sin mucho riesgo de mi persona.

15. Acuérdome que, preguntando al que esto pedía la causa por qué demandaba estos hábitos, dijo que porque le parescía único remedio e manera mejor que todas para ser gobernada e poblada la tierra, y en más breve tiempo, y los indios mejor tractados y antes convertidos e bien industriados que por otra vía alguna de cuantas se habían intentado por otros gobernadores.

16. Many of the licenses and terms for these positions are in the AGI (Indiferente 415, L. 1 ff. 51–52, 66–69, "Real Cédula de asiento y capitulación tomados" [1523], "Real Cédula de capitulaciones de Capitán Gonzalo Fernández de Oviedo para la

pacificación y población de Cartagena" [1525]; Panama 233, L. 1., f. 235, "Real Provisión concediendo un regimiento de Santa Marta," [1519]). For more on these positions, see Otte's classic article "Documentos inéditos," 40–46, and Alexandre Coello de la Rosa's more recent analysis, *De la naturaleza,* 158–163.

17. Otte, "Aspiraciones," 43.

18. See Pérez de Tudela's summary of Otte's work on this case, "Vida," cxxxv–cxxxvi.

19. Mi deseo fue siempre servir a Sus Magestades con mi persona e lo demás.

20. A rough outline of the chapters is as follows: 1–6, the history leading up to Pedrarias's taking over Núñez de Balboa's governorship; 7–13, Pedrarias's arrival and dealings with Balboa; 14–25, Oviedo's attempts to curtail Pedrarias's power (trips to Spain, term as *teniente,* and litigation); 26–32, ethnographic information on Native Americans and a brief description of the region's natural world and riches; 33–34, later updates on the fates of captains, governors, and *adelantados.*

21. E dicho aquesto, arrimé la vara en aquel consistorio, e púsela encima de la silla principal, sobre que yo estaba e presidía en su lugar del gobernador, e paséme a otra silla más baja, e dije: "Este es mi lugar, que el César me dio, e desde aqueste serviré yo a Sus Majestades, como su oficial, e no como teniente del señor gobernador; en todo lo que yo le pudiere contentar al señor gobernador con mi persona, e lo que yo alcanzare que sea en servicio de mi Rey y en pro e utilidad desta república, lo haré como lo tengo jurado e soy obligado." E hice juramento de nunca tomar vara de justicia por Pedrarias ni por otro, si no fuese por Sus Majestades, con su expreso mandado o de su Real Consejo; e pedilo por testimonio, e así lo hice asentar por auto.

22. Many of these petitions and lawsuits are housed in the collections at the General Archives of the Indies in Seville; see chapter 1, "A Man Between Two Worlds," for specific references to these documents and those dealing with Pedrarias Dávila.

23. Much of book 42 on Nicaragua concerns Oviedo's firsthand experiences there. Unlike books 26 and 29, however, 42 is characterized by a more scientific reporting style. Oviedo describes the lagoons and volcanoes and illustrates them. Much of book 42 was written in 1548, more than fifteen years after Pedrarias's death, so Oviedo may have had more distance from his situation with Pedrarias.

24. Yo le puse catorce o quince demandas, en que tuve creído que, guardándome justicia, yo le condenara en más de ocho mill pesos de oro.

25. Oviedo details his appointments in book 29. For a brief overview of them, see Turner's introduction, *Oviedo,* xiv.

26. Animosity between Corral and Oviedo surfaces frequently in book 29. Corral was Pedrarias's attorney and coconspirator. Among other things, according to Oviedo, Corral had a hand in legalizing Balboa's execution. When given the chance, Oviedo as *teniente* sent Corral back to Spain in chains. Ultimately, Oviedo paid the price for this punishment. Soon Corral and Oviedo were on the same ship as members of the new governor's staff, and he had to pay a fine for imprisoning Corral. The chronicler claims that Corral was one of the men who orchestrated the attempt on his life. The AGI contains many documents from these lawsuits between Oviedo and

Corral. For example, one document orders Oviedo to pay damages to Corral for his wrongful banishment, and another orders Oviedo's son to return Corral's slaves to his heirs (Panama 233, L. 2, f. 99v, 1526, and ff. 147v–148v, 1534). Perhaps more significant to our study in this chapter, there is a letter in response to Oviedo's request for more safety measures to be taken after the attempt on his life, "A Royal Decree by means of which Gonzalo Fernández de Oviedo, his wife, children, relatives, and property are granted a letter of safe conduct, protection, and royal defense at his request, as he is fearful that because of the hatred of Pedrarias Dávila's wife and son . . . they might kill him or take his person or his property" (Panama 233, L. 2, ff. 22r–23r, 1524). [Real Provisión por la q se da darta de segur, amparo y defensa real a Gonzalo Fernández de Oviedo, su mujer, sus hijos, parientes, y bienes a petición del mismo, temeroso de que por odio de la mujer e hijo de Pedrarias Dávila . . . le maten o le prendan sus persona o bienes.]

27. Anthony Pagden notes in his chapter entitled "The Autopic Imagination" that the concept of the independent, detached spectator did not exist yet, so authors looked to other genres for discursive models, *European Encounters,* 60–62. Both Oviedo and Las Casas, for example, drew upon the language of Christian martyrdom, 67.

28. Me llevó Dios uno de mis hijos, en edad de ocho años; enterré a mi mujer, que había diez días que estaba enferma. E con el dolor de pérdida tan triste para mí, transportado e fuera de sentido, viendo muerta a mi mujer, que yo amaba más que a mí, estuve para perder el seso.

29. See Turner, "Biblioteca."

30. Lo primero, porque por hacer yo lo que debía e hacer justicia . . . lo otro porque San Pablo fué sin comparación mejor que yo, e no negaba sus azotes . . . lo tercero, porque Cristo, Nuestro Redentor en Dios, e no se despreció de su pasión (puesto que estas comparaciones son muy altas e desproporcionadas . . . e yo soy y he sido pecador). Pero no permitió la bondad divina que mis enemigos saliesen con su intención.

31. Mas paresce ser que me tenía Dios guardado para otros trabajos. . . . Yo no me desacordaba que estos trabajos me venían de la mano de Dios por mis méritos, pues que dice Sanct Gregorio: "Cuando en esta vida padescemos lo que no queremos, necesario es que inclinemos los estudios de nuestra voluntad a la de aquel que ninguna cosa injusta puede querer." Grand consolación es en lo que nos desplace pensar que todo se hace por la dispusición de Dios.

32. Non obstante esta auctoridad del glorioso dotor que tengo alegada, sospechaba yo que por industria de Pedrarias se acumulaban mis trabajos.

33. In a similar fashion, Oviedo undoes his portrait as a just man who would have helped the Native Americans. When one cacique rebeled during Oviedo's time as *teniente,* he captured him and burned him alive (bk. 29, chap. 16).

34. [No] se me niegue el loor del trabajo que en tanto tiempo y con tantos peligros yo he padescido, allegando y inquiriendo, por todas las vías que pude saber lo cierto destas materias, después quel año de mill e quinientos y trece de la Natividad del redemptor nuestro, Jesucristo, el católico rey don Fernando, de gloriosa memoria,

abuelo de Vuestra Cesárea Majestad, me envió por su veedor de las fundiciones de oro a la Tierra-Firme, donde así me ocupé cuando convino en aquel oficio, como en la conquista y pacificación de algunas partes de aquella tierra con las armas, sirviendo a Dios y a Vuestras Majestades, como capitán y vasallo en aquellos ásperos principios que se poblaron algunas cibdades e villas que ahora son de cristianos; donde con mucha gloria del real cetro de España, allí se continúa e sirve el culto divino. . . . Y destos dos mil y quinientos hombres que he dicho, no hay al presente en todas las Indias ni fuera dellas cuarenta hombres, a lo que yo creo; porque para servir a Dios y a Vuestras Majestades, y para que viviesen seguros los cristianos que después han ido a aquellas provincias, así convenía, o mejor diciendo era forzado que se hiciese. Porque la salvajez de la tierra y los aires della y la espesura de los herbajes y arboledas de los campos, y el peligro de los ríos e grandes lagartos e tigres, y el experiementar de las aguas e manjares fuese a costa de nuestras vidas. Oviedo continues: "Yo acumulé todo lo que aquí escribo, de dos mill millones de trabajos y nescesidades e peligro en veinte dos años y más que ha que veo y experimento por mi persona estas cosas, sirviendo a Dios e a mi rey en estas Indias" (*Proemio,* part I, 1535).

35. In Oviedo's own manual about Prince Don Juan's household staff, *Libro de la cámara,* he describes the position of chronicler: "It is an Evangelist's occupation, and it is proper that he should be there in person and fear God, for he must write of very important matters." [Oficio es de evangelista y conviene que esté en persona y que tema a Dios porque ha de tractar cosas muy importantes.]

36. Cansado quedará el lector de algunas materias de las que hasta aquí habrá leído . . . pero en éste verá la justicia de Dios, y la cuenta que tuvo para punir en esta vida a todos los que fueron en se la quitar. Muéstranos, Señor, tu rostro, y seremos salvos.

37. See Turner, *Gonzalo Fernández de Oviedo,* xv.

38. Las Casas continued to block the publication of Oviedo's work and Sepúlveda's in 1550.

39. Lewis Hanke describes each man's respective plans, *The Struggle for Justice,* 63.

40. Oviedo petitioned for additional salary and a *repartimiento* of two hundred Indians (AGI, Santo Domingo 868, L. 1, ff. 25r–26r, 1536).

41. Pedrarias died during his term as governor of Nicaragua. Oviedo discusses this in book 42, chap. 14.

42. The Spanish court upheld Pedrarias's decision to execute Balboa and his men on the charge of treason. Moreover, he was not punished for his failure to uphold the king's instruction about the fair treatment of natives.

43. This is evident in the "Relación autógrafa de Fernández de Oviedo, exponiendo el mal estado en q se hallaban las cosas en Tierra Firme, atribuyéndolo a la mucha edad, a la codicia y la constancia del gobernador Pedrarias Dávila" (AGI, Patronato 193, R. 9, ff. 116–125, 1523).

44. Porque él e sus ministros e capitanes asolaron e destruyeron la tierra con robos e crueldades, sin los castigar . . . e lo que él y ellos llaman pacificar, era yermar e asolar, e matar e destruir la tierra de muchas maneras, robando e acabando los naturales della.

45. "[Espinosa] even invented an atrocity unknown in those parts . . . at a distance of ten or twelve paces he ordered set up a small cannon and had [the Indian] shot in the chest. The entry wound was the size of a nut, but the exit wound in his back was the size of a ten-gallon jug" (bk. 29, chap. 13).

46. Comenzarse la destruición de la tierra (a que ellos llamaban pacificación e conquistar); y no bastaría papel ni tiempo a expresar enteramente lo que los capitanes hicieron para asolar los indios e robarlos e destruir la tierra . . . había dos millones de indios . . . se acabó tanta gente. . . . Muchos capitanes . . . aunque hubiesen fecho mill desatinos e crueldades, eran defendidos con el favor de los mismos oficiales. . . . No quedase ninguna provincia ni parte de la tierra sin dolor.

47. Las Casas provided numerous historical details in his *Historia de las Indias,* which was published posthumously.

48. In a similar vein, Patricia Galloway argues that through overt commentary and silent emphasis, Oviedo displaces Las Casas's criticisms of Oviedo onto De Soto, *The Hernando de Soto Expedition.*

49. Oviedo finally sailed for Spain in 1548 and left the manuscript in a monastery in 1549. According to Daymond Turner, after 1547, Oviedo added at least seventy-nine more chapters to the history, "Gonzalo Fernández de Oviedo y Valdés, prosista," 121.

50. The preface and chapters 1 through the first part of chapter 7 are missing, but the rest of the chapters are extant in the Salazar Collection at the Real Academia de Historia (9/553).

51. Esta ciudad de Santo Domingo donde estoy.

52. Indeed in the autograph manuscript a folio was ripped out of chapter 17, the account of the attempt on Oviedo's life, and there are more changes in this passage than in any other in the extant manuscript (RAH 9/553 ff. 51r, 51v).

53. "The first appeal which I refused to grant the Bachelor, when I arrested him, requested that it be sent to Pedrarias (I sent it to Spain to the Royal Council of the Indies), and the other one [was] that when I ordered chief Corobarí to be burned, I decreed that the Indians who were taken prisoner with him were to be slaves, and parceled them out among the company who had captured them. It was on behalf of the Bachelor that this was appealed before the Governor." [La una [apelación] que no quise otorgarle al bachiller, cuando le prendí, que pedía ser remitido a Pedrarias (e lo envié a España al Consejo Real de Indias); e la otra que, cuando mandé quemar al cacique Corobarí, adjudiqué por esclavos sus indios que con el se tomaron e los repartí por la compañía, que los habían tomado, e fue por parte del bachiller apellado para ante el Gobernador.]

54. Todo lo que a mi me toca y he dicho de mis trabajos e diferencias con Pedrarias, e con aquel licenciado Diego de Corral, fue la causa principal por do se despobló el Darién; porque, en la verdad, aquella cibdad se sostuviera si yo no fuera primero destruído e perseguido por la forma que está dicho. De manera que aquella población duró desde el año de mill e quinientos y nueve hasta el de mill e quinientos e veinte y cuatro. E no fue menos deservido a Dios e al Rey dejarla perder Pedrarias, de cuanto

fue muy señalado e grande haberla ganado Enciso e los que con él se hallaron; ni sería menor bien restaurarla e reedificarla, por la fertilidad e riqueza de su asiento e comarcas.

55. Other changes dealing with the governor or his administrators are apparent in RA 9/553. ff. 51r, 51v, 53r, 53v, 54v, 56r, 57v, 82r, 83v, 86v, 88r, and 88v.

56. In the autograph manuscript one clearly sees "libro XXVI" crossed out and replaced with "libro XXIX" (RAH 9/533).

57. Sentid e mirad entre estas generasciones e diferentes calidades de hombres si habrá pecadores, e no de los comunes asaz, sino de los más perversos e desechados de sus proprias patrias, e de otras desterrados por su méritos.

58. Chapters 1–12 (1539–1540); chapters 13–15 (1541–1542); chapters 16–17 (after 1542); and the final twelve chapters on El Nuevo Reino de Granada (1548).

59. No me detengo en decir puntualmente los trabajos que este teniente y los españoles padescieron siguiéndole: basta que, como hombre que ha treinta y cuatro años que ando por Indias, merezco crédito, e oso decir que son tan excesivos los que en Indias padescen los cristianos, que ninguno los puede pasar tan grandes nin tan intolerables en todas las otras partes que hay cristianos por el mundo.

60. See chapter 5 below for more detail on the stages of composition of the *History*.

61. As mentioned above, it may also reflect his own deepening disillusionment after a fourth unsuccessful bid for a governorship in 1546.

62. For an excellent analysis of the political context of Bernal Díaz's work, see Rolena Adorno's "Discourses on Colonialism."

63. No quiso [Dios] que en España quedase, aunque me crié en la casa real de Castilla, sino que llevándose Dios al serenísimo príncipe don Joan, mi señor, e faltándome su real presencia, de quien esperaba ser remunerado y heredado en mi propria patria, por mis servicios fuese peregrinando por el mundo e viniese a parar en estas tierras tan extrañas e desviadas de donde nascí e soy natural.

FOUR

1. The impulse to record physical reality in the form of drawings is already apparent in Oviedo's first work about the New World, the *Sumario* (1526), which includes four woodcuts based on sketches he made. The first edition of the *History* (1535) includes three of these woodcuts and adds twenty-nine more, which were modified and republished in the 1547 edition. The 1557 publication of book 20 of the *History* includes a new woodcut of a Patagonian camp. See Turner, "Forgotten Treasures," for valuable information on manuscript drawings.

2. Parts II and III (the final thirty-one books of the *Historia*) have less than one-third of the illustrations found in part I (the first nineteen books).

3. A study of Amador de los Rios's manuscript, held at the Hispanic Society of America (HC: NS5/604/1), reveals that his intention was to include the illustrations

within the narrative. He either copied Oviedo's illustrations or left a blank space about the size of the original drawing, indicating that the illustrations would be included in their original places. Perhaps cost-conscious editors decided to place all the illustrations in the appendix.

4. By far the majority of the surviving illustrations are at the Huntington Library (HEH-HM 177). There are twenty-four pen-and-ink drawings. The Royal Academy of History in Madrid owns the only other known section of the autograph manuscript that contains original drawings (RAH 9/553–9/557). Other manuscript copies from the seventeenth and eighteenth centuries apparently faithfully transcribe Oviedo's illustrations, sometimes coloring them in. These partial copies, at the library of the Royal Palace in Madrid and the Biblioteca Colombina in Seville, provide us with an idea of the extent of Oviedo's drawings. There is no autograph manuscript or sixteenth-century copy of the drawings in book 12 of part I, which contains illustrations of New World fauna. My discussion of these drawings is based on the eighteenth-century copy made by Juan Bautista Muñoz, currently held at the Royal Academy of History. The first scholars to discuss the manuscript drawings were William C. Sturtevant, "First Visual Images of Native America" (1976), which mentions the whereabouts of Oviedo's drawings (447n23), and Daymond Turner's *Forgotten Treasures from the Indies* (1985), which provides an initial study of all extant sixteenth-century autographs and copies, except the section at the Royal Palace. For more information on the manuscript history and its copies, see the introduction to this book, note 7. For a complete list of the illustrations, see the table in appendix D. Notably, one image is far more elaborate than the others: it illustrates the method for ferrying horses across water. The illustration, however, reflects the style used in Oviedo's *Batallas*. Nonetheless, it is possible Oviedo had assistance in drawing this illustration. One document in the archive even reflects Oviedo's request for help: "Y que Vuestra Majestad hiciese merced a Oviedo de alguna ayuda de costa cada año, por el trabajo que en ello ha de poner y para ayuda a un scriviente que consigo ha de traer (*Petición al consejo,* 1532, as quoted in Muñoz's copy, RAH, A/102, f. 78v).

5. Turner's "Forgotten Treasures" (1985) is an exception to the generally brief comments on Oviedo's drawings. My article "The Representation of New World Phenomena" (1993) expanded on Turner's conclusions. Antonello Gerbi's extensive section on Oviedo in *Nature* (1978), for example, mentions only in passing the importance of the sense of sight and the role of art and illustrations in Oviedo's text, 181–85, 226–231, 390. Jesús Carrillo's doctoral dissertation, "The Representation of the Indies" (1997), contextualizes Oviedo's illustrations within early modern figurative culture. Carrillo published a revised version of his thesis, *Naturaleza e Imperio* (2005).

6. Paul Hulton and David Quinn are among the few researchers who have noted the novelty of Oviedo's approach. In *The Drawings of John White,* they mention the liveliness of Oviedo's drawings and say they are a "revolutionary achievement" not soon to be paralleled (I: 32).

7. Ni el ciego sabe determinar colores, ni el ausente así testificar estas materias, como quien las mira.

8. Sin dubda los ojos son mucha parte de la información destas cosas.

9. Although sight and experience are not quite of the same order, sight being a part of experience, Oviedo equates the two in his preface.

10. Many Italian Renaissance painters wrote treatises that discuss this relationship; see, for example, Leon Battista Alberti's *Della Pintura* and Leonardo da Vinci's *Treatise on Painting.* Moreover, as treatises by Juan Luis Vives and Cabrera de Córdoba demonstrate, the historian was encouraged to help the reader understand the subject depicted by evoking mirrorlike scenes and the use of the sight of the mind's eye.

11. Diré lo que de él he comprendido, remitiéndome a quien mejor lo sepa pintar o dar a entender, porque es más para verle pintado de mano de Berruguete u otro excelente pintor como él, o aquel Leonardo de Vinci, o Andrea Manteña, famosos pintores que yo conocí en Italia, que no para darle a entender con palabras. Es muy mejor que todo esto es para visto que escripto ni pintado.

12. On Oviedo's knowledge of Italian Renaissance art, see García Sáiz, "Acerca de los conocimientos pictóricos."

13. Robinson explains this phenomenon: "In a sense the Renaissance artist and scientist gave a local habitation to the airy nothingness of a predominately verbal philosophical tradition. They incorporated forms into their pictures, made concepts into visible objects, and thought of Ideas as things easily converted to images and emblems. The characteristic dissatisfaction with things unseen resulted in the belief that everything, including the activity of the mind, could be represented to the sense of vision" (94).

14. Quiero decir otra cosa muy notable, que los que no han navegado por estas Indias no la pueden haber visto . . . [hay] cuatro estrellas en cruz, que andan al derredor del círculo de las Guardas del polo antártico, de la forma que están en esta figura puestas; las cuales la Cesárea Majestad me dio por mejoramiento de mis armas, para que yo e mis subcesores, las pusiésemos juntamente con las nuestras antiguas de Valdés, habiendo respecto a lo que yo he servido en estas partes e Indias e primero en la casa real de Castilla, desde que hobe trece años.

15. Si la he sabido dar a entender, esta cama es desta manera que aquí está pintada.

16. Y porque mejor se entienda esto, pongo aquí la manera o figura del caney, como baste a ser entendido.

17. Porque allá en algunas provincias son de otra forma, y aun algunas dellas nunca oídas ni vistas, sino en aquella tierra. Pero pues se debuxó la forma del caney o casa redonda, quiero así mismo poner aquí la segunda manera de casas que he dicho, la qual es, como aquesta que está aquí patente, para que mejor se entienda lo que en la una y en la otra tengo dicho.

18. Baste a ser entendido.

19. Como aquí se ve la figura della; segund aquí está pintado el nahe o remo y canoa.

20. Esto a lo menos del sacar fuego de los palos pónelo Plinio en su *Natural Historia* . . . de manera que lo que Plinio dice y aquestos indios hacen (en este caso), todo es una mesma cosa. . . . Mas para qué quiero yo traer auctoridades de los antiguos en las cosas que yo he visto, ni en las que natura enseña a todos y se ven cada día?

21. Así que, esto es cosa que se ve e es natural.

22. La figura de lo qual es de la manera que lo enseño debuxado, puesto que sin tal pintura basta lo que está dicho, para lo entender. Pero todavía es bien en lo que fuere possible usar de la pintura, para que se informen della los ojos e mejor se comprendan estas cosas.

23. Como aquí está pintado.

24. Porque la figura que llevaron pintada para que la Cesárea Majestad la viese, es muy diferente de la carta, la cual pongo aquí.

25. Porque mejor se entienda este golfo, pongo aquí la figura dél, si lo supe entender todavía, so enmienda de quien más particularmente lo hubiere comprendido.

26. Cuando yo le vi; es cosa muy notable de ver.

27. Ojo de este ave se pintará la talla.

28. Puse la forma de la una e de la otra aquí debuxadas, non obstante que en las mismas maneras de hojas hay particularidades y diferenciadas suertes o generaciones de yuca.

29. The actual drawing of the pineapple reveals, to a degree, Oviedo's confusion about how to represent it. He renders an image that is partially inspired by the pinecone.

30. A unas llaman yayama; a otras dicen boniama; e a otras yayagua.

31. Ninguna otra da tal contentamiento; no tiene comparación con ella otra fructa en las que yo he visto.

32. The naming of American flora coincided with new efforts to delineate natural classifications. By the mid–eighteenth century this activity had its effect in the abundant production of herbals. See Joseph Ewan, "The Columbian Discoveries," and Jonathan Sauer, "Changing Perception."

33. No pueden la pintura de mi pluma y palabras dar tan particular razón ni tan al propio el blasón desta fructa, que satisfagan tan total y bastantemente que se pueda particularizar el caso, sin el pincel, o debuxo, y aun con esto serían menester las colores para que más conforme (sino todo en parte) se diese mejor a entender que yo lo hago y digo, porque en alguna manera la vista del lector pudiese más participar desta verdad: non obstante lo qual, pornéla, como supiere hacerlo, tan mal debuxada como platicada; pero para los que esta fructa ovieren visto bastará aquesto, y ellos dirán lo demás. Y para los que nunca la vieron sino aquí . . . les certifico que si en algún tiempo la vieren, me avrán por desculpado, si no supe, ni pude justamente loar esta fructa.

34. Y si, por falta de colores y del debuxo, yo no bastare a dar a entender lo que querría saber decir, dese la culpa a mi juicio, en el qual a mis ojos es la más hermosa fructa de todas que he visto y la que mejor huele y mejor sabor tiene.

35. La que llaman yayama es algo en su proporción prolongada e del talle de la

que aquí he pintado, e las otras dos maneras o géneros, de quien he hablado, son más redondas.

36. La hoja vera desta planta, al natural, es como aquesta que aquí esta debuxada.

37. Y por ser nueva forma de edificios pinté aquí una de la misma forma queste capitán me la dio a entender.

38. Indeed, in the chapters he revised or added to the history after its first printing, Oviedo took ever greater care to render the text and image as one. Sections of the manuscript copy at the Huntington Library show that the later illustrations were more often drawn first and the text fitted in around the image (see fig. 20, for example). Earlier illustrations are usually embedded in the narrative, but the words of the text are not as carefully interlocked with the image.

39. Arguing in a similar but different vein, Stephanie Merrim asserts in "Un mare magno" that Oviedo's empirical *yo* is a subtext of the history, serving to assert his authority, which is achieved by establishing two "rhythms": the chronological passing of time and the revelation of life's mysteries (111–112). Furthermore, she suggests that Oviedo's natural history can be viewed as a teratology: "A teratology, or study in marvels (and monstrosities), the natural history submits the mysteries of its subjects to the reader's eyes as *herygma,* an ongoing parade of revelations, with the intent that reading about these mysteries should produce the same awe and reverence as the original reading of these miracles" (106).

40. Porque es más para verle pintado . . . que no para entender con palabras. The seventeenth-century Andean chronicler Guaman Poma de Ayala arrived at a similar, albeit more covert, theory of the relationship between words and images. In *Guaman Poma,* Rolena Adorno argues that the chronicler uses visual images to mediate between (Andean) oral and (European) written tradition and in doing so asserts that the message in his drawings is more powerful than that in the written chronicle.

FIVE

1. One of Oviedo's sources, Erasmus of Rotterdam, wrote a famous text discussing *imitatio, Ciceronianus* (1528).

2. The 1535 edition contained only part I (bks. 1–19) and what later became book 50 of part III, published originally as book 20 of part I, the "Naufragios." Unlike part I, judging the extent to which parts II and III have been layered by successive revisions often depends on an even closer reading of the text, since there is no revised edition with which to compare it. Salas notes how the changes in verb tenses often signal to the reader when a passage has been added later by Oviedo (*Tres cronistas*). In addition, narrative sequences often make clear Oviedo's accumulation of accounts over the period 1542 to 1548. The final chapters in book 33, on New Spain, serve as a good example. Chapter 53, a 1542 letter to Viceroy Mendoza discussing Oviedo's departure for Spain to publish the revised history, was clearly intended to be the concluding chapter of the book. Two years later, however, Oviedo appends another

chapter, explaining why he has not yet sailed for Spain, and he includes more information about Mexico in an interview with Juan Cano. Three years later, in 1547, Oviedo adds two more chapters that mark significant events: the end of Mendoza's tenure as viceroy and the death of Cortés. The final chapter of book 33 comes only with Oviedo's arrival in Spain in 1548 and the deposit of the manuscript in a monastery.

3. The new chapters generally augment the representation of the natural world, although book 17 (Cuba) adds eight chapters on the Hernando de Soto expedition. Book 14 (Birds) adds two new chapters, book 12 (Animals) includes thirty-two new chapters, book 11 (Herbs) adds 7, books 8 and 9 (Trees) grow by eighteen chapters each, book 7 (Agriculture) adds 6, and, finally, book 6 ("Depósitos") expands by forty chapters.

4. Oviedo's official charge was to write "complidamente e por buen estilo" about the Indies. See Juan Pérez de Tudela's introduction to the history (cxxn381). Although Oviedo inserts new information, he rarely removes overlapping material, which often accounts for the unevenness of his style. When Oviedo refers to events, the inclusion of the year often clues the reader that the account is revised, but the elaboration of descriptions of the natural world often is not apparent to the reader of only the final edition of the *History.* The chapter on the pineapple, for example, provides only one clue about the addition of new material; there are two sections that deal with the role of the senses—the first is added, the second is original.

5. Porque para la segunda impresión desta primera parte o historia, vamos añadiendo y enmendando lo que le compete y el tiempo va obrando.

6. Aquí llegué con esta materia, quando esto se escribía en limpio, en fin de marzo del año de mill e quienientos e treinta e nueve.

7. Quiero decir que estos indios, aunque ignoren tales preceptos, la Natura les enseña lo que conviene en este caso.

8. Podría ser que Plinio no lo vido de todas estas colores.

9. Oviedo even adds his own experience to the account: he has cultivated maize and has seen it grown in the coldest city of Spain (Ávila). Moreover he comments on its use as a nutritional source (bk. 7, chap. 2).

10. See Daymond Turner, "The Aborted First Printing," 113. In the mid–eighteenth century Juan Bautista de Muñoz made a list of Oviedo's additions to part I (RAH Muñoz A/34).

11. This aspect of the history is also seen in the manuscript's blank spots; Oviedo often left a place in the manuscript for outstanding information on the exact names of people and towns as well as dates. As Oviedo gathered more information he returned to these blanks and filled them in with the correct information.

12. See Stephanie Merrim's "The Apprehension of the New."

13. As an Erasmian convert, Oviedo may well have been acquainted with philological studies and treatises, such as Erasmus's *Ciceronianus,* which discussed the concept of historical anachronism, suggesting that the language of the ancients was no

longer historically decorous. Erasmus argues that if Cicero were writing in 1500, he would use words more in keeping with the new historical age. Erasmus raises the question of the appropriateness or role of imitating the ancients. See G. W. Pigman's "Imitation and the Renaissance."

14. ¿Para qué quiero yo traer auctoridades de los antiguos en las cosas que yo he visto, ni en las que Natura enseña a todos cada día?

15. See Merrim's discussion of Oviedo's use of Pliny, "The Apprehension," 174–175.

16. No he sacado de dos mil millares de volúmines que haya leído, como en el lugar suso alegado Plinio escribe, en lo qual paresce que él dijo lo que leyó . . . pero yo acumulé todo lo que aquí escribo de dos mill millones de trabajos y nescecidades e peligros en veinte e dos años más que ha que veo y experimento por mi persona estas cosas . . . ; una cosa terná mi obra apartada del estilo de Plinio, y será relatar alguna parte de la conquista destas Indias, e dar razón de descubrimiento.

17. Also see Michel Foucault, *The Order of Things,* 17–25. He argues that *aemulatio* was one of the types of repetition used in the sixteenth century in order to seek the underlying resemblance of all the things in the world.

18. Another strategy, dialectical imitation, at once criticizes the model and opens itself up to criticism; the model is used to examine cultural meaning in both eras. "Just as heuristic imitation involves a passage from one semiotic universe to another, so dialectic imitation, when it truly engages two eras or two civilizations at a profound level, involves a conflict between two *mundi significantes,*" Greene, *The Light in Troy,* 46.

19. Cuanto más que son en sí estas cosas tan apartadas e nuevas, que no hay nescesidad de ficciones para dar admiración a las gentes ni para dejar de dar infinitas gracias al Maestro de la Natura.

20. Deletions are rare in the manuscript, except in book 29 (see chapter 3 above), so when the reader is able to decipher the text beneath lines that have been stricken, curiosity is piqued. Amador de los Ríos notes many of these changes made in chapter titles and some of those that deal with Oviedo's role in various circumstances. The majority of deletions, however, go unnoted, as in this case in the chapter on Amazon women.

21. Ellas mismas enbiaron mensajeros a los españoles amonestándoles que no fuesen osados de entrar en su tierra porque aunque eran mujeres . . . les paresiesen sus obras de varones de grande valor e esfuerzo.

22. E otro día llegó a vista de la población e hallo cerca de aquella cibdad un grande exército de mujeres en el campo al punto de guerra, esperando a los cristianos e todas ellas con sus arcos e flechas e carcajes. Vestidas de camisas blancas . . . las más dellas no tienen más de una teta siniestra.

23. E quando son pequeñas quítanles o quémanles la teta derecha para el exercicio de armas que son los arcos e flechas en que son muy diestras.

24. Yo me quise después, en España, informar del mismo Nuño de Guzmán . . .

e me dijo que es burla, e que no son amazonas. . . . Digo yo que ya podría ser que, pues las halló casadas, fuese en el tiempo desos sus allegamientos; pero dejemos eso e pasemos adelante.

25. Oviedo returns to this same report in bk. 34, chap. 8. The narrative maintains this same representation of Amazon-like women and Oviedo's rather ambivalent stance.

26. En griego *a* quiere decir "sin" e *zona* quiere decir "teta", y por esto, amazona quiere decir "sin teta." . . . Así los cristianos las comenzaron a llamar amazonas sin serlo.

27. Mujeres que viven a imitación de las amazonas.

28. Algunos cronistas dicen que [Matinio] era poblada de amazonas, e otras fábulas muy desviadas de la verdad . . . por los que habemos visto . . . es todo falso lo que desta se ha dicho cuanto a ser poblada de mujeres solamente, porque no lo es ni se sabe que jamás lo fuese.

29. Las amazonas (si amazonas deben decir).

30. Pero porque la claridad e particular intelegencia no se sabe más puntual al presente, quise poner aquí esto . . . para acuerdo de lo que adelante subcediere e conviniere escribirse, cuando estas regiones e provincias mejor estén sabidas e vistas. . . . E así, para lo mejor entender, consejaría yo al lector que, llegando con su lección hasta aquí, sin proceder adelante, vea el capítulo XXIV del último libro de esta *General Historia de Indias,* para que quede más satisfecho del descubrimiento.

31. No discrepaba de lo que . . . decían otros indios . . . traemos esta noticia por muy cierta.

32. Paresce que imitan a aquellas que los antiguos llaman amazonas.

33. It is also possible Oviedo was influenced by his contemporaries' curiosity and by accounts of New World Amazons. A Spanish account from 1534 reported that ten thousand Amazon women met seventy Spanish ships and offered fifty ducats for each pregnancy contracted (Otis Green, *Spain and the Western Tradition* 3:40). Rodríguez de Montalvo's sequel to the *Amadís* locates Amazon women on an island to the right of the Indies. In the New World, Juan Díaz de Grijalva (in the Yucatán) and Cristóbal de Olid (in New Spain) report seeing Amazon women (Leonard, *Books of the Brave,* chaps. 4–5, Johnson, *Women in Colonial Spanish-American Literature,* 10–13). Or perhaps Oviedo was actually inspired by parallel native American legends of republics of women. These stories may have intermingled with Old World legends, producing an interpenetration of medieval/Renaissance myths with what the chronicler saw and heard in the New World.

34. Salas observes that with Oviedo's history myths acquired verisimilitude in the New World, *Tres Cronistas,* 115.

35. Of course Oviedo's theory on the link between the Indies and the Hesperides is yet another example of this. See Álvaro Félix Bolaños, "The Historian and the Hesperides."

36. Enrique Pupo-Walker suggests that "poblar a América con leyenda y mitos era una manera de europeizarla y de conocerla," *La Vocación literaria,* 52.

SIX

1. Robert Alter explains in *The Art of Biblical Narration* that in biblical narrative "meaning, perhaps for the first time in narrative literature, was conceived as a process, requiring continual revision—both in the ordinary sense and in the etymological sense of seeing-again—continual suspension of judgement, weighing of multiple possibilities, brooding over gaps in information provided" (12).

2. Oviedo held a Ciceronian idea of history as the mother of human nature and, therefore, a subject full of moral and ethical lessons. For a well-developed analysis of this theme, see Álvaro Félix Bolaños, "Ambigüedad narrativa."

3. Among the other sources included in the chapters preceding the dialogue in book 33 are accounts by soldiers that support Cortés's account of the conquest (chaps. 45–47) and a passage about indigenous lawsuits and customs based on Fray Diego de Loaysa's writings (chap. 49).

4. For example, Thucydides employs dramatic monologue in his *History of the Peloponnesian War.*

5. Pero irá arrimada a la simplicidad e forma de hablar que deben concurrir en la verdadera historia. E llamo simplicidad a lo que el gramático atribuye tal verbo, que es decir sencillamente, sin lagotería ni lisonjas, lo que hace el caso.

6. In her article "The Castle of Discourse," Stephanie Merrim argues convincingly that even in the *Claribalte* Oviedo is working through the problems of multiple accounts and the representation of events.

7. Furthermore, the book that contained the history was perceived as a receptacle of information through which one would be able to determine truth from falsehood. As Foucault observes in *The Order of Things,* beginning in the sixteenth century there was a tendency to believe that order could be found if only the right order of words could be constructed to represent man in his world (11).

8. Donald R. Kelly also discusses this tendency in particular and its emergence in the work of Lorenzo Valla, one of the Quattrocento dialogists. See *Foundations of Modern Historical Scholarship,* 40–46.

9. Also see Cristina Barbolani's article "Los diálogos de Juan de Valdés: ¿Reflexión o Improvisación?" She maintains that the nature of dialogue is not systematic and that it consists of "observaciones siempre opinables" (147). For an overview of dialogue in Spain during this period, see Luis Andrés Murillo, "Diálogo y dialéctica en el siglo XVI español." Of course, Oviedo no doubt would have also been familiar with the moralistic forms of Spanish medieval dialogue.

10. M. Bataillon notes the particularly strong influence of Erasmus's *Colloquies* on Oviedo. They provided an ideal model of "verosimilitud, verdad psicológica, ingeniosidad de la composición, sustancia filosófica, respeto de la moral" (224).

11. For information on this topic consult Antonello Gerbi, *Nature,* 157–76, and Turner's "La Biblioteca de Gonzalo Fernández de Oviedo."

12. En el cual el auctor da razón por qué cesó su camino e ida a España; e hace relación de otras cosas e subcesos de la Nueva España; e dice algunas particularidades

que a su noticia han venido, las cuales son del jaez de las que la historia ha contado e para más verificación e verdad de algunos pasos que quedan escriptos de otra forma, no le aviendo tan puntualmente informado, como agora se dirá. E cuéntanse otras cosas del jaez destas materias, así enmendando algunas cosas hasta aquí apuntadas, como declarando e perficionando otras de que hay nescesidad que los lectores sean advertidos.

13. La Noche Triste was the routing of the Spaniards from Tenochtitlan on June 30, 1520. While Cortés was away dealing with Pánfilo de Narváez's rebellion, the Spaniards who had stayed in the city under the supervision of Alvarado massacred the young nobles at a ceremony, angering the population. The Spaniards managed to survive, according to Cortés's account, only thanks to his timely arrival. Montezuma was unable to control the situation and was murdered. (There are different versions of how this happened: he was stabbed by Spaniards or stoned by his own people.) The Spaniards were forced to flee the rioting city. The night of the escape Cortés sat under a tree in Tacuba and wept, hence the name La Noche Triste.

14. Obidiente e fiel alcaide e criado.

15. Joanis Carionis, i.e., Johannes Carion, 1499(?)–1537, was a historian and court astrologer for Elector Joachin I. He wrote, with the support of Philipp Melanchthon, a well-respected world chronicle, *Chronica* [Wittenberg, 1532].

16. Relátenlas los que allá se hallan.

17. Los puse en este volúmen con buena fe, creyendo que decían lo cierto, e aun así lo afirmaban aquéllos; pero como el entendimiento de los hombres sea mucho mejor en unos que en otros, no es de maravillar que discrepen en sus dichos e aun en sus hechos, en especial en cosas semejantes, en quel intento e afición e interese particular causa esas diversidades en la información.

18. En verdad paresce que Nuestro Señor permite que mis ojos no se cierren e que alcancen más claridad en la historia que entre manos tengo.

19. E así yo preguntando e Joan Cano respondiendo, diré aquellas cosas en que platicamos, porque no hobo tiempo para más.

20. Examples of words found on the boundaries of dialogue that are considered semantic reversals are "good," "bad," "ugly," "important," etc. See Mukařovský, *The Word,* 89.

21. Señor Joan Cano, suplícoos que me digáis ¿porqué mató Hernando Cortés a Guatimucín? ¿Rebelóse después, o qué hizo para que muriese?

22. Pues escriba Vuestra Merced lo que mandare, y el marqués Hernando Cortés lo que quisiere: que yo digo en Dios y en mi consciencia la verdad, y esto es muy notorio.

23. Porque he oído sobre esto muchas cosas, e muy diferentes las unas de las otras, e yo querría escribir verdad, así Dios salve a mi ánima.

24. Señor alcaide, eso que preguntáis es un paso en que pocos de los que hay en la tierra, sabrán dar razón, aunque ello fué muy notorio, e muy manifiesta la sinrazón que a los indios se les hizo.

25. Y con mucha razón que tenían para ello.

26. Montezuma, ¿cómo murió? Porque diversamente lo he entendido, e así lo he yo escripto diferenciadamente.

27. Grand lástima fué perderse tanto tesoro e ciento e cincuenta e cuatro españoles, e cuarenta e cinco yeguas, e más de dos mill indios. . . . Yo así lo tengo escripto en el capítulo XIV de esta historia.

28. Señor alcaide, en verdad quien tal os dijo, o no lo vido ni supo, o quiso callar la verdad. Yo os certifico que fueron los españoles muertos en eso . . . más de mill e ciento e septenta, e así paresció por alarde; e de los indios nuestros amigos de Tascaltecle que decís dos mill, sin dubda fueron más de ocho mill.

29. Para mucho ha seído el marqués, e digno es de cuanto tiene e de mucho más; e tengo lástima de ver lisiado un caballero tan valeroso, e manco de dos dedos de la mano izquierda, como lo escribí e saqué de su relación, e puse en el capítulo XV; pero las cosas de la guerra así son, e los honores e la palma de la victoria no se adquieren durmiendo.

30. Tuvo Dios poco que hacer en sanarle; e salid, señor, dese cuidado: que así como los sacó de Castilla, cuando pasó la primera vez a estas partes, así se los tiene agora en España, porque nunca fué manco dellos ni le faltan; e así nunca hobo menester cirujano ni miraglo para guarescer de ese trabajo.

31. Señor Joan Cano, ¿es verdad aquella crueldad que dicen que el marqués usó con Chulula?

32. Cortés's descent from popularity began in 1524 when he engaged in the disastrous expedition to Honduras (Las Hibueras). Soon the Crown began to limit his influence, and Cortés was forced to return to Spain to defend his rights in 1528. At this time he was given the title of Marqués del Valle and granted a generous encomienda. Upon his return to Mexico in 1530, however, the territory was in chaos and the *Audiencia* did not support his claims, so he retired to his estate in Cuernavaca and continued his exploration of the Pacific. By 1541 he returned to live in Spain, where he surrounded himself with humanists, such as López de Gómara. Cortés died in 1547.

33. Demás desto, digo que yo tengo cédulas reales para que los gobernadores me envíen "relación de lo que tocare a la historia en sus gobernaciones, para estas historias. Y escribí e avisé al marqués del Valle, don Hernando Cortés, para que me enviase la suya . . . e remitióme a unas cartas misivas, que le escribió a Su Majestad . . . e no curó de más.

34. For more on this incident between Las Casas, the bishop of San Juan, and Oviedo, see Gerbi, *Nature,* 357, and Amador de los Ríos, "Vida," lxxix.

35. El señor obispo de Sanct Joan . . . holgaba . . . que todo lo que dije e lo que dejé de decir se probaría fácilmente. . . . Y como el señor obispo de Sanct Joan es tan noble, e le consta la verdad e cuán sin pasión yo escribo, el obispo de Chiapas quedó satisfecho: aunque yo no ando por satisfacer a su paladar ni otro, sino por cumplir con lo que debo, hablando con vos, señor, lo cierto.

36. Y por tanto, cuanto a la carga de los muchos frailes me paresce en verdad que estas tierras manan o que llueven frailes . . . parescía una devota farsa, e agora la co-

mienzan; no sabemos en qué parará. The only full translation of the *History* during Oviedo's lifetime was the Italian edition. Selections of the history were translated into French and Latin. Oviedo, however, claims "aquel libro [the first part of the *Historia general*] estaba ya en lengua toscana e francesa e alemana e latina e griega e turca e arábiga, aunque yo la escribí en castellana" (bk. 33, chap. 42).

37. Pero pues van [Las Casas and his friars] hacia aquellos nuevos vulcanes, decidme, señor, qué cosa son, si los habéis visto, e qué cosa es otro que tenéis allá en la Nueva España, que se dice Guajocingo.

38. Like Lorenzo Valla, Oviedo believed that historical truth could be extracted from conflicting testimony. See Eric Cochrane's *Historians and Historiography in the Italian Renaissance,* 485. Among other works, one could also include Juan Luis Vives's "Veritas fucata, sive de licentia poetica, quantum Poetis liceat a Veritate abscedere."

SEVEN

1. See Hanke, *All Mankind,* 34.

2. For portraits that Oviedo and Las Casas paint of each other, see Oviedo's *History* (bk. 7, chap. 1, and bk. 19, chap. 5) and Las Casas's *History of the Indies* (chap. 42).

3. See Hanke, *The Struggle for Justice,* 54–60.

4. For more, see ibid., 58–66.

5. Hanke, *All Mankind,* 47.

6. See Turner, *Fernández de Oviedo,* xv, and Hanke, *The Struggle for Justice,* 41–43.

7. See Hanke, *The Struggle for Justice,* 19–20.

8. Oviedo paints this bishop as being greedy and untrustworthy in book 29; see, for example, chapter 10.

9. For an excellent brief study of Sepúlveda's and Las Casas's positions, see Rolena Adorno, "Los debates sobre la naturaleza de los indios."

10. For an excellent article about the encomienda, see Patricia Seed, "Taking Possession and Reading Texts."

11. For a similar argument about how knowledge of another culture is bound up with the imperial project, see José Rabasa, "Writing and Evangelization."

12. Tornando al propósito del tequina que los indios tienen, y está para hablar con el diablo, y por cuya mano y consejo se hacen aquellos diabólicos sacrificios y ritos y ceremonias de los indios, digo que los antiguos romanos, ni los griegos, ni los troyanos, ni Alejandro, ni Darío ni otros príncipes antiguos, por no católicos estuvieron fuera de estos errores y supersticiones.

13. Han pasado a aquellas partes personas que, pospuestas sus conciencias y el temor de la justicia divina y humana, han hecho cosas, no de hombres, sino de dragones y de infieles, pues sin advertir ni tener respeto alguno humano, han sido causa que muchos indios que se pudieran convertir y salvarse, muriesen por diversas formas y maneras; y en caso que no se convirtieran los tales que así murieron, pudieran ser útiles, viviendo, para el servicio de vuestra majestad, y provecho y utilidad de los

cristianos . . . [y] han sido causa de aqueste daño llaman pacificado a lo despoblado; y yo más que pacífico, lo llamo destruído; pero en esta parte satisfecho está Dios y el mundo de la santa intención y obra de vuestra majestad en lo de hasta aquí, pues con acuerdo de muchos teólogos y juristas y personas de altos entendimientos ha proveído y remediado con su justicia todo lo que ha sido posible, y mucho más con la nueva reformación de su real consejo de Indias.

14. Se me ocurre una cosa que he mirado muchas veces en estos indios, y es que tienen el casco de la cabeza más grueso cuatro veces que los cristianos. E así cuando se les hace guerra y vienen con ellos a las manos, han de estar muy sobre avisos de no les dar cuchillada en la cabeza, porque se han visto quebrar muchas espadas.

15. La nueva reformación de su real consejo de Indias.

16. Copiosamente apuntadas en mi *General historia de Indias.*

17. Estaban pobladas de indios flecheros llamados *caribes,* que en lengua de los indios quiere decir bravos e osados. Estos tiran con hierba tan pestífera y enconada, que es irremediable; e los hombres que son heridos con ella mueren rabiando. . . . Estos flecheros destas islas que tiran con hierba, comen carne humana, excepto los de las isla de Boriquén. Pero, demás destos de las islas, también la comen en muchas partes de la Tierra Firme, como se dirá en su lugar.

18. Nunca había ni acaescían guerras o diferencias entre los indios desta isla sino por una destas tres causas: sobre los términos o jurisdición, o sobre las pesquerías, o cuando de las otras islas venían indios caribes flecheros a saltear.

19. In 1516 Cardinal Cisneros sent Jeronymite friars to Hispaniola to investigate the Indians' ability to live on their own.

20. Pero, en fin, estos indios es gente muy desviada de querer entender la fe católica; y es machacar hierro frío pensar que han de ser cristianos. Y así se les ha parescido en las capas, o, mejor diciendo, en las cabezas; porque capas no las traían, ni tampoco tienen cabezas como otras gentes, sino de tan rescios e gruesos cascos que el principal aviso que los cristianos tienen cuando con ellos pelean, es no darles cuchillada en la cabeza, porque se rompen las espadas. Y así como tienen el casco grueso, así tienen el entendimiento bestial y mal inclinado, como adelante se dirá de sus ritos e ceremonias e costumbres e de otras cosas las que al mismo propósito me ocurrieren. The final version of the *History* slightly revises the 1535 passage. It is noteworthy that Oviedo adds certain qualifiers and further insists on his eyewitness role and his increased interest in the particular characteristics of certain native groups; he also adds the word "idolatrías" (added sections are in italics in the following quote): "Pero, en fin, estos indios, *por la mayor parte* de ellos es nación muy desviada de quere entender la fe católica; y es machacar hierro frío pensar que han de ser cristianos, *sino con mucho discurso de tiempo,* y así se les ha parescido en las capas, o, mejor diciendo, en las cabezas; porque capas no las traían, ni tampoco tienen las cabezas como otras gentes, sino de tan rescios e gruesos cascos, que el principal aviso que los cristianos tienen cuando con ellos pelean *e vienen a las manos,* es no darles cuchilladas en la cabeza, porque se rompen las espadas. Y así como tienen el casco grueso, así tienen el entendimiento bestial y mal inclinado, como se dirá adelante, *especificando*

algunos de sus ritos e ceremonias, *e idolatrías* e costumbres, e *otras particularidades* que al mismo propósito ocurrieron *e yo tuviere noticias dellas hasta el tiempo presente*" (*Proemio,* bk. 5).

21. El historiador prueba que en otras partes del mundo se usaron los sacrificios de matar hombres e ofrescerlos entre los antiguos, a sus dioses, y en muchas partes, asimismo, se acostumbró comer carne humana y al presente se hace en muchas partes de la Tierra Firme destas Indias, y en algunas islas.

22. Bartolomé de Las Casas wrote at length about Don Enrique, and later, in 1882, Manuel de Jesús Galván wrote the foundational Dominican novel, *Enriquillo,* about this heroic indigenous figure.

23. Cuanto al cacique don Enrique, me paresce que él hizo la más honorosa paz que ha hecho caballero o capitán o príncipe de Adam acá, y quedó más honrado que quedó el duque de Borbón en el vencimiento e prisión del rey Francisco de Francia en Pavia, segund la desproporción e desigualdad tan grande que hay, del mayor príncipe de los cristianos y Emperador del universo, a un hombre tal como este don Enrique. . . . Por cierto, don Enrique, si vos los conoscístes y supístes sentir, yo os tengo por uno de los más honrados y venturosos capitanes que ha habido sobre la tierra en todo el mundo hasta vuestro tiempo. Note that the 1535 edition lacks a chapter 6; thus chapters 6–11 in the modern edition correspond to chapters 7–12 in the 1535 edition.

24. Note that the 1535 edition of book 6 contained only the first thirteen chapters.

25. In the case of book 17, some ethnographic chapters, such as 8 and 9, were added later.

26. Olor de caballería prometida y fábulas.

27. See Álvaro Félix Bolaños, "A Place to Live," 276.

28. Por no dar pesadumbre a los letores, repitiendo algo de lo que está dicho, se tocarán en suma en este libro XXIX algunas materias que en los libros precendentes se hobieren memorado, declarando las diferencias que hobiere de lo que está dicho en la primera parte, a lo que se dice en esta segunda en cosas semejantes.

29. Nonetheless, Oviedo still homogenizes many elements. For example, he calls native songs in different parts of America *areitos,* even though the term originated with indigenous groups in the West Indies.

30. También hay en estas mujeres de Cueva algunas que públicamente se dan a quien las quiere, e a las tales llaman *irachas,* porque por decir mujer, dicen *ira;* e la que es de muchos o amancebada, dícenlas iracha (como vocablo *pluralitèr,* que se extiende a muchos). Hay otras tan amigas de la libídine, que si se hacen preñadas, toman cierta hierba, con que luego mueven e lanzan la preñez; porque dicen ellas que las viejas han de parir, que ellas no quieren estar ocupadas para dejar sus placeres, ni empreñarse para que, en pariendo, se les aflojen las tetas, de las cuales se prescian en extremo, e las tienen buenas.

31. Hay asimesmo en esta provincia de Cueva sodomitas abominables, e tienen muchachos con quien usan aquel nefando delicto.

32. E tráenlos con naguas, o en hábito de mujeres; e sírvense de los tales en todas las cosas y ejercicios que hacen las mujeres, así en hilar como en barrer la casa y en todo lo demás; y éstos no son despreciados ni maltractados por ello; e llámase el paciente, *camayoa.*

33. E acuérdome que me referí a esta *General Historia,* que aunque no estaba copiada regladamente en las minutas e memorias que yo tenía de aquestas cosas, no carescía en mi deseo la esperanza de traerla a este estado que agora está. . . . Y así iré discurriendo, por lo que allí escribí . . . le quiero avisar que no los topará aquí a reo como allí los puse, pero estarán en sus lugares convinientes.

34. Y así hice yo en aquel sumario, que muchas cosas de las que allí se acumularon, no se entienden puntualmente dónde están.

35. Indeed, chapters 30 and 31 clearly place the date of composition as 1540–1542 and 1548–1549, respectively.

36. Para considerar que estos tractados se fundan principlamente en loor de Dios, que de tantas novedades e diversidad de cosas es el Hacedor, . . . y lo segundo, porque la clemencia de César quiere que por su mandado se sepan e comunique al mundo todo; y lo terecero, porque es un grand contentamiento a los hombres, de cualquier estado que sean, oír cosas nuevas.

37. Son tantas e tan diferenciadas las costumbres destas gentes, que no se pueden aun entender ni saberse, sin que el tiempo dé lugar a ello e pasen más años.

38. Yo tengo hasta agora visto grandísimo número destos indios en treinta y cinco años que ha que tracto estas partes e veo esta generación, e ninguno perfecto cristiano he hallado.

39. Muy reverendos obispos e perlados, que examinéis bien vuestros ministros, porque a veces os engañáis en la elección e os engañan. ¿Quereíslo ver? Mirad las bolsas a algunos, e los negocios particulares, y el caudal con que entraron en sus granjerías; e veréis cuán apartado anda el ejercicio del oficio del sacerdocio.

40. Alexandre de Coello notes that Oviedo made a fourth bid for a governorship in 1546, that of Cartagena, *De la Naturaleza,* 186. See also Pérez de Tudela, "Introducción," cxxxv.

41. The year before his appointment as chronicler, Oviedo petitioned for a *restitución* of Indians because he was one of the first settlers of Tierra Firme (AGI, Panama 233, L. 5, f. 1r, 1531). A royal decree to the officials in Santo Domingo in 1536 replies to Oviedo's petition for a *repartimiento* of two hundred Indians. Oviedo argues that *alcaides* in the past received *repartimientos* and that with his salary of two hundred thousand maravedís "no se puede sustentar según la carestía de la tierra" (AGI, Santo Domingo L. 1, ff. 25r–26r, 1536). To put Oviedo's complaint in context: the rate of inflation from about 1510 to 1550 was approximately 100 percent.

42. See Pérez Tudela's summary of Enrique Otte's work, "Vida," cxxxv–cxxxvi.

43. In "Empowerment through Writing" Santa Arias convincingly argues that Las Casas uses the same constructs as Oviedo but arrives at a different conclusion, 170.

44. See Louise Bénat-Tachot's introduction to her French translation of Oviedo's

book 42 on Nicaragua; she briefly discusses Oviedo's approaches, *Singularités de Nicaragua,* 31–40, 66.

45. Preguntando yo a los indios que significaba aquella señal.

46. Rolena Adorno and Patrick Pautz in their *Alvar Núñez Cabeza de Vaca* and Patricia Galloway in her study of the De Soto expedition meticulously compare sections of Oviedo's *Historia* with his original sources; all three scholars conclude that Oviedo was fairly faithful to his sources.

47. En el cual se tracta de la idolatría e diabólicos sacrificios de los indios de la Nueva España.

48. Algunos trajes e ritos e condenados sacrificios.

CONCLUSIONS

1. Ande verdad sobre todo; . . . pues sin elegancia ni circunloquios ni afeites ni ornamento de retórica, sino llanamente, ha dejado llegar a tal estado esta *General e Natural Historia de Indias,* conforme a verdad.

APPENDIX C

1. Don Alfonso de Madrigal, bishop of Avila, 1404?-1455.

2. Oviedo uses the Spanish word for "world," when, to be consistent, he should have used the Latin term *mundus*.

3. The drumstick tree, used for medicinal purposes.

4. A purple dye.

5. Spaniards.

6. For a definition of this term, see above, chap. 3, n 1.

7. Oviedo is most likely referring to Lucius Munatius Plancus (87 BCE–15 BCE), one of Caesar's and also Augustus's supporters. One of Plancus's enemies was said to be preparing an oration against him, which was to be pronounced after Plancus's death, so that he could not answer it; upon learning of this, Plancus is reported to have said, "cum mortuis non nisi larvas luctari" (It is only ghosts who fight with the dead). Oviedo's rendition of this is similar, but not quite the same, but we know his command of Latin was shaky. I am indebted to Teresa Ramsby for this information.

8. Another medieval Spanish churchman.

9. According to two professors of Latin whom I consulted (Teresa Ramsby and George Ryan), a literal translation of the Latin passage would be as follows: "Never by means of victory is a traveler or similar person found in Spanish lands," which does not make a lot of sense. According to them, the original Latin is very unclear and again may reflect Oviedo's lack of expertise in this language.

10. Oviedo uses the word "piña" in his original text, which in Spanish has the

dual meaning of "pinecone" and "pineapple." Since this whole chapter focuses on the fruit, I have chosen to use the term "pineapple" almost exclusively throughout.

11. I have been unable to determine which fruit this is.

12. Footnote in Tudela Bueso's text: Justin, book II.

13. The supposed etymology of this word was "breastless."

14. Footnote in Tudela Bueso: Pliny, book 5, chapter 18.

15. Footnote in Tudela Bueso: *Cives vocatique in unum coeuntes, vivat, et utita comes et ornatior fiat et tutior. Ethim.*, book 4, chapter 4.

BIBLIOGRAPHY

PRIMARY WORKS BY FERNÁNDEZ DE OVIEDO

Archives

AGI	Archivo General de las Indias (Seville)
AGS	Archivo General de Simancas
BC	Biblioteca Colombina (Seville)
BE	Biblioteca del Monasterio de El Escorial
BN	Biblioteca Nacional (Madrid)
BUS	Biblioteca de la Universidad de Salamanca
HSA	Hispanic Society of America (New York City)
HEH	The Huntington Library (San Marino, California)
PR	Biblioteca del Palacio Real (Madrid)
RAH	Biblioteca de la Real Academia de Historia (Madrid)

Works Published during Oviedo's Lifetime

1519 *Libro del muy esforçado y invencible Cauallero dela Fortuna propiamente llamado don Claribalte.* Valencia: Juan Vinao. Republished in 1956. More recent editions include Alberto del Río Nogueras (Alcalá de Hernares: Centro de Estudios Cervantinos, 2001) and María José Rodilla León (Mexico: Universidad Autónoma Metropolitana-Iztapalapa, 2002).

1526 *Oviedo de la natural hystoria delas Indias.* Toledo: Ramón de Petras. Republished multiple times; the most recent: *Sumario de la natural historia de las Indias,* ed. Juan Bautista Avalle-Arce. Salamanca: Ediciones Anaya, 1963.

1535 *Historia general de las Indias,* Part I (bks. 1–19 and what would become bk. 50 of part II). Seville: Juan Cromberger. Republished several times in Oviedo's lifetime, 1547 and 1557. The first full edition of all three parts with the author's extensive revisions is the *Historia general y natural de las Indias,* ed. José Amador de los Ríos. Madrid: Imprenta de la Real Academia de la Historia, 1851–1855. Vols. 1–4. This was reprinted with a new introduction by Juan Pérez de Tudela, Madrid: Real Academia Española, BEA, 1956 and 1992.

Posthumous Publications and Unpublished Manuscripts

ca. 1528 *Libro primero del blasón. Tratado de todas las armas e diferencias dellas e de los escudos e diferencias que en ellos hay . . .* (RAH 9/4023).

ca. 1532 *Relación de lo sucedido en la prisión del rey de Francia . . .* (BN, ms. 87756). Published in *Colección de documentos inéditos para la historia de España XXXVIII.* Madrid: Imprenta de la Vda. De Calero, 1861. 404–492.

1535 *Epílogo real, imperial y pontifical* (BN, ms. 6224)

1532/1535 *Catálogo Real.* Parts I–III. (BE, ms. h-I-7). Only the first volume survives (1532). Published as a dissertation, "Transcripición y edición del *Catálogo Real de Castilla,*" by Evelia Ana Romano de Thuesen, University of Santa Barbara, 1992.

1547 *Libro de la cámara del Príncipe don Juan,* final draft (various versions in BS, ms. 2149; BE, e-iv-8; and PR, VII Y 6). First published in Madrid, 1870, and more recently by J. M. Escudero Peña, Madríd, 1987.

1548 Translation of an Italian text, *Regla de la vida espiritual y Teología secreta.* Seville: Domingo Robertis. No copy of this work seems to have survived.

1548/1549 Last additions made to the three-part *Historia* (partial original "Monserrate manuscript": RAH, Colección Salazar, 9/551–9/557 and HEH, Hm-176-177; sixteenth-century copy "Gascó" or "Truxillos" copy: PR, ms. II/3041-42 and BC ms. 83-6-15. See publication information above.

1552 Last additions made to *Batallas y quinquagenas* (BS, ms. 359; RAH 9/5387). Vol. I was published by Juan Pérez de Tudela, Madrid: Real Academia de la Historia, 1983; Vol. II, by Juan Bautista Avalle-Arce, Salamanca: Ediciones de la Diputación de Salamanca, 1989; Vol. III is still unpublished.

1552? *Libro de linajes y armas* (RAH, c-24, a contemporary copy); a work related to the *Batallas.*

1555 *Las Quincuagenas de los generosos e ilustres y no menos famosos reyes, príncipes, duques.* Vols. I–III (BN, ms. 2217-19). Vol. I was published by Vicente de la Fuente, Madrid: Imprenta y Fundición de Manuel Tello, 1880; selections from all three volumes were edited by Juan Bautista Avalle-Arce, Chapel Hill: University of North Carolina Press, 1974.

1851–1855 *Historia general y natural de las Indias,* ed. José Amador de los Ríos. Madrid: Real Academia.

1945 *Historia general y natural de las Indias,* ed. J. Natálico González and José Amador de los Ríos. Vols. 1–14. Asunción, Paraguay: Editorial Guaranía.

1959 [1992] Pérez de Tudela Bueso, Juan. *Historia general y natural de las Indias.* Biblioteca de Autores Españoles. Vols. 117–121. Madrid: Atlas.

SECONDARY SOURCES

Abbot, Don Paul. *Rhetoric in the New World: Rhetorical Theory and Practice in Colonial Spanish America.* Columbia: University of South Carolina Press, 1996.

Adorno, Rolena. "On Pictorial Language and the Typology of Culture in New World Chronicles." *Semiotica* 36 (1981): 51–106.

———. "Discourses on Colonialism: Bernal Díaz, Las Casas, and the Twentieth-Century Reader." *Modern Language Notes* 103 (1988): 239–258.

———. *Guaman Poma: Writing and Resistance in Colonial Peru.* Austin: University of Texas Press, 1986.

———. "Los debates sobre la naturaleza del indio en el siglo XVI: textos y contextos." *Revista de Estudios Hispánicos* 19 (1992): 47–66.

———. "The Discursive Encounter of Spain and America: The Authority of Eyewitness Testimony in the Writing of History." *William and Mary Quarterly* 49 (1992): 210–238.

———. Rev. of *La naturaleza de las Indias nuevas: de Cristóbal Colón a Gonzalo Fernández de Oviedo,* by Antonello Gerbi, trans. by Antonio Alatorre. *Hispánica* 63.2 (1980): 438.

———. "The Negotiation of Fear in Cabeza de Vaca's *Naufragios.*" *Representations* 33 (1991): 163–199.

———. "Visual Mediation in the Transition from Oral to Written Expression." *New Scholar* 10 (1986): 181–195.

Adorno, Rolena, and Patrick Pautz. *Alvar Núñez Cabeza de Vaca: His Account, His Life, and the Expedition of Pánfilo Narváez.* 3 vols. Lincoln: University of Nebraska Press, 1999.

Albanese, Denise. *New Science, New World.* Durham: Duke University Press, 1996.

Alter, Robert. *The Art of Biblical Narration.* New York: Basic Books, 1981.

Álvarez López, Enrique. "La historia natural en Oviedo." *Revista de Indias* 17 (1957): 541–601.

———. "El Dr. Francisco Hernández y sus comentarios a Plinio." N.p.: n.p., 1942. 251–290.

Álvarez Rubiano, Pablo. *Pedrarias Dávila: Contribución al estudio de la figura del "Gran justador," gobernador de Castilla de Oro y Nicaragua.* Madrid: Consejo Superior de Investigaciones Científicas, 1944.

Amador de los Ríos, José. "Vida y escritos de Gonzalo Fernández de Oviedo." In *Historia general y natural de las Indias,* ix–cvii. 1855. Repr. Madrid: Imprenta de la Real Academia de Historia, 1992.

Arias, Santa. "Empowerment Through the Writing of History: Bartolomé de Las Casas's Representation of the Other(s)." In *Early Images of the Americas: Transfer and Invention,* ed. Jerry M. Williams and Robert E. Lewis, 163–182. Tucson: University of Arizona Press, 1993.

Arrom, José. "Gonzalo Fernández de Oviedo, Relator de Episodios y Narrador de Naufragios." *Ideologies and Literature* 17 (1983): 133–145.

Avalle-Arce, Juan Bautista. *Las memorias de Gonzalo Fernández de Oviedo.* 2 vols. Chapel Hill: University of North Carolina, Department of Romance Languages, 1974.

Bakhtin, Mikhail. "The Word in Dostoevsky." In *Problems of Dostoevsky Poetics,* trans. R. W. Rotsel, 150–227. Ann Arbor: Ardis, 1973.

Bakhtin, Mikhail. *Rabelais and His World.* Trans. H. Iswolsky. Bloomington: Indiana University Press, 1984.

Ballesteros, Manuel. *Gonzalo Fernández de Oviedo.* Madrid: Fundación Universitaria Española, 1981.

Banfield, Ann. *Unspeakable Sentences.* Boston: Routledge and Kegan Paul, 1982.

Barbolani, Cristina. "Los diálogos de Juan de Valdés: ¿Reflexión o improvisación?" In *Doce consideraciones sobre el mundo hispano-italiano en tiempos de Antonio y Juan de Valdés,* 138–151. Bolonia: Actas del Coloquio Interdisciplinar Bolonia, 1976.

Barreto, Luis Filipe. "Ananas versus cacao: un exemple de discours ethnographique dans la Historia Gerneral y Natural de las Indias de Gonzalo Fernández de Oviedo." *Entre dos mundos: fronteras culturales y agentes mediadores,* ed. Berta Ares Queija and Serge Gruzinski. Seville: Escuela de Estudios Hispanoamericanos, 1997.

Barthes, Roland. *Mythologies.* Trans. Annette Layers. New York: Hill and Wang, 1972.

Bataillon, Marcel. *Erasmo y España.* Mexico City: Fondo de Cultura Económica, 1982.

Beckjord, Sarah H. "Stranger than Fiction: Narrative Reliability in the Early Historiography of the Indies." Diss., Columbia University, 2001.

Beer, Jeanette. *Narrative Conventions of Truth in the Middle Ages.* Geneva: Droz, 1981.

Bénat-Tachot, Louise. "El relato corto en la *Historia general y natural de las Indias* de Gonzalo Fernández de Oviedo." In *La formación de la cultura virreinal.* Frankfurt, Madrid, Vervuert: Iberoamericana, 2000.

———. Introduction to *Singularités de Nicaragua,* by Gonzalo Fernández de Oviedo, 7–72. Paris: Chandeigne, 2002.

Blake, Jon Vincent. "Libro de cámara real del Príncipe don Juan e officios de su casa e servicio ordinario de Gonzalo Fernández de Oviedo y Valdés: según el manuscrito autógrafo Escorial e.iv. 8: estudio, transcripción y notas." Diss., University of North Carolina, 1976.

Bolaños, Álvaro Félix. "El líder ideal en el libro de caballerías y las crónicas de indias de Gónzalo Fernández de Oviedo." Diss., University of Kentucky, 1988.

———. *Barbarie y canibalismo en la retórica colonial: Los indios pijaos de Fray Pedro Simón.* Bogotá: CEREC, 1984.

———. "A Place to Live, A Place to Think, and a Place to Die: Sixteenth-Century Frontier Cities, Plazas, and 'Relaciones' in Spanish America." In *Mapping Colonial Spanish America: Places and Common Places of Identity, Culture, and Experience,* ed. Santa Arias and Mariselle Meléndez, 275–293. Lewisburg: Bucknell University Press, 2002.

———. "La crónica de Indias de Fernández de Oviedo: Historia de lo general y natural, u obra didáctica." *Revista de Estudios Hispánicos* 25 (1991): 15–34.

———. *Panegírico y libelo del primer cronista de Indias, Gonzalo Fernández de Oviedo,* 1–73. Bogotá: Instituto Caro y Cuervo: 1990.

———. "Milagro, peregrinación y paraíso: narración de naufragios del cronista Fernández de Oviedo." *Revista de Estudios Hispánicos* 9 (1992): 163–178.

———. "The Historian and the Hesperides: Fernández de Oviedo and the Limitations of Imitation." *Bulletin of Hispanic Studies* 72 (1995): 273–288.

Branch, Michael. *Reading the Roots: American Nature Writing Before Walden*. Athens: University of Georgia Press, 2004.

Bucher, Bernadette. *Icon and Conquest: A Structural Analysis of the Illustrations of de Bry's Great Voyages*. Trans. Basia Miller Gulati. Chicago: University of Chicago Press, 1981.

Cabrera de Córdoba, Luis. *De historia: para entenderla y escribirla* [1611]. Ed. Santiago Montero Díaz. Madrid, 1948.

Campbell, Ysla. *Historia y ficción: crónicas de América*. Colección conmemorativa quinto centenario del encuentro de dos mundos 2. Ciudad Juárez, México: Universidad Autónoma de Ciudad Juárez, 1992.

Cañizares Esguerra, Jorge. *How to Write the History of the New World: Histories, Epistemologies, and Identities in the Eighteenth-Century Atlantic World*. Stanford: Stanford University Press, 2001.

Carbia, Rómulo D. *La Crónica Oficial de las Indias Occidentales*. Buenos Aires: Ediciones Buenos Aires, 1940.

Carrillo Castillo, Jesús María. *Naturaleza e Imperio: La representación del mundo natural en la* Historia general y natural de las Indias *de Gonalo Fernández de Oviedo*. Madrid: Fundación Carolina, 2005.

———. *Oviedo on Columbus*. Ed. Jesús Carrillo. Trans. Diane Avalle-Arce. Turnhout, Belgium: Brepols, 2000.

———. "The Representation of the Indies in Gonzalo Fernández de Oviedo." Diss., King's College, Cambridge University, 1997.

Chavolla, Arturo. *La idea de América en el pensamiento europeo: de Fernández de Oviedo a Hegel*. Guadalajara: Universidad de Guadalajara, 1993.

Cochrane, Eric. *Historians and Historiography in the Italian Renaissance*. Chicago: University of Chicago Press, 1981.

Coello de la Rosa, Alexandre. *De la naturaleza y el nuevo mundo: maravilla y exoticismo en Gonzalo Fernández de Oviedo y Valdés (1478–1557)*. Madrid: Fundación Universitaria Española, 2002.

Colie, Rosalie L. *The Resources of Kind: Genre-Theory in the Renaissance*. Ed. Barbara Lewalski. Berkeley and Los Angeles: University of California Press, 1973.

Collins, J. L. "Antiquity of the Pineapple in America." *Southwestern Journal of Anthropology* 7 (1951): 145–155.

Columbus, Christopher. *Diario de abordo*. Ed. Luis Arranz. Madrid: Historia 16, 1985.

Cuart Moner, Baltasar. "La historiografía áulica en la primera mitad del siglo XVI y los cronistas del emperador." *Antonio de Nebrija: Edad Media y Renacimiento*, ed. Carmen Codoñer, 39–65. Salamanca: Ediciones de la Universidad de Salamanca, 1994.

Elliott, John H. *The Old World and the New, 1492–1650.* London: Cambridge University Press, 1970.

———. "Voces nahuas en la *Historia general y natural* de Gonzalo Fernández de Oviedo: testimonio histórico y pervivencia actual." *II Encuentro de lingüistas de España y México,* ed. José María Enguita Utrilla. Salamanca: Junta de Castilla y León, Consejería de Cultura y Turismo, Ediciones Universidad de Salamanca: 1994.

Emilfork, Leónidas T. "Letras de fundación: estudio sobre la obra americana de Oviedo y la crónica de las siete ciudades de Cíbola." Diss., Johns Hopkins University, 1981.

Ewan, Joseph. "The Columbian Discoveries and the Growth of Botanical Ideas, with Special Reference to the Sixteenth Century." In *First Images of the New World,* ed. F. Chiappelli, 2:807–812. Berkeley: University of California, 1976.

Fernández de Oviedo y Valdés, Gonzalo. "1544: Primera entrevista en suelo americano (excerpt from book *Historia general y natural de las Indias*)." *Correo de los Andes* 44 (1987): 24–29.

———. *La llegada de Gonzalo de Oviedo y de Pedrarias Dávila a la bahía de Santa María, año de 1514.* Santa María: n.p., 1950.

———. *The Journey of the Vaca Party: The Account of the Narváez Expedition, 1528–1536, as related by Gonzalo Fernández de Oviedo y Valdés.* Trans. Basil C. Hedrick and Carroll L. Riley. Carbondale: University Museum, Southern Illinois University, 1974.

———. *Oviedo on Columbus.* Ed. Jesús Carrillo. Trans. Diane Avalle-Arce. Turnhout, Belgium: Brepols, 2000.

———. *Sucesos y diálogo de la Nueva España.* Prol. Edmundo O'Gorman. México: UNAM, 1946.

———. *Writing from the Edge of the World: The Memoirs of Darién, 1514–1527.* Trans. G. F. Dille. Tuscaloosa: University of Alabama Press, 2006.

Ferro, Donatella. "Oviedo/Cabeza de Vaca: 'debito testuale e tarea de acumulacion e correcion.'" In *El Girador: studi di letterature iberiche e ibero-americane offerti a Giuseppe Bellini,* ed. Giovanni Battista de Cesare and Silvana Serafin. Roma: Bulzoni, 1993.

Foucault, Michel. *The Order of Things: An Archaelogy of Human Sciences.* New York: Random House, 1973.

Franklin, Wayne. *Discoverers, Explorers, Settlers: The Diligent Writers of Early America.* Chicago: University of Chicago Press, 1979.

Fuentes, Vicente de la. "Advertencia preliminar acerca de las *Quinquagenas* del capitán Gonzalo Fernández de Oviedo." In *Las quinquagenas de la nobleza de España,* Vol. 1, v–xxxvi. Madrid: Real Academia de Historia, Imprenta y Fundación de Manuel Tello, 1980.

Galloway, Patricia. *The Hernando de Soto Expedition: History, Historiography, and "Discovery" in the Southeast.* Lincoln: University of Nebraska Press, 1997.

García Anoveros, Jesús María. Rev. of *Fernández de Oviedo e il problema dell'indio,* by Giuliano Oreste Soria. *Revista de Indias* 50.189 (1990): 646–648.

García Pinilla, I. J., et al. "Las fuentes clásicas de *General y natural historia de Indias* de Gonzalo Fernández de Oviedo." *Anuario de Estudios Americanos* 48.1 (1991): 13–40.

García Sáiz, María Concepción. "Acerca de los conocimientos pictóricos de Gonzalo Fernández de Oviedo." *América y la España del siglo XVI: Homenaje a Gonzalo Fernández de Oviedo,* Vol. 1, ed. Francisco de Solano and Fermín del Pino, 65–71. Madrid: CSIC, Instituto Gonzalo Fernández de Oviedo, 1982.

Gerbi, Antonello. *La naturaleza de las Indias nuevas: de Cristóbal Colón a Fernández de Oviedo.* Mexico City: Fondo de Cultura Económica, 1978.

———. *Nature in the New World: From Christopher Columbus to Gonzalo Fernández de Oviedo.* Trans. Jeremy Moyle. Pittsburgh: University of Pittsburgh Press, 1985.

Gil, Juan. *Mitos y utopías del descubrimiento.* Vol. 1. Madrid: Alianza, 1989.

Gombrich, E. H. *Art and Illusion.* New York: Pantheon, 1960.

González-Boixo, José Carlos. "Plinio y Pedro Mexía, como modelos narrativos en la *Historia* de G. Fernández de Oviedo." In *El Girador: studi di letterature iberiche e ibero-americane offerti a Giuseppe Bellini,* ed. Giovanni Battista de Cesare and Silvana Serafin. Roma: Bulzoni, 1993.

González-Echevarría, Roberto. "The Law of the Letter: Garcilaso's *Comentarios.*" In *Myth and Archive: A Theory of Latin American Narrative.* Cambridge: Cambridge University Press, 1990.

Grafton, Anthony. *New World, Ancient Texts.* Cambridge: Harvard University Press, 1992.

Green, Otis. *Spain and the Western Tradition.* Vol. 3. Madison: University of Wisconsin Press, 1965.

Greenblatt, Stephen, ed. *New World Encounters.* Berkeley: University of California Press, 1993.

Greene, Thomas M. *The Light in Troy: Imitation and Discovery in Renaissance Poetry.* New Haven: Yale University Press, 1982.

Hanke, Lewis. *All Mankind Is One.* De Kalb: Northern Illinois University Press, 1974.

———. *The Spanish Struggle for Justice in the Conquest of America.* Dallas: Southern Methodist University Press, 2002.

———. *Bartolomé de las Casas, Historian: An Essay in Spanish Historiography.* Gainesville: University Press of Floria, 1952.

Hart, Johnathan. "Strategies of Promotion: Some Prefatory Matter of Oviedo, Thevet, and Hakluyt." In *Imagining Culture: Essays in Early Modern History and Literature,* ed. Johnathan Hart. New York: Garland, 1996.

Hernández, Francisco. *Quatro libros de la naturaleza, y virtudes de las plantas, y animales que estan recevidos en el uso de la medicina en la Nueva España, y el methodo, y correcion, y preparacion, que para administrallas se require con lo que el doctor Francisco Hernandez escrivio en lengua latina.* México: Diego López Dávalos, 1615.

Hulton, Paul, and David Quinn. *The Drawings of John White.* 2 vols. Chapel Hill: University of North Carolina Press, 1964.

Ife, B. W. "Alexander in the New World: Fictional Archetype and Narrative History." *Renaissance and Modern Studies* 30 (1986): 35–44.

Johnson, Julie. *Women in Colonial Spanish-American Literature.* Westport, CT: Greenwood Press, 1983.

Kagan, Richard L. "Clio and the Crown: Writing History in Hapsburg Spain." In *Spain, Europe and the Atlantic World,* ed. Kagan and Parker, 73–101. Cambridge: Cambridge University Press, 1995.

Kamen, Henry Arthur Francis. *Philip of Spain.* New Haven: Yale University Press, 1997.

Kelly, Donald R. *Foundations of Modern Historical Scholarship.* New York: Columbia University Press, 1970.

Kohut, Karl. "Fernández de Oviedo: Historiografía e Ideología." *Boletín de la Real Academia Española* 73.259 (1993): 367–381.

Kohut, Karl, and Sonia V. Rose, eds. *Pensamiento europeo y cultura colonial.* Frankfurt, Madrid, Vervuert: Iberoamericana, 1997.

Krieger, Margery H. *We Came Naked and Barefoot: The Journey of Cabeza de Vaca Across America.* Austin: University of Texas Press, 2002.

Kushinsky, Martin. *Oviedo: On the Conquest of New Spain.* Philadelphia: n.p., 1953.

Las Casas, Bartolomé de. *Historia de las Indias.* Ed. Isacio Pérez Fernández et al. Madrid: Alianza, 1994. Vols. 3–5 of *Obras Completas.* 14 vols. 1994.

Lens Tuero, Jesús. "Fernández de Oviedo (*Historia general y natural de las Indias,* libro VI, cap. LI) y la etiología clásica." *Anuario de Estudios Americanos* 54 (1997): 187–198.

Leonard, Irving. *Books of the Brave.* New York: Godian Press, 1964.

Lerner, Isaías. "La visión humanística de América: Gonzalo Fernández de Oviedo." In *Actas del III Congreso Argentino de Hispanistas "España en América y América en España,"* ed. Luis Martínez Cuitiño and Elida Lois. Buenos Aires: Instituto de Filologías y Literaturas Hispánicas, Facultad de Filosofía y Letras, Universidad de Buenos Aires, 1993.

Lloyd, David, and Paul Thomas. *Culture and the State.* New York: Routledge, 1998.

López-Baralt, Mercedes. "La iconografía política de América: El mito fundacional en las imágenes católica, protestante y nativa." *Nueva Revista de Estudios Hispánicos* 31 (1983): 448–461.

López Pinciano. *Philosophia antigua poética.* Ed. Alfredo Carbaleo Picazo. Madrid: Biblioteca de Antiguos Libros Hispánicos, 1953.

López Piñero, José María. *Ciencia y técnica en la sociedad española de los siglos XVI y XVII.* Barcelona: Labor Universitaria, 1979.

Manzotti, Vilma A. "Rememorias de una peregrinación en el historiar del cronista Gonzalo Fernández de Oviedo." Diss., Temple University, 1988.

Maravall, José Antonio. *Carlos V y el pensamiento político del renacimiento.* Madrid: Instituto de Estudios Políticos, 1960.

———. *Antiguos y modernos: la idea de progreso en el desarollo inicial de una sociedad.* Madrid: Sociedad de Estudios y Publicaciones, 1966.

Marsh, David. *The Quattrocento Dialogue: Classical Tradition and Humanist Innovation.* Cambridge: Harvard University Press, 1980.

Martínez, José Luis, ed. *Entrevista de Gonzalo Fernández de Oviedo a Juan Cano.* Mexico City: Editorial Ambos Mundos, 1986.

Martire d'Anghiera, Pietro. *Décadas del Nuevo Mundo.* 1516. Trans. Joaquín Torres Asensio. Madrid: Polifemo, 1989.

Méndez, Ángel Luis. "Estudio y análisis del discurso narrativo en la *Historia general y natural de las Indias* de Gonzalo Fernández de Oviedo y Valdés." Diss., New York University, 1992.

Merrim, Stephanie. "The Apprehension of the New in Nature and Culture: Fernández de Oviedo's *Sumario.*" Spec. issue of *Hispanic Issues* 4 (1989), ed. René Jara and Nicholas Spadaccini, 165–199.

———. "The Castle of Discourse: Fernández de Oviedo's *Don Claribalte* (1959) or 'Los correos andan más que los caballeros.'" *MLN* 97 (1982): 329–346.

———. "'Un mare magno e oculto:' Anatomy of Fernández de Oviedo's *Historia general y natural de las Indias.*" *Revista de Estudios Hispánicos* 11 (1984): 101–119.

Mignolo, Walter. "El metatexto historiográfico y la historiografía indiana." *MLN* 96 (1981): 358–402.

Mojica, Rafael H. "Fortuna Auri: The Dialectics of Gold in Gonzalo Fernández de Oviedo's Imperial Discourse." *Revista de Estudios Hispánicos* 23 (1996): 125–135.

Mujica, Barbara Louise. *Women Writers of Early Modern Spain: Sophia's Daughters.* New Haven: Yale University Press, 2004.

Mukařovský, Jan. *The Word and Verbal Act.* Trans. J. Burbank and E. Steiner. New Haven: Yale University Press, 1977.

Murillo, Luis Andrés. "Diálogo y dialéctica en el siglo XVI español." *Revista de la Universidad de Buenos Aires* 4 (1959): 55–66.

Myers, Kathleen A. "History, Truth, and Dialogue: Fernández de Oviedo's *Historia general y natural de las Indias* (Book XXXIII, Ch. XLVI)." *Hispania* 73 (1990): 616–625.

———. "Imitation, Authority, and Revision in Fernández de Oviedo's *Historia general y natural de las Indias.*" *Romance Language Annual* 3 (1991): 523–530.

———. "The Representation of New World Phenomena: Visual Epistemology and Fernández de Oviedo's Illustrations." In *Early Images of the Americas: Transfer and Invention,* ed. Jerry Williams and Robert Lewis, 183–213. Tucson: University of Arizona Press, 1993.

Nader, Helen. *The Mendoza Family in the Spanish Renaissance.* New Brunswick: Rutgers University Press, 1979.

Nava, María Teresa. "La Real Academia de la Historia como modelo de unión formal entre el Estado y la Cultura." *Cuadernos de Historia Moderna* 8 (1989): 127–155.

———. "En torno a la historiografía indiana (1764–1768)." *Revista de Indias* 185 (1985): 111–133.

Nelson, William. *Fact or Fiction: The Dilemma of the Renaissance Story Teller.* Cambridge: Harvard University Press, 1973.

O'Gorman, Edmundo. *Cuatro historiadores de Indias, siglo XVI: Pedro Mártir de Anglería, Gonzalo Fernández de Oviedo y Valdés, Fray Bartolomé de Las Casas, Joseph de Acosta.* Mexico City: Sep Diana, 1979.

———. *La invención de América.* 1958. Repr. Mexico City: Fondo de Cultura Económica, 1984.

———. Prólogo. *Sucesos y diálogo de la Nueva España.* By Gonzalo Fernández de Oviedo. México: UNAM, 1946.

———. *The Invention of America: An Inquiry into the Historical Nature of the New World and the Meaning of Its History.* Bloomington: Indiana University Press, 1961.

O'Rourke, Marjorie. *Erasmus on Language and Method in Theology.* Toronto: University of Toronto Press, 1977.

Otte, Enrique. "Aspiraciones y actividades heterogéneas de Fernández de Oviedo." *Revista de Indias* 71 (1958): 9–61.

Oviedo Pérez de Tudela, Rocío. "*Una paradoja* en la corte europea: José Fernández." *Cuadernos Hispanoamericanos* 560 (1997): 79–88.

Pagden, Anthony. *European Encounters with the New World: From Renaissance to Romanticism.* New Haven: Yale University Press, 1993.

———. *Lords of All the World: Ideologies of Empire in Spain, Britain and France c. 1500–c. 1800.* New Haven: Yale University Press, 1995.

Panofsky, Erwin. "Iconography and Iconology: An Introduction to the Study of Renaissance Art." In *Meaning in the Visual Arts: Papers in Art and History,* 26–54. Garden City: Doubleday, 1957.

Pardo Tomás, José. *El tesoro cultural de América: colonialismo y ciencia en el siglo 16.* Madrid: Nivola, 2002.

Pastor, Beatriz. *Discurso narrativo de la conquista de América.* La Habana: Ediciones Casa de las Américas, 1983.

Peña y Cámara, Isabel de la. "Indice onomástico de la *Historia natural y general de las Indias* de Fernández de Oviedo." *Revista Historia* 29 (1966).

Peña y Cámara, José. "Contribuciones documentales y críticas para una bibliografía de Gonzalo Fernández de Oviedo." *Revista de Indias* 17.69–70 (1957): 603–705.

Pérez de Tudela y Bueso, Juan. "Vida y escritos de Gonzalo Fernández de Oviedo." In *Historia general y natural de las Indias de Gonzalo Fernández de Oviedo,* Vol. 1, vii–clxxv. Madrid: Biblioteca de Autores Españoles, 1959.

Pérez de Tudela y Bueso, Juan, and Pedro Lain Entralgo. *Sabiduría de Fernández de Oviedo.* Madrid: Instituto de España, 1979.

Pigman, W. G. "Imitation and the Renaissance Sense of the Past: The Reception of Erasmus' *Ciceronianus.*" *Journal of Medieval and Renaissance Studies* 9 (1979): 155–177.

Pupo-Walker, Enrique. *La vocación literaria del pensamiento histórico en America.* Madrid: Gredos, 1982.

Rabasa, José. *Inventing America: Spanish Historiography and the Formation of Eurocentrism.* Norman: University of Oklahoma Press, 1993.

———. *Writing Violence in the Northern Frontier: The Historiography of Sixteenth-Century New Mexico and Florida and the Legacy of Conquest.* Durham: Duke University Press, 2000.

———. "Writing and Evangelization in Sixteenth-Century Mexico." In *Early Images of the Americas: Transfer and Invention,* ed. Jerry M. Williams and Robert E. Lewis, 65–92. Tucson: University of Arizona Press, 1993.

Restrepo Uribe, Fernando. "Gonzalo Fernández de Oviedo, primer cronista de Indias." *Boletín de Historia y Antigüedades* 74.752 (1987): 245–257.

Río Nogueras, Alberto del. "Diálogo e historia en las *Batallas y quinquagenas* de Gonzalo Fernández de Oviedo." *Criticón* 52 (1991): 91–109.

———. *Claribalte, de Gonzalo Fernández de Oviedo: (Valencia, Juan Viñao, 1519): guía de lectura.* Alcalá de Henares: Centro de Estudios Cervantinos, 2001.

Robinson, Forrest. *The Shape of Things Known.* Cambridge: Harvard University Press, 1972.

Rodríguez, Ligia. "El discurso moral en la historia general de Gonzalo Fernández de Oviedo." Diss., City University of New York, 1990.

Romano de Thuesen, Evelia. "Transcripción y edición del Catálogo Real de Castilla, autógrafo inédito de Gonzalo Fernández de Oviedo y Valdés." Diss., University of California, Santa Barbara, 1992.

———. "Un autógrafo inédito de Gonzalo Fernández de Oviedo y Valdés: la historia de España escrita desde el nuevo mundo." *Actas Irvine-92, Asociación Internacional de Hispanistas.* 5 vols. Ed. Juan Villegas Morales. Irvine, Calif.: AIH, 1994.

Ross, Kathleen Ann. "Carlos de Sigüenza y Góngora's *Parayso occidental*: Baroque Narrative in a Colonial Convent." Diss., Yale University, 1985.

Salas, Alberto M. *Tres cronistas de Indias: Pedro Mártir de Anglería, Gonzalo Fernández de Oviedo, Fray Bartolomé de Las Casas.* Mexico City: Fondo de Cultura Económica, 1959.

Sampedro, Benita. "Historia oficial versus historia personal: las fronteras del 'yo' en la crónica de Indias de Gonzalo Fernández de Oviedo." *Actas del XIII Congreso de la Asociación Internacional de Hispanistas,* ed. Florencio Sevilla Arroyo and Carlos Alvar. Madrid: Castalia, 2000.

Sampedro Vizcaya, Benita. "Bajo bandera inmóvil: Gonzalo Fernández de Oviedo escribiendo desde y sobre la conquista." Diss., New York University, 1997.

Sánchez Jiménez, Antonio. "Memoria y utilidad en el *Sumario de la natural historia de las Indias* de Gonzalo Fernández de Oviedo." *Colonial Latin American Review* 13 (2004): 263–273.

Sauer, Carl O. *The Early Spanish Main.* Berkeley: University of California Press, 1966.

Sauer, Jonathan D. "Changing Perception and Exploitation of New World Plants in Europe, 1492–1800." In *First Images of America,* Vol. 2., ed. Fredi Chiappelli, 813–825. Berkeley: University of California Press, 1976.

Seed, Patricia. *American Pentimento: The Invention of Indians and the Pursuit of Riches.* Minneapolis: University of Minnesota Press, 2001.

———. "Taking Possession and Reading Texts: Establishing the Authority of Overseas Empires." In *Early Images of the Americas: Transfer and Invention,* ed. Jerry M. Williams and Robert E. Lewis, 111–148. Tucson: University of Arizona Press, 1993.

Solano, Francisco de, and Fermín del Pino. *América y la España del siglo XVI: homenaje a Gonzalo Fernández de Oviedo en el V centenario de su nacimiento.* 2 vols. Madrid: CISC., Instituto Gonzalo Fernández de Oviedo, 1982.

Soria, Giuliano. *Fernández de Oviedo e il problema dell'indio.* Roma: Bulzoni, 1989.

Struever, Nancy S. *The Language of History in the Renaissance: Rhetoric and Historical Consciousness in Florentine Humanism.* Princeton: Princeton University Press, 1970.

Sturtevant, William C. "First Visual Images of Native America." In *First Images of America,* Vol. 1, ed. Fredi Chiappelli, 417–454. Berkeley: University of California Press, 1976.

Tate, Robert Brian. *Ensayos sobre la historiografía peninsular del siglo XV.* Madrid: Gredos, 1970.

———. "La historiografía del reinado de los Reyes Católicos." In *Antonio de Nebrija: Edad Media y Renacimiento,* ed. Carmen Codoñer Merino y Juan Antonio González Iglesias. Salamanca: Ediciones Universidad de Salamanca, 1994.

Turner, Daymond. *Forgotten Treasure from the Indies: The Illustrations and Drawings of Fernández de Oviedo.* Charlotte, N.C.: E. Daymond Turner, 1985.

———. "Forgotten Treasure from the Indies: The Illustrations and Drawings of Fernández de Oviedo." *Huntington Library Quarterly* 48 (1985): 1–46.

———. *Gonzalo Fernández de Oviedo: An Annotated Bibliography.* Chapel Hill: University of North Carolina Press, 1966.

———. "Gonzalo Fernández de Oviedo's *Historia General y Natural*: First American Encyclopaedia." *Journal of Inter-American Studies* 6.2 (April 1964): 267–274.

———. "Gonzalo Fernández de Oviedo y Valdés, prosista." *Revista de Indias* 43.171 (1983): 327–334.

———. "Gonzalo Fernández de Oviedo y Valdés: First Spanish-American Author." *Studies in Language and Literature: The Proceedings of the 23rd Mountain Interstate Foreign Language Conference,* ed. Charles L. Nelson. Richmond: Department of Foreign Languages, Eastern Kentucky University, 1976.

———. "La Biblioteca de Gonzalo Fernández de Oviedo." *Revista de Indias* 31 (1971): 139–198.

———. "Los libros del alcaide: la biblioteca de Gonzalo Fernández de Oviedo y Valdés." *Revista de Indias* 31.125–126 (1971): 139–198.

———. "The Aborted First Printing of the Second Part of Oviedo's *General and Natural History of the Indies.*" *Huntington Library Quarterly* 46 (1983): 105–125.

Tuttle, Edward F. "Borrowing versus Semantic Shift: New World Nomenclature in European Languages." In *First Images of America,* Vol. 2, ed. Fredi Chiappelli, 595–605. Berkeley: University of California Press, 1976.

Valdés, Juan de. *Diálogo de la lengua.* Ed. José Fernández Montesinos. Madrid: Ediciones de La Lectura, 1928.

Vázquez, Josefina Zoraida. "El Indio americano y su circunstancia en la obra de Oviedo." *Revista de Indias* 17.69–70 (1957): 483–520.

Vives, Juan Luis. "De disciplinis." *Obras completas*. Vol. 2. Ed. and trans. Llorenç Riber. Madrid: Aguilar, 1948.

———. "De ratione dicendi." *Obras completas*. Ed. and trans. Llorenç Riber. Vol. 2. Madrid: Aguilar, 1948.

———. "Veritas frucata, sive de licentia poetica, quantum poetis liceat a Veritate abscedere." *Opera omnia*. Valentiæ Edetanorum: In officina Benedicti Montfort, 1782–1790.

White, Hayden. *Metahistory*. Baltimore: Johns Hopkins University Press, 1974.

Zamora, Margarita. *Language, Authority and Indigenous History in the "Comentarios Reales de los Incas."* Cambridge Iberian and Latin American Studies. Cambridge: Cambridge University Press, 1988.

Zavala, Silvio. *La filosofía política en la conquista de América*. Mexico City: Fondo de Cultura Económica, 1972.

———. Las instituciones jurídicas en la conquista de America. Mexico: Porrua, 1971.

INDEX

Page numbers in *italics* indicate illustrations.